Making
Contemporary Sculpture

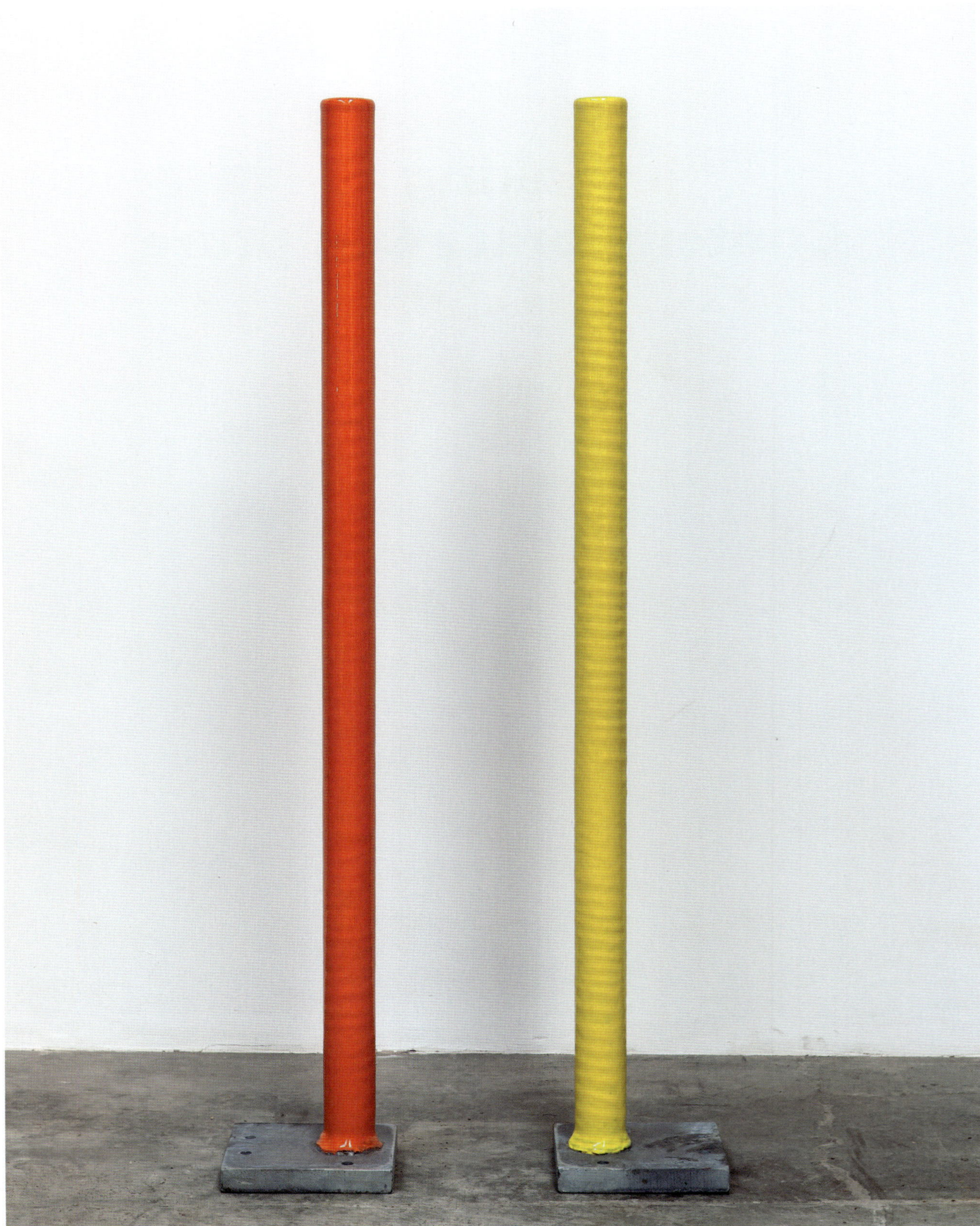

Making Contemporary Sculpture

Ian Dawson

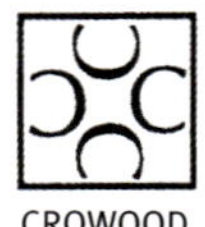

CROWOOD

First published in 2012 by
The Crowood Press Ltd
Ramsbury, Marlborough
Wiltshire SN8 2HR

www.crowood.com

British Library Cataloguing-in-Publication Data
A catalogue record for this book is available from the British Library.

ISBN 978 1 84797 430 3

Frontispiece: Keith Wilson, *Posts* (2008). PU elastomer-coated galvanized steel, height 2m.

Dedication
To Helen, Ava and Nancy Hayward.

Graphic design and layout: www.peggyandco.ca
Printed and bound in India by Replika Press Pvt Ltd

Contents

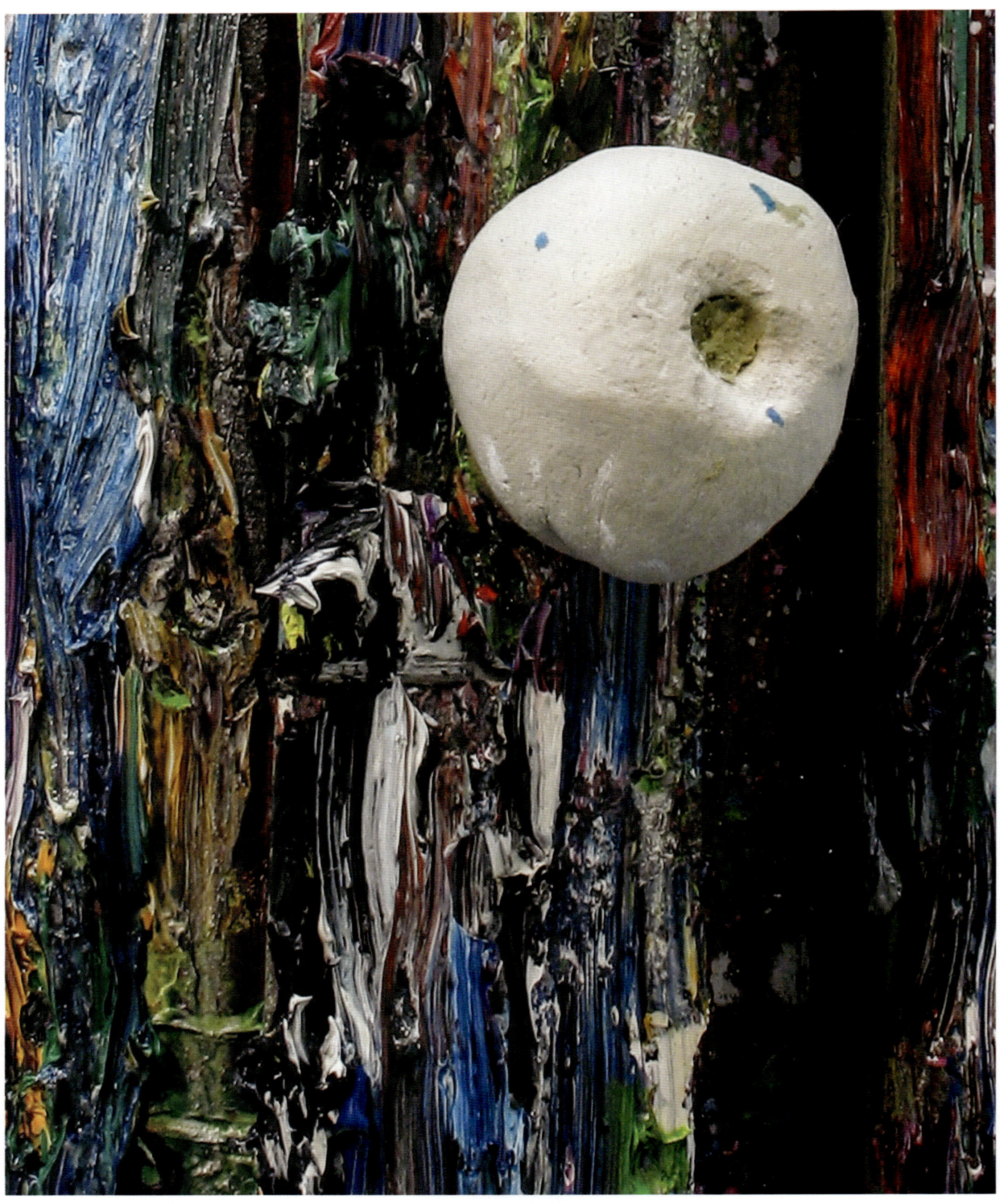

Introduction

The Paris study visit is a staple of an English art school course. The whole year group getting shipped off to stay in a tatty Gare du Nord hotel, a weary and gruff hotelier managing the chaos of backpacks and key deposits in the confines of the cramped lobby. The itinerary is crammed: the Louvre, the Pompidou, Musée Picasso, Musée Rodin, Musée d'Art Moderne, Gare d'Orsay and the Grand Palais. Sore feet and sagging eyes, riding on the euphoria of youthful bewilderment. I remember my Paris study visit. With a miniscule budget, mostly spent on postcards (pictures of my favourite works, treasuring them like actual cultural artefacts), living off baguettes and wine. Rushing to *The Raft of Medusa*, hightailing it to Monet's *Water Lilies*. And then, at a place I can't remember, an obsessive and impatient tutor by the name of John Gibbons pointed out a Venus figurine, a small stone sculpture, palm sized, worn and rounded with voluptuous breasts. Here was an object dating back towards the Ice Age, the point 50,000 years ago when humans across the whole world started to sculpt: to chop, carve, whittle, polish and engrave bits of stone, wood and bone, creating stylistically varied sculptures. These hunter-gatherers were beginning to accrue a sense of the world through object-making. By all accounts the Ice Age was an unforgiving environment and these first sculptures were part of developing rituals and customs to help build strong social bonds in order to survive. From stone tools – axes and arrow heads, the very earliest objects that identify our species – came small sculptures, every human sharing this compulsion not just to make implements to negotiate the world but to make objects to help describe it. Objects like these are a reminder of this basic human prerogative; it is another 45,000 years before the earliest forms of writing emerge in the shape of accountancy tablets documenting the dispersal of commodities through the burgeoning civilization of Mesopotamia.

The study visit and frequent outings to the British Museum were once a core requirement, to view objects from previous centuries that had performed particular purposes: ceremonial, memorial, moral and ornamental, sculpture fulfilling communal functions. It was also where sculpture students would sketch African masks, delving into the ethnographic collections to understand the great modernists such as Picasso. To absorb his cultural plundering, to consider this a source for his playfully direct energy, placing a bike seat and handlebars together to create a bull's head replete with horns, or casting a model car as a baboon's head. Beginning to comprehend a modern sculpture that had begun to ditch certain Western traditions to reconstitute itself out of cubist collage.

The previous 400 years had seen a continuation of a Renaissance ideal, of the artist as philosopher, who, where possible, worked in an urbane environment often to the accompaniment of music, a cultured setting for the mental exertions of transferring three dimensions to two. Sculpture, however, was a different matter: it required a lot of manual labour, covering the wearied worker in dust and chippings, complemented only by the mindless cacophony of hammering. This wasn't considered compatible with a higher level of thinking. Sculptors were mostly categorized with masons, with the guilds, not with the higher arts. But those twentieth-century sculptures were different altogether, and heralded the emergence and pursuit

OPPOSITE PAGE
Ian Dawson, *Yon Yonson* (2011). Steel, oil and clay (detail), 244cm high.

of new levels of object-based experimentation. In this modern era it was now good to get dirty, to physically toil with an object, to exploit folk vernacular and use ready-made materials. And sculptural activity began to be conducted as impulsively and spontaneously as any other art form, becoming un-tethered from the deliberate and calculated act, responding directly to materials and processes of the modern world.

In the Sixties, Anthony Caro, taking his lead from the energy of American abstract expressionism, began to sculpt intuitively, to draw in space with the immediacy and abandon of a pencil line on a piece of paper, aspiring to search for ways to retain a freshness and vibrancy: a form of spatial mark-making not previously associated with sculptural endeavour. Just as painting had previously signalled its own vitality with the self-portrait, so now had sculpture as the embodiment of modern artistic principles. We now take it for granted that art works inhabit floor and airspace so definitively.

These values of material integrity, mastery and uniqueness were soon subsumed by postmodern ones of collage, chance, anarchy, repetition, surface and irony. Modernism's preference for connoisseurship and universals gave way to Postmodernism's embrace of commodity and its incorporation of as many circumstances as the world contained. Gilbert and George asked whether they themselves could be the objects, that they were more complex than any sculpture could ever be. They coined the term 'living sculptures'; dressing in sober suits, feigning polite *English* personas and performing durational pieces, the pair would coat themselves in metallic make-up and stand on a table shifting slowly with robotic styled movements. Through these awkward performances the line between life and art was ever further blurred, between what constitutes the living and the sculpted form, and continued the major innovation of art – that

it exists in and consists of the same space as the viewer.

The public appeal of these feats and exploits had remained generally unfavourable. When in 1974 Carl André's minimalist piece *Equivalent VIII*, a layer of house bricks solemnly arranged in a low-lying grid, was purchased and exhibited by the Tate, it became symbolic for a language that could not be appreciated by an unfriendly and intimidated public, but this was about to change. Charles Saatchi had boldly purchased a Richard Wilson installation: a room filled with sump oil, this pitch black material perfectly reflecting the ceiling so that the sheet metal corridor hovered in perceived limbo. Queues began to form to marvel at the experience and, invigorated by this success, Saatchi embarked on a sequence of commissions, including a vitrine framing a great-white shark; a portion of the public became newly enthralled by the theatre of the art gallery. And at the turn of the new millennium the Tate opened in a converted power station with magisterial views of St Paul's Cathedral. In the turbine hall at the Tate the vast, cavernous vestibule became a site to be humbled by contemporary art; *The Weather Project* by Olafur Eliasson transformed the space into a never-ending sublime sunset, or sunrise depending on your preference, millions of visitors flocking to participate in the work.

And in 2010 in the Duveen Galleries, the grand gallery of Tate Britain, Fiona Banner suspended a Harrier jump jet from its neoclassical arches. A dull weathered aluminium grey, etched with feathered markings, its wings spanned the entire distance of the room almost touching the sides, its matt black nose cone hovering a matter of inches from the Portland stone floor. The gallery goers, captivated by the juxtaposition of this a sleek anthropomorphic object strung from the ceiling of this imposing venue with imperial overtones, shimmy and shuffle into positions before photographing themselves and their companions in a selection of poses, later posting them onto their Facebook profiles.

The gallery has become only one kind of space as art practice has become more expansive: Richard Woods 'piggy-backing' off architecture, for example, as others make work under the guise of a workshop, sculpture vibrantly entering the public domain once again with humour that maintains its spirit in a place that had previously been staid. Two decades after the pile of bricks entered the public consciousness, Keith Wilson proposes a puddle as a piece of public art.

Sculpture Has Transformed

But what of the artists, the makers, how do they make decisions? Sculpture departments in art schools across the world maintain their foundries, ensuring that an essential principle is practically available, but now an artist is as likely to atomize or extrude or draw; print, wear or perform with objects as part of an adaptable practice. And since art has been transformed into aesthetic communication it is no longer traditions but messages that count, reflecting the information age. From the printing press to the Internet, this point of the development fuelled Keith Tyson to construct a three-hundred-object extravaganza: an enlarged skull, a bust of Thomas Edison, a barbecue, a giant house of cards, an Indian yogi squashed inside a Perspex case, a dry-stone wall, Magic Johnson, a penguin on a pile of books, a stack of turtles, a plinth with giant snails and slugs crossing trails, mushrooms, a two-bar electric fire, an elephant made of mice, a typewriter, a target and a top hat – graphic representations, scaled-up sculptures, models – laid out on an enormous grid, an interrelated lattice of material, titled *Large Field Array*, after a range of high powered telescopes aimed at a single spot in space. How did Tyson start with such a

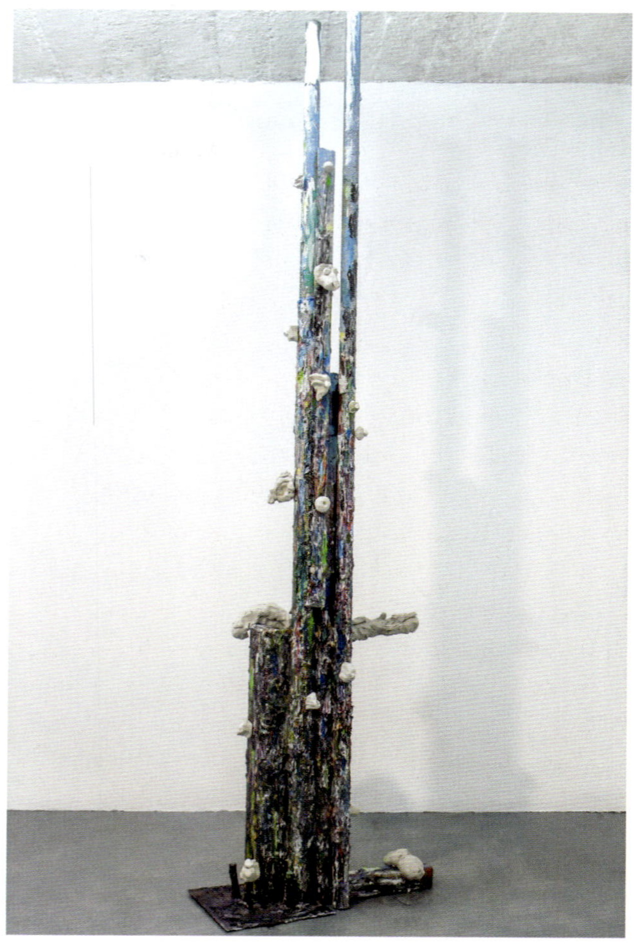

Ian Dawson, *Yon Yonson* (2011). Steel, oil and clay (detail), 244cm high.

complex piece? He looked out of his window early one morning, noticing a seagull perched on a chimney, and he decided to start there.

So I can only thank the artists immeasurably for their contributions to the book, to acknowledge their often unequivocal, always articulate assertions that they make clear choices to work unsystematically, that the processes they are involved in can be both simultaneously mindful and mindless, and that gestures that later might become iconic are sown from simple intuitive responses, and come from a stance of not knowing; that artists, irrespective of the scale of their work, endeavour to work from a position of unfamiliarity, the act of discovery still the bedrock of the making process.

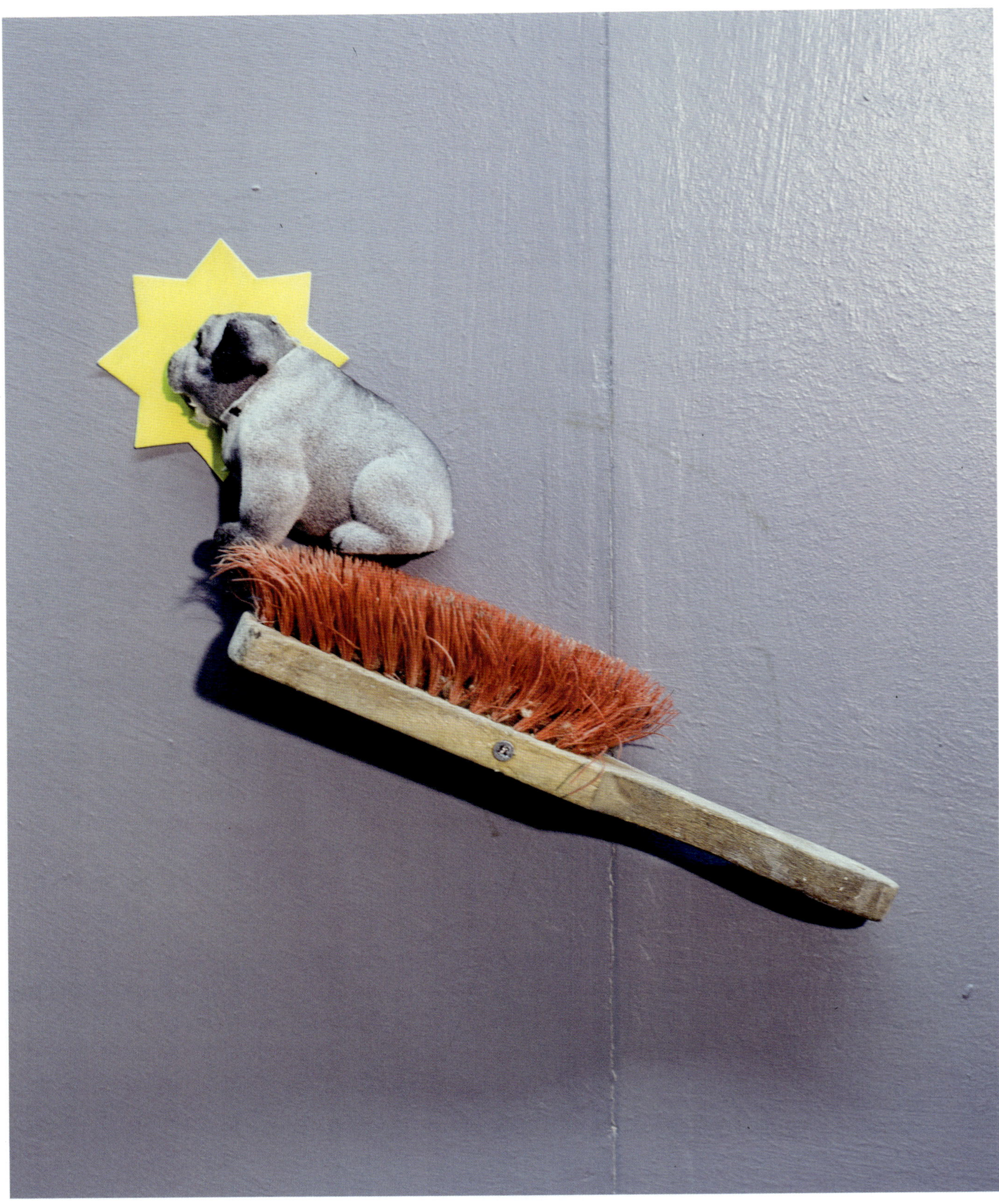

1 Material

In 1912 Pablo Picasso and Georges Braque began using pre-existing materials and objects to create collages. At first two-dimensional, Picasso soon began cutting, folding, threading and gluing material such as cardboard, paper, string and wire to create three-dimensional works. Natural and manufactured material began to be combined into assemblages that had very few antecedents. Prior to this, Western sculpture was either carved or modelled. The following year Marcel Duchamp mounted a bicycle wheel on a stool; from this point on sculpture and the modern world began a dynamic dialogue about material. Indeed, from this point on sculpture has explored, celebrated and critiqued the world through materials.

Recent sculptures are listed here, described only by their material content. Each coloured section is a different sculpture.

The list here illustrates the freedom artists currently have to use an unashamedly abundant array of materials; the freedom to be able to use materials that are bought, that are found, scavenged, swapped, even loaned, materials that are crafted or mass-produced, organic or man-made, solid or liquid. The sheer array and combinations of material and material references shuns the idea of purity of form and purity of medium. Indeed, the list emphasizes an openness to be able to use material without precepts, other than the decision to use material at all.

Following Picasso and Duchamp's early experimentation with collage, artists such as Kurt Schwitters and the Dada movement began to utilize

FUR COAT, POLYURETHANE, MIRRORED ACRYLIC, WOOD
WHITE MARBELIZED RESIN, GOLD LEAF, BARBED WIRE
SALT DOUGH, PINS, RIBBON, DOLLS EYES, POLYSTYRENE,
COLOURING, PAINT, SYNTHETIC HAIR
SCREEN PRINT SUCTION PLATE, ALUMINIUM GLOBE, CONCRETE
TWO WAY SECURITY MIRROR, STEEL, BRASS
TIMBER, ALUMINIUM FOIL, GLOSS PAINT, GERMAN BEER MUGS
COPPER POWDER IN RESIN AND PEACOCK FEATHER
CELLOPHANE, SELLOTAPE, PETROLEUM JELLY, PAINT,
PLASTER POWDER, GLASS, POLYTHENE BAGS, CONCEALER
STICK, LIPGLOSS, HAIR CONDITIONER, BATH CREAM,
TRACING PAPER, GLITTER, HAIRSPRAY, LIPSTICK
FABRIC, LATEX, CARDBOARD, PAINT AND PLASTIC
TIMBER, STEEL, PLASTIC, ELECTRIC, FANS, LIGHTING,
PAINT AND TAPE
ONE HUNDRED AND TWENTY-FIVE CARVED LIMESTONE ROCKS
THREE HUNDRED SPEAKERS, PIANOLA, VACUUM CLEANER,
AUDIO AMPLIFIERS, HARD DISC RECORDER,
SPEAKER WIRE, SUCTION HOSE, PIANO ROLL
OAK TABLE, LEATHER BOUND BOOKS, CUSTOMISED BOOKS
NEON STICK, STRIP LIGHT, JESMONITE, PLY AND GLOSS PAINT
ABACUS RUG, IKEA TORIM LAMP, NOGUCHI REPLICA TABLE,
ROBIN DAY CHAIR, NIKE DUNK SUPREMES, BUDDHA HEAD,
PANTON MINIATURE, RASHID LIGHTER
SUGAR PAPER, CHALK, RIBBON, LIPSTICK, GLITTER
SILICON CARBIDE, PAINT, ARTEX, POLYSTYRENE, CAN,
CIGARETTE BUTTS
WOODEN PEDESTAL, TWO POLYESTER ELEPHANTS, TWO
PLASTIC DICE, SHELL PLAYING CARDS, TWO SMALL PLASTIC
FIGURINES, PAPER BIRD, STAINLESS STEEL PERFORATED
PLATE, C-PRINT WITH ADHESIVE TAPE, LAQUER AND SPRAY

OPPOSITE PAGE
Dan Coombs, *Pollen* (2001), detail. Mixed media.

A list of materials.

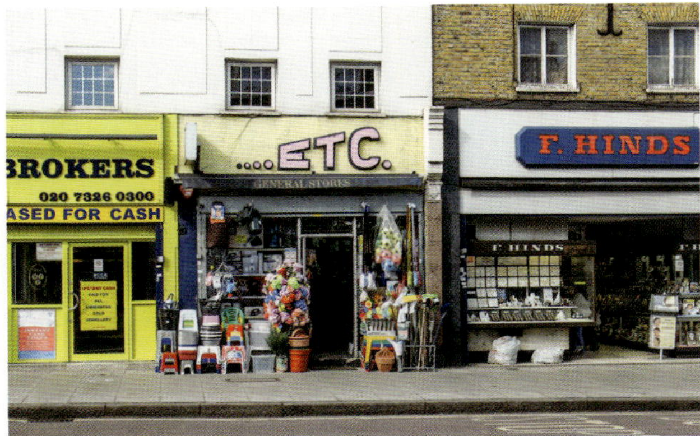
ETC general store.

fragments of used, damaged and reclaimed material. The inherent abject qualities of these materials were retained and were combined in absurd ways to characterize the notion of a senseless world. Dada was committed to disregarding rational material combinations in an attempt to politicize art. To revel paradoxically in a nihilistic act was the means to question the logic of a society at war.

The essence of this febrile period, which formed the foundation for Surrealism, remains in contemporary sculpture: the use of cheap, readily available material that enables making with spontaneity, whim and verve without having to rely directly on any specialist skill, or craft, to realize the work. In continuing to combine real materials and real objects it has the capacity to explore the complexity and confusion of contemporary life. In an increasingly digital age, there appears to be ample justification for a method of creation rooted in the material and the physical.

Meaning and Material

In 1996 I had recently moved studios and I remember passing Woolworths every morning and becoming interested in the changing palette of colours: mustard- and salmon-coloured packing crates, jelly shoes, fluorescent clothes hangers, picnic plates in pastel. The charity shop next door had an ever-growing bucket of brash toys, Disney merchandise, happy-meal giveaways. I began making work with these things and started to become engrossed with the plastic 'backstory'.

Metal, stone, wood, ceramic, glass, skin, horn, and fibre – these eight kinds of materials had provided previous civilizations with the material for most of their objects and possessions. Ambitions had remained within the parameters of those materials. That situation changed in the twentieth century when chemists learned to synthesize substances that had never before existed and began to specify properties.

In 1862 at the Great Exhibition in Crystal Palace, Alexander Parkes unveiled the first man-made plastic. Parkesine was a cellulose-based material that unfortunately in this instance proved more expensive than rubber to manufacture. Early plastic innovation was about finding substitutes, replacing scarce and expensive materials. Billiards, for example, had become so popular that it was significantly contributing to the endangerment of elephants; thus an alternative for ivory snooker balls was necessary – and in 1869 John Wesley Hyatt invented one. Then came the first fully synthetic resin, Bakelite. Unlike previous plastics this substance would not melt, burn or dissolve. Then rayon, nylon, cellophane, Teflon, PVC, polyethylene, polyurethane, polystyrene, neoprene and polyester arrived, and to an ever-increasing degree the things of everyday life became moulded, extruded, blown, foamed, stamped and vacuum-formed. The stuff of the world became synthesized in chemical refineries from petroleum. Objects, appliances and furnishings began to take on a completely new visual appearance and tactile quality.

Plastics are polymers: they are large molecular chains built up from small simple chemical units. The simplest, polyethylene, is a long chain of carbon atoms with two hydrogen atoms attached to each carbon atom. The substitution of a chlorine atom for a hydrogen atom creates polyvinyl chloride; introducing oxygen and nitrogen produces nylon. By adding to these chains, chemists were creating novel and complex properties replete with possibilities. To shape and mould stuff at a fundamental chemical level, to inject it with properties, textures, and colours unknown to earlier generations, to mould it into objects and environments unknown to prior civilizations – all these marked a degree of human control over nature. The developments of the synthetic chemical industry compared favourably with the idea of a pliant planet open to human influence. And reconfiguring manufactured plastic with heat by instantly remoulding everyday plastic objects was a way for me to explore those analogies.

'I want to say just one word to you, just one word. Are you listening? Plastics.' This is the secret given to Ben, played by Dustin Hoffman, in the opening of the 1967 film *The Graduate*. Generations have grown up with Airfix and Lego, hula-hoops and frisbees, Action Men and Barbies, Lino and Formica, biro pens and carrier bags. The evolution of plastic during this period typified a culture interested in the pursuit of material goods.

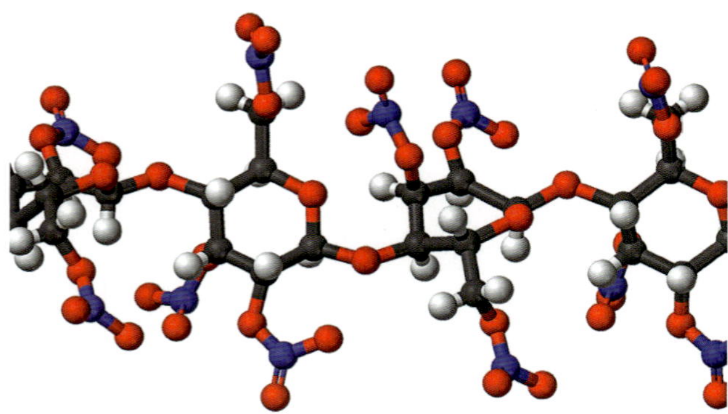

The chemical structure of a cellulose-based product (nitrocellulose).

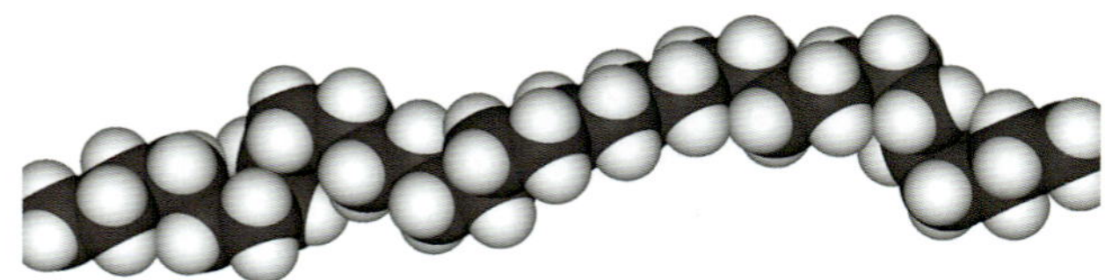

The polymer chain of polyethylene.

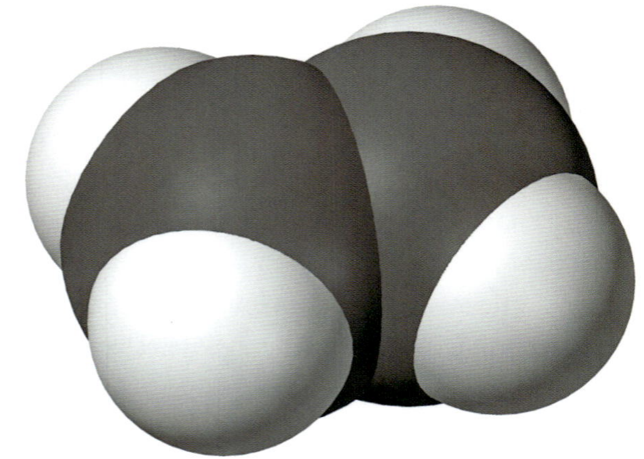

The ethylene molecule.

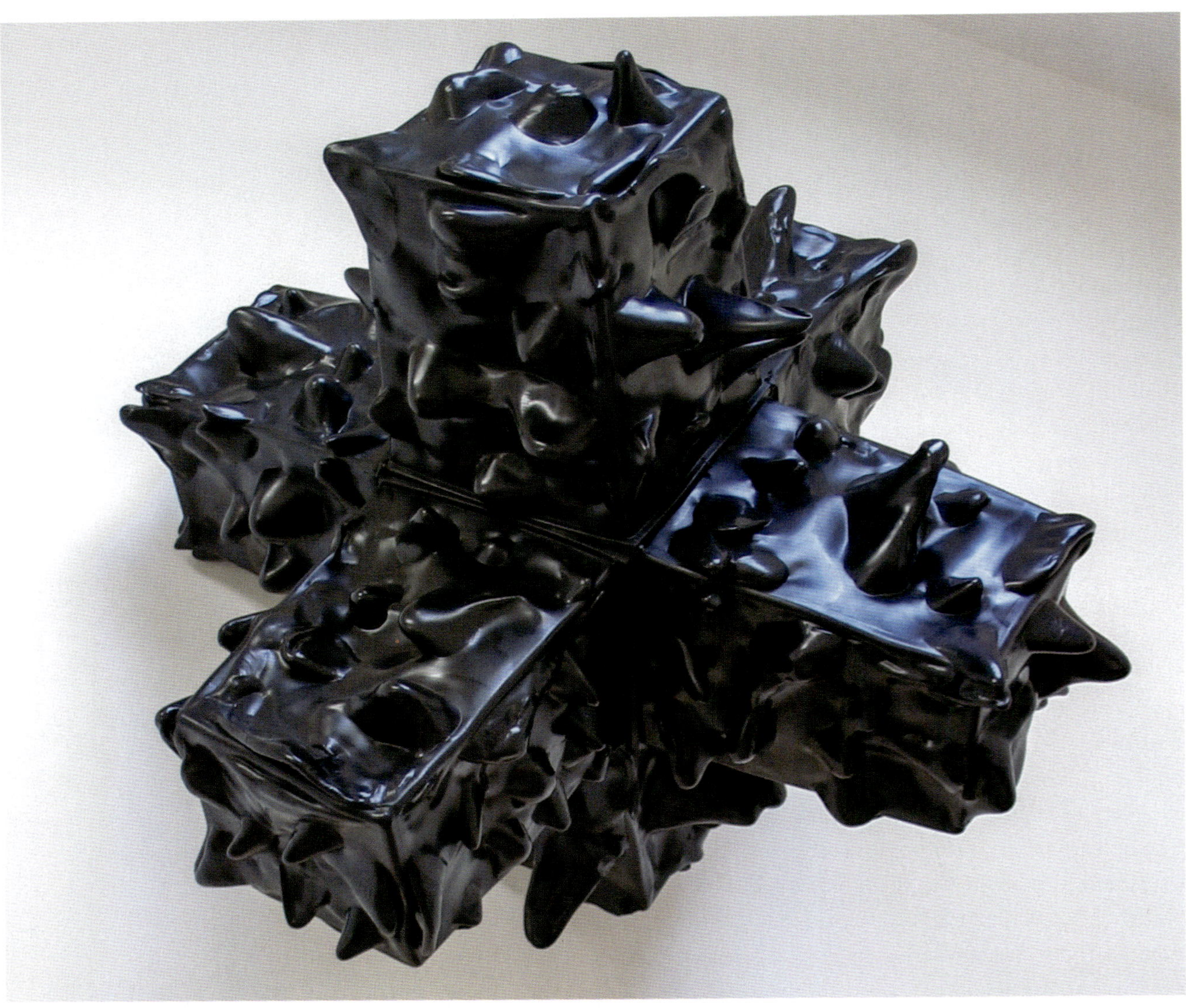

Ian Dawson, *Blackbins* (2002). Plastic, 182 × 182 × 182cm.

Health scares and the toxicity of various materials have added to the negative connotations of plastic. Though plastic is relatively inert it is apparent that some are unstable, for example the garden chair that becomes brittle after a season in the sun. On a molecular level some chemicals when added to the polymer chains do not bind strongly. Phthalates, for example, are added to provide added flexibility to a host of plastic products, including the ubiquitous credit card. However, phthalates have been found to leach into the environment and are considered to be an endocrine-disrupting chemical, which can disrupt the hormone system.

During this period these reflections on plastic motivated and inspired me: our evolving relationship towards it and our contradictory assumptions of it. It has an ability to be both wonder stuff and environmental evil. The proliferation of cheap plastic continues to affirm unromantic symbolism against those products that continue to enter everyday life with value.

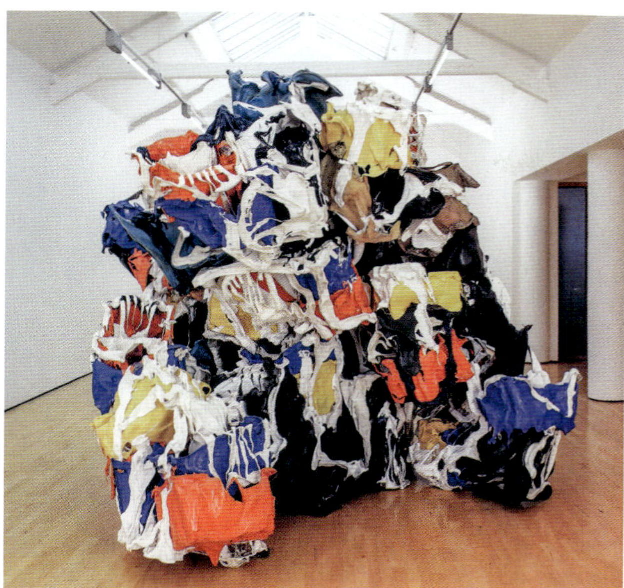

Ian Dawson, *166 Elements* (1998). Plastic, 265 × 374 × 323cm.

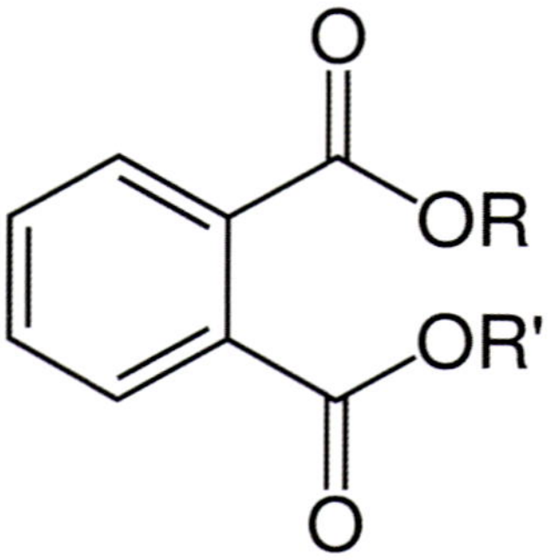

The chemical structure of a phthalate.

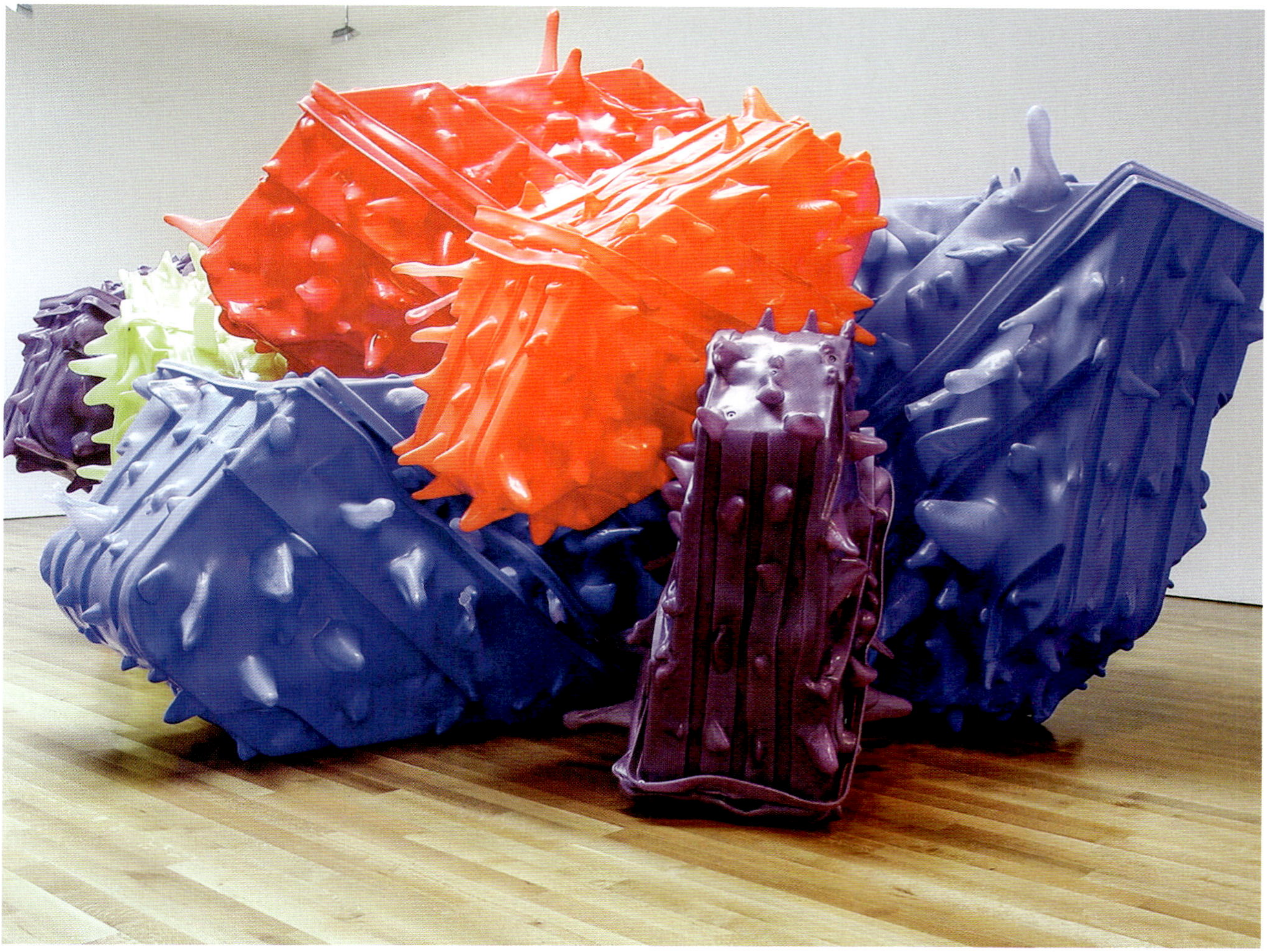

Ian Dawson, *24 Tilt Trucks* (2002). Plastic, 427 × 746 × 304cm.

Detergent bottles and a strip light, mounds of cable, pools of rippling paint on paper, sunglasses and cable ties, a McDonalds trolley and coloured perspex, Dexion shelving and light boxes, wheelie bins, neon lights. Combinations of bright cheap consumer goods sidle alongside the light industrial. The by-products and left-overs from the making process also become subsumed into the work. This is David Batchelor's studio where materials act as catalysts, as starting points in a speculative open-ended practice. Here Batchelor discusses his practice.

IAN DAWSON: *So where does it all start?*

DAVID BATCHELOR: Stuff. It starts with stuff rather than ideas. That's it! The reason why I say it starts with stuff is because people ask me how do I have my ideas. And it is not necessarily that the ideas come first, it is often that I see something and I think that maybe I can use that. For example, when I first visited São Paulo I noticed that the warning signs for their road-works consisted of an upright steel rod, a coloured plastic bucket atop of the rod and a light inside the bucket. Seeing this on the street inspired me to think that I could adapt something along those lines. But of course I only noticed the road-works signs because I had been thinking about colour in the city, so the two – the idea and the work – come along in unison. I have a sense of what I am doing, some sort of sense of focus but I can't predict what will happen within that range; anything I see can trigger some development in the work.

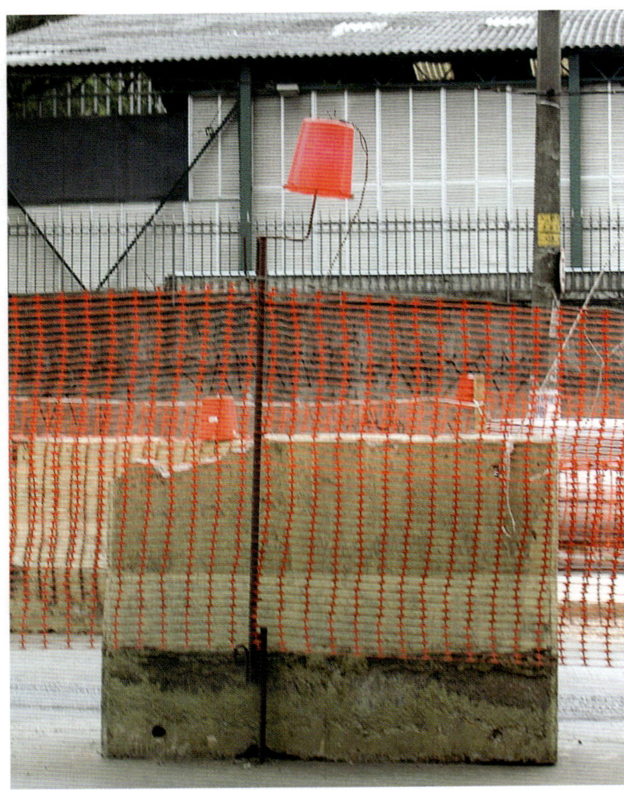

David Batchelor, São Paulo street scene.

ID: *Is there a particular method that you use when you collect materials?*

DB: It has to be quite unsystematic, because you don't know where it is going to go and what it is going to deliver. So if there is a methodology, it is 'suck it and see'. So there is no method particularly. I am always on the look out for brightly coloured material that is found in the city. So then anything within that range I would drag back to the studio and see what, if anything, comes of it. That's how I found these very cheap sunglasses in a street market, again in São Paulo, and it was plastic – check, brightly coloured – check , cheap – check. Right, buy fifty pairs, take them home and I didn't know what I was going to do with them. Initially I thought I might be able to make a screen out of them, something that hung, then I don't know how it happened but I started tying them together and they started to form globes, so that's what triggered making these so called 'eyeballs'.

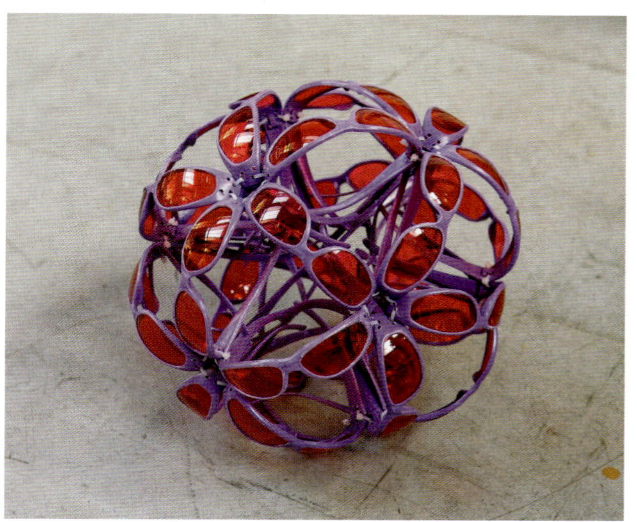

David Batchelor, *Eyeball* (2007). Thirty pairs of plastic sunglasses, 300mm diameter.

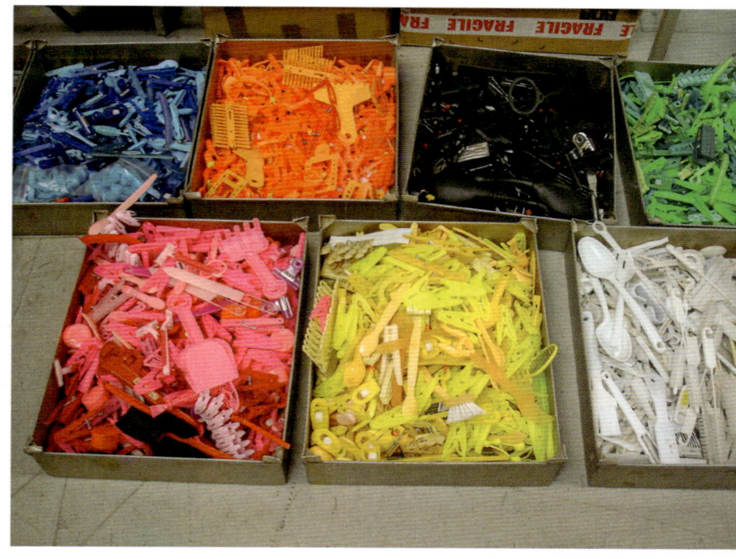

David Batchelor collecting for *Parapillars* (2006–7).

ID: *You have become more discerning with your material choices?*

DB: When I was less focused I would have my head in a skip and I would drag something back to the studio like a demented hunter-gatherer and it would sit there for ten years and not do anything. Sometimes things are too intrinsically interesting in their own way and you can't do anything with them. Sometimes just nothing happens; sometimes something happens after it's been lying around for five years. You never quite know.

ID: *Are you interested in the back-stories to the materials you choose?*

DB: In lectures I tend to talk about where the materials come from and I've written about where you find colour in the city: it is in pound-shops and on supermarket shelves. And I tend to talk about those things and put it in writing but I don't make it part of the work *per se*. I prefer to let the work sit on its own, and let people make their own minds up about it. I have made a whole series of works that came from pound-shops. A series of works that became pillars made with about four hundred individual objects. I started to get interested in the whole phenomenon of pound-shops – they are everywhere, in every city, selling identical goods. The market is global and it appears to be all from one source. The function of the pound-shop, it seems to me, is for people who can't afford to consume to go there to consume and to join the economy. I find this all very interesting but I don't include that as a part of the work when it is being shown.

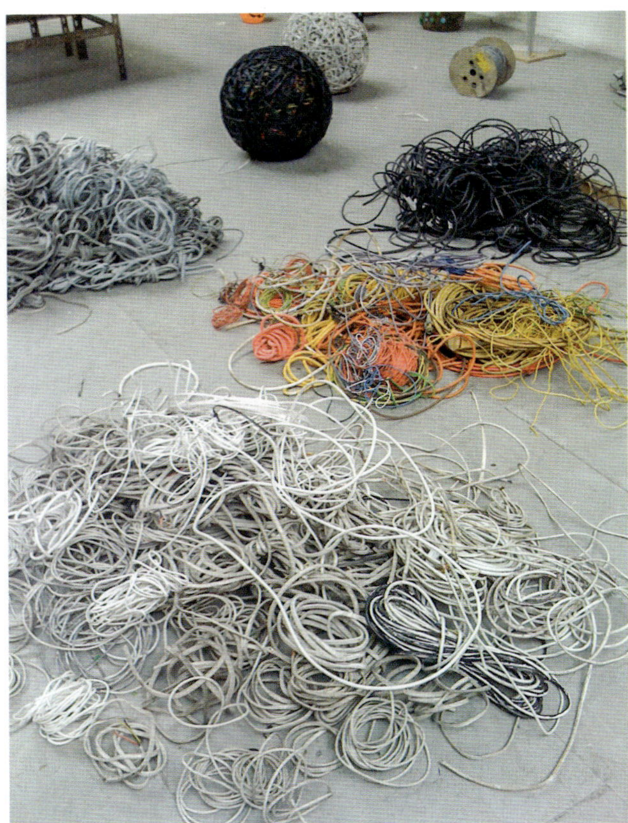

David Batchelor, flex.

ID: *And these balls of electrical cable?*

DB: The first ones were made from the flex I had left over from stripping out old light boxes; it just accumulates in the studio. It's one of those materials that gets totally overlooked, flex and cable, that if it were to suddenly disappear the whole world would fall apart. Every building must contain hundreds of thousands of metres of this stuff, you sort of know about it but it's all hidden and concealed. I didn't really intentionally do this but one aspect of my work is about drawing attention to overlooked things, the overlooked everyday stuff of the city that is so ubiquitous that you don't really see it. That is not the whole intention in the work; it is a part of it, I guess. This particular pile of cable came from Bloomberg, all of their defunct cable goes to a depot by London City Airport, to be stripped down. I'm always on the look-out for old cable, in order to make these rather slow lumbering balls, and usually you have to pay for it because of the copper in it. This flex has been here for three months – it may or may not get transformed into more balls, I will find out at some point whether or not it's got more life or not, and if not I will end up chucking it.

ID: *So the work develops from having materials in the studio?*

DB: Yes, that's why I very rarely have my work made, only occasionally when it has to be. I strongly believe that the studio is a site to work, where you learn and find things out and it's only by fumbling around with things, trying to make two things stick together that don't particularly want to, that's when you stumble across something that does stick together both in your mind and physically. It is in the process of working with materials that new ideas get generated. If you have something in mind that you think you are going to do, the chances are you are going to get to the studio and it doesn't happen, but something else may do, and it's that sort of irregularity that I depend upon in which the work begins to instruct you and you learn what needs to be done from the materials instead of imposing on the materials what you want done. You have to follow the material in a funny kind of way; you can't make materials do what they don't want to do, somehow. Sometimes you can work with a material with a given idea in mind for a couple of years and it just doesn't happen. That's part of the deal.

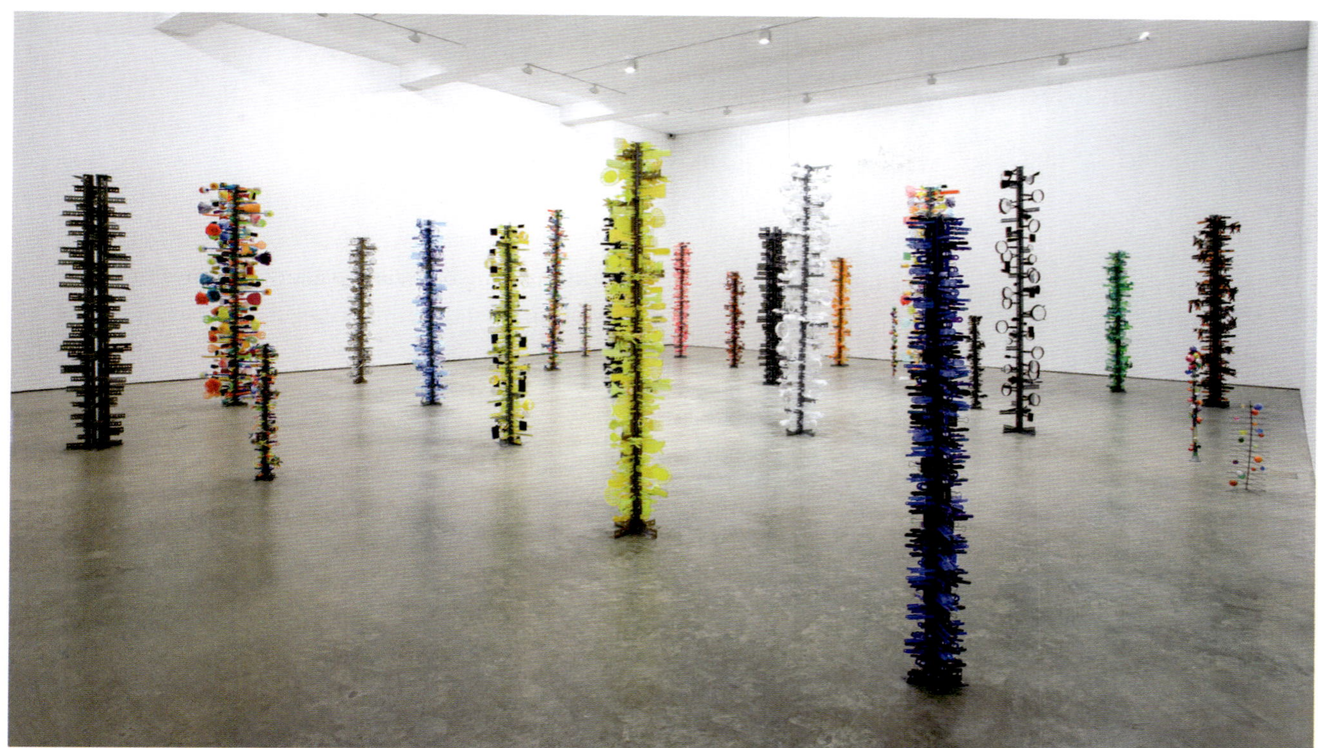

David Batchelor, *Parapillars* (2006). Plastic household items, toys, bric-a-brac, Dexion shelving uprights.

ID: *How do you edit your work?*

DB: When I make something, the first one of a type, what I think about it when I've just made it, those thoughts are not to be trusted. So if I think, 'Fuck, that's good', I go home, watch telly, and then go back the next day. The chances are I will think it is kitsch. Sometimes I have to turn things to the wall for weeks, or months even, and when I look at it again I start to see it for what it is rather than what I have aspired for it to be.

ID: *This way of working must make you prolific?*

DB: I guess I get prolific at certain moments when I have a deadline. It took me at least eighteen months to make the pillar series, and I got totally obsessed with them, as you have to. I was desperate to make the next one and the next one and I was going around pound-

shops, leaving with ten carrier bags worth of stuff, with the owner waving goodbye, saying, 'Come back soon'. At that point I was driven.

ID: *You tend to work with groupings in pieces.*

DB: I tend to make quantities of a related thing and stick them together. I think it's to do with the phenomenon that when you stick a lot of things closely together they lose their individuality; they lose their specific individual presence and they gain a different kind of character. If you stick five hundred plastic bottles together, you don't immediately see them as individual bottles, you see them as a cluster. Equally with the pillars you first see a furry pole, where the colour is the dominant thing. It's only when you get up close to it that you realize it's made from pegs and knives and forks and things. That's the reason for me to work with quantities, amassing things together, to

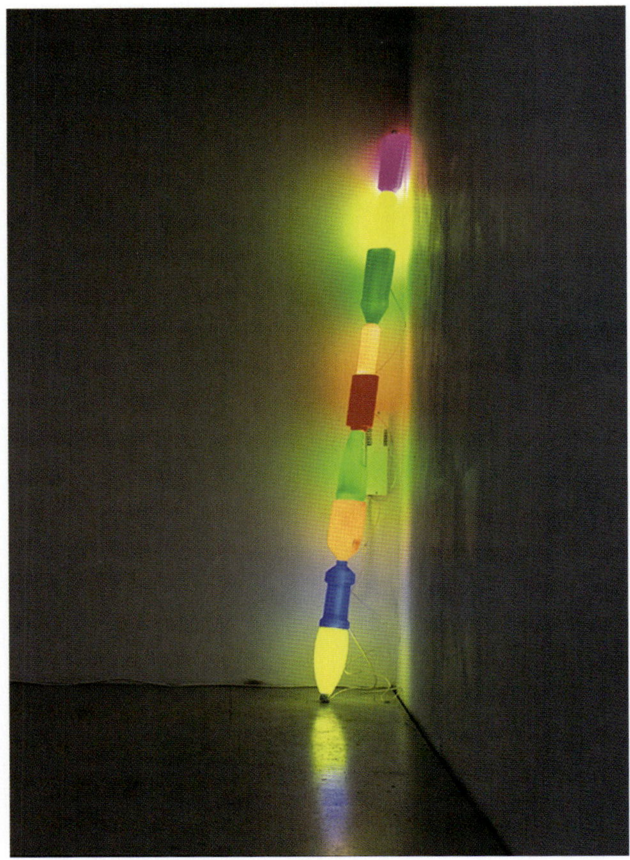

David Batchelor, *Idiot Stick* (2006). Plastic bottles, polycarbonate, fluorescent light, cable, 179 × 10 × 9cm.

suspend the identity of the objects for a bit, so that the colour takes over. So that you see the colour first, rather than the object. Whereas normally you might go, 'That cone is yellow', here you can say, 'That yellow is a cone'.

ID: *Do you also work across groups of pieces in the studio?*

DB: I tend to like to have more than one thing on the go at once: to have some drawings on the go, to be working on a sculpture, to be building something for a show and to be thinking through a new idea, all at the same time. I tend to like having a few things ticking over and move between them. I guess I want

to keep a number of balls in the air at the same time. I have always thought there are two main ways of working as an artist. One is the Piet Mondrian way, to have one thing and work on it ruthlessly, with an extraordinary focus, to get everything else out of the way and to narrow it down and narrow it down. And the other way is the Robert Rauschenberg way, which is to say, 'Let's see how much shit we can throw at this and see what doesn't fall off.' I am drawn to the Mondrian way but I am not capable of working like that. I am too impatient, and I also believe in the ethos of Arte Povera. I recollect the Alighiero Boetti show at the Whitechapel Art Gallery and it was like he would choose to work with a material only until he had got good at it. It was an acknowledgement that once you've got good at something, that's when it becomes slick or knowing, and it isn't about finding your way anymore and I thought that was a really wonderful ethos.

You know you have to work against yourself sometimes, work against your good taste, your habits of thought. It is so easy to fall into habits, tending to use a certain coloured material, knowing that it behaves in a particular way, rather than to try to use materials that you aren't drawn to, that you don't find easy, otherwise it is just mannerism in the end. So you have to do two very contradictory things: work against yourself, as well as following your nose – it's psychologically odd. I don't think that's just me but everyone who works with materials in the studio. But that in the end is what is interesting, because in the end that is how you find things out about yourself.'

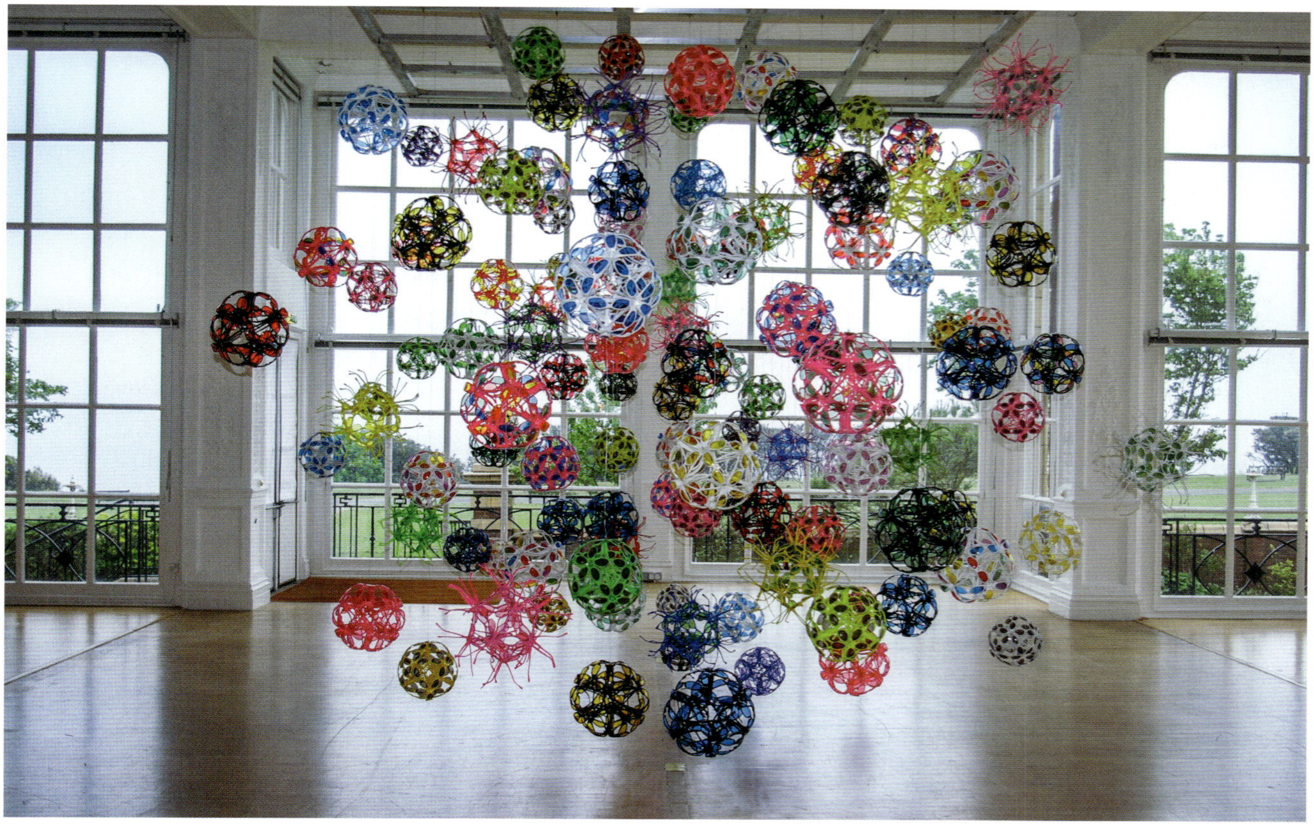

David Batchelor, *Disco Mécanique* (2008). Plastic sunglasses.

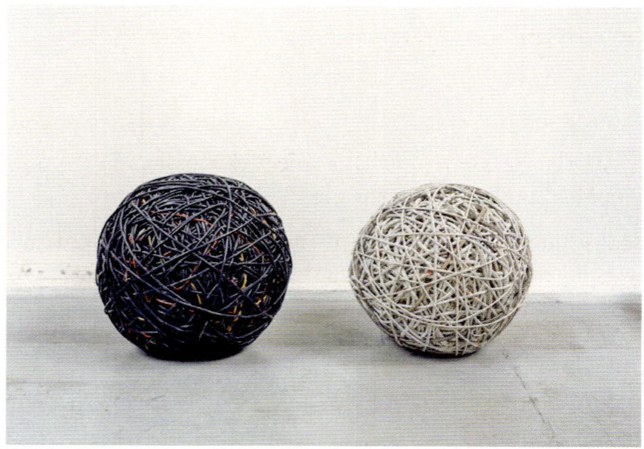

David Batchelor, *Dog Day* (2005, left). Electrical flex, 430mm.
Doris Day (2006, right). Electrical flex, 390mm.

DB: That's absolutely right. I want something to happen. I don't want to disguise the materials I work with. I don't want to hide the fact it's a trolley, but I want to do something to it that just takes it out of itself.

ID: *But not too far?*

DB: No, its still a trolley, it's still of the City, of everyday life. But it's different enough to be interesting to look at. So in a sense they are like adapted ready-mades. They are ready-made materials but something is done to them; a light is added or a panel of colour, or they are formed into a shape. Something is done, but not much. And almost nothing is done that cannot be undone.

ID: *So elements come back to the studio and are reconfigured?*

DB: Yes. It drives galleries mad! They ask where a certain piece is and one component is over here, another is over there. The only reason for the pieces to become fixed is if and when they are sold and they become someone else's property. In a way I do believe in the dignity of everyday materials: if you pay attention closely almost anything is or could be interesting, interesting enough to look at. And it's trying to do just enough to hold someone's attention for a bit. ▪

Material Choice

The recycling centre is where the stuff of domestic refinement and excess begins its cycle of re-conversion. It is the place to go to recover and reclaim objects and materials; much like charity shops and car boot fairs, these are places to rescue objects whose original value has stalled, for whatever reason. It is replete with the broken, the unwanted and the outmoded.

The scrapyard is an industrial version of the recycling centre. This is an evocative place: it's dirty, and oil oozes drearily across the muddy ground. Car bodywork is a mound of convoluted metal, contorted and twisted. Vehicles appear tossed with abandon onto piles. There is an imposing scale and inherent energy to the site. Heaps of rubber tyres cascade from corners of the yard and a crate of car batteries recalls the purpose of the site. The yard is active: men etched with grease are busy but how it works is never quite clear – how does this area of apparent chaos assist in converting the car back into its constituent parts? At another yard, length after length of imperial-gauge steel lies rusting in racks with little value beyond its scrap price. Copper, bronze, lead, aluminium, cast iron, mild steel, all have fluctuating prices depending on global demand.

These are some of the accessible places where materials are scavenged and the artist can rummage. This experience alone is insightful into the way materials are cast aside, parked waiting for the next step in the cycle.

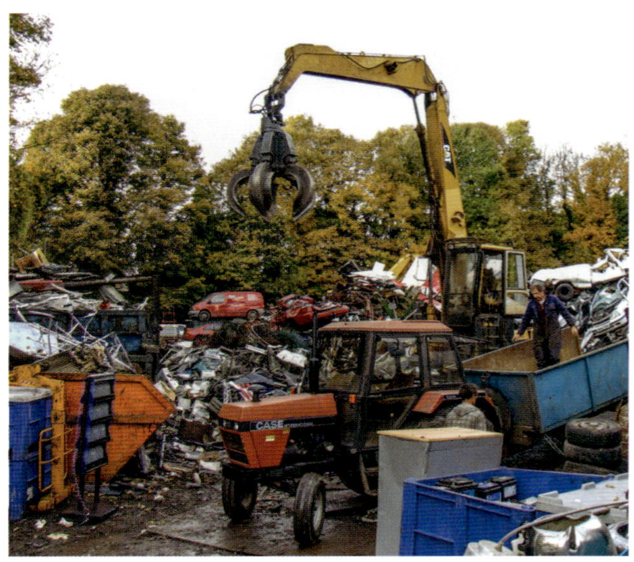

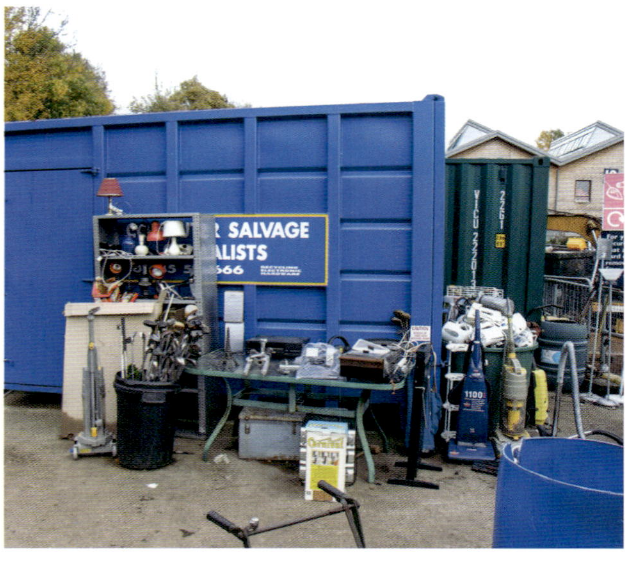

Recycling centre.

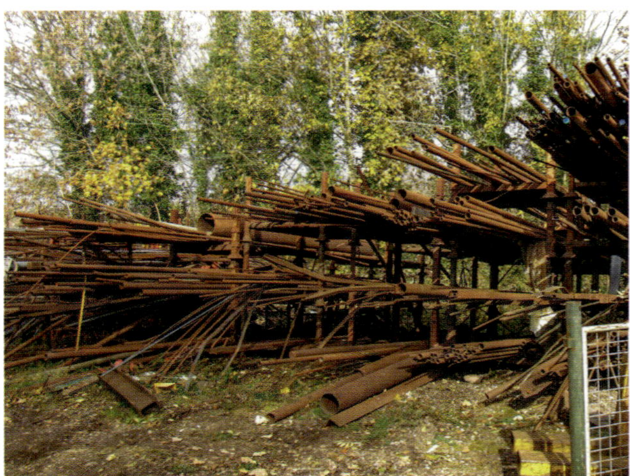

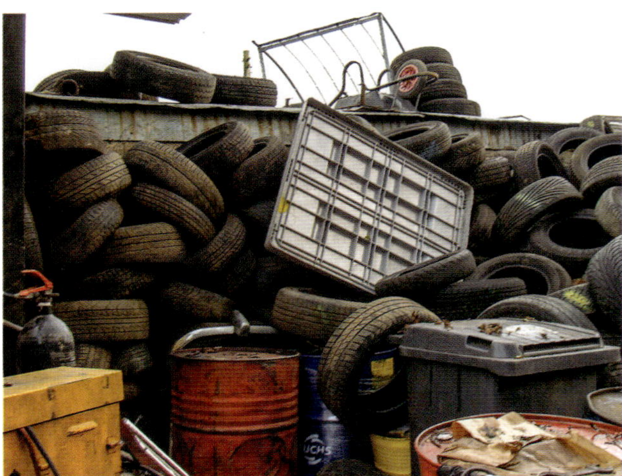

Images from a scrapyard.

The Material Library

With the expansion of material science another resource is fast becoming available: the material library. Material libraries are predominantly databases of material swatches to assist in material choices in design and industry. The Institute of Making, however, is an altogether more tactile resource, which houses the world's lightest solid and the blackest black.

In 2005 the artist and designer Martin Conreen was at a materials conference for academics. Sitting in the gloomy lecture theatre, he was bored and about to fall asleep when Dr Mark Miodownik stood up, rose to the lectern, and started to talk passionately about materials. Miodownik was a materials scientist from King's College, London, and had come with a suitcase-sized wooden box containing samples of a variety of known materials such copper, lead, tin and glass as well as some newer ones, including a viscosity-altering ferrofluid and alloys that remember their previous shapes. Conreen sat up and started to pay attention: this was a selection of materials that immediately had a resonance, that seemed physically to connect the past with the present.

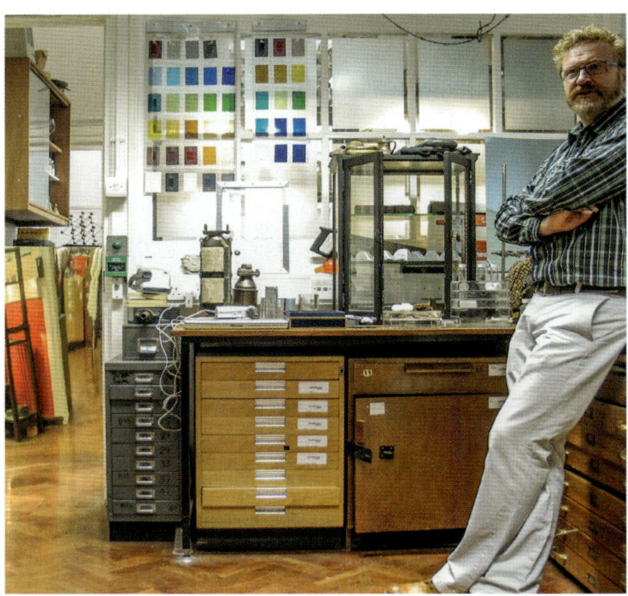

The material library with Martin Conreen.

Along with the artist Zoe Laughlin, he started to put a material library together. And in two small basement rooms below the Strand the library began to take shape with an eclectic and eccentric collection of objects and 'stuff'. An assortment of shelves, plan chests and cabinets began to be filled with an abundance of different materials, including an aerogel that is 99.8 per cent air (it doesn't just resemble a hyper-real cloud, it *is* ethereal). There is also a strip coated with the world's blackest black, which absorbs 99.9 per cent of light.

Material libraries are the conduits of materials science, a new repository for the study of both the molecular and physical qualities of materials, appreciating that traditional forms of classification are not sufficient with the growing plethora of invented plastics and biomaterials. However, most other material libraries are swatch-based and supply a service to product designers and manufacturers, a database for locating materials with specific properties for specific purposes, with a literal relationship toward product design methodologies. But here, there was a conscious decision to collect materials as objects, to ensure a physical response to them, to make the resource more pertinent to artists, who have a more lateral interest in material questions. Miodownik, Conreen and Laughlin felt it was important to assert that art and aesthetics should continue to offer inspiration to technology. Artists utilize materials with a tacit knowledge that helps them to recognize their value, and an understanding that materials scientists have become ever more involved in a realm of expertise dominated by data sheets.

There is a container of translucent cubes, a row of tuning forks, and bells, so as to explore sonic material references physically. Conreen acquired the largest piece of silly putty that he was able to export from a trip to North America; this became a signifier of metamorphosis, of how solids become runny, to enable discussions about the science behind material states. It was also symbolic of how a material languishes between applications; invented in the Sixties without any purpose, becoming a plaything before being harnessed as protective equipment.

The archiving system is chronological and there are quite deliberately no labels, so that each object is encountered first, touched and reacted to instinctively; in one cabinet aluminium and carbon vie for attention. A dense black ingot of pressed peat displays a primitive physicality – dense, evocative of the stored energy within it. It comes as no surprise that religious icons, Irish artefacts and souvenirs have previously been moulded from this stuff. Nearby is a piece of polyester chainmail produced by a starch printer.

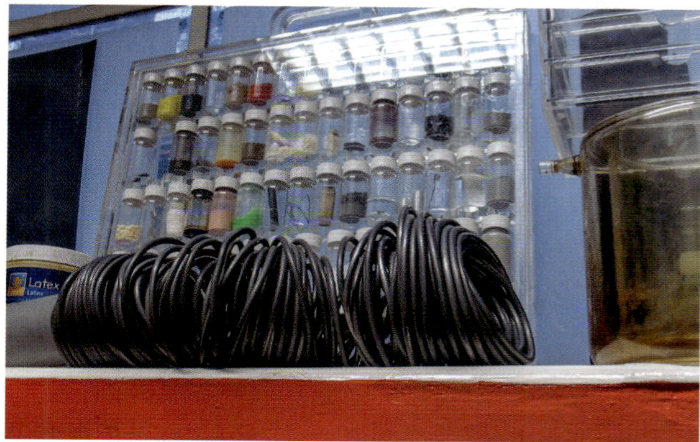

The material library (ledge).

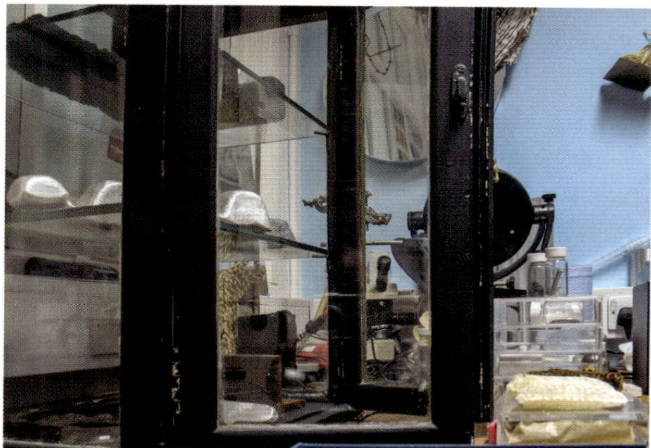

The material library (cabinets).

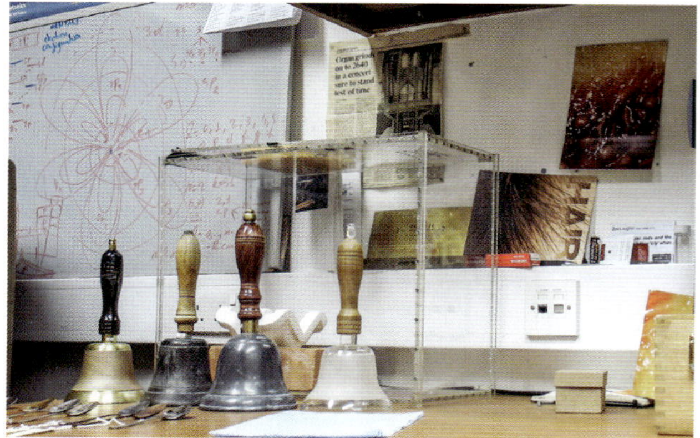

The material library (bells).

Sustainability is constantly debated, whether it be current trends for recycling or presumptions on mining landfill. There is a history of recycling resources: in Ancient Rome, kilns once surrounded the main architectural sites in order to turn marble statues into lime for building, and the library has an optimistic outlook – it acknowledges life cycles of materials. Whole periods are named after materials – the Stone Age, the Iron Age and now the Silicon Age – each period defined by how that particular material has impacted on humankind and how civilization has made the most of that material. And the library is evolving, continuing its objectives to work broadly, without specific outcomes, and without a commercial remit. It has aligned itself to the Institute of Making in order to assist its growing membership of creators who are coming to the library because they want to make something.

▶ Dan Coombs

A broken hand basin, a row of Sunny Delight orange juice bottles, a tape measure, a packet of paracetamol, insulating tape, a broken window, an extractor flue, some chair legs, an old bed, a toy spider, and reconstituted toilet tissue: all coalesce in Dan Coombs' uncomfortable and psychologically charged sculptures. Here he discusses his thinking behind working with objects in an uncomfortable and uncompromising way.

IAN DAWSON: *Shall we talk about your assemblages?*

DAN COOMBS: What I find interesting is that until I made these pieces I couldn't make collages. I was too overwhelmed by the possibilities; I thought I wouldn't know where to stop. It also seemed cheap, it seemed without enough coherence and too random – it's something where anything could happen, it's something anyone can do. Prior to this all those things were unattractive to me. I couldn't get to grips with the psychology of collage, because with collage you can just keep going for ever; it's like a psychosis in a way, you can use anything, it's a kind of madness. So I really put a lid on it, I thought, 'I don't want to go there.' And then it just sort of exploded. With these pieces it was a Pandora's box really.

ID: *Was there a sequence of events that made you turn to collage in this way?*

DC: I became interested in Eva Hesse: she had the phase in between being a painter and a sculptor. *Hang up* (1965–66), for example, is a frame on the wall with a big loop stretching down to the floor. I really responded to this piece because it didn't quite know what it was – it wasn't a sculpture or a painting. Hesse had somehow made the artwork's own lack of identity the subject of the work.

Dan Coombs, *It's Raining* (1999), detail.

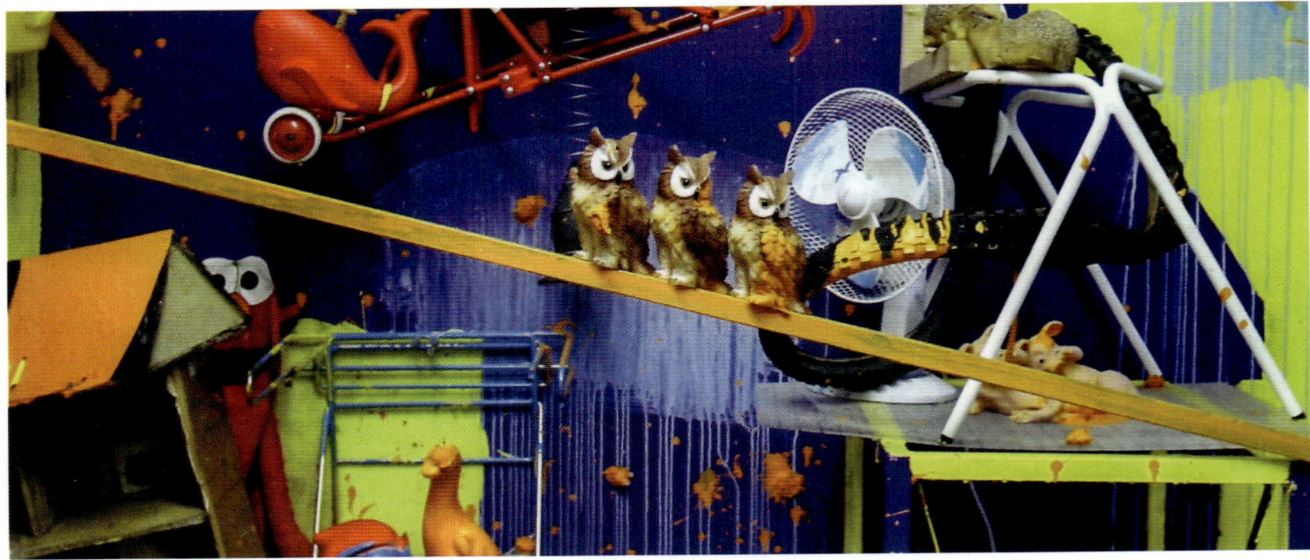

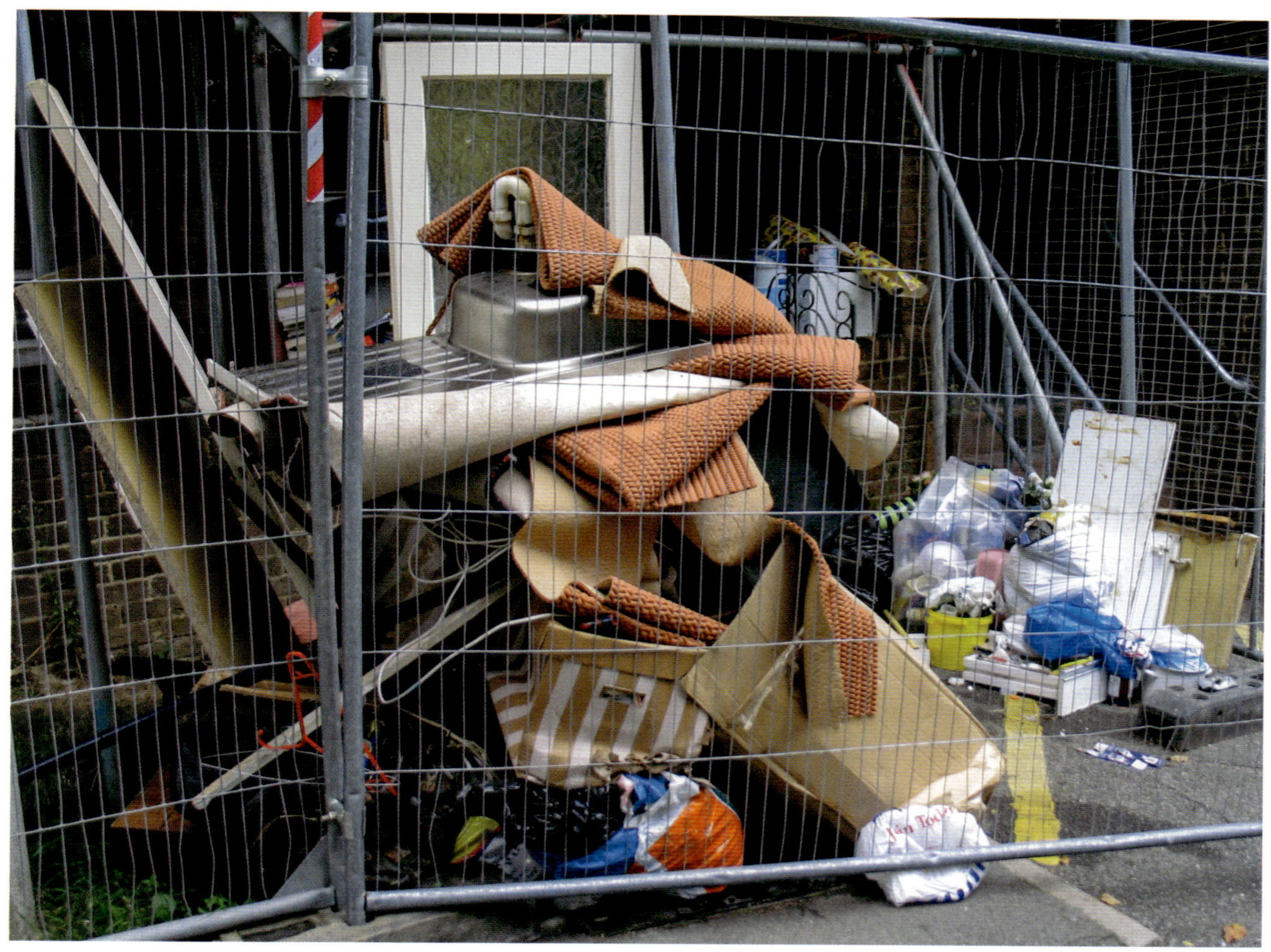

Material pile 2 (2010). Loughborough Junction estate, Brixton, South East London.

DC: I had started to become interested in these pathetic piles of objects that people throw out. Bits of furniture and domestic detritus, piled up outside blocks of flats and they seemed really poignant. I was looking for something at the time that would get under the skin a bit more and these piles to me seemed very real. I felt that some of the objects look back at you. So I would see something, think that it was fascinating and take it back to the studio, and just have it in the studio. I started finding things. Some were incredible finds: I remember finding nine film canisters, and a small roll of film. The film was a scene from Jim Jarmusch's *Down By Law*. The prison scene when Roberto Benigni draws a window onto the wall of his cell. And you start thinking about coincidences and randomness and what that means. And then the objects start building up, and the objects start to go together in different ways that are beyond what you could first imagine.

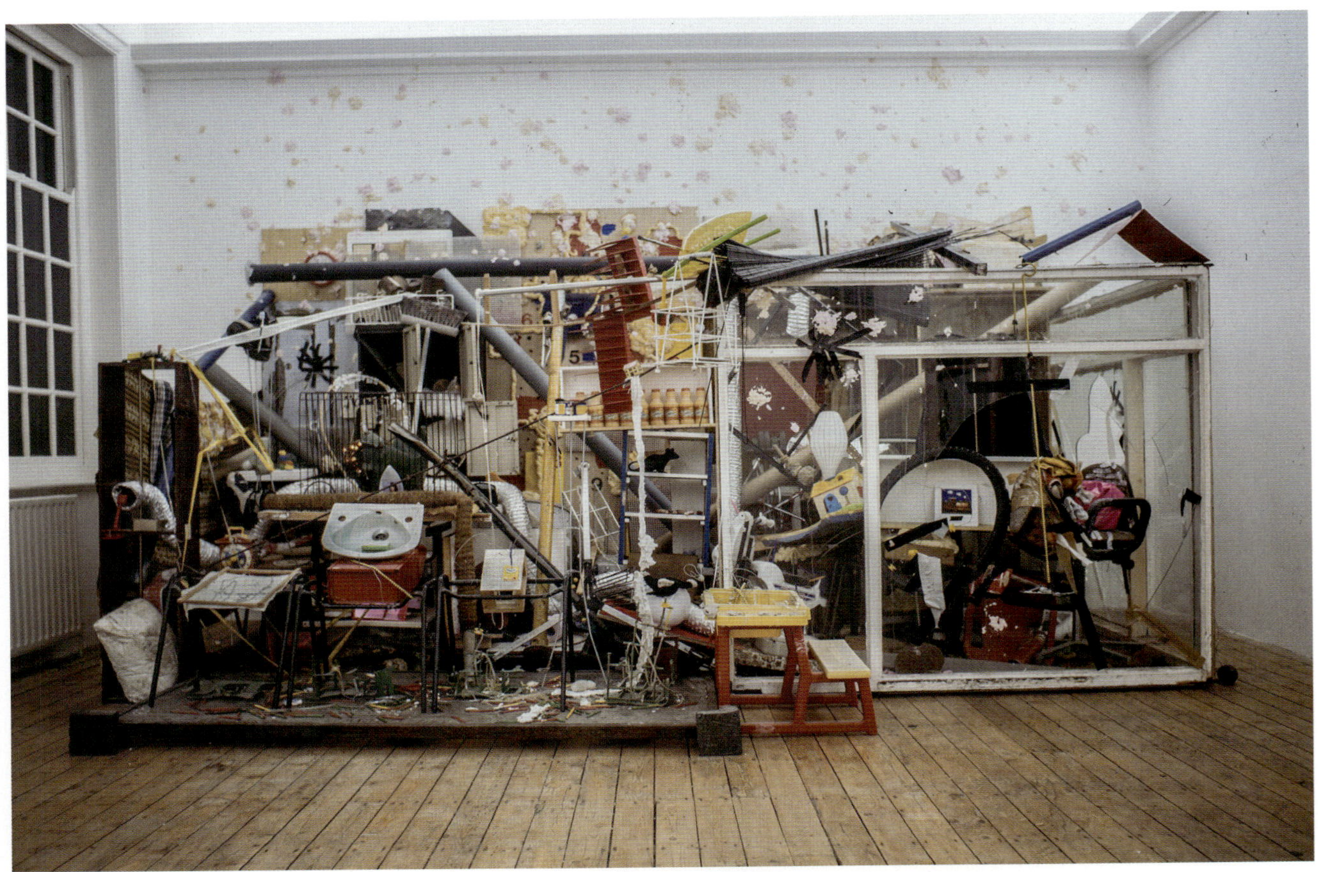

Dan Coombs, *It's Raining* – installation at The Approach, E2 (1999).
Mixed media, 488 × 366 × 244cm.

ID: It is quite an extensive range of objects.

DC: I was interested in the psychology of the objects, or the human quality, or their abject quality, or their narrative quality. I remember thinking when I was making this that it was incredibly important that every object was different. Another artist might focus on using narrow groups of items; I didn't want to do that. There are the odd multiples – a packet of fake pencils, for example – but on the whole everything is different.

ID: It is a real mixture – Sunny Delight cartons, broken washbasin, tubing, window frames, railings…

DC: It was only when I started moving all these objects against the wall, using the objects in a pictorial format, that it began to make sense for me. I then salvaged a set of windows from a nearby renovation, and once the stuff had been sectioned off through the windows it really started to work. Until then it had been a struggle for the thing to find its own overall form. It nudged the piece back into being a whole room. I liked the idea of looking in through a window, the voyeuristic nature. And then I couldn't resist throwing a brick through the glass as well.

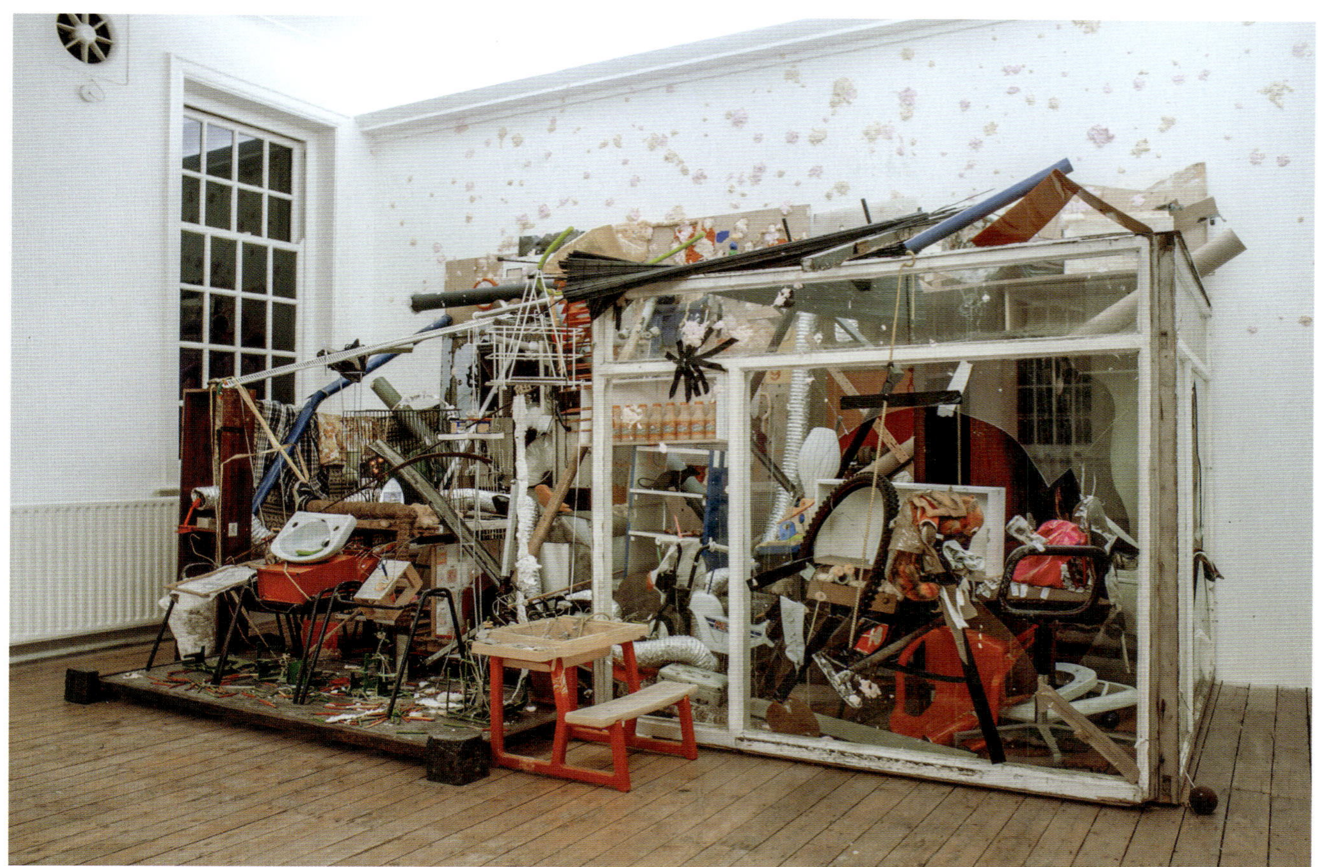

Dan Coombs, *It's Raining* 2 – installation at The Approach, E2 (1999).
Mixed media, 488 × 366 × 244cm.

DC: My studio partner came in and went, 'What this piece needs is this,' and just lobbed some wet toilet roll at it, and it went splat on the wall. There were a lot of things I liked about that gesture, the totally juvenile quality of that. It felt like it underpinned how anarchic it was. It also helped create an 'overallness' that I was interested in – two influences at the time were Peter Doig and Jackson Pollock. Both were exhibiting at the time and both shows helped me with the idea of this overallness.

When looking at the piece I sometimes see something that is highly structured and sometimes I see something that is just a pile of rubbish; the fact that it flips between just a load of rubbish and being constructed is really important. I think if you were only aware of it as being constructed, it would not have any psychological edge. That's why a lot of the juxtapositions have to be random and gestural as well as built. It was a way of exploring the idea that maybe you can actually give up on having intentions, creating the illusion that things just occur, that you can give up on your own intentions and just let things happen. That is always an illusion.

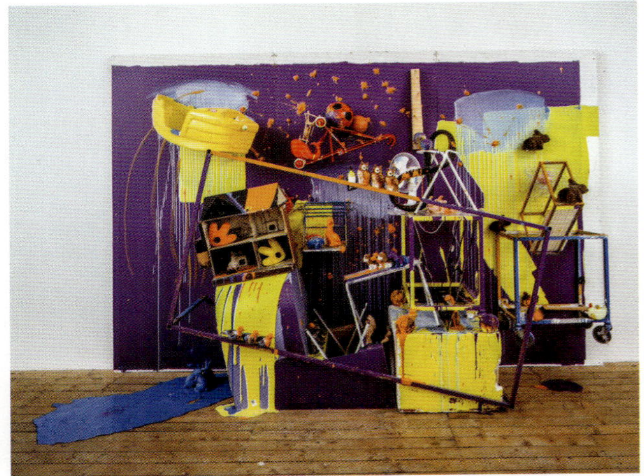

Dan Coombs, *Moon River* (2001). Found objects and mixed
media on board, 244 × 379 × 106cm.

ID: *Is that how you work out when a piece of work is
finished?*

DC: I look for a totality, and also to be led somewhere.
When a piece is unresolved, the 'why' hasn't been
answered; also it feels that I am being led on a wild
goose chase. Whereas with a piece that is finished there
is a set of relationships that hold together, like a film.
It's the feeling of having the total structure.

ID: *Your interest in film is important?*

DC: Yes, cinema is important. David Lynch has been
very important to me. All his films are built up from
fragments – he doesn't necessarily start off with an
overview, he starts off with fragmented ideas and
hopes that they will gel. I do think the way he works is
interesting: he does collage his films.

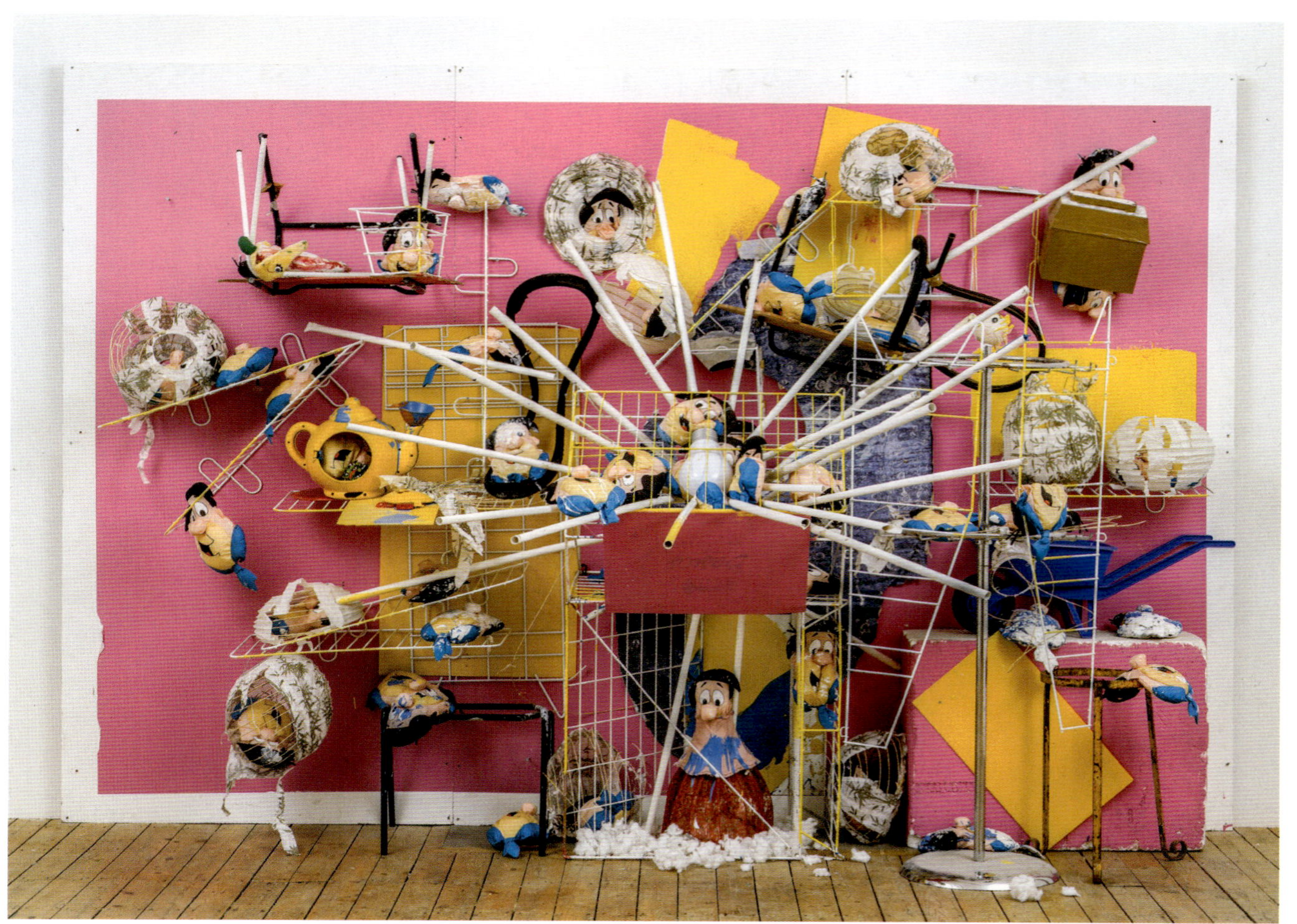

Dan Coombs, *Self Portrait as a Light Bulb* (2001). Mixed media on board, 244 × 366 × 200cm.

ID: *There is a clear similarity of principles.*

DC: I also think there is some political element to working in this way. I think they are about seeing things: seeing possibilities in juxtapositions that you wouldn't normally imagine of things coexisting. It is incredibly important that you want the subject to come out implicitly rather than explicitly. Or that your ideas inform the work but that they are not necessarily the programme that makes the work. For me it was important to be able to collage things that are radically opposed together. I think it is really important to emphasize the discontinuity of things; it might seem that you are revelling in a kind of anarchy but it's making you recognize, helping you to understand, how different people are from each other, and what a huge gap exists between people and things, as opposed to imagining that everybody or everything is cut from the same bit of cloth, which is what politicians do. There seems to me something completely corrupt about trying to be as universal as possible, aspiring to make art that is universal. There is a certain capacity for art to have an ethical dimension, and it often comes in surprising forms and I think in a way David Lynch fulfils this concept. Because he has absolutely looked at his dark side and has pronounced that difference is the key. It may sound obvious but it is really important. It is when you don't look at that, that is problematic. ∎

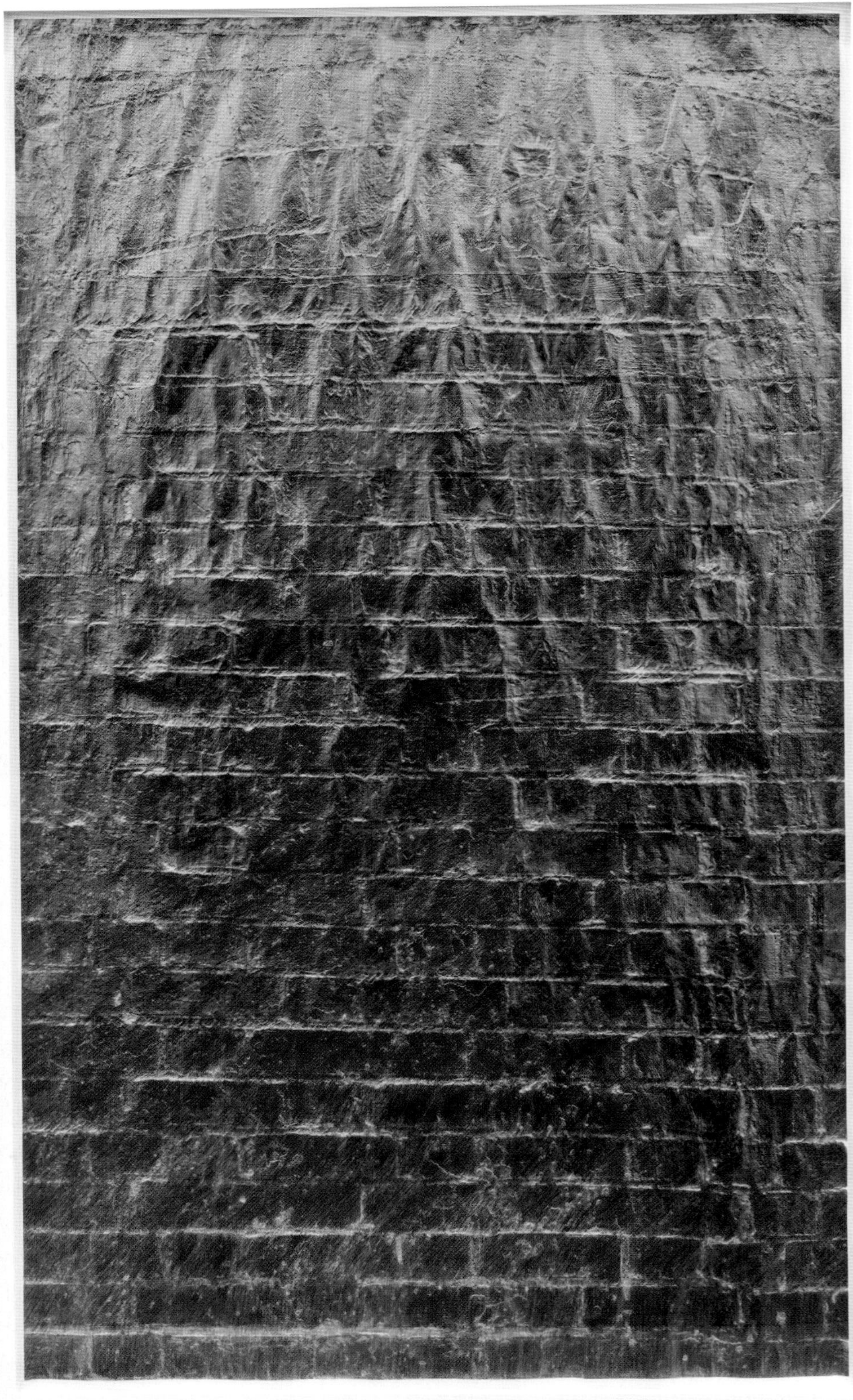

2 Process

In 1950 Jackson Pollock picked up a paint pot and reached over a strip of canvas draped across his studio floor and began to drip paint onto it, stretching and straining first with his arms and then with his whole body, creating tracks and trails of dribbled paint that captured the trajectory of his hand, leaving an indelible trace of all that had gone on in that moment of synthesis.

In conceding to the fluidity of the material, Pollock directed the essence of his work back towards the natural world; through accident and gravity and with the paint congealing on the horizontal plane of the floor, it moved the activity of making into a direct engagement with natural circumstances and states. Process became the work.

Subsequently, artists such as Robert Smithson, Eva Hesse and Robert Morris started to approach work from a position of chance, contingency and indeterminacy; predetermined plans were eschewed as they elaborated on notions of change and transience. They allowed actions such as cutting, hanging, stacking, piling and dropping to affect their work.

Morris termed his work of this period 'Anti Form' and in an essay and exhibition from 1968 suggested a basis for making art in terms of process and time. In *Continuous Project Altered Daily*, Morris visited Leo Castelli's warehouse space every day to create a fluctuating installation. Here he would work playfully and randomly with materials such as felt, threads and grease alongside physical props such as timber frames and platforms. On some days strata of rolled felt would droop and drape over timber armatures; on other days piles of timber, rubble and dust were scattered and strewn across the panorama, the tools (a leaning shovel and broom) contributing to the dynamism of the scene.

Morris made a diary of his activities: 'First day of the Continuous Project in the Warehouse. Dumped out 200lb of wet clay out of 50lb cans onto floor. No idea what to be done with it. Began aimlessly – throwing it around.' Morris was also photographing the location at the end of each day, adding a new image to the wall for the duration of the show. And on the last day of the exhibition Morris tape-recorded the de-installation and clean-up, playing back the recording whilst shooting the final photograph, a scene of the lone tape deck in the vacated space. *Continuous Project Altered Daily* was an unambiguous denial of a composition based on linear progress.

> There is no reality except in action.
>
> Jean-Paul Sartre

OPPOSITE PAGE
Anna Barriball, *Untitled* (2009). Pencil on paper, 218 × 134cm.

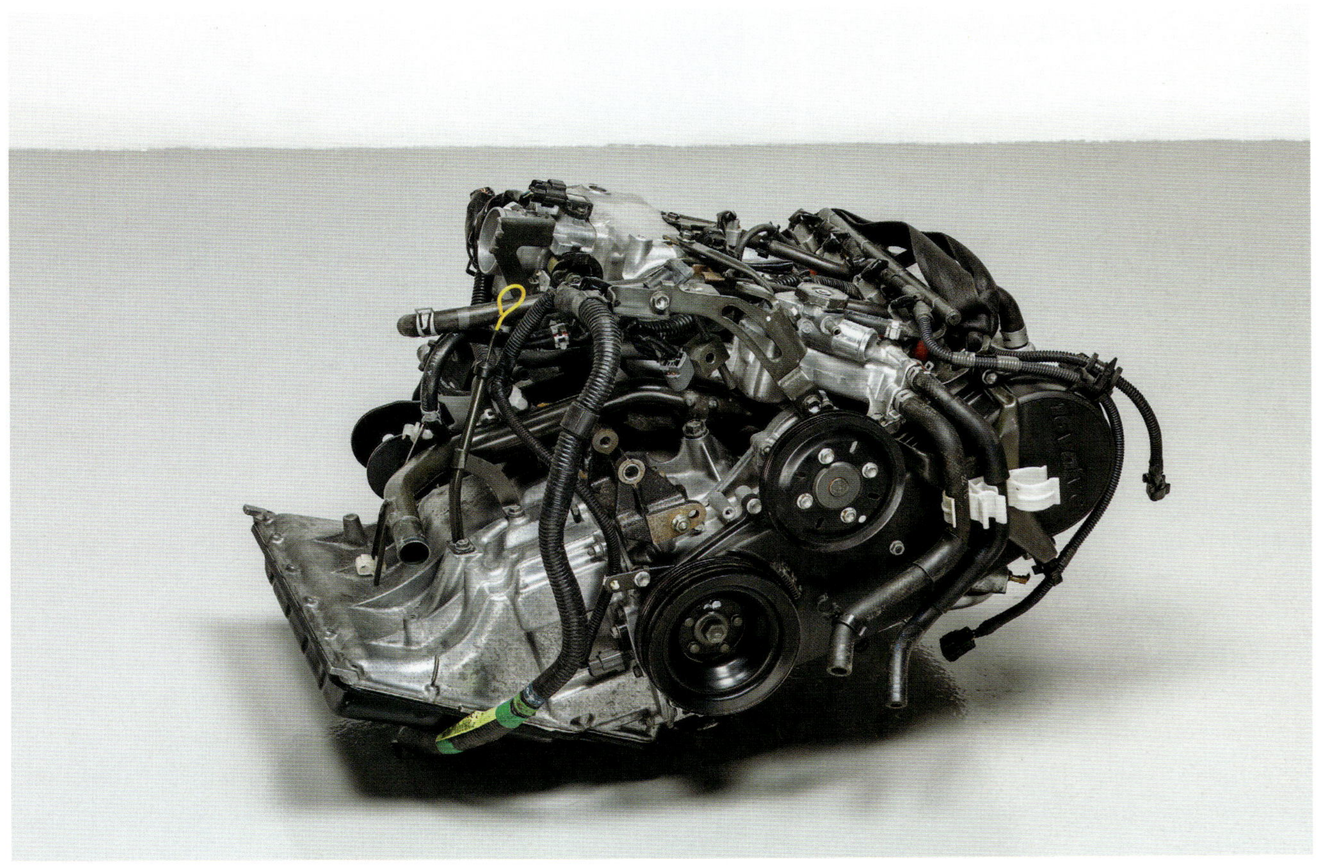

Roger Hiorns, *Untitled* (2008). Toyota engine, brain matter, 76 × 61 × 50cm.

Energy and Entropy

In 1970 Robert Smithson arrived at Kent State University, Ohio, for a one-week residency and with the aid of a bulldozer, he and the students proceeded to bury a timber and stucco shed that stood on a secluded part of the campus. Scooping bucket-load after bucket-load of earth and soil over this disused building until the central beam creaked and collapsed, Smithson immediately announced the piece finished and titled it *Partially Buried Woodshed*. Using a nursery rhyme he articulated his motivation in what had become a serious subject of sculptural enquiry: decay, and in particular its central relationship to energy.

North America was on the verge of its first oil crisis,

Humpty Dumpty sat on a wall
Humpty Dumpty had a great fall
All the King's horses
and all the King's men
Couldn't put poor Humpty
together again.

and energy transformation – a fundamental aspect to the world – was becoming a conscious subject for artistic discourse. The advancement of industrial civilization had entirely been determined by the

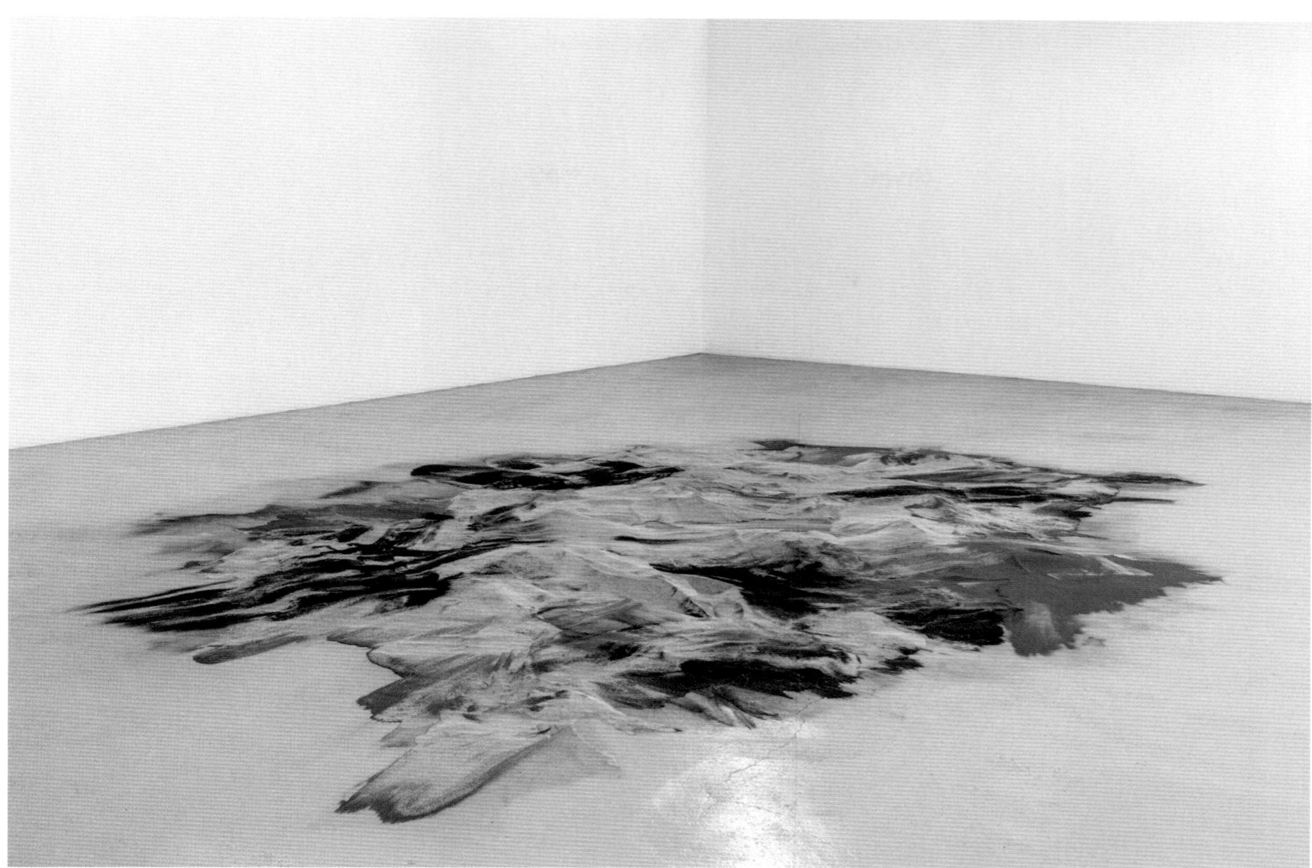

Roger Hiorns, *Untitled* (2008). Atomized passenger aircraft engine, dimensions variable.

imperative for energy and the apparatus to transform it, from waterwheels and windmills to steam turbines, the electric grid and the nuclear reactor. Improvement in quality of life is proportional to increased energy consumption, and entropy, a condition of the second law of thermodynamics, became a significant symbolic reference that artists have explored ever since.

The first law of thermodynamics explains the conservation of energy: it cannot be made or destroyed, just converted from one state to another – from light to heat, for example. And then the second law emerged: it describes how this flow of energy will always tend towards a more chaotic state, that it is an inexorable slide towards formlessness. Entropy was the measure of this, and became the buzzword for this principle, and it helped shift a vision of the world from a stable entity governed by rigid and deterministic physical laws to an inevitable mutable state in an expiring universe. And as artists began to look at temporal processes, they began to explore the concept of entropy. In Roger Hiorns' 2008 untitled installation, the viewer is confronted with undulating dull grey dunes spreading across the floor, an absorbing landscape of atrophy. These ash-like granules are the remains of a passenger aircraft engine; atomized by the artist and scattered across the floor in its most disorganized and implausible state; an example of a final state of macroscopic uniformity and microscopic disorder.

There is also no physical way to return to the earlier position of the aircraft engine unimpaired, a categorical physical statement of the universe's tendency towards a more disordered state. Death in

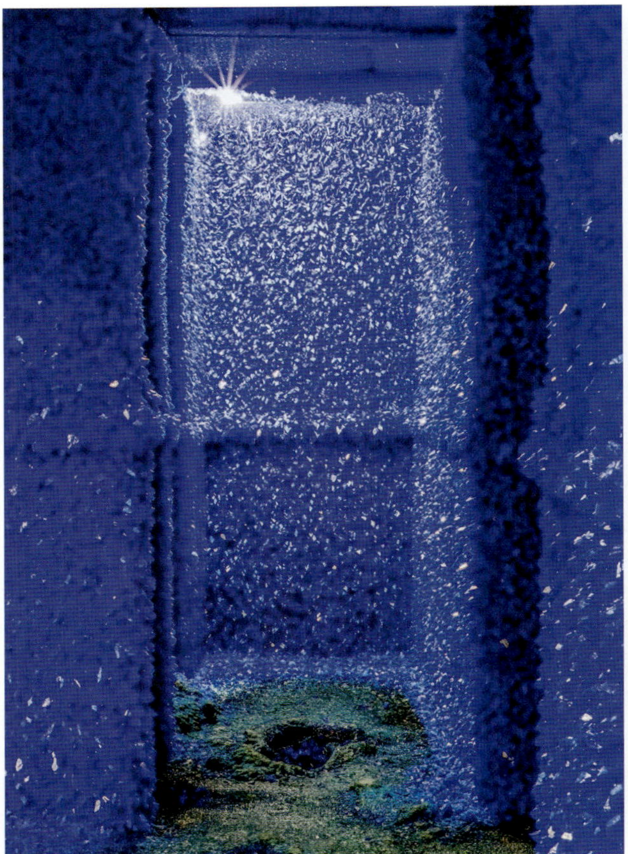

Roger Hiorns, *Seizure* (2008). An Artangel/Jerwood Commission, Harper Road, London.

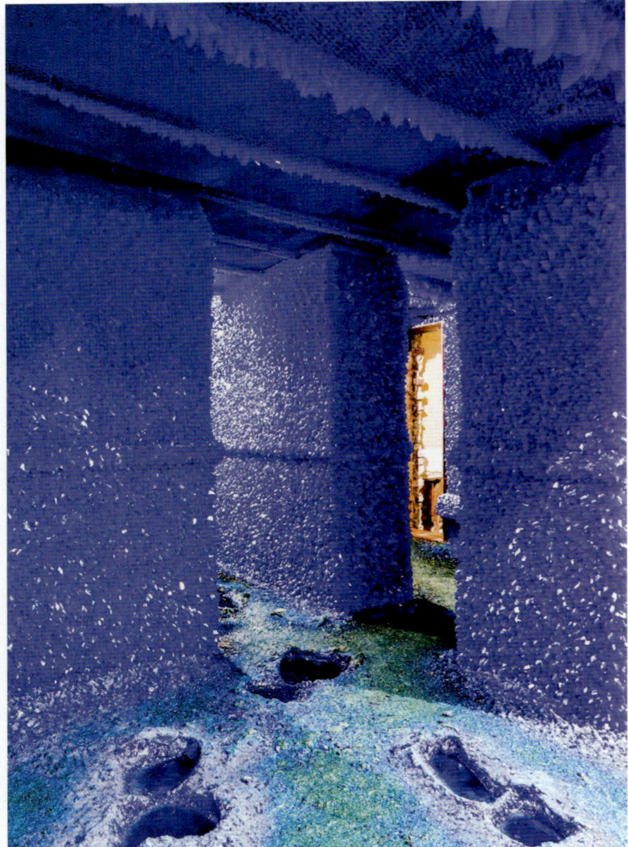

Roger Hiorns, *Seizure* (2008). An Artangel/Jerwood Commission, Harper Road, London.

physical terms is inescapable; time, a one-way street. This idea was no more arrestingly rendered than when Hiorns chose to fill a complete flat on a derelict estate with copper sulphate crystals; the rooms transforming into a glowing cave of calcification.

Entropy and its connotations extended beyond energy to information. Like energy, information became a vital principle pervading every facet of the physical world. From simple origins in the telephony industry the idea of information with a basic unit of a bit has permeated through life; DNA became a piece of information, 6 billion bits to form a human. 'If you want to understand life, don't think about vibrant, throbbing gels and oozes, think about information technology,' declared the evolutionary theorist

Richard Dawkins. And the universe came to be seen as an entanglement of information; the black hole an information-swallower.

In 2011 Erik Kessels printed every photo that had been uploaded in a 24-hour period to Flickr, the photo-sharing website, and sprawled them across a gallery space, relaying the ultimate contradiction that encompasses entropy and information. Millions of images, a barrage of digitized data; a tsunami of family snaps, landscapes, portraits, pets, occasions, all indiscriminately scattered and heaped. It's the total noise of *The Library of Babel*, a Jorge Luis Borges story that portrays a library containing all books, in all languages, on all subjects. This library preserves all information, the true alongside the false, and precisely because of this, no knowledge will ever be found there.

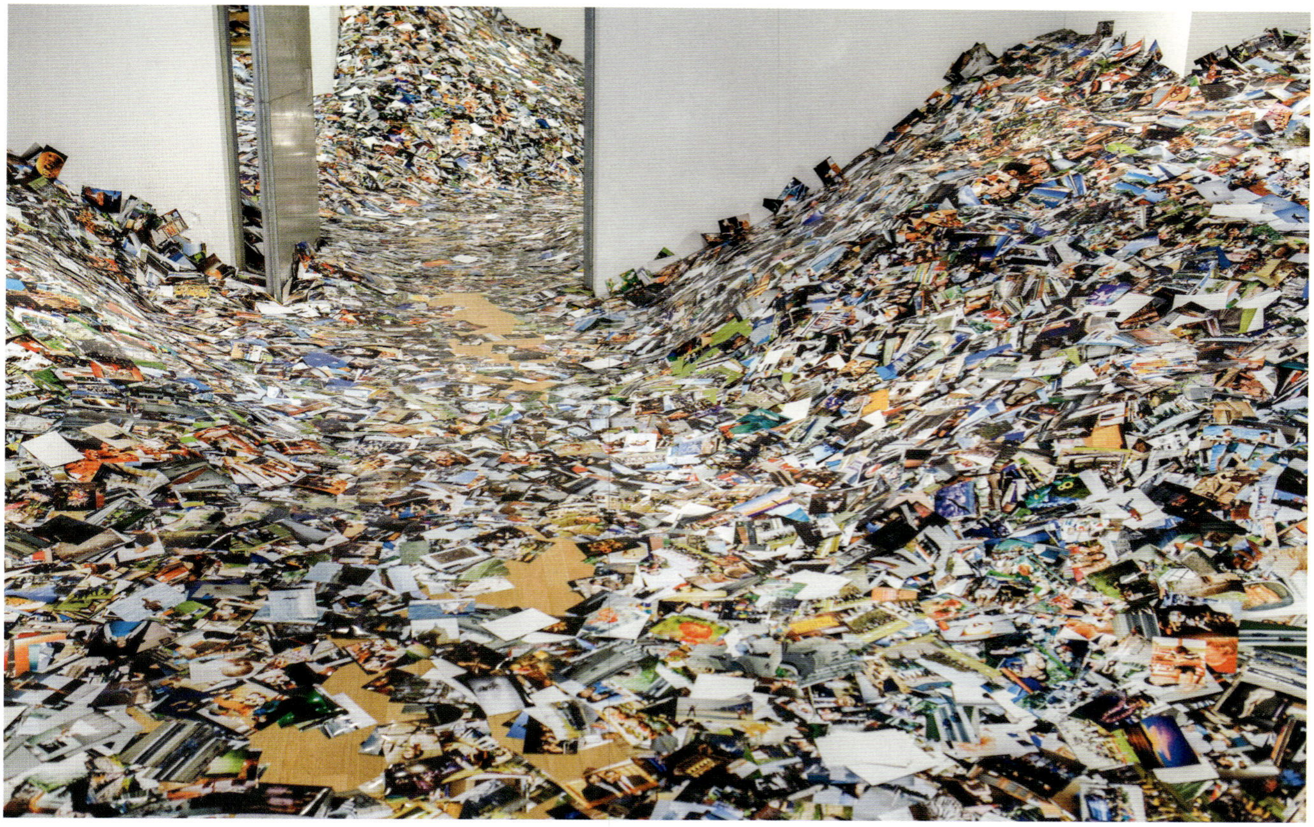

Eric Kessels, *24 hrs in Photos* (2011). 'What's next?' Exhibition, Foam, Amsterdam (2011).

Resin and Polystyrene

One day I accidentally dropped some paint thinners onto a piece of polystyrene; it was reminiscent of a scene in Ridley Scott's *Alien* movie when the crew of the *Nostromo* manage to draw blood from the monster. The blood drips onto the floor of the spaceship. To the consternation of the watching crew the fluid eats aggressively through the metal grating, emitting acrid-looking fumes, dissolving the structure like warm water on snow. The crew clamber to the lower deck of the vessel, watching as the fluid eats through level after level, giving a huge sigh of relief as it finally comes to a halt before it breaches the hull.

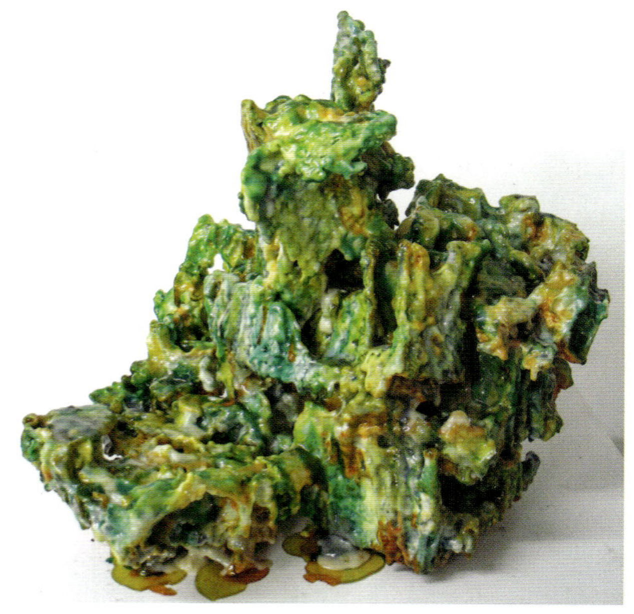

Ian Dawson, *Acidscape (green)* (2004). Resin and polystyrene, 71 x 42 x 37cm.

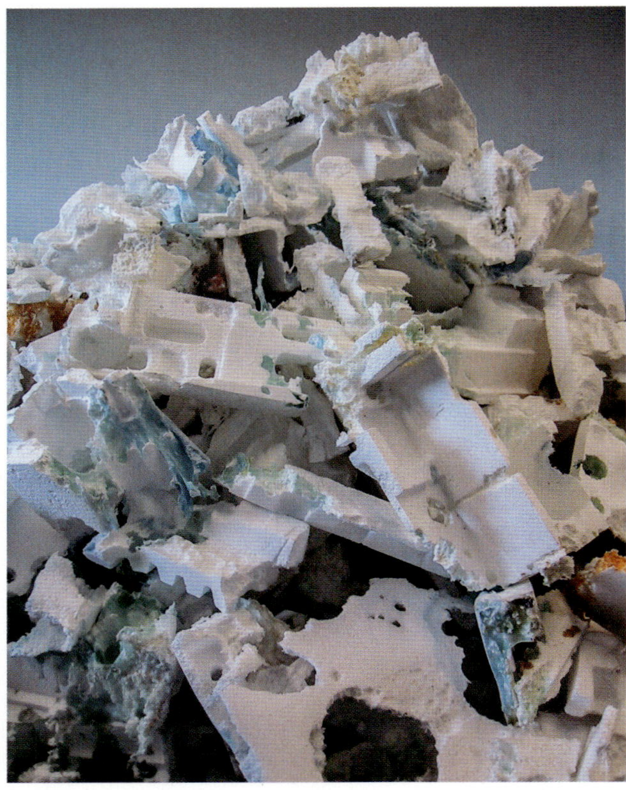

Ian Dawson, polystyrene and solvent pile (in progress), 2003.

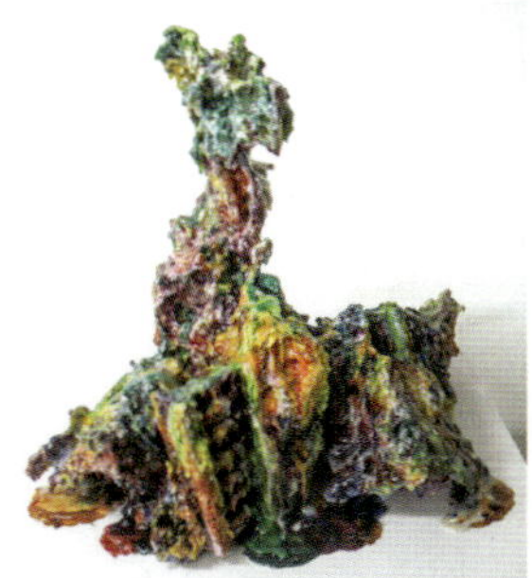

Ian Dawson, *Acidscape* (2004). Resin and polystyrene, 83 × 47 × 51cm.

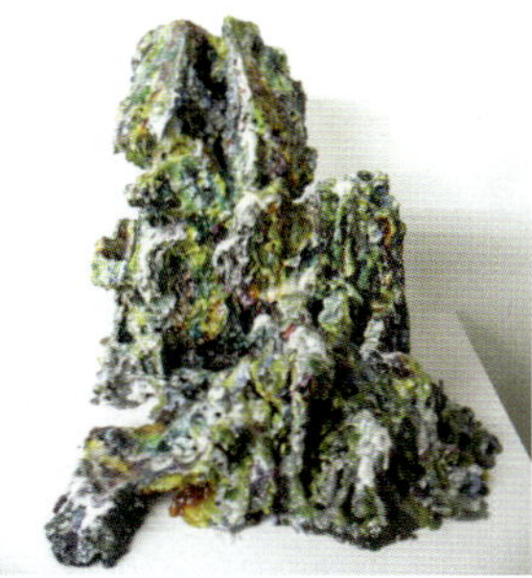

Ian Dawson, *Acidscape (silver)* (2004). Resin and polystyrene, 68 × 40 × 46cm.

This is what happens when resins and thinners, cellulose-based fluids, come into contact with polystyrene. It is a corrosive relationship. I was fascinated that this substance – which no known

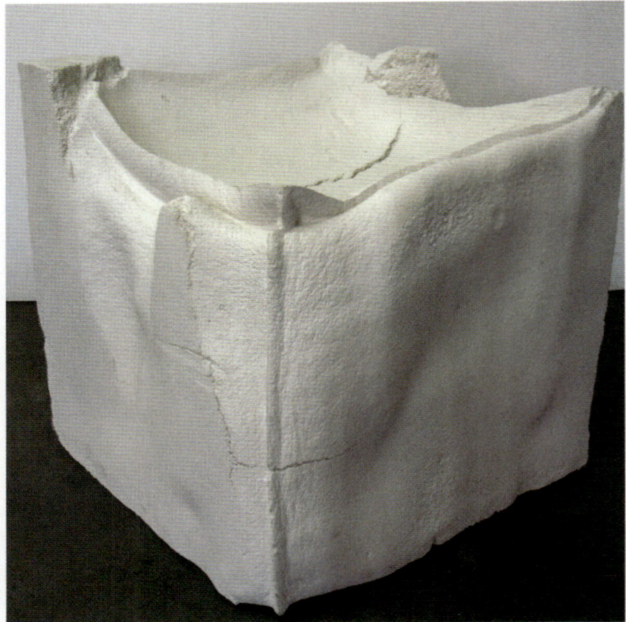

Ian Dawson, *Styrocube*, (2005). Cast jesmonite, 120 × 120 × 120cm.

micro-organism can biodegrade, which languishes in the sea in ever greater quantities – can be violently distressed and distorted. And I became charmed with the process, with the chemical reaction, the instant incompatibility between both materials: a way of making an object out of an adverse process. This process wasn't a mimetic act; there is no representation. They are literally what they are, pure substance and materiality.

I began pouring a combination of solvents, spirits and tinted resins over polystyrene garnered from the bins of the local electrical goods shop. The polystyrene was a non-material, used to package white goods, a value-less filler of space. With each successive pour the shape of object changed, transforming over days and months. Solidifying in a contorted torpor. White spirit was less aggressive than the solvents and would gently dissolve large cubes of polystyrene from the inside out; over several weeks a cube would gently implode, cracking and slumping, sometimes disappearing into a stodgy lump on the floor, a slow death, victims of my initial exuberance with the mineral spirits.

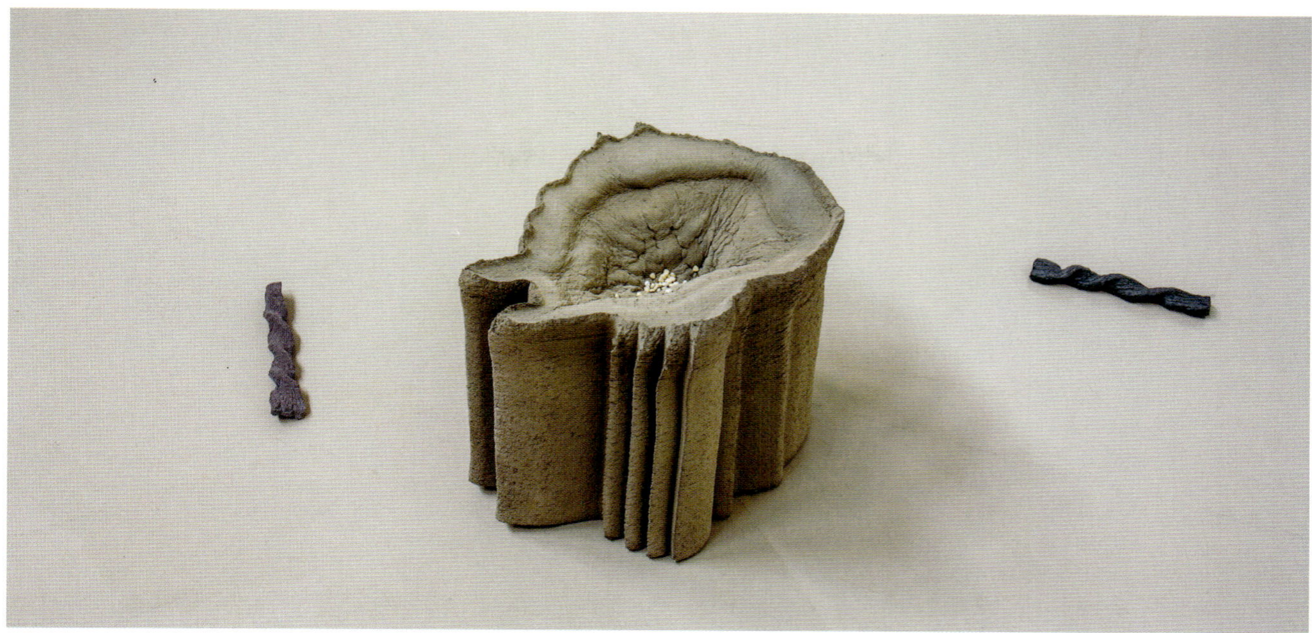

Martin Westwood, *These Hands Are Models, Rehearsing, Relaxing, Snacking* (2011). Fired-clay extrusion and press-casts of Smints and cheese twists, dimensions variable.

▶ Martin Westwood

Martin Westwood's recent thinking has evolved from a print process, in the sense that the recent clay extrusions are as much prints as sculptures. They are just very fat physical prints; what separates them from the drawings sprayed through paper profiles that he executes is quantity of material, but essentially to Westwood they are one and the same.

IAN DAWSON: *You began by making these extrusions at a ceramic workshop in Holland?*

MARTIN WESTWOOD: Yes. The extruded clay forms were made by bottle jacking the clay through a big box that had a metal profile on the bottom. It sits on a stand and I car-jack the clay through. It's a rudimentary, non-automated process. In both industry and ceramic workshops, extrusion on any kind of scale starts to become an automated activity and I went to the workshop because I needed technical help. The non-automation was important: I didn't want to end up with a facile object achieved through the velocity of machinery; I wanted the physical pressure required in making these to be announced within the object.

ID: *How did you become interested in the process?*

MW: I kind of got led to it; I was looking at office equipment and I came across an octagonal extruded aluminium channel used in wall and partition infrastructure. I had a piece knocking around for ages – I found it a really beautiful object. At one point I looked at the cost of getting something made, of extruding some aluminium, which was phenomenal, so that was a no-goer. I am quite happy that it did close it down – something else happened in the work because of having to go about it another way.

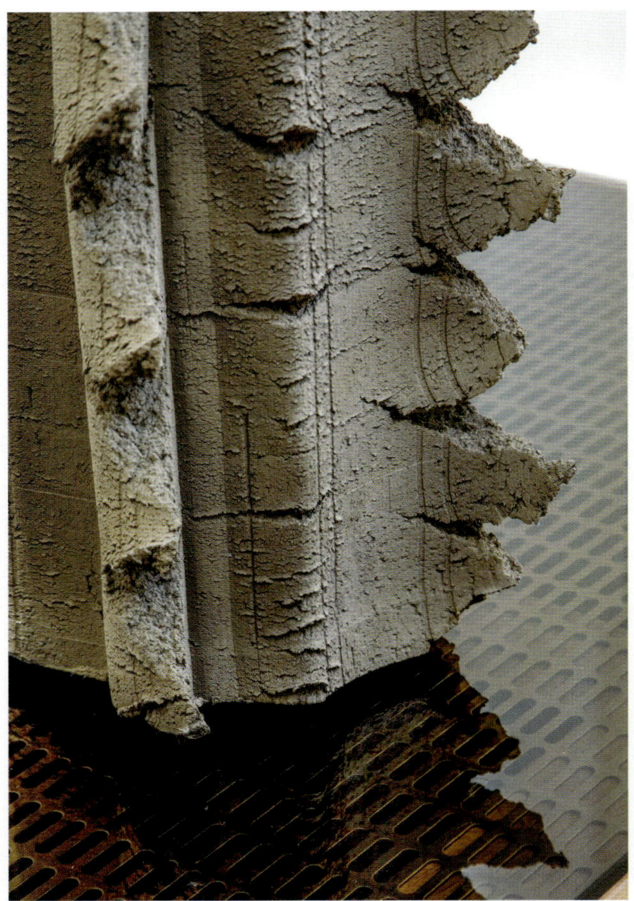

Martin Westwood, *These Hands Are Modelled, Fingered, Numbered* (2011), detail. Fired-clay extrusions and press-casts of donations box and stone, toughened bronze glass, perforated steel, walnut box-section, 113 × 112 × 60cm.

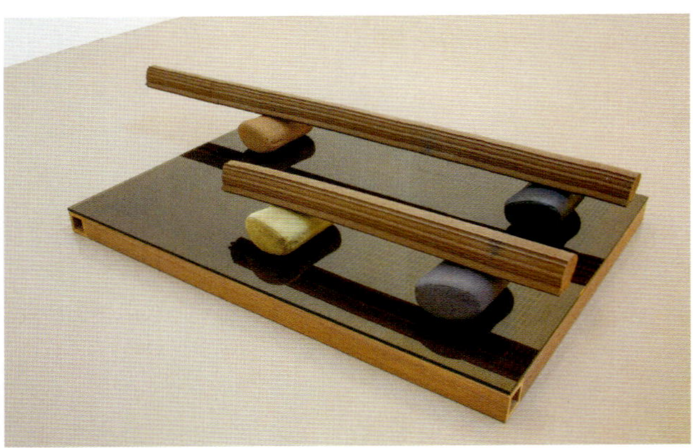

Martin Westwood, *These Hands Are Matching Models* (2011). Fired-clay extrusions and press-casts of Range Rover headrests, toughened bronze glass, perforated steel, walnut box-section, 27 × 186 × 100cm.

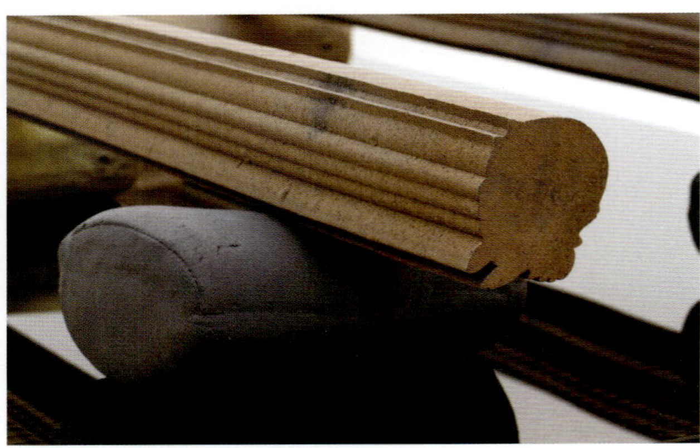

Martin Westwood, *These Hands Are Matching Models* (2011), detail. Fired-clay extrusions and press-casts of Range Rover headrests, toughened bronze glass, perforated steel, walnut box-section, 27 × 186 × 100cm.

ID: *Were you working in clay prior to these?*

MW: I had no experience and I came to it because it seemed the most useful material; once I started working with the clay it led me to a lot more spontaneous collaboration with the material. I went there thinking I was going to make a lot cleaner extrusions, a lot less about the qualities of the clay, but I was pleased to accept things that I wasn't anticipating.

ID: *It seems right that they are made of mud rather than aluminium; they look both primitive and technical. Were there other considerations?*

MW: I was also thinking about extrusion as a diagram of quantity, of how it is a quantitative system for statistical information. Commonly you would extrude different lengths of bars, on a chart for example, to represent different number values. So that was important, this idea that it is the language of quantity and thus linked to the idea of currency, commodity and valuation. In simple terms of scale or length, if it's bigger it's worth more, if it's smaller its worth less, that's the appropriated language of the commercial measure (if you go to a timber yard that bit of wood will cost more because it is longer), and that's kind of how I wanted the compositional sense of them to be.

ID: *It's interesting to have the idea of value attached to such fecal lumps.*

MW: In Marxist terms we are still in a primitive and superstitious state. Money is the most superstitious object and it's our relationship to money that is the confirmation of the primitive world we still live in.

ID: *You have also introduced into the sculptures a variety of other objects: Range-Rover headrest, charity boxes, bread.*

MW: They are press-moulded. An object such as the bread bloomer has originally been made into a two-part plaster mould and then clay is pressed into the mould and as the plaster starts to draw some of the moisture out of the clay it shrinks, releasing itself from the plaster; it's a low-tech casting process. It's very manual: pushing clay in with my thumbs then gluing the two sides together. You can glue the two sides together at the end, but I tend to squash the two sides together, leave them for a while and then release them.

ID: *When did you introduce this to the work?*

MW: I started doing them in Holland too, as an aside, press-moulding travel pillows, then I press-moulded the cheese twist. Then largely I've been doing it since I got back.

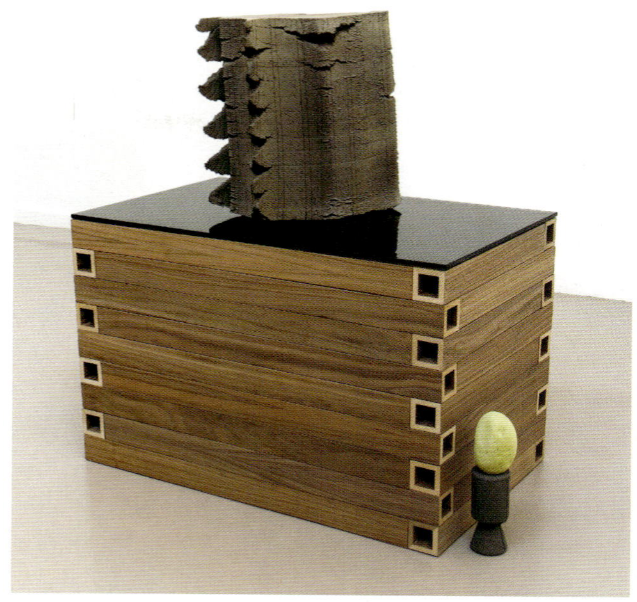

Martin Westwood, *These Hands Are Modelled, Fingered, Numbered* (2011). Fired-clay extrusions and press-casts of donations box and stone, toughened bronze glass, perforated steel, walnut box-section, 113 × 112 × 60cm.

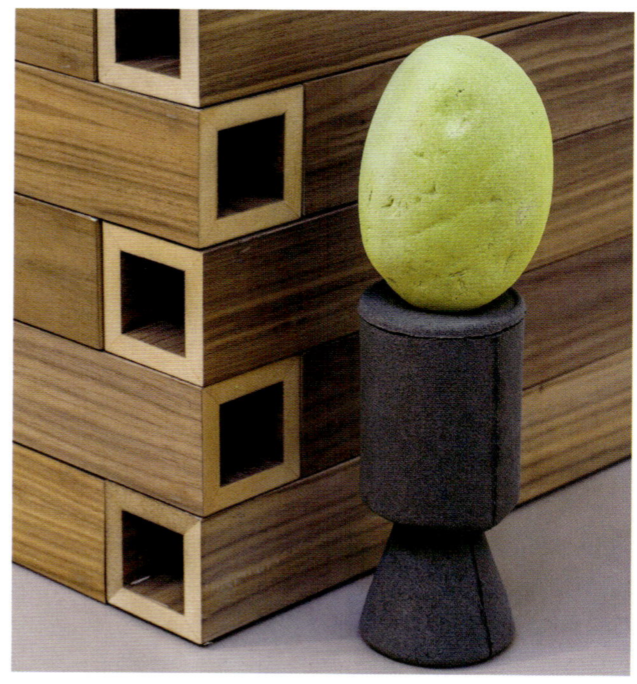

Martin Westwood, *These Hands Are Modelled, Fingered, Numbered* (2011). Fired-clay extrusions and press-casts of donations box and stone, toughened bronze glass, perforated steel, walnut box-section, 113 × 112 × 60cm.

ID: *And their relationship to the extrusions?*

MW: Well, the extrusions carry an idea of process with them, of flow; the cast then is a counter-argument, its proposal is to do with identity – the formed identity of an object – it has received value, it is a Range-Rover headrest, it's an incorporation of something that is about identity, and is able to be placed in a context, as opposed to something which is about the impossibility of the context being found or formed because it is about a system of flow and duration, that the identity of the objects in the extrusions is put under a kind of question mark, and contingency and arbitrariness.

ID: *So it's an expanded conversation?*

MW: The press moulds are arresting the identity of a pre-formed found object and have been incorporated into a charged relationship with the extruded objects, which are about non-identity and duration.

ID: *When did they begin to come together?*

MW: I had been making the press mould alongside the extrusions but I wasn't certain they were going to have such proximity. They have tended to find each other. It has almost been like two conversations, which have started to be layered together, it wasn't something that was clear until quite recently. The air fresheners have only just been included. It pushed it into that more allegorical territory, and slightly more light hearted about the relationship to them in terms of a relationship to a history of abstraction, or history of form, because the press moulds are clearly a mimetic object, they are copies of something and in that way they don't announce a relationship to the history of material abstraction the way that one might read some of these extrusions. It is at the crossover point between those things that something interesting starts to happen to them. Yes, there is a bit of a joke in there, an air freshener next to a turd-like extrusion. All the press moulds do shift the dialogue.

ID: *The charity boxes continue to delve into this narrative.*

MW: You are involved in this fairly abstract notion; the activity of putting coins in a slot is how one constructs the object called charity. There is a different kind of economy that you expect to get back from it, something that is more traditionally to do with the soul, to do with the whip-round after the church service, so there is something that is meant to be received from it, but it is a different exchange than the exchange of tokens for objects or identities.

ID: *The stones that are perched on top?*

MW: They are all igneous rather than sedimentary rocks, smooth and soft-contoured, formed by a repetitive process of being rubbed against other stones over millennia; they are all wholly original things that are completely unrepeatable, yet within a metaphorical language they represent deadness. So it interested me to replace the coin, a unit of print, which is the origin of reproductive technology, with an arbitrarily unique thing formed by such a repetitive natural process. So this metaphor for inertia is thrown back upon a token, and talks about the deadness of the token and not necessarily the inertness of the stone. But I just put these things into play; I can't direct the flow of an idea. I replace a token in a charity box with a stone atop a charity box, but I can't determine the direction of the metaphor. I can put them into play, though I can't govern how somebody is going to read them.

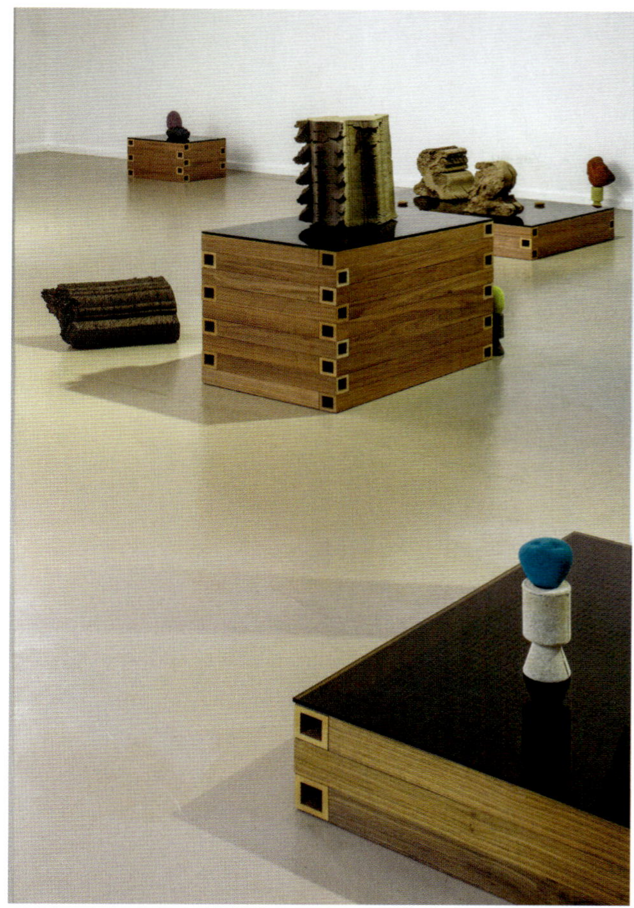

Martin Westwood, *These Hands are Models*, installation view (2011). Stanley Picker Gallery, UK.

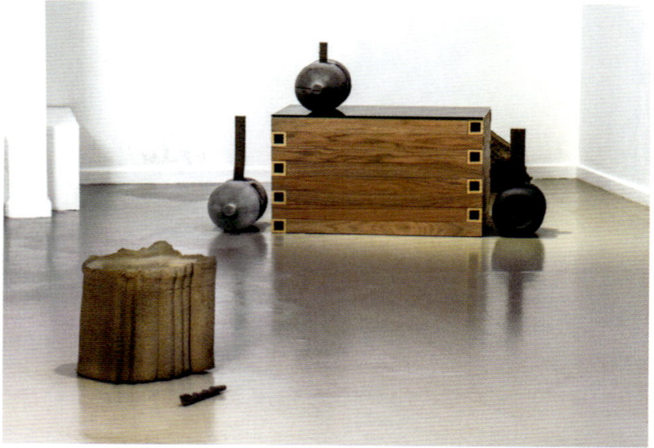

Martin Westwood, *These Hands are Models*, installation view (2011). Stanley Picker Gallery, UK.

ID: *The bases are also rich with associations.*

MW: I wanted to play around with ways of elevating them without being monolithic, for the plinths to appear as a standardized exchangeable system that could be reconfigured and recombined. And to have something that looks as though it has the potential to perform a function, to be able to organize and channel air.

ID: *They are highly aestheticized.*

MW: The choice of walnut veneer goes way beyond function and is about a type of conspicuous consumption. The combination with smoked glass and perforated steel sheeting was to create an executive environment and associations with the company boardroom, a contractual space, which is about seduction and a fetishistic use of material to charm the environment and create a certain ambience of authority and taste.

ID: *The water bottles also?*

MW: They are a particular type of bottle for quite a formalized group of individuals, employees of a company. But they are also about the delivery system of a basic unit of survival. It is called *Fawcetts smother Fountain*, which asks a question towards Duchamp's readymade, the upturned urinal titled *Fountain*. I suppose there is an allegorical aspect that is about ascension about water going up and water going down. By Duchamp titling it *Fountain*, he was proposing a cleansing of this sanitary object that is all about gravity and makes it talk about some kind of idealism, a metaphor for some kind of conceptual arrangement. He moves it away from a form of materiality, which the function binds it into.

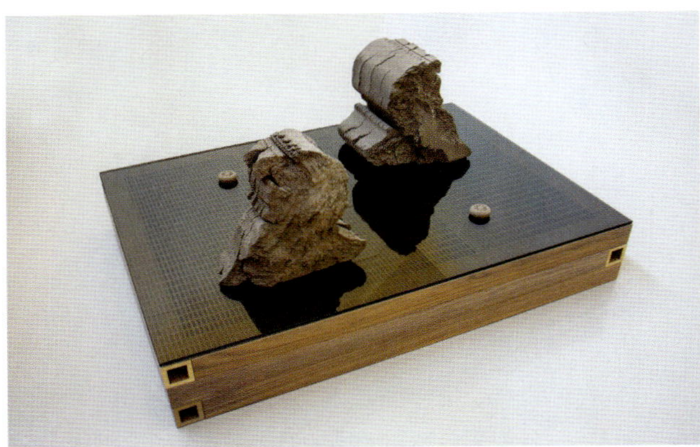

Martin Westwood, *Pere and Terre Hang Out In Bistro RePeTere*
(2011). Fired-clay extrusions, press-casts of air freshener,
toughened bronze, glass, perforated steel, walnut box-section,
60 × 139 × 100cm.

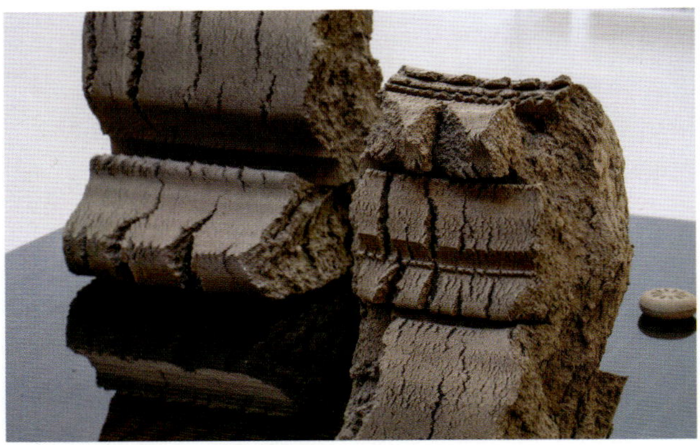

Martin Westwood, *Pere and Terre Hang Out In Bistro RePeTere*
(2011), detail. Fired-clay extrusions, press-casts of air freshener,
toughened bronze, glass, perforated steel, walnut box-section,
60 × 139 × 100cm.

ID: *Do the others have allegorical titles?*

MW: For example, *Pere and Terre hang out in Bistro
RePeTere*. Which is like, father and earth hang out in
café repetition. I got interested in the word *repetition*; it
had come from the French with a Latin root, *repetere*.
I like playing around with words and finding different
ways of using them within a title, the idea of father and
earth; in Western identity the father-figure evaluated
subjectivity. He is the main subject in the same way as
gold was for commodities. I was toying around with
what I find in loose etymological associations, in order
to tease some poetic and structural possibilities out of
these combinations of words and objects. ■

Bronze: Pangolin Foundry

A short distance into the picturesque countryside from
Stroud, Gloucestershire, some imposing old double-
height industrial buildings loom. Here is the Pangolin
Foundry. Housed within an old asbestos factory, this
foundry has been here since Lynn Chadwick helped
establish it in the heartlands of arts and crafts country
nearly a quarter of a century ago.

In the yard outside the gigantic building that houses
the furnace stands a magnificent cast, a 10m-tall
figure by Eduardo Paolozzi – a classic Paolozzi figure,
its human features modelled and suffused with the
geometric and the angular. The figure faces out, a
symbol and testament to the industry and human craft
alive in this place, a place capable of taking an artist's
piece of work and reproducing it perfectly down to
the fingerprints, but also able to work on the grand
theatrical scale as demanded by some of the main
artists today. 'It makes it a very dynamic and exciting
place to work,' says Rungwe Kingdon, and I don't doubt
him whatsoever.

Rungwe Kingdon and Claude Koenig are the
husband-and-wife team who have established this
foundry as a viable producer for contemporary
sculpture. It is clear that it has evolved from a
remarkable passion towards object-making as he
gestures with his lithe and elegant hands. 'That's what
these are for,' says Kingdon, 'and it's how you use these
in conjunction with your ideas that makes art, you can
delegate a lot of it, and use technology but at the end
of the day it comes down to what gets manufactured by
somebody's hands and then what that object stimulates
in the viewer.' This is the spirit and the enthusiasm of
Rungwe, an eloquent and articulate man who lives for
objects. He continues:

If you pick up even a cast of the Venus of Willendorf, 30,000 years old, it's a direct communication, in your hand, your mind, your eye, a prehistoric sculpture and there is something fantastic about that, really magical about being able to hold that much knowledge. You pick it up and it is just a writhing little knot of a sculpture, a fantastic bundle of energy, and it's a time capsule, a capsule for ideas, for me that's what sculpture is; you look at a sculpture and it sets off a chain of thoughts and ideas, and to be able to do that across time is something that is quite specific to sculpture. It is so direct, you can feel what a prehistoric sculptor felt, and that's an astonishing connection.

Visiting Pangolin Editions is an acknowledgment that at a certain point artists will employ other artists and artisans to free themselves from the constraints of production and that through this they will often want to produce something more durable. The comparison is drawn with Rodin's studio, which would have had fifty or sixty artisans carving, enlarging his squidged bits of clay, making elaborations that Rodin would only influence at the end. This is similar to how Pangolin works with some of its artists. Quite often it will be a double-headed development, where the artist is leading the foundry and then the processes that are being developed will lead the artist.

This is an ideal set-up for both Kingdon and Koenig, trained artists who were experimenting with casting techniques but decided that their talents were better served realizing other people's visions. 'I could have made objects, no problem, and I still do for artists but I am much better at taking up someone else's language and speaking that language with them rather than trying to create a voice of my own,' says Kingdon.

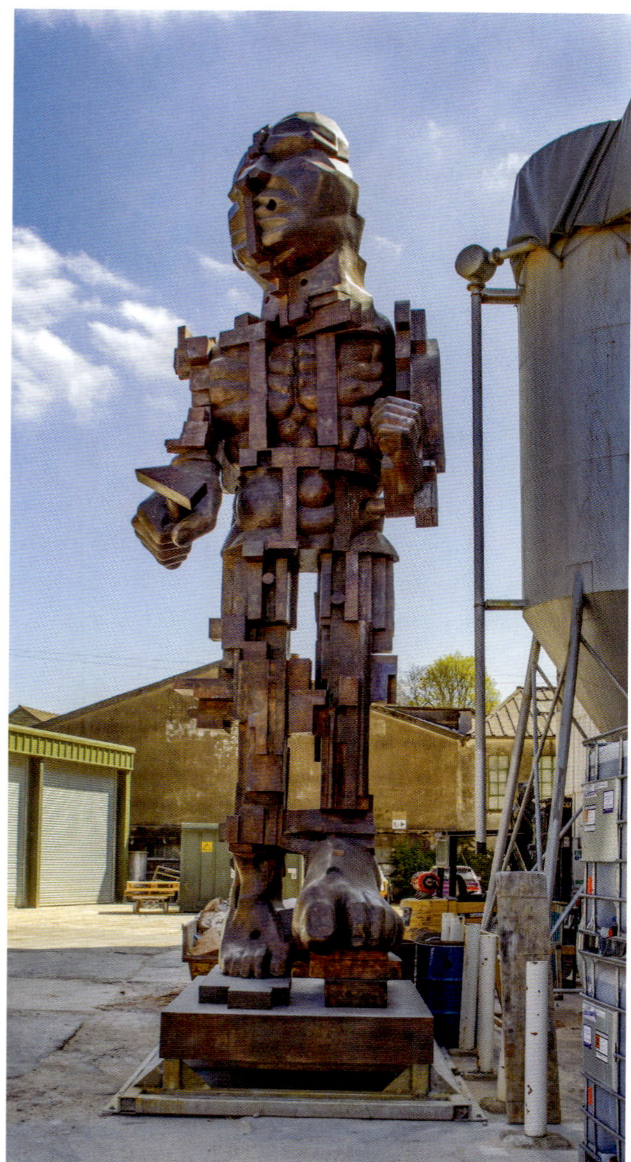

Pangolin Foundry, Paolozzi.

Their first foundry was fashioned in his parents' back garden; it was in a greenhouse made from recycled windows rescued from a skip. Claude had welded up the kiln, and had lined it with bricks; the furnace was an old tin lined with refractory concrete and the flame was powered by an old paraffin weed-killer. It used the lost-wax process, on a very simple scale. 'That is the beauty of lost wax: you can do it on an ant-hill in the middle of Africa – it's low-tech and high-skill and that just seems to suit the way I think,' Kingdon says. And with this he begins to explain the enduring nature of both the material and the process, from the first development of lost-wax casting 6,000 years ago with the production of high value ritual objects – sceptres and crowns – bound by the brittleness of arsenical copper. 'You can't make an axe head out of it. We have tried; we've made arsenical copper – it breaks, it snaps very easily, so it can only be used for these art objects,' he explains. It was only later with the advent of bronze that weapons such as axes and arrowheads began to be made. Bronze casting then developed independently across several cultures in Africa. It was a unique expression: 'We know that because it has an enclosed crucible which none of the European cultures had, so it was a separate concept of how to cast – it was their own system.' Rungwe continues, 'and then there is the South American culture casting predominantly in gold. In fact pre-Colombian South and Central American lost-wax casting also developed independently.'

I ask how it has been, to come from a makeshift garden foundry to then run a huge facility that now employs 120 highly skilled craftspeople. 'It's sort of been accidental, its not been designed like that at all.' He says, with a glint in his eye, 'If I am honest with you, to begin with the elemental thing of controlling fire was quite a big attraction.' It is clear he lives for the magic of this kind of transformation of taking something often fragile, insubstantial and non-permanent and transforming it into a durable and seductive material. And the growth of the foundry is testament to an enduring relationship to bronze. The past century has seen numerous cycles of rejecting bronze, then accepting it, rejecting then accepting, and Rungwe points out that it is very difficult for successive generations to reject it entirely because it is so appropriate for making objects. The foundry

has presided over such a cycle, from working with Chadwick, Armitage and Paolozzi as elder men, and then seeing a new generation of Caro, King and Tucker eschew it for steel and fibre-glass before returning to it on their terms.

This has also been a reason why Pangolin remains true to the traditional lost-wax method as opposed to a more modern ceramic-shell process. Lost wax is adaptable to the changing needs of the artist, whereas with ceramic shell process, more often than not the object has to be adapted to the process. It's a subtle difference but Rungwe is adamant about its impact:

Over the 6,000 years it has been in existence, lost wax has adapted and adapted to different types of sculpture; it makes it supremely suitable to an evolutionary process. By comparison, ceramic shell is a set process that doesn't really change so you are always adapting a sculpture to the process. I just feel it's the wrong way round.

It is, however, a slower process, involving more labour and thus affecting costs, but it is a price worth paying in order to remain ultimately flexible and hence sympathetic towards the subtleties and the differences of each object.

We begin our tour; Pangolin is spread through numerous interlinking buildings. We start in the model-making studio – for some artists, this is the beginning point where skilled clay modellers interpret their ideas; then into the rooms dedicated to creating the rubber moulds. Then the wax area, where hollow wax models, the replicas of the original, are made, chased and sprued; the whole thing is then 'invested' – covered in a casing of plaster. The work now arrives in the furnace area, and the tone of the tour changes dramatically, from the soft to the hard. The tranquil, precise and clean studio environment is transformed

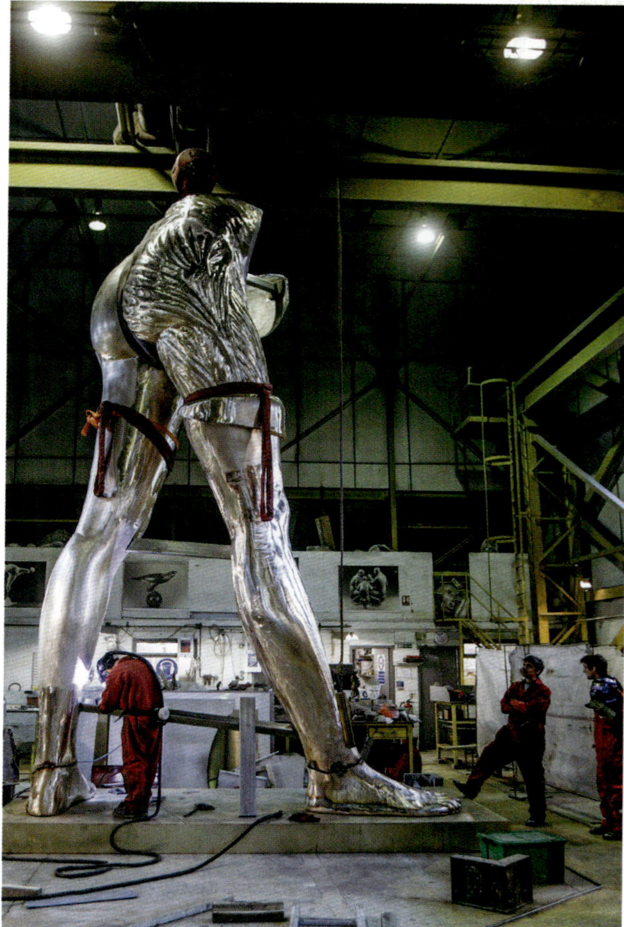
Pangolin Foundry, monumental sculpture.

into the noisy cacophony of the factory floor. Huge home-made kilns burn out the wax, as workers sweating in suede smocks prepare for a pour.

We pass a part of a Damien Hirst, the head of a unicorn, a rotating mobile by Lynn Chadwick, an Angus Fairhurst being put together as we come out into the chasing area, punctuated by the high-pitched squeal of grinding equipment as the runners and risers are removed. It is here that one begins to realize the range of objects that is being cast, from the photorealistic to abstract. A polythene spray booth has been erected to accommodate a Michael Joo sculpture, which is a cast of his rubber mould. Joo had visited and observed the piece just as they were about to make the fibre-glass jacket and said 'I want you to

cast the whole thing as a sculpture, I love it as it is.' So the whole thing, complete with drips, and on its wooden frame, was cast into bronze. It is reminiscent of the Hirst bronzes that were produced here for *In-A-Gadda-Da-Vida* at Tate Britain in 2004 – *trompe l'oeil* sculpture that Hirst started to experiment with when one too many of his pharmaceutical pill pieces were returned with only a gloop of gelatinous material at the bottom of the box. Rungwe observes, 'When you get someone like Damien taking on the material you get all the other contemporary artists suddenly looking at the potential of bronze. Up to that point it was a complete no-no. Who was using bronze before then? A few people, but he does it and does it big, and recreated a sense that this was an exciting material to use, and it has been great, a real renaissance in bronze, but tackling it from a different point of view.' There are so many genres being made here, I imagine at other periods there would have been a single dominant style. A table in the metal chasing area has work by Antony Gormley, Jonathan Kenworthy, Sarah Lucas, Jon Buck and Damien Hirst, competing for space, alongside a historical artefact and an ancient Japanese object being restored – they are all waiting to be worked on. The table is a post-modern feast of styles.

We continue through to the patina workshop, a smelly room filled with chemicals that are applied to colour the bronze. This is where Rungwe is often found late into the night searching for a new tarnish. When Pangolin first started there were only three available patinas for bronze: brown, green and black were the only colours available from foundries. An exhibition of Chinese bronzes at the Ashmolean Museum in Oxford altered his appreciation:

There were pinks in there and blues, subtle greens, greys. It was just fantastic, and I thought, if nature can do that to bronze we must be able to find a

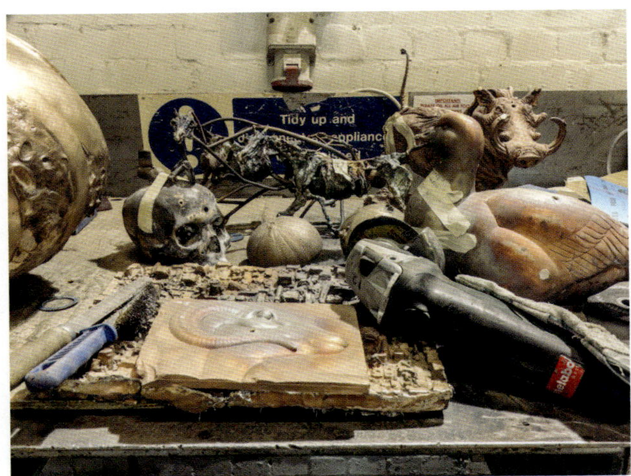

Pangolin Foundry, metal work bench.

way to replicate that, so I devoted some time to experiment. I began by just buying some random chemicals; I knew it had to be an acidic salt, so I just looked up everything I could with that and I just played and experimented. It took us years to get a stable white and much longer still to get a stable blue. I could get blue but it was always fugitive, changing back to green, or changing to mud, and when I got it, they are like eureka moments. Of course you get one colour and then you can mix it with other ones and you can double the range of your palette instantly. So they are very exciting moments. To go from green, brown and black to then being able to patinate bronze with such an array of colours, it's a radical change and it is part of what has made bronze relevant again. If bronze had stayed just those three colours I don't think contemporary artists would have embraced it the way that they have.

It is this preparedness for the whole team to innovate with all aspects of the process that is so inspiring. It might have been regarded as impossible to get bronze to flow all the way down a thin, spindly vein, but by experimenting with the alloys Pangolin are able to get bronze to flow like water, so that they can cast in an extremely delicate way:

By upping the percentage of tin, for example, or taking out the amount of lead, reducing the zinc, adding phosphorous to make a bronze with different properties, then we can do different things. And this is where we are interacting with what the artist's ambition is to do, so if an artist comes in with a stick, for example, and says, 'Will you be able to cast that?', we find a way to do it.

The team has even modified a pressure barrel and vacuum pump in order to create a negative atmosphere inside the moulds, so that when the molten metal is poured in it can spread to the extremes of the mould – a way of getting added detail into the cast.

It's now time for the pour. A sense of anticipation starts to hang over the furnace area; the groan of the furnace becomes more pervasive. A level of anxiety creeps in as a safety trench of sand is constructed around the pour area. Suddenly the roar stops and the crucible emerges, glowing an incandescent orange; it sits there until it becomes a dull cherry-red. Pouring the metal at the right temperature is crucial: if it's poured too hot it burns the plaster; pour it too cold and the bronze won't get to the bottom of the mould. The sense of expectation mounts. The crucible is lifted into position and is gradually tipped and a mesmerising line of molten bronze disappears down a hole. That's it – show over and work resumes, the whine from the grinders and the hammering of metal starts up again. The valley drowned in the noise of industry once more.

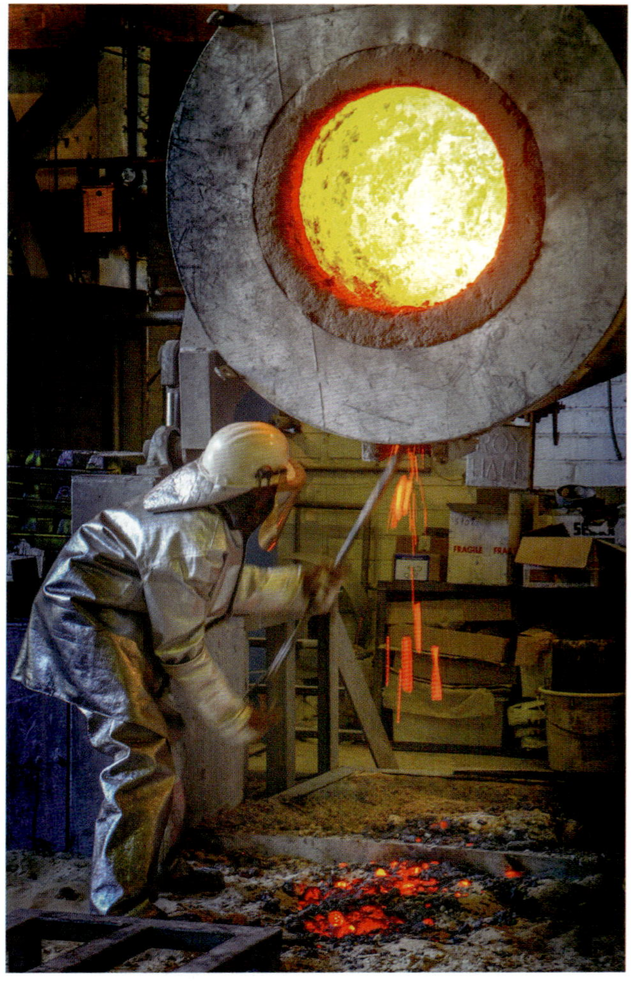

Pangolin Foundry, pour (1).

Rungwe sums it up:

It's like non-stop development: every penny the foundry earns goes back into getting it into a better place, looking after our people a bit better, making it safer, making a nicer environment for the artists and a better environment for ourselves. Improving the quality of what we can do and the range of what we can do. To be able to go from that little tiny twig to something the size of the Paolozzi, all in-house, we don't have to subcontract anything – it's a great sense of being able to make anything. Bring us your idea, we can make it work. That's a very exciting place to be for us. And that means we attract artists who are keen to push contemporary sculpture to an extreme of their language and expression and our process. It's great to be a partner to some of the great artists of our age.

Pangolin Foundry, pour (2).

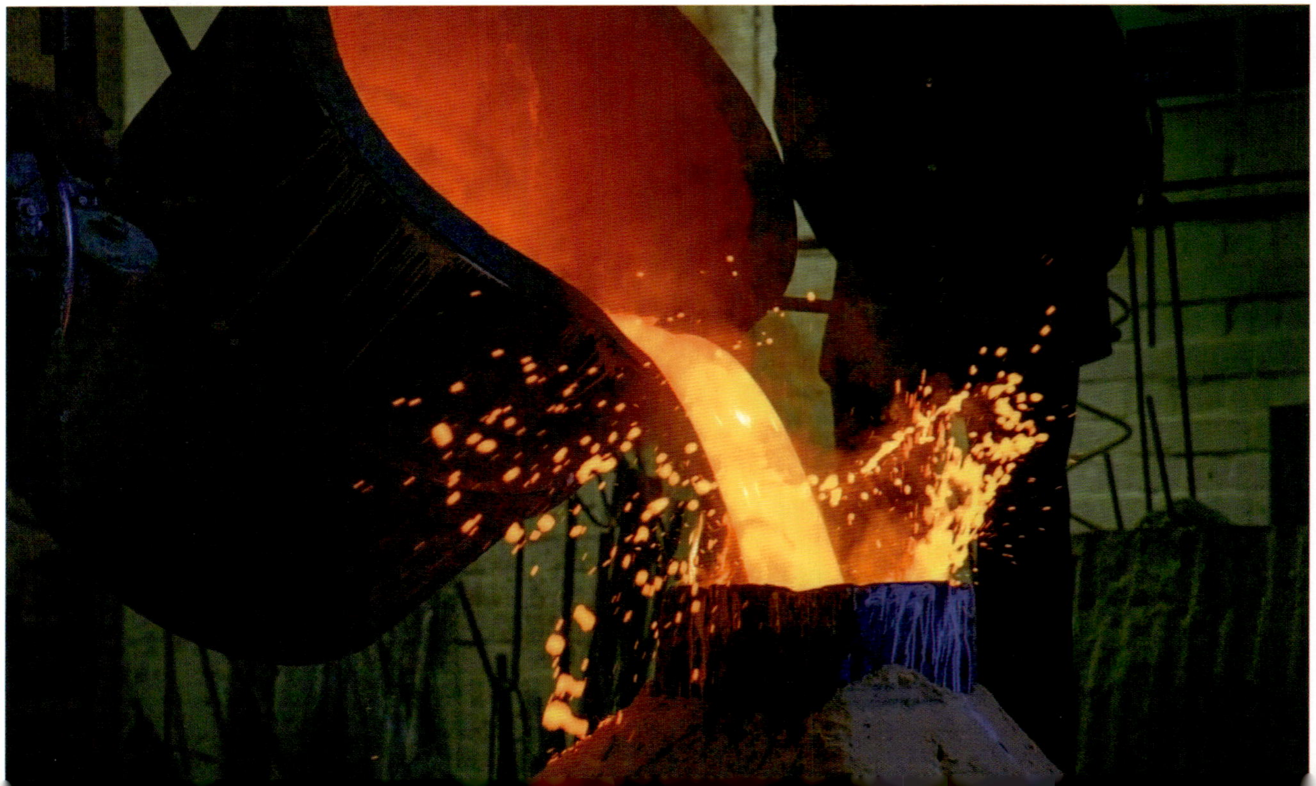

▶ Anna Barriball

Inside Anna Barriball's studio are the remnant marks of her activity, a defined pile of pencil shavings lingers as the residue of an accomplishment. A roll of paper unfurls onto the floor, becoming physically a part of the space. Charcoal, and graphite traces intersect the undulations of the floorboards and brick walls. Here I talk to Barriball about her work.

IAN DAWSON: *The bag drawing was quite significant?*

ANNA BARRIBALL: It concisely brought together lots of things that I had been thinking about; about drawing and describing form. Where the object and the drawing meet, where one thing starts and another thing stops; what's acceptable to be called a drawing.

ID: *What had you done?*

AB: I had taken a white carrier bag and coloured it in with a red marker pen. The surface was covered all over, inside and out. And it hung on the wall like a makeshift bin, waist height. From a distance it was intensely red and then when you looked closely, you were drawn in to see the individual pen marks, to see that the surface had been completely drawn over.

ID: *It was a very intense piece.*

AB: It was about bringing the object up close to meet the drawing, of not having that translation between looking at something and describing something. And that set off quite a lot of work after that, things that I still think about in terms of two dimensions and three, and the forensic level of scrutinizing surfaces.

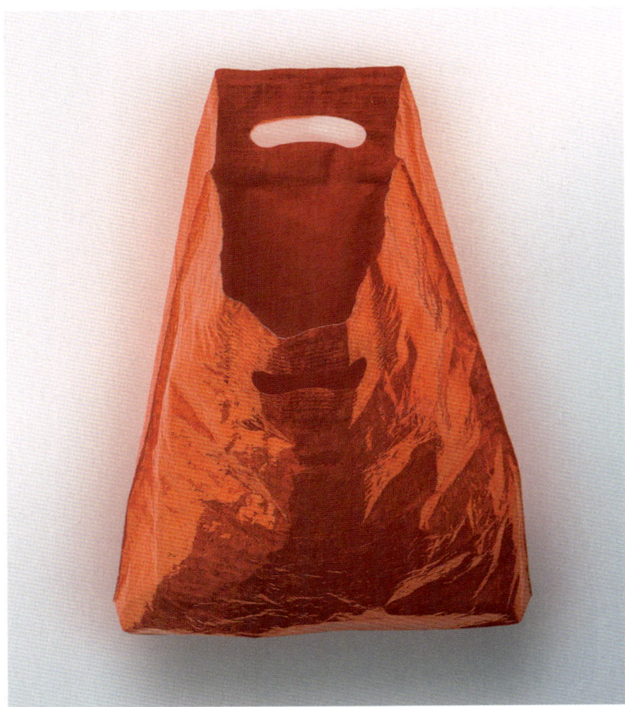

Anna Barriball, *Bag Drawing* (2000). Marker pen on carrier bag, 46 × 37 × 21cm.

ID: *It was a very particular surface too.*

AB: I enjoyed making it; the feel of the marker pen on the plastic. The marks are held apart by the polythene, the very slim material between two sides of pen marks. It's playful and a bit ridiculous.

ID: *Which continued with a subsequent piece.*

AB: I covered the surface of a five-pound note with a gold marker pen. From a distance it looks like a piece of rolled gold, but on closer inspection you can see all the embossing of the five-pound-note. This piece wasn't just relating to value: it also described incidental things like the way the note had been creased in countless different pockets. All these marks had become much clearer once it had been covered. The pen pushes back the printed information on the note and makes the marks made by handling, the piece of paper's exchange more visible.

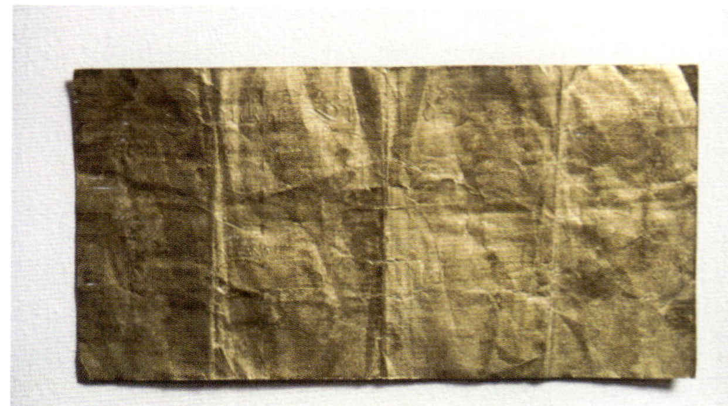

Anna Barriball, *Money Drawing* (2000). Gold pen on five pound note, 13 × 7cm.

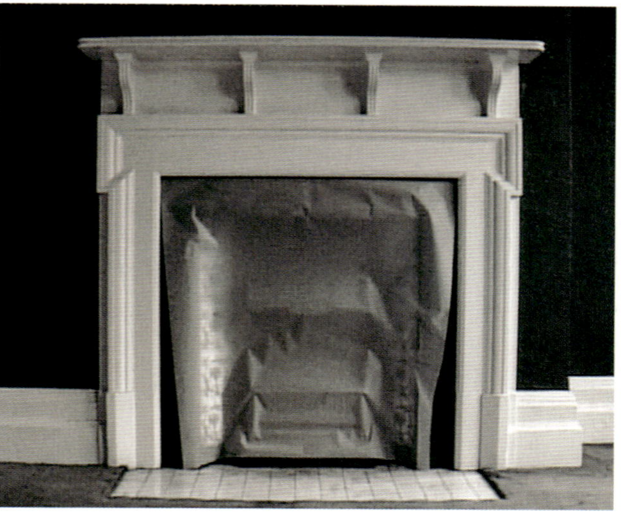

Anna Barriball, *Draw (fireplace)* (2005). DVD projection, 10 min 30 sec, edition 1/3.

ID: *They must be quite time-consuming works to deal with.*

AB: Some are and some aren't. Some are executed quite quickly. Yes, some things are very slow and meditative.

ID: *That must be the case with these larger rubbings?*

AB: I recently made one of a bricked up doorway that was roughly 7 feet by 3 or 4. So I started off – high up on a ladder with a normal pencil, and it's just pencil after pencil, hour after hour, very densely worked. That took a relatively long time to make. Day after day being that close to a brick wall is quite an unforgiving practice. It goes from being contemplative to being testing and durational until I end up lying on the floor trying to get the last bit done.

ID: *There must be a sense of completeness when they are finally finished.*

AB: That is one of the things I like about the process, that once I have filled in the last bit of the drawing then it instantaneously becomes an autonomous, and in this case confrontational, physical thing that then breaks down when you look very closely into the marks.

ID: *Its physicality is an illusion?*

AB: In a way, yes, but I hope the drawing holds the physical nature of its making. I am interested in a drawing when it has a physical presence which takes it into the language of sculpture, so you are standing with it, as well as looking at it, you're physically confronted by it. It's a thin piece of paper that has been densely worked on so that it seems to become heavy with the cumulative weight of marks. At the same time they have an indexical, causal relationship with surface which is photographic in its level of detail.

ID: *It reminds me of a video you made of a breathing membrane placed over a fireplace.*

AB: I was about to move from my flat. I had always liked the tiles around the fireplace and wanted to make a record of them for myself. So I put a piece of tracing paper over the fireplace to just draw, make a record of the tiles and it was an incredibly windy day, and the wind must have been in exactly the right direction and exactly the right force to make the tracing paper literally suck in and out, and I was so totally taken aback at how animated it had become. I just sat watching it for ages and thought, 'I've really got to do something with this somehow.' I like responding directly to things that I notice, being receptive to whatever is around or gets thrown up for one reason or another.

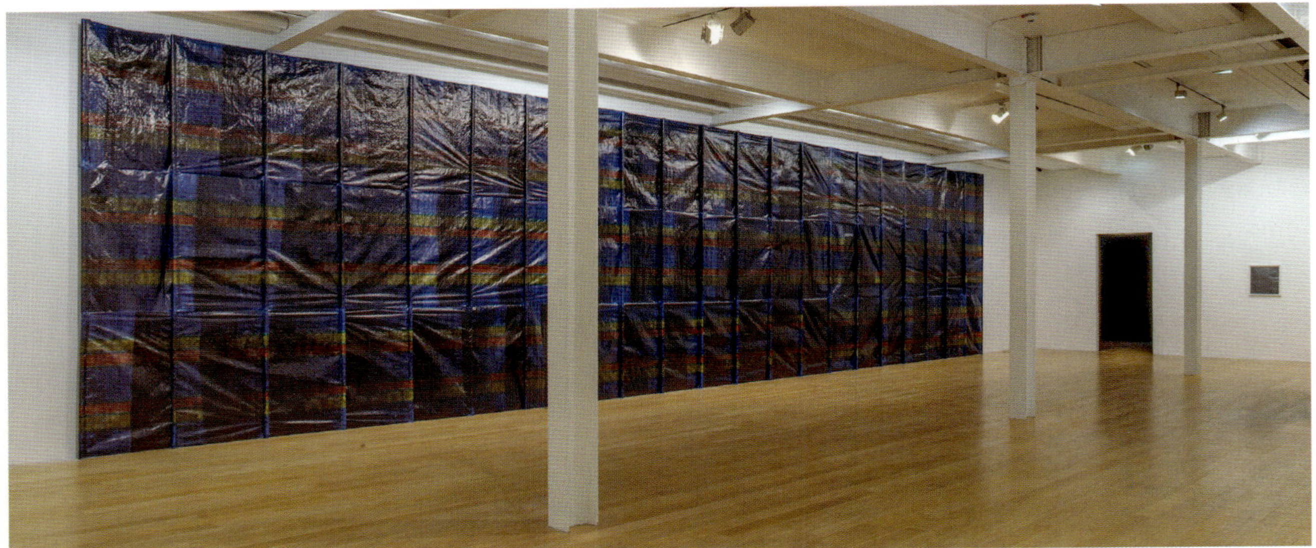

Anna Barriball, *Untitled* (2011). Marker pen on windbreaks, metal poles, dimensions variable. Installation view, The Fruitmarket Gallery, Edinburgh.

ID: *You are also working on a piece that appears like a screen.*

AB: It's a sequence of windbreaks coloured in black marker pen. Again, I have started at one end and as the pen runs out, you get a less dense mark. So you get this undulating surface and I like how it appears that there is light within the piece somehow. It has a weird translucence; I like the fact that it feels like it's hiding something. It is installed 10cm away from the wall. Behind it, coloured light, a kind of rainbow from the stripes on the windbreak is projected onto the wall.

ID: *I didn't initially recognize it as a beach windbreak.*

AB: I like that it's not immediately recognizable, but I enjoy the connotations, that it's a protective barrier, you put it up in different configurations to create a form around you according to the way the wind is blowing.

ID: *So the origin of it is this kind of portable, flimsy, everyday sculptural item which then made it into this dense curtain.*

AB: Also, the thing about what you can see and what you can't. I think that underlies quite a lot of things I make or qualities I recognize – what's there and what's covered; what's hidden and what's revealed. Again you're faced with this thing visually and physically. But that there is something implied behind it.

ID: *It also appears to be growing across the wall.*

AB: I am thinking about covering a whole wall, so it relates to the architecture.

ID: *In your studio there is evidence of tracings everywhere, of testing things out.*

AB: I often do something and stand back, think about it, do something else and have the patience to wait for something else to join it. Pieces come about in a round-about sort of a way; most work does. In this instance I intended to make a drawing that had just started to peel away from the wall. Just enough so that it was just starting to edge into three dimensions, to become slightly more tangible than something flat on the wall. I put a sheet of paper up and covered it in Chinese ink, then with a rubber, I pushed into the paper to pick up some texture, some sense of the wall behind it. And it started pulling away from the wall and I wasn't sure how I felt about it.

ID: *How did you resolve it?*

AB: It was there for a bit, and then I had to make room in the studio to get on with something else, so I pulled it off the wall, rolled it and leant it in the corner, stood back. It had such a strange presence, it was much stronger than it had been. It started doing what I had hoped it would do, but more so. It had incorporated a denseness; a weight. It had shifted materially. I made a series of five, they all hold themselves quite differently.

ID: *It is such a subtle transformation.*

AB: The thing that changed the way the paper felt, what shifted the materiality of the it, was the application of the rubber against the paper.

ID: *Also allowing for the build up of time.*

AB: It's not easy describing my way of going about things but I come into the studio and there's a real day-to-day-ness about it in lots of ways, where being around things, leaving things, trying out stuff, letting things settle in a reductive process, getting to a point where nothing is superfluous. I like the evidence, the residue, what's left. ■

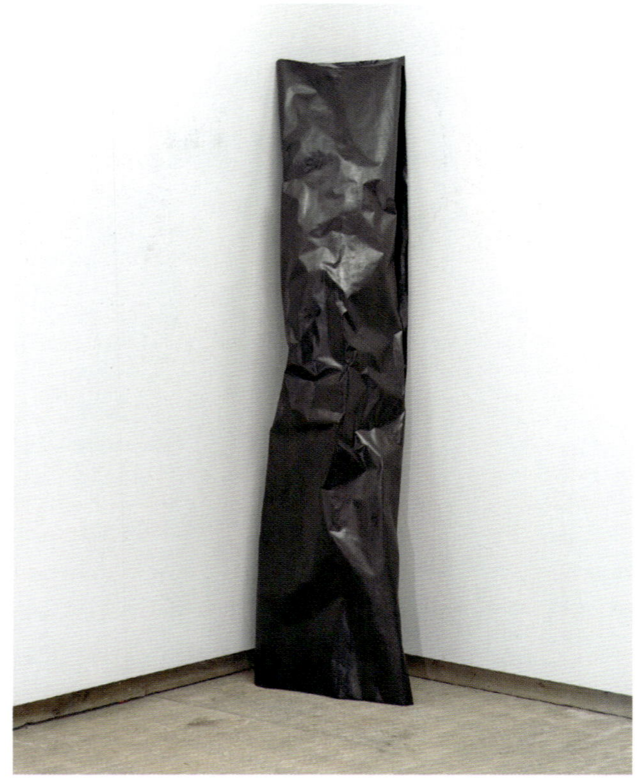

Anna Barriball, *Untitled II* (2008). Ink on paper, 239 × 66 × 22cm.

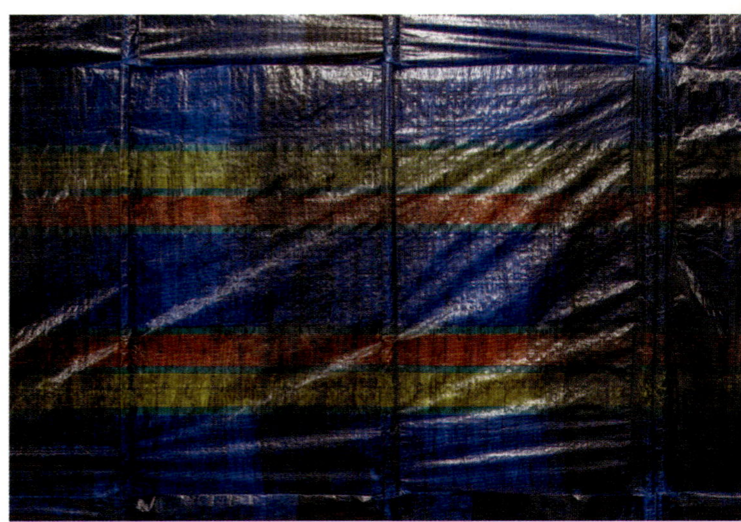

Anna Barriball, *Untitled* (2011). Windbreak detail.

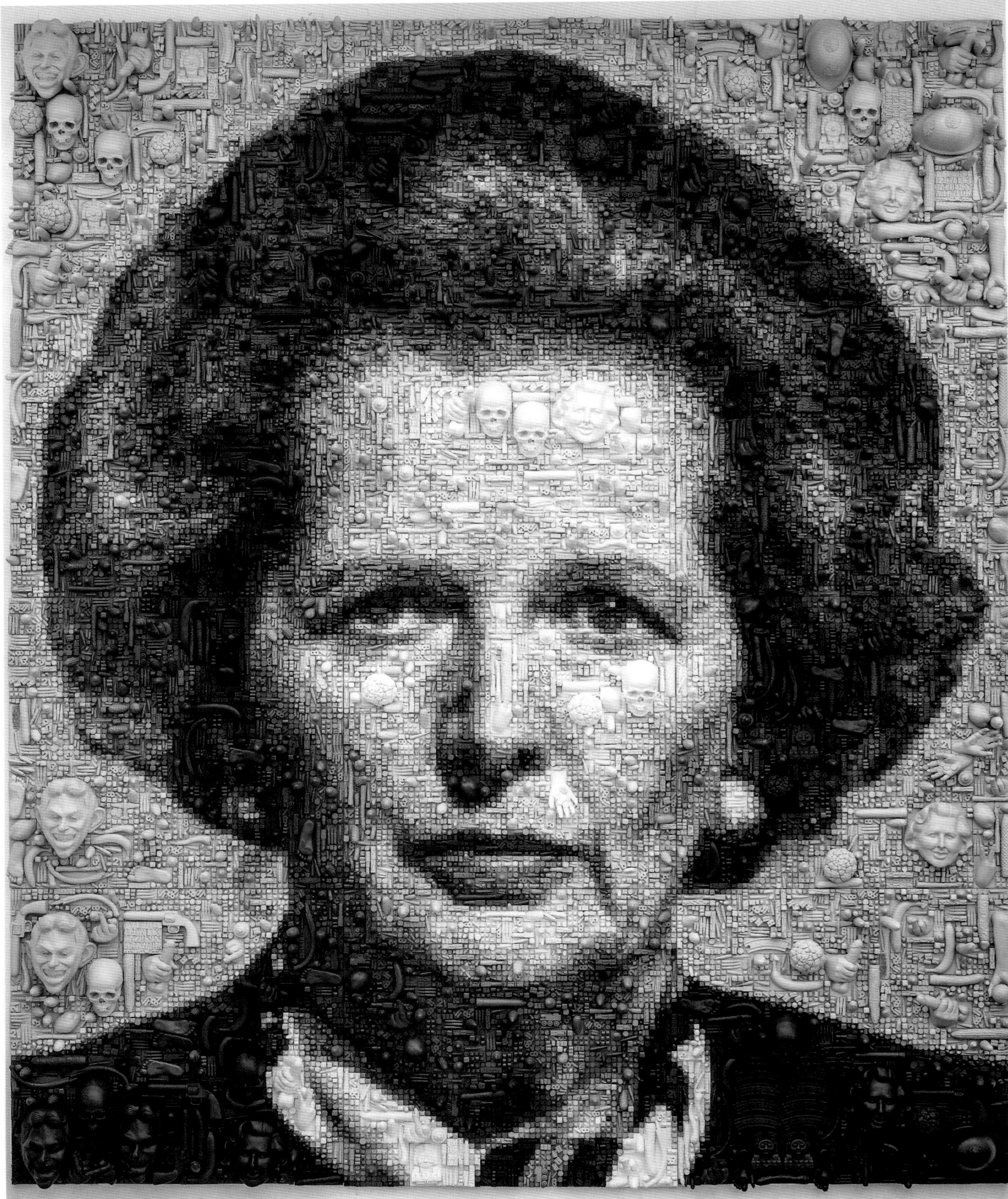

3 Narrative

The Elgin Marbles currently reside at the British Museum, plundered from the ruins of the Parthenon in Greece; these fragments depict mass ceremonies and celebrations in honour of Athena, the goddess of wisdom. The carvings feature waves of rhythmic interlocking horses rearing in a tumult, with figures and limbs wrestling, inter-cut with fabric folds.

In historical terms this is narrative sculpture, existing in the form of relief, a flattened space where a story can be expressed across a linear plane. Narrative sculpture can be incorporated into scenes and, unlike sculpture in the round, it doesn't have to stand up. These compressed depths allowed themes to be played out along stretches of architectural detail; it was an effective vehicle for commemorative narratives and valiant themes.

The tradition of the frieze continued into the twentieth century, most notably with Rodin's *Gates of Hell*, a seething and writhing uproar of figures based on Dante's cathartic journey through the inferno. But the idea of a sculptural frieze supporting a singular event was counter to anti-triumphal sentiments.

Another tradition was also developing, that of the cabinet of curiosity – collections of accumulated objects. Rocks, shells, corals, skeletons, stuffed animals, religious relics, books, manuscripts, paintings, and sculptures began to be presented together in rooms. Known as a *Wunderkammer*, a 'wonder room', these spaces were filled floor to ceiling with specimens of the physical world. This was a place to contemplate strange synergies between different forms, whilst symbolically communicating the power of the patron. Imaginatively piecing together what one had found in order to chronicle and tell a tale, like the relief, relied on constrained space, in this instance that of a room or cabinet that allowed juxtapositions to be part of a narrative. These rooms became part of a growing museum culture, and collections such as Elias Ashmole's would become the Ashmolean Museum in Oxford. The partitioning of disciplines ensured that collections were separated and subsumed into grand institutions such as the British Museum and the Natural History Museum.

In the 1940s the idea of creating lateral collections attracted attention again with the collector Joseph Cornell, who with the aid of small boxes began to build himself a world out of marbles, bells, feathers and wire. At his parents' house on Utopia Driveway in New York, Cornell would file anything that he found into hundreds of boxes. The basement was a vast archive of memorabilia, souvenirs and objects, scraps from the shores of the river Hudson and from second-hand stores. Here he would file his collection of oddities and allow them to gestate and to cohere. The revival of interest continues: in 2001 Mark Dion turned the whole of the Weisman Art Museum into an imaginative display, countering an institutional preference towards isolating objects for singular consideration.

Artists are reconsidering the narrative of how to assimilate subject matter in order to address events particular to this time; that there can be a narrative within which we can place ourselves; that there is a past and a present and we are able to imagine a future.

OPPOSITE PAGE
Marcus Harvey, *Maggie* (2009). Plaster and acrylic on aluminium, 440 × 366cm.

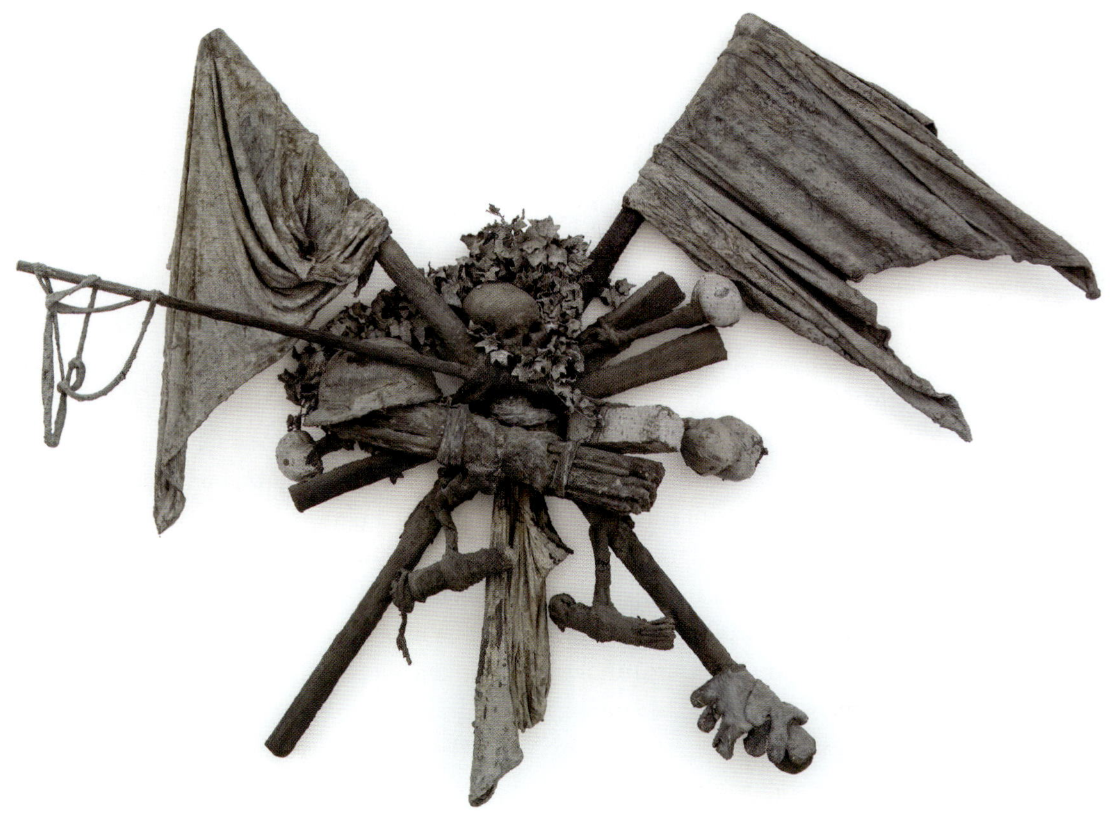

Sophie Newell, *Spoils* (2007). Mixed media.

▶ Sophie Newell

It's the final scenes of *Planet of the Apes* (1968) and Taylor (Charlton Heston) is about to gallop off to his hard-fought freedom. He is still searching for answers about how in this alter-universe apes have evolved from men. 'Don't look for it too hard, you may not like what you find,' shouts Dr Zaius, the orangutan-like religious zealot. Taylor sets off with those words ringing in his ears along a desolate, untouched stretch of coastline. As he rides through the surf an angular wiry edifice overshadows him and Taylor bellows, 'You have finally gone and done it, you've gone and blown it, damn you all to hell!' as he pounds his fists in the sand in front of the relic – the Statue of Liberty, buried in the sand. This is no alter-universe: it is the future.

The use of ruins as a sculptural *memento mori* goes back to antiquity, the contemplation of ruins an enduring preoccupation of being human; backdrops of renaissance paintings cast the shadow of architectural decline, of human feats that offer only a very brief position on earth. The ruins of Rome have been carefully preserved since 1462 for visitors to marvel at a collapsed civilization, Pope Pius II declaring their 'exemplary frailty' worthy of such consideration. And by the nineteenth century an enthusiasm for erecting mock-classical ruins spread through Northern Europe, with fallen colonnades and weather-beaten stone slabs and pedestals being arranged in formal considerations of a former catastrophic act, where the viewer could wonder when it might happen next.

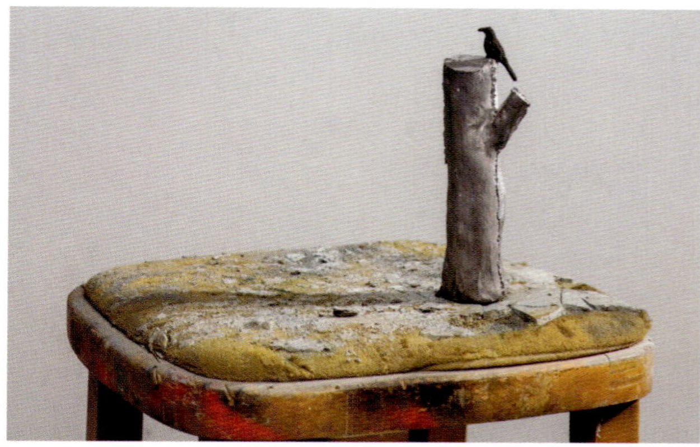

Sophie Newell, *Small Sentinel* (2008). Cast lead, clay.

Inside Sophie Newell's studio, breeze blocks, bags of cement, polythene and decorator's dust-sheets are strewn across the floor – everything has a dense dusting of grey matter. At first glance I am stepping into some kind of building site or reclamation zone. Neoclassical sections vie with building materials and only when I inspect more closely does it becomes clear that within the mess of construction material and alongside the architectural fragments there is a careful choreography of elements.

Out of this environment develops the *mise en scène* of ruins. Theatrical sets of judgement day.

IAN DAWSON: *How did the work first develop?*

SOPHIE NEWELL: I remember I was never quite satisfied with making flat imagery. There was something about the impact of a piece in a room, an architectural impact, its drama or presence. So I began using bits of architrave, doorknobs and other bits of found architectural elements and then manipulating them to become like marks. There was quite a lot of melodrama in these pieces. I began to explore a kind of frisson between the material and its capacity to become more transcendent. I was attracted to that kind of intensity of images and of wanting to present some kind of escapism through using low-grade material to create high drama.

ID: *And it was from this that you began to develop this language utilizing building materials?*

SN: I started dipping dustsheets in quick-drying cement and then throwing them over breezeblock structures. I found it a versatile material and process, to get that kind of architectural reference that I was after – a kind of ghostly imprint. There is something about dipping a piece of material, and it dries quickly and records that movement, the action; it kind of holds it. You know it's not a carving – it's a swift thing that's happened.

ID: *The breezeblocks?*

SN: Someone told me they are the remnants of the sewage process: when you look at them they are all bubbly, light and fluffy, like aerated sludge. The idea that they are tampons and toilet paper, I don't know if that is true or not, but it confirmed my interest in them as a material to use, they transcend into something else quickly but they also remain what they are. They are quick to carve, it was an interesting process – when does a breezeblock become a mountain? Some became too mountain-like; others were too blocky.

ID: *You began to create theatrical scenes?*

SN: It happened through a sequence of exhibitions, particularly the Lawrence O'Hana show. For this show an architect had made a large plywood structure, and I was invited to respond to this architectural motif. And that fitted the ideas of the work at the time, in terms of providing a stage set and of wanting to present some sort of sculptural imagery. This box was a useful device, and the exhibition helped to crystallize the work that I had been making in the studio, having a structure that I could utilize and turn into a romantic landscape

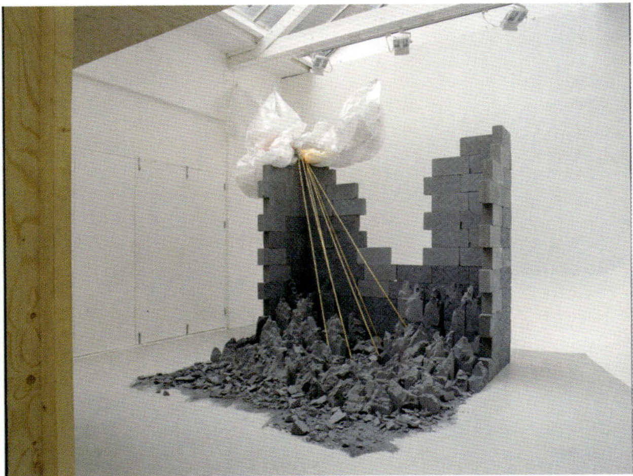

Sophie Newell, Lawrence O'Hana installation (5) (2004).
Mixed media.

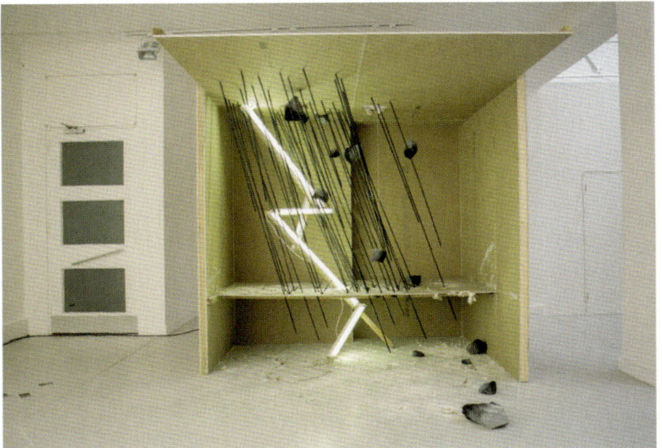

Sophie Newell, Lawrence O'Hana installation (7) (2004).
Mixed media.

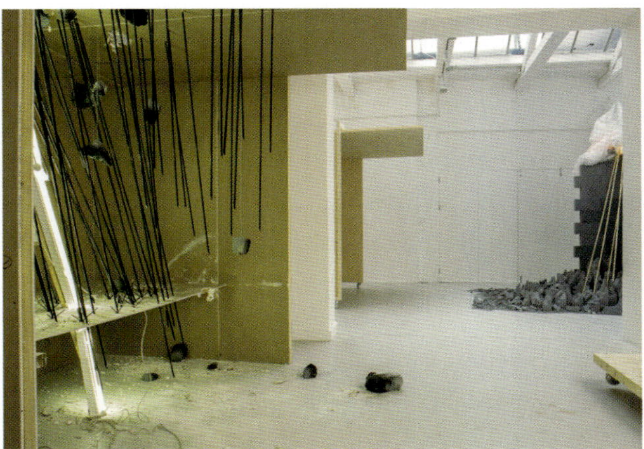

Sophie Newell, Lawrence O'Hana installation (4) (2004).
Mixed media.

by using the most basic building materials: plastic dustsheets, copper pipes and breezeblocks.

There was a second section to the show, made from plasterboard with neon tubes as lightning. Because the plywood structure was a given, that was quite useful in throwing up what the imagery could be within that. Using the idea of a meteor storm as the most ridiculous thing that could happen in a white cube – it was my way of introducing high drama into that. Bits of dust that became the surface of a landscape; detritus that became moon rocks.

ID: *You are choreographing a destructive moment.*

SN: I remember for my MA, I knocked a big hole through a wall and exposed another space, a corridor that had needle-cord grey carpet and chipboard lining paper. I remember becoming concerned with the shape of the hole. On the one hand I was essentially just smashing through plasterboard but on another level I was became interested with creating an image with that hole, of wanting the imagery to be more involving.

ID: *And the nature of the imagery?*

SN: I am attracted to that kind of intensity of images and the melodrama that you get in Bernini. And wanting to present some kind of escapism through the materials I am choosing.

Drawing has always been a big part of the process. That's how all the work starts out – as a series of sketchbook drawings, mainly line drawings. It becomes quite interesting when you look back at the drawings and realize that I executed what I was planning to do, in a way that often surprises me.

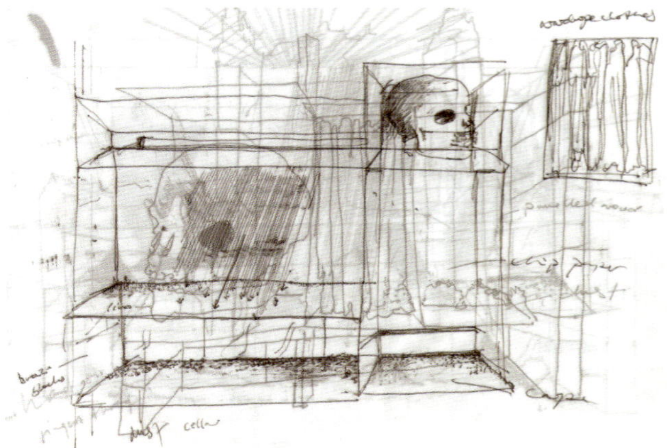

Sophie Newell, drawing on layout pad (1).

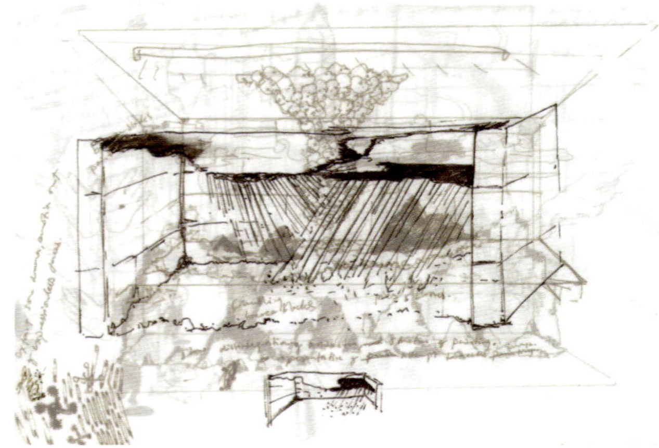

Sophie Newell, drawing on layout pad (2).

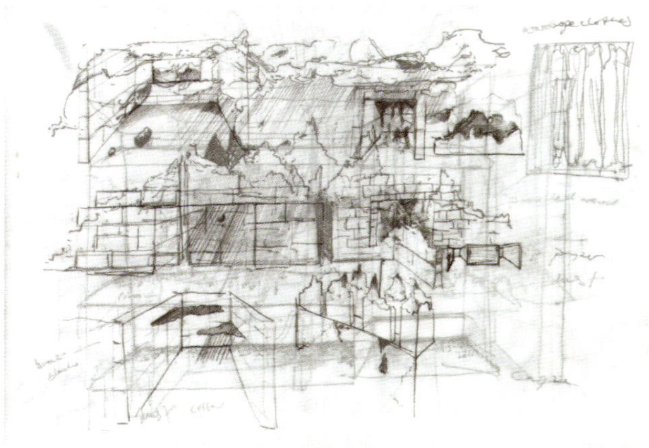

Sophie Newell, drawing on layout pad (3).

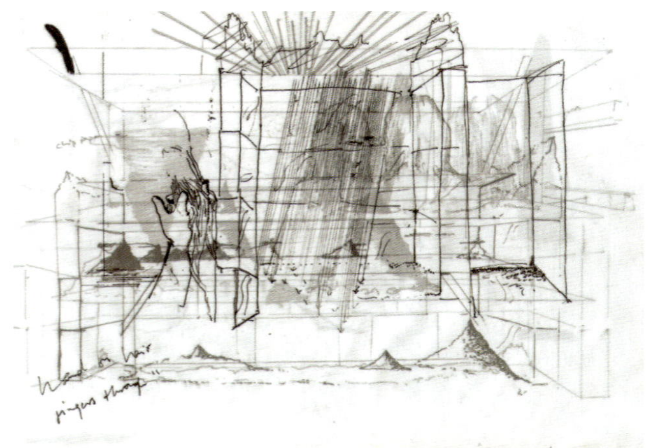

Sophie Newell, drawing on layout pad (4).

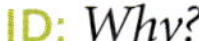

ID: *Why?*

SN: Because it is an intuitive process in terms of how the sculptures relate to the drawings and like everything it always involves a bit of this and a bit of that. But rather than an intuitive sculptural process, I think I have an intuitive drawing process that then becomes translated into objects. That's the thing that anchors all the pieces.

ID: *The drawings have a clear link with the vitrines in the studio.*

SN: Yes, it allowed the material to become imagery because it is housed in a framework. And that it means I can sort out the imagery because I didn't have to worry about the structure itself. The structure is a given.

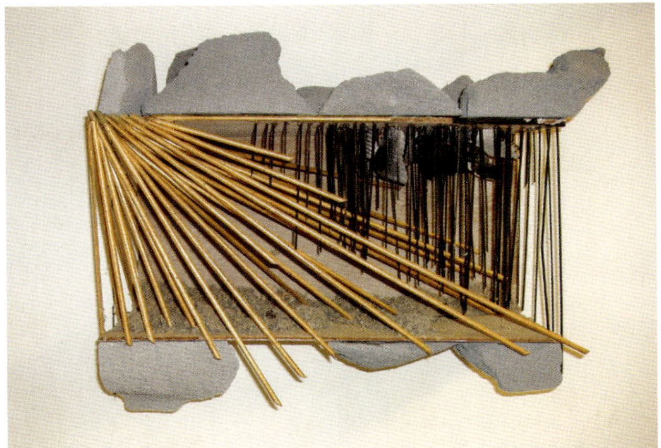

Sophie Newell, *Birdcage*.

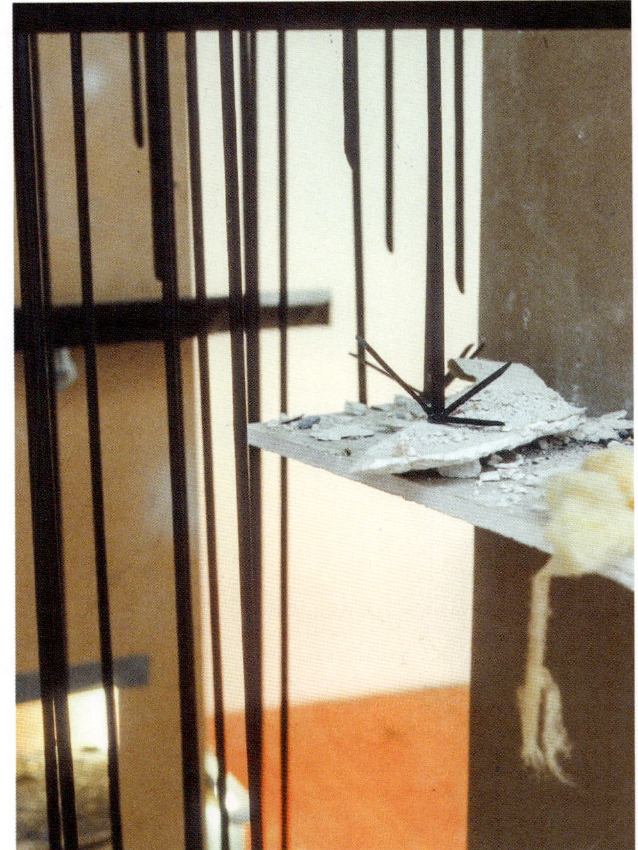

Sophie Newell, *Ancoats Hospital* (detail).

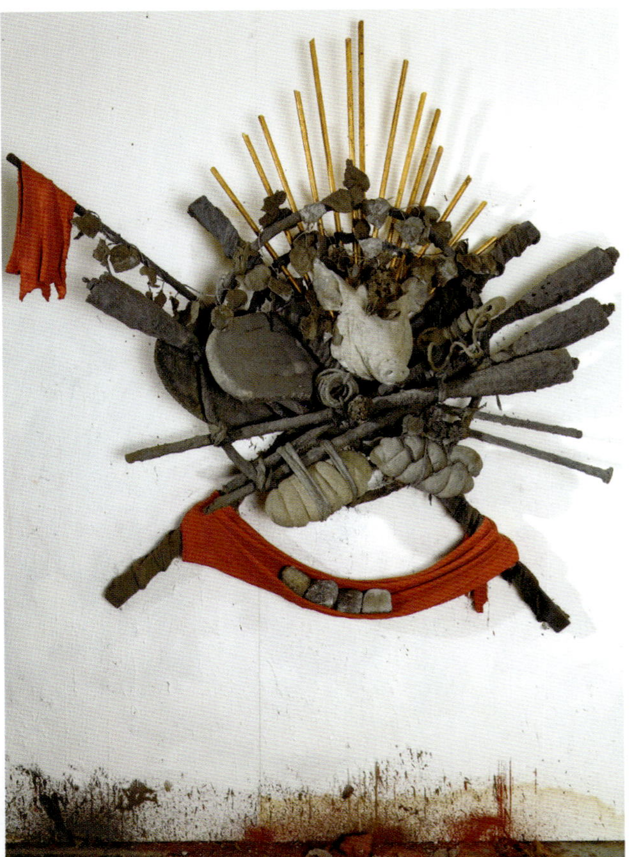

Sophie Newell, *Pig God* (2007). Cement, cast pig's head, cast bread, garden torches, plastic ivy, gold leafed copper piping.

ID: *In Ancoats Hospital waiting room you have responded to a Lowry painting of the same name. You seemed to have successfully made work to a set of imposed criteria.*

SN: The Lowry show was weird. Respond to a Lowry? What do you mean? But then it is good because you have to rethink Lowry and look a bit harder at what the proposition is. And it was interesting to be given an image that I wouldn't necessarily have used to generate an atmosphere from, rather than to hack it out from somewhere else. I was using all those motifs anyway. Sometimes it's handy, sometimes it's not. There was a show where every contributing artist had to construct a birdcage. That's spurred on a lot of future work; for me that was a good example of a themed show that sent me somewhere interesting through its restrictions.

ID: *The work became wall-based again.*

SN: I had started to look at Victorian engravings of trophies. Originally Athenian armies would nail their spoils of war together and hang them from a tree. By the seventeenth century these had become aestheticized, as woodcarvers would mimic them by hanging whatever the patron or occasion would demand.

I became interested in these commemorative objects and that notion of being able to combine lots of objects in a recognizable form. Like a tattoo, I suppose.

ID: *It was a form of ordering much like the vitrine.*

SN: I guess what I did was use an aesthetic structure to hang the shape of the work on; both metaphorically and physically. I felt it was more important to sift out the objects in order to see what might be important. I wondered what would be important in society if certain structures were not there any more, in terms of people's basic needs, so for example you have bread and weapons. Sieving through those things so you have the object can contain that kind of evocative meaning. But then it's a parody of that: it's a 99p shop bit of tat, they are not symbolic in that way, they no longer have that kind of currency. I suppose I was looking for that kind of symbolism with the banality of the cheapness.

ID: *A whole range of objects are combined.*

SN: Chunks of polystyrene, weird mastic lumps, a builder's helmet, plastic ivy – that very simple process of dipping something in cement was an easy way of getting that transcendence from a bunch of bits of MDF to some other more loaded thing. There is some humour there when you start to recognize a builder's

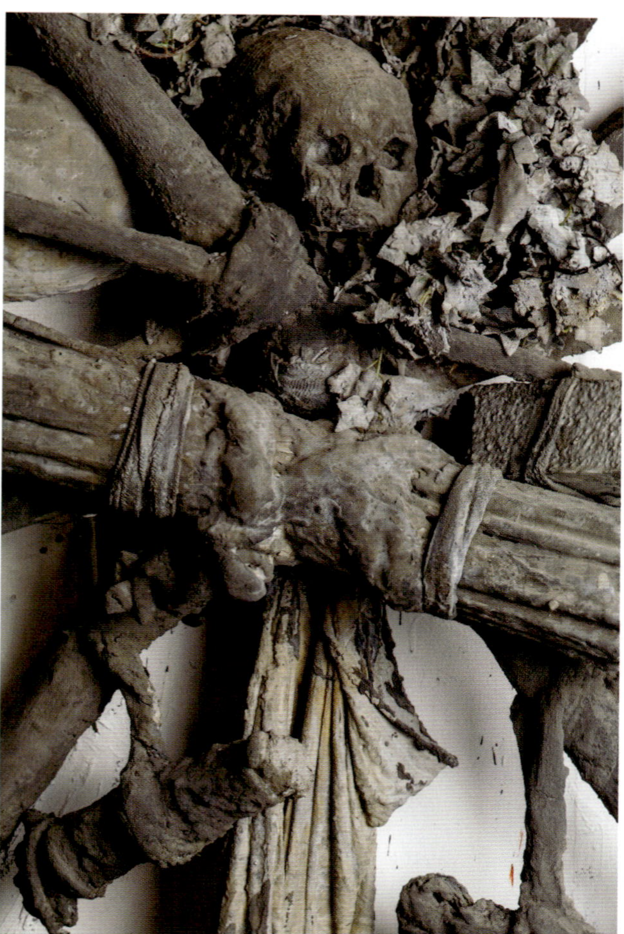

Sophie Newell, *Spoils* (2007, detail). Mixed media.

glove. I was dipping and then letting the objects dry then binding the pieces together. They were like drawings really, the swiftness of them.

ID: *The pieces become unified like calcified lumps.*

SN: Yes there something archaeological about the process, the artifice of giving a history to the object. The illusion of age, that these objects transcend the present.

There is also a transience to it: there is no longevity to the materials, they get packed into these crates that are going to last longer than the work's going to last.

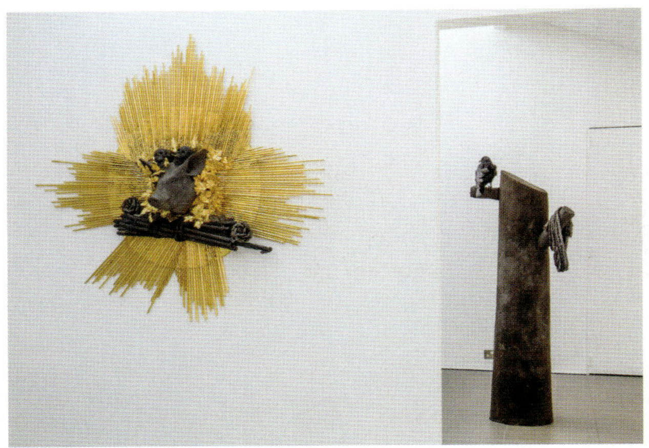

Sophie Newell, installation shot at Cell Project Space, London, (2008).

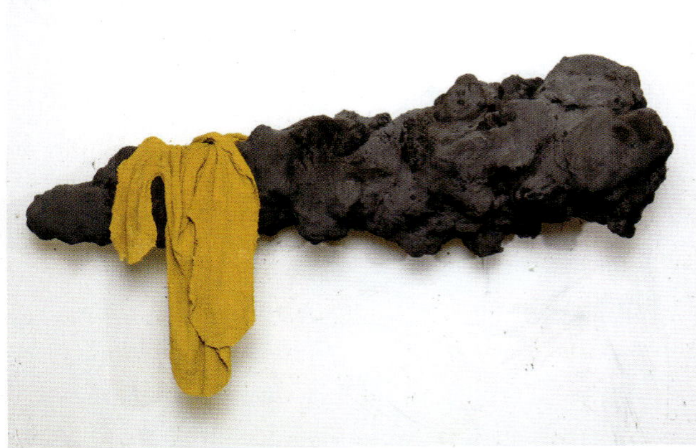

Sophie Newell, *Club* (2008). Cement, polystyrene, towel, length 160cm.

ID: *They are constructed with a distinct sense of purpose. In terms of the process, the visual language that was being crystallized within them, using the bread and the plastic guns and the pig heads.*

SN: I felt guilty at the ease of finding the objects but at the time it was the right combination of pressure and practice. When I was making these pieces, I had two dedicated days in the studio per week. It was brilliant: there was no procrastination, I couldn't sit there for half a day making a million drawings but not making a decision. I had to go, 'first thought best thought' – I would have probably ended up at the same place anyway, because I was using the same amount of information and knowledge to make that decision anyway. So not having too much time to doubt myself was a really invaluable thing.

ID: *There is the sculpture of a club.*

SN: I think this was the most successful piece of the show in terms of its simplicity. Very different, not as pictorial in terms of how the other works existed within a space frame. It's more sculptural yet also exists on a wall. It is almost like a painting as well – the nature of its shape, its dumbness. I remember making

it and thinking, 'Is it possible to make a piece this simple, this blunt?' That was liberating: an object that contains an element of drawing, an element of surface, but communicates that set of ideas about filtering out what is important, necessary, to pare it down to this very simple image of a tool, a basic tool. And the pelt, a towel dipped in coloured cement, was there to balance the shape, but also added humour to it.

ID: *When was* Club *made?*

SN: It was the last piece made of the series. It was a response to the complexity of the others, struggling with the amount of imagery in the others. I guess it was a condensing of all that was in the others, militaristic. It's the kind of piece that when it happens it then spawns a whole set of other works.

ID: *I understand what you were saying about the club being important.*

SN: Pieces like this are like a door. They spur on the next body of work. ■

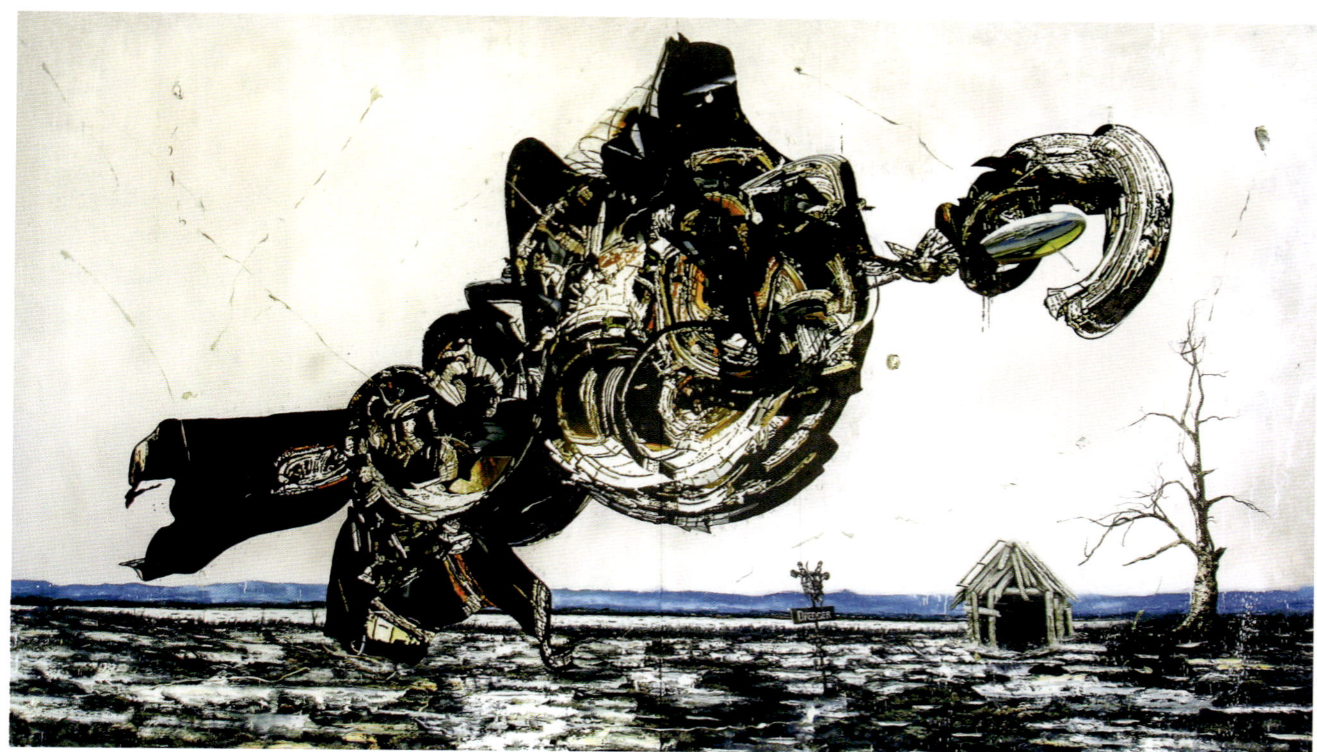

Chris Hawtin, *Dredger* (2011). 336 × 198cm, oil on canvas.

▶ Chris Hawtin

I even saw it once, at least I think so. Its shape was indistinct in that it was impossible to look at. As soon as it came under your direct gaze it would disappear, and therefore could only be glimpsed in peripheral vision. It moved, seemingly flying or hovering slowly, yet with definite purpose. One could never be certain of its material existence, although its appearance was that of something corporeal, almost organic, yet with the callous functionality of an engine. Light was reflected from it, which suggests it has material form, even if only the finest membrane. Although I can only claim one encounter, they say it can be often seen, when it is near dark, or against a backdrop of intense bright light. It invokes both anxiety and nostalgia, and though instinct tells you it is not meant to exist, not here at least, we need it.

This is Hawtin's description of the central character in his recent paintings, it is a partly fluid, a partly architectural spectre, that dominates the horizon line. Its origin unexplained. Along the vista and in the distance and overshadowed by the apparition is a shed, a temporary structure fused into the landscape, a symbol of human activity, a marginal element against the main subject. With an urge to understand these structures that exist as narrative subplots, Hawtin has rendered these models with lollipop sticks, hamster bedding, straws and sackcloth; these fictional spaces made real. Made quickly with a glue gun, they personify the structures that they represent.

I imagine the artist as the character played by Richard Dreyfuss in Spielberg's *Close Encounters of the Third Kind*, who has experienced a UFO and has become ever more obsessed by a space that he is impelled to attempt to describe. He too has modelled a mountain using household items, attempting to

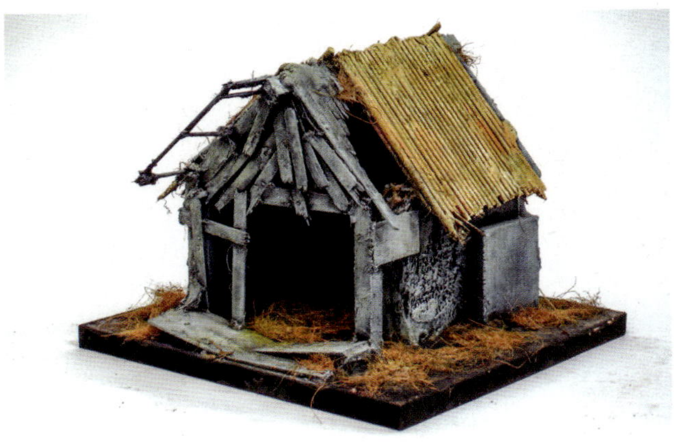

Chris Hawtin, *Gregor's Shack* (2011). Wood, styrofoam, clay, dried plants, oil and acrylic, 30 × 30 × 24cm.

make it correspond to his subliminal vision. At last he manages to contrive to make the object *right* and then in a frenzy of activity using flowers and shrubs from the garden, and earth from a wheelbarrow, he makes the mountain until it fills the front room and the flat crater hugs the ceiling.

The television is on, showing a rolling news report about Devils Tower in Wyoming. The subconscious image that has been rendered real by him in his sitting room is identical to the projected image on the television set. His actions are vindicated as he begins to comprehend the implications. ■

▶ Cathy de Monchaux

Cathy de Monchaux's often extravagant and ornamental objects trap the viewer's gaze with their luscious folds, spiky metalwork and dense thickets of wire. With a coating of powder or tarnish they appear out of time.

Meaning is lodged on the surface of the work; the image, whether it references genitalia or mythical horses, is as a result of a process. The meaning does not precede the experience of viewing, of being drawn into the mass of wire or ruffled velvet, the externalization of the image meeting the imprint of her hand as she shaped the work with an apparently obsessive attention to detail.

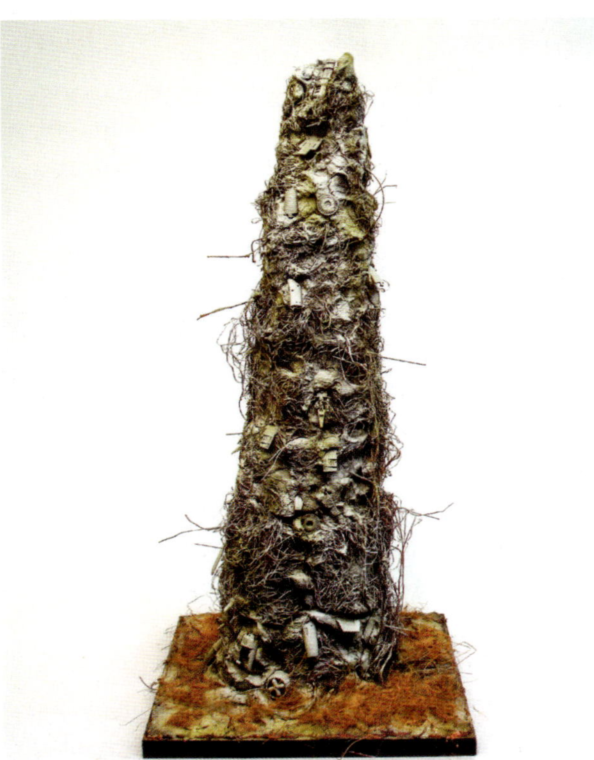

Chris Hawtin, *Ennio's Spire* (2011). Clay, metal, plastic, dried plants, oil and acrylic, 30 × 30 × 65cm.

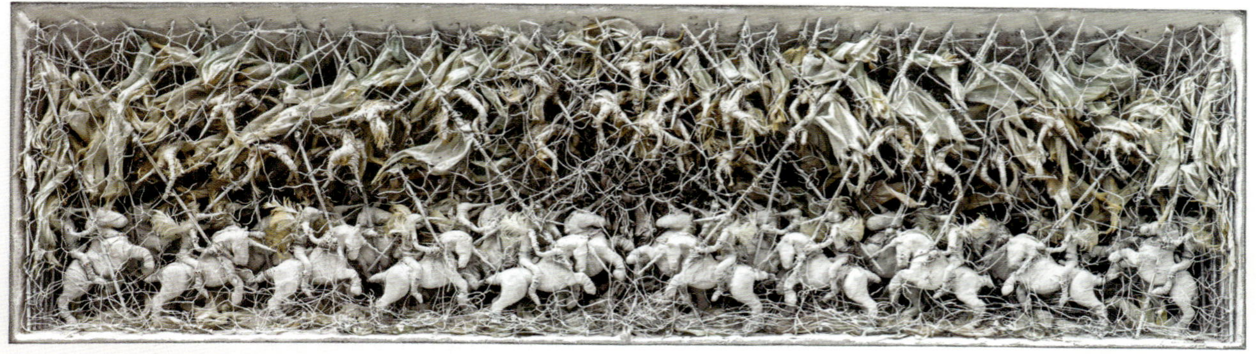

Cathy de Monchaux, *Sweetly The Air Flew Overhead – Battle With Unicorns no. 9* (2010). Leather, copper, brass, bandage, perspex, gesso, silk, wood and glass, 86 × 154 × 11cm.

CATHY DE MONCHAUX: I left art school in 1984, it was a completely different time, it doesn't feel a long time ago, but the imperatives were completely different. In terms of sexual politics alone it was a completely different sort of drive. When I was 24, there was an importance in gender politics; it is still a pressing concern that has not been dealt with by the world we live in.

ID: Your concerns have evolved?

CDM: The notion of global conflict seems to have become more pervasive. That might be due to globalization and how we look at the world – that I am now much more conscious of an act of violence in Kosovo, say. It comes into your retina somehow, so for me, it has become increasingly pressing to think about that.

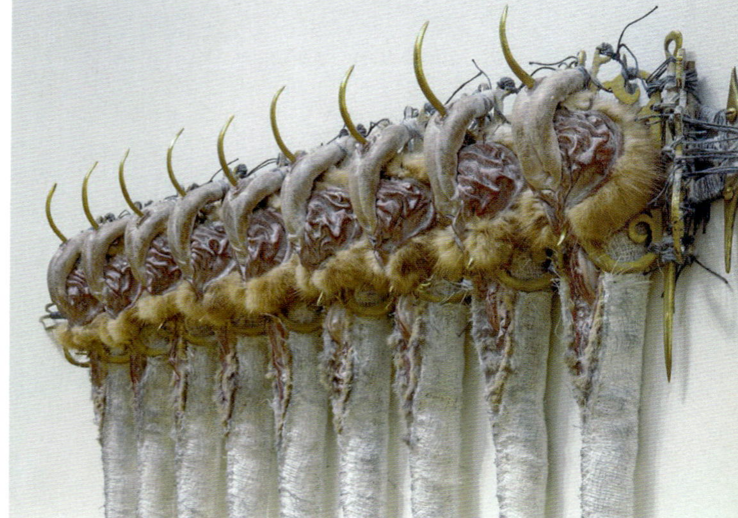

Cathy de Monchaux, *Don't Touch My Waist* (1998) detail. Brass, leather, fur and scrim, 117 × 106 × 8cm.

ID: How do you go about trying to express this?

CDM: I think it's problematic to articulate it because it's like, 'What can you say about that, except that it's bad?' Which in a sense is, 'So what? That's obvious.' But to try and have some tenderness of thought towards the dilemma that we're in is how I then try to make artwork. I don't have an articulated script for what it is that I'm trying to do; it's just that I find myself doing it.

ID: *So in a way you rely on your thoughts entering in an implicit way.*

CDM: There's an imperative to do it, but I am not able to articulate those reasons. I'm not doing it to save the world, I'm doing it because it's a way of talking about the world that I'm in. So I can't really say why am I making a battle scene, other than it seems the correct thing to do for me right now.

ID: *There also appear to be references to Assyrian sculptures, for example?*

CDM: The conscious references that I'm making to art, that's just the cultural plundering that I do in my head. Other times I might be thinking of Islamic pattern-making – a cultural artefact is always loaded with meaning even if we don't know what the meaning is.

ID: *The battle scenes are in a series.*

CDM: There are currently eight in the series. Each one gets more and more complicated and refined about a notion of depth. I am interested in depicting something that doesn't look like now at all. I'm inventing this place that is somewhere else, but talks about where we are in a different sort of way.

ID: *Is there a prerogative for that?*

CDM: I'm not interested in obviously mirroring the world because to replicate it would become problematic; it's how to make something that might still have a resonance in twenty years' time.

ID: *It displays the hallmarks of earlier works that have the sense of being arrived at.*

CDM: I start with the frame, the space if you like. And then I make the horses and the riders; I start composing with the background, which almost becomes completely obscured. It becomes a dense layer. What is interesting is that you can't completely lose what you started: once you've made those initial marks, they always have a bearing even if they're hidden.

ID: *I find it interesting that the practical side of making it, the layering and the loss of those initial marks corresponds to aspects of your subject matter.*

CDM: Some of it is to do with forgotten memories. I am questioning what I do with this information that's returned to me, that I've had hidden in my head that I just didn't really want to know about, and that's coming back to me.

ID: *That is fascinating.*

CDM: It's intriguing because the brain hides things; it's fascinating what it will do to protect you. You're living your life and suddenly its starts to reveal memories. How can that be? The brain wants to release this information. And then is that information real? Do you then have to rewrite your own thinking about those things? So for me that's fascinating as an artist because in the past I was making work that was about hiding something I didn't know about. And now I know about it, it's how to make that into art.

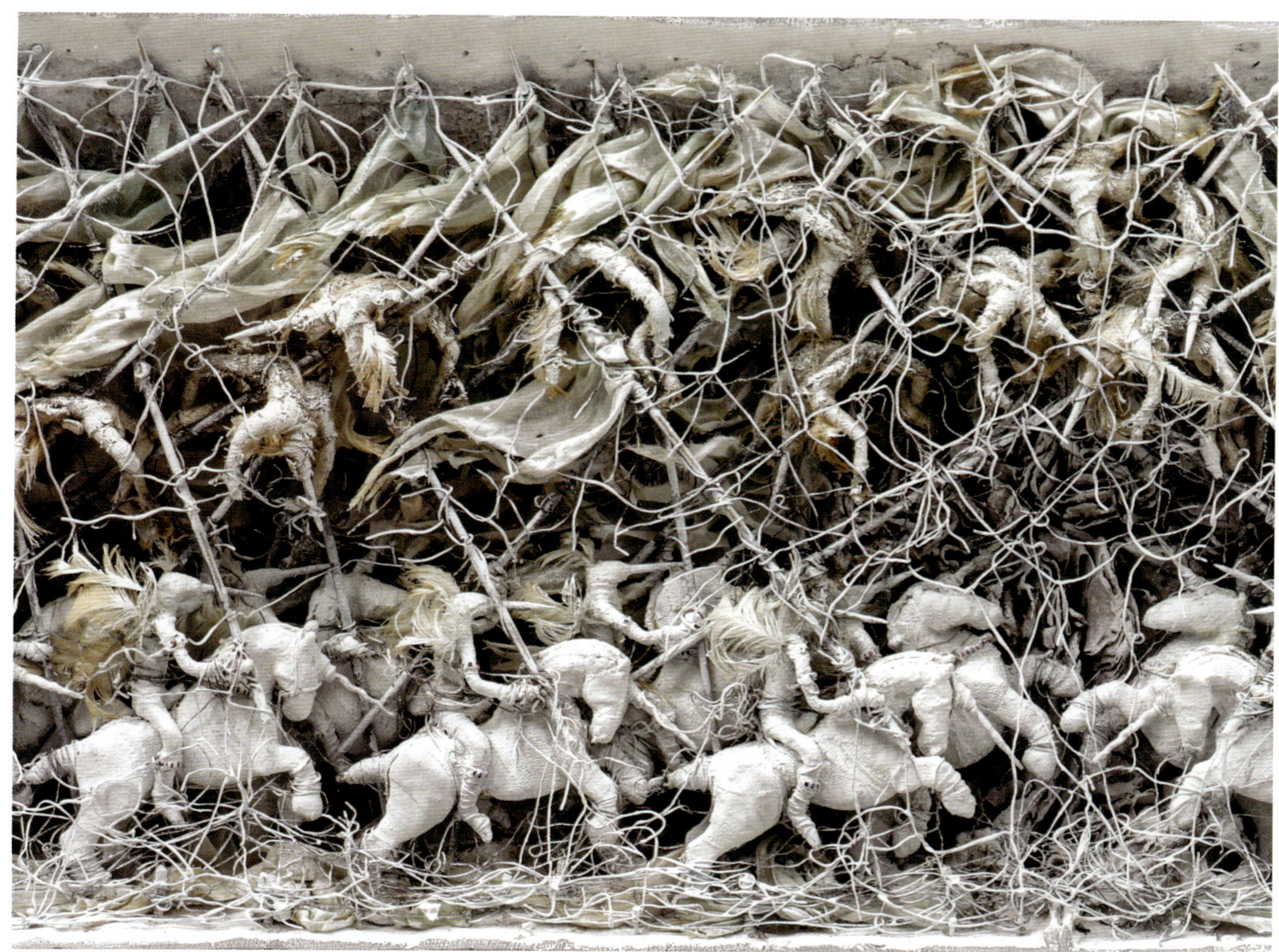

Cathy de Monchaux, *Sweetly The Air Flew Overhead – Battle With Unicorns no. 7* (2007, detail). Leather, copper, brass, bandage, perspex, gesso, silk, wood and glass, 86 × 154 × 11cm.

ID: Have you been looking back and re-assessing earlier works?

CDM: Yes, I recently moved studio after working in the same place for many years and I've unearthed this piece from 1999, for example. I had found a dead frog and it looked liked it was praying. So I had the frog cast in silver and had an idea of placing it in a vagina-like box. It was around the time of the Balkan conflict; there was this whole sudden realization that people were raping and pillaging, with permission, for want of a better way of putting it, in a Western environment, women becoming this bounty of war.

ID: That's what you were thinking about at the time of making that piece?

CDM: At the time I would never have said that to anybody. I was also thinking very much about the broader idea of being violated. And the frog is praying in supplication.

CDM: I had a show in New York, so I travelled to America with the cast frog, a bit of wood and some leather and I worked, making this piece in the gallery at night, trying to explain to myself what I thought – and the urgency of it probably permitted me to make it like this. If I was sitting in my studio I would've been thinking, 'you can't do that, that's too fucking weird!'

ID: *So working with such pressures allows you to make those difficult decisions?*

CDM: I was almost at a point where I had to dare myself to do this really weird thing that I had in my head. I'm not convinced that necessarily makes it better art. It is just that there is a point where I have to switch off the questions – and I use the urgency of the occasion for that. There seems to be a point where I let something in which is bizarre, these things appear from the back brain, from the unconscious and are not nameable. I suppose I'm interested in that.

ID: *So switching off the questions.*

CDM: And of doing it quite urgently and also quite innocently. To give myself permission to do something, that probably comes from a certain naivety. I am having a conversation in my head: 'I can't do it like that because of this or that.'

ID: *That's an interesting way to work, like you short-circuit yourself.*

CDM: The urgency to make things comes after quite a long period of what appears to be slovenliness! The sitting back and waiting is an important moment.

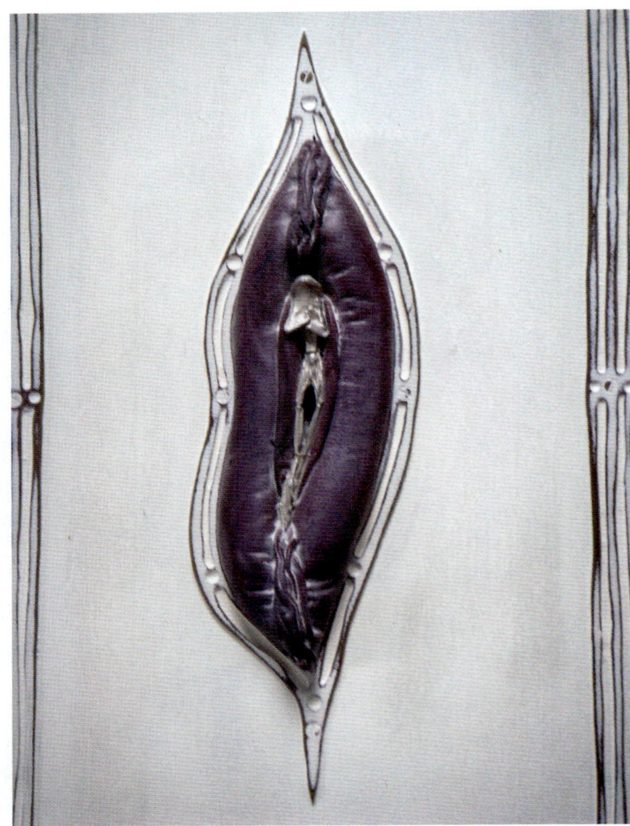

Cathy de Monchaux, *Mayflower (Warbride)* (1999). Cast silver frog, leather, wood, paint, chalk.

Waiting and thinking: it's not like your mind goes to sleep – the nature of the activity demands it.

ID: *I wouldn't think that of the work. I would think that it was produced more evenly.*

CDM: As soon as you pick something up and start making you're somewhat hijacked by what you've picked up and by what mood you're in and how the day started; it has all got to be perfect for me before I start. When you're making work as opposed to the thinking about working, you think in a different way – your mind wanders, so you have to be convinced enough about what you're working on. Especially when there's a process involved, because it would be really boring if that was all I did. It's much more interesting to say, 'I'm

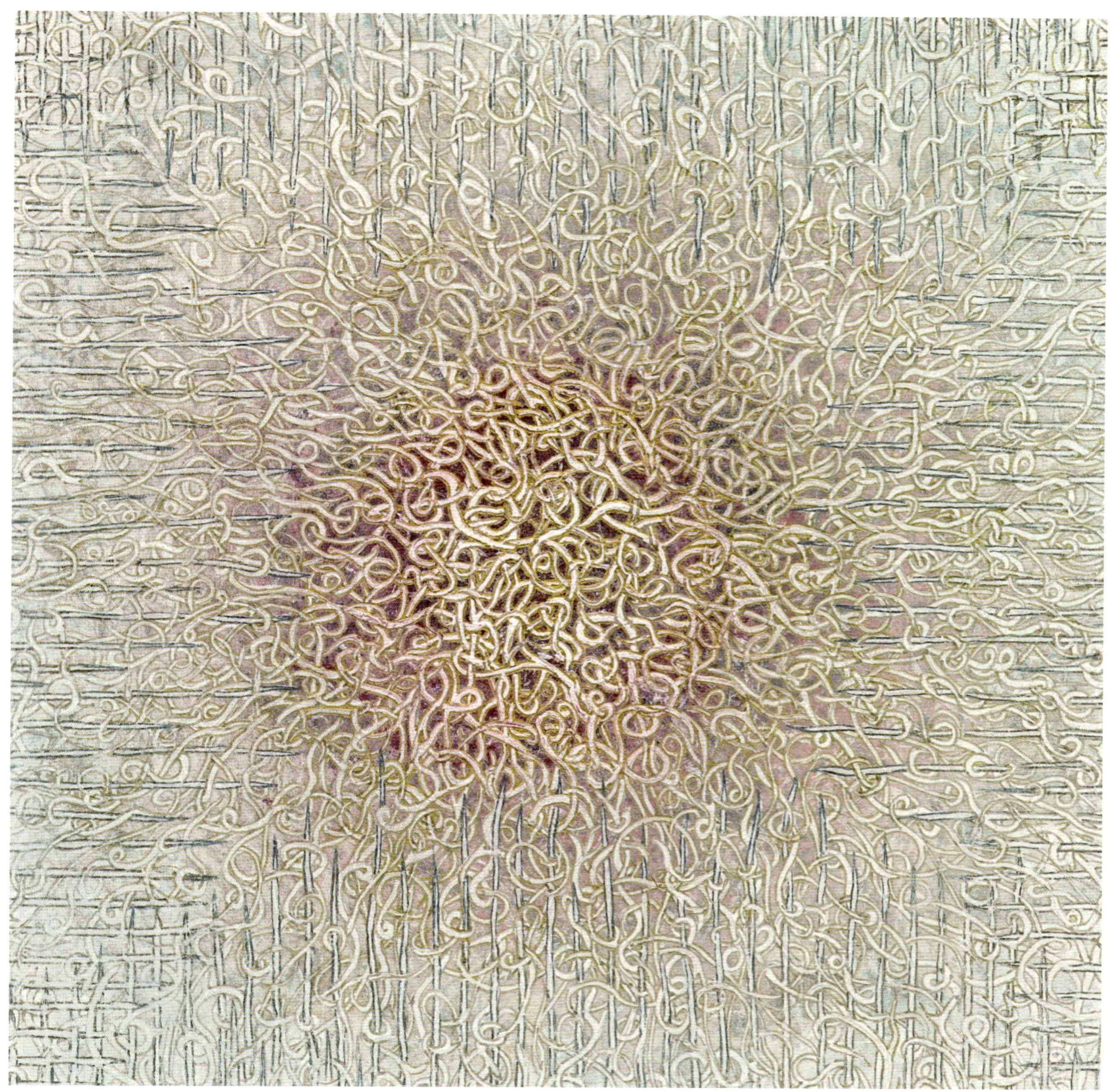

Cathy de Monchaux, *I'm So Scarred, I'm So Scared* (2008). Drawing.

going to make thirteen horses in the next three days.'
Because there isn't any time for prevarication at that
point – you just do it! And do it just well enough, but
not too well.

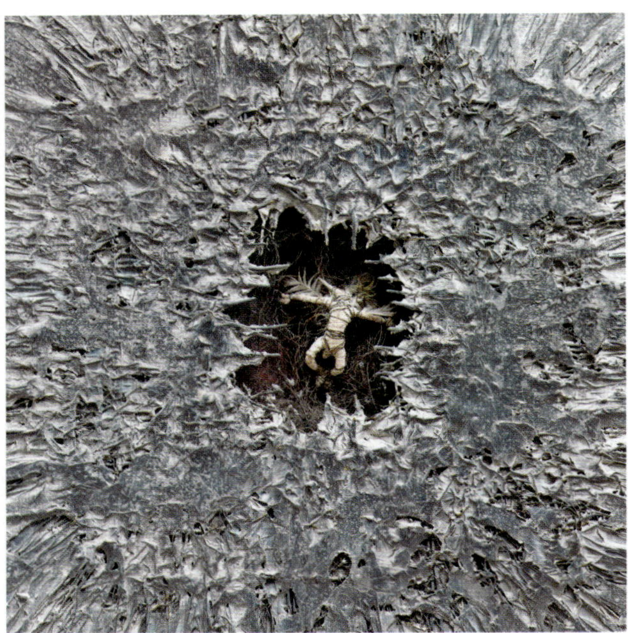

Cathy De Monchaux, *You Had No Right To Take My Spirit* (2008). Tissue paper, pigment, watercolour, copper wire, elastoplast, feathers, 123 × 108 × 11cm.

ID: *That makes sense of your activity.*

CDM: Otherwise it would be really tiresome. It's finding that point where it almost unravels but it just holds in place, so I don't just keep on covering things up. Sometimes urgency gives that to you because there is that place where you have to stop.

ID: *So again that's a practical way of defining the end.*

CDM: For me, it's finished when I can't physically unravel it anymore. It's fixed enough so that it's not going to fall to pieces.

ID: *You have described a practice that is questioning itself. That is a brave position.*

CDM: For my part there's often an anxiety about stating something. I know how I did things, but I don't know how I'm going to do things. Particularly because I have moved studios, after working for so long in the same place. It's quite difficult for me now to say to myself that this is my practice – because I've taken away the habit of my normal routine and place. So what do I do today? What do I do? So I am asking myself those quite difficult questions. To which I don't know the answers. I don't really know what I will arrive at.

ID: *To question the why.*

CDM: That's what I'm curious about. What if you take away the habits that you think feed what you do? Then is there room for something else to come in? I am starting from a forest fire position right now and I am waiting for the new shoots to grow.

ID: *That feels pertinent right now.*

CDM: I am becoming more engrossed with how artists might be able to get power back in terms of trying to make things that are fundamentally interesting. To me, the only reason to be an artist is to at least have a go. Maybe that's our hope, to say, 'Let's go back to the drawing board', and find out what it is that we can convey to the rest of humanity. ∎

▶ Marcus Harvey

In 2009 Marcus Harvey exhibited an enormous pixelated relief portrait of Margaret Thatcher. Consisting of thousands of cast objects coloured in tonal gradations and painstakingly arranged, this frieze captured a media image of the former Prime Minister in her prime. The frontal nature of the piece ensured the total confrontation with the iconic status of the image, replete with all those memories. The array of objects, an agglomeration of skulls and hands, cauliflowers, corn on the cobs, dildos and lipsticks, and masks of Tony Blair are all devolved to the historical significance of the image. *Maggie* supports the conventions of narrative relief with its clarity of message.

The exhibition *White Riot* also featured a towering bronze of the Churchill statue from Parliament Square sporting its famous Mohican strip of turf from a millennium Mayday riot. There was also a deflated football and a painting of the white cliffs of Dover.

Shorn of colour and planned before the global financial crisis, it was a powerful exhibition of dominant imagery. His work continued with direct incorporations of figures such as Punch and Judy into ceramic sculptures.

I arrange to meet Marcus in the Hermit's Cave pub close to his studio.

IAN DAWSON: *You've come from a painting background.*

MARCUS HARVEY: Essentially I have always been interested in two-and-a-half dimensions.

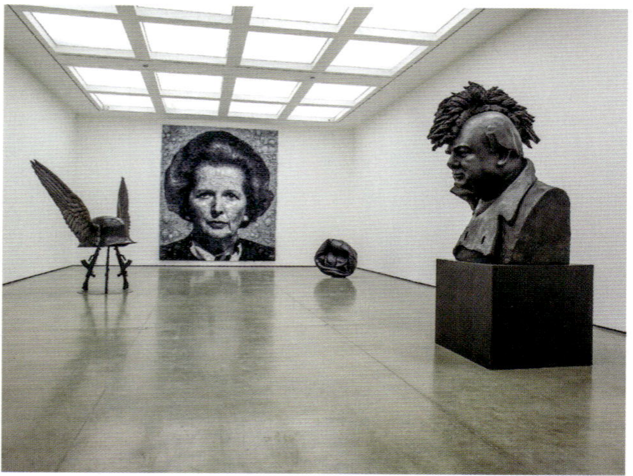

Marcus Harvey, *White Riot* exhibition (2009). Gallery installation view, White Cube, Hoxton Square, London.

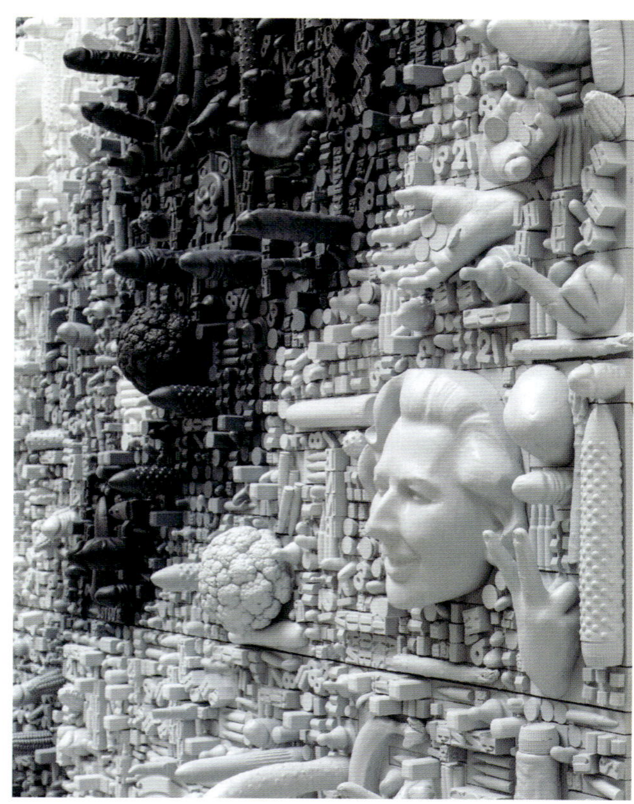

Marcus Harvey, *Maggie* (2009, detail). Plaster and acrylic on aluminium, 440 × 366cm.

ID: *How do you describe that?*

MH: A three-dimensional object, incorporated into something wall-based – like a frieze – this seems to be my point of interest. It's not sculpture in the round as such. So a lot of the sculptures that I've made, you don't really look at them from behind, they're all against the wall. In a way that's church-like, where they literally would be against the wall.

ID: *In your paintings prior to the* White Riot *show you have worked with constructed and reconstructed historical narratives, theatrical scenarios that included Hitler and Mussolini.*

MH: There was an important moment when I decided to look at my own culture and experience rather than a historical exploration of dictators and historical figures; to start looking at nationalism and icons closer to home. Then to explore it in a sculptural way was part of the synthesis of ideas and material.

ID: *You often talk of a triangle with an apex, the meeting point between the subject, on one side, and the material on the other.*

MH: Some people start with material and the material suggests the idea, and some people start with an idea and then they find the appropriate material and you are either on one side of that or the other – we all have different starting points. But there seems quite a lot of hostility half way down that triangle from different sides. I mean, the great insult which always hurt me was that the subject's doing all the work.

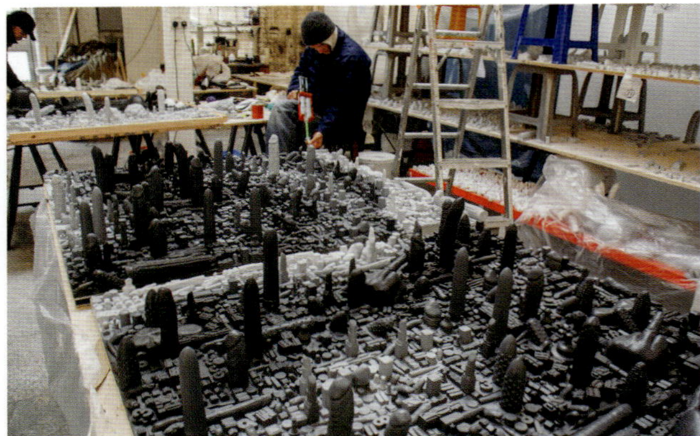

Marcus Harvey, *White Riot* production.

ID: *Was that the case with* White Riot?

MH: Well, in that show the subject was the most important thing for me. It was an opportunity to present this static image, although it was sculpturally very involving and a lot of fun to do. But I was very aware of it being a static fixed image that was executed over a year. There were a lot of creative decisions in the making of it. But I was very aware that I was now going to need something with more of an immediate plasticity and I wasn't going to continue to use the foundry and other sets of assistants.

ID: *So it was the end of something.*

MH: It capped off a way of working and an adherence to the photographic icon. I needed to make those images, but I knew full well it was a cul-de-sac of sorts. They're not cul-de-sacs in terms of your life's works, but in terms of what people might perceive in terms of a connected progression. It was something that I needed to exhaust, the crystalline clarity, the phenomenon and events that are only ever told through photographs. And then try and supply the human angle through the materiality.

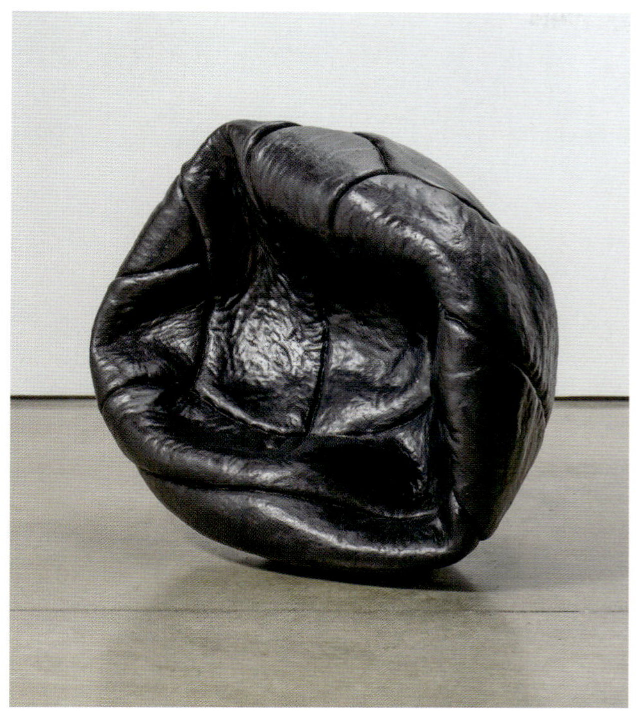

Marcus Harvey, *Victoria* (2008–9).

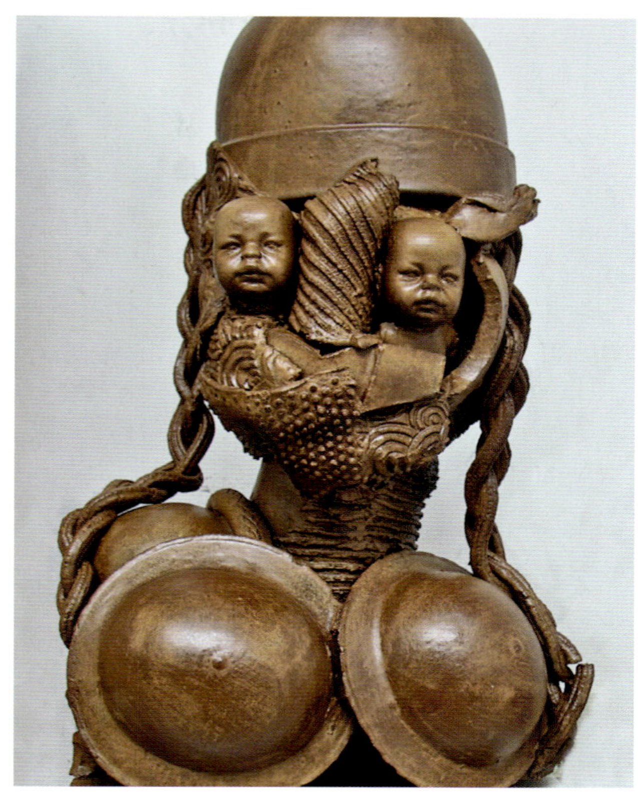

Marcus Harvey, work in progress. Fired stoneware, unique.

ID: *I found the deflated football poignant.*

MH: I tried to get it into a recent exhibition but I couldn't get it down the stairs – I thought it was a lot lighter than it is. It's really fucking heavy!

ID: *It was first exhibited at the same time as growth was being questioned within the economy.*

MH: That show had some poignant images. There was an image looking at the Thatcher piece through the closed doors of White Cube. But I've always resisted using or celebrating those specific readings and I was a bit frustrated with the timing of the show. I think people thought I'd had my fifteen minutes of fame and were loath to give me any more. It wasn't intentional: these are subjects I am interested in.

ID: *How do you go about negotiating that?*

MH: Gilbert and George said a good thing: that they wanted to bring the bigot out of the liberal and the liberal out of the bigot – I appreciate that sentiment.

ID: *You started to use ceramics.*

MH: Bronze was too expensive. It was good, translating an object into the hard metal material, but it's such a protracted process. Then when I was using the clay in preparation for the bronze I realized that was the exciting part where I had much more immediate control.

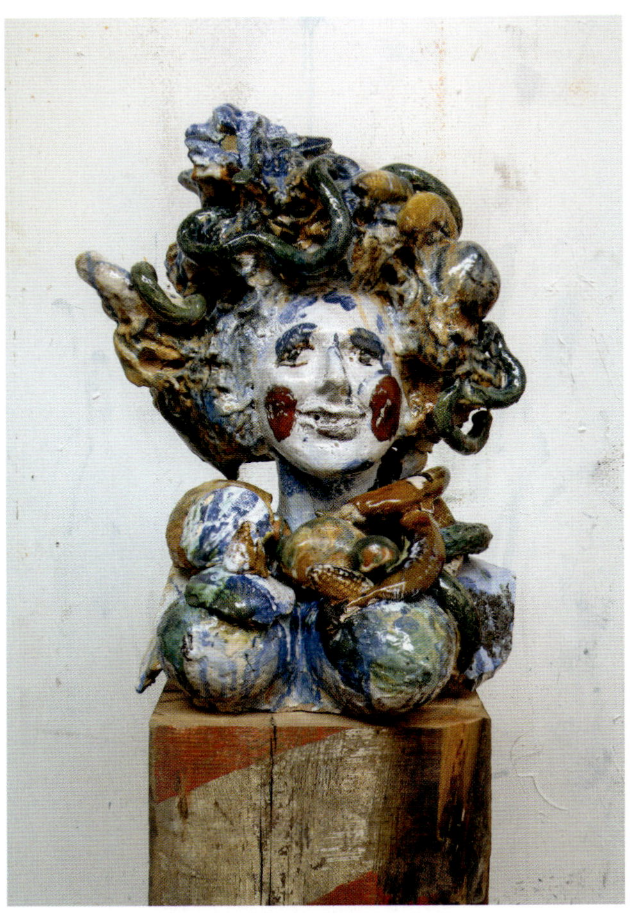

Marcus Harvey, *Female bust*. Fired stoneware, unique.

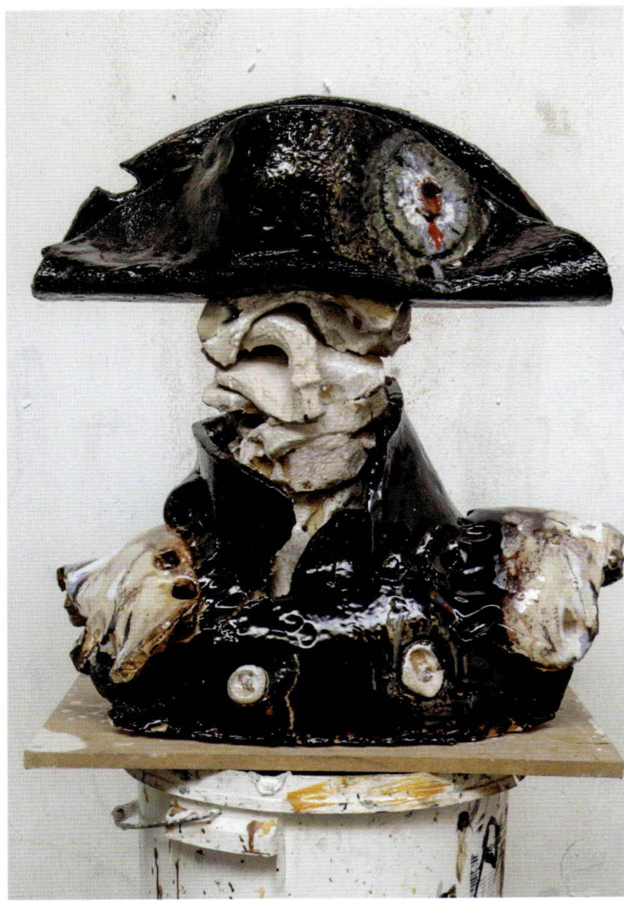

Marcus Harvey, *Napoleon* (2010). Fired stoneware, unique.

ID: *So it was from that experience that you began experimenting?*

MH: Opposite my old studio in Greenwich there was a gallery shop selling little clay things and I had always marvelled about what a creative media it was, it was all colour and physical substance, but because I didn't know anything about the process I was put off by the idea of the kiln.

ID: *How did that change?*

MH: As it happened I moved studio next to a ceramicist's. I visited them during an open studio and it was only then, with a kiln next door, that I realized how simple it was, painting on clay and then baking it. So that answered years of anxiety – I felt a bit stupid for not having explored it in the past, but it came at just the right time. A subject matter and a new process arriving at the same time was fantastic.

MH: It was a stupidly simple solution to the years of trying to synthesize an idea of colouration and plasticity that I had been previously attempting through casting things onto paintings.

ID: *More responsive?*

MH: There was something about painting the clay and then putting it into the fire rather than casting and painting it, an organic aspect to the process but with a limit to what you can do as well, so that the material asks you to treat it with colours and colouration in a certain way, whereas previously those two processes had always been separated.

ID: *And to explore your subject matter.*

MH: I had always been drawn to these little baked clay artefacts in the British Museum – they were always such a point of focus and over the years I've been into African masks, ever more obsessively.

I had become much more sensitized into how some of these objects had been carved and wrapped in lime- and plaster-soaked canvas and then painted and worn, and it had a similar quality and patina to those on little puppets, on Punch and Judy, for example.

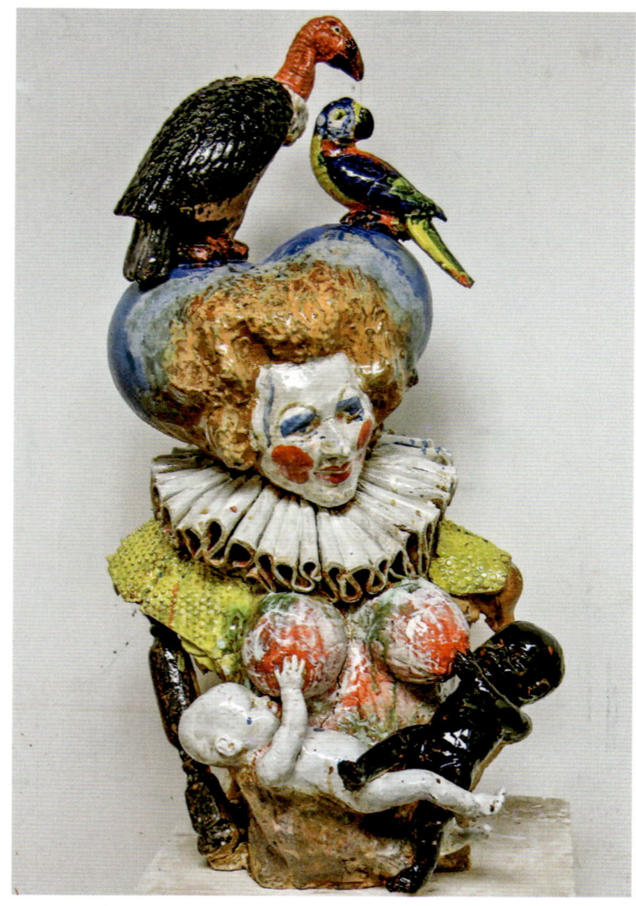

Marcus Harvey, *Female Bust* 2. Fired stoneware, unique.

ID: *The Thatcher relief took over a year to execute; how long do the new ceramics take?*

MH: They usually happen on the day, or a couple of days, because you can't join anything after a couple of days because it will dry out and it won't fuse. The origins are in drawings that appear over six months to a year, or even a two-year period. And then when I find the form that's suitable, I can just pour in all these ideas.

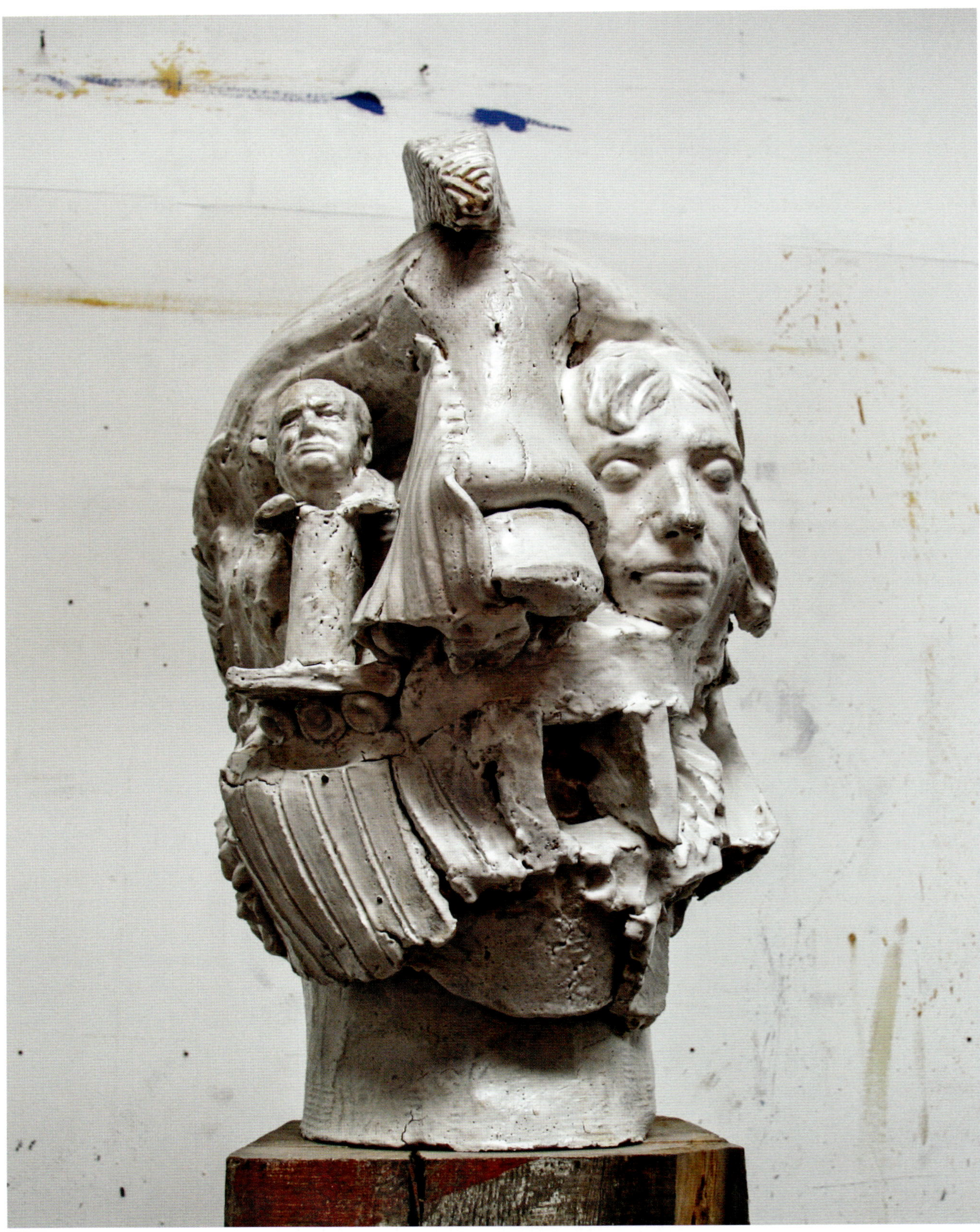

ID: *How do you get a Nelson or a Churchill-type mould?*

MH: The Nelson was a death mask. So I cast it and made a press-mould out of it. It's such a strange thing – it's a flat, rolled-out bit of clay squashed into it and then peeled out.

ID: *How do you go about constructing the object?*

MH: I create a tube, let it go hard enough to support the clay and then wind more onto it and push it around so you get more of a presence of the head. But you can only do so much otherwise it will collapse under its own weight (it's quite a heavy material). Then the next day, come in and see how much else it will tolerate. And once I've got a certain sort of dryness and it will actually support its own weight, then I will chuck some slip and glaze on it and there you go. So I have quite a physical attitude towards it – lifting great sheets of inch-thick clay. There is an art to playing about without ripping it. I make a lot of things that don't work – I throw most of them away, and some hang around waiting to be fired. Sometimes I look at them and think: oh, they're not as bad as I thought – I'll have another go at that.

ID: *It's quite clear that there is a great playfulness.*

MH: When I was doing it I was thinking people might just laugh at these: I'm having fun. We all have a bit of fun but I don't know if that's enough to make a point. It was only when people started getting it that it reinforced that satisfaction I had.

OPPOSITE PAGE
Marcus Harvey, *Heroic Head*. Fired stoneware, unique, height 65cm.

ID: *You are learning the limitations of the material too.*

MH: I made six sculptures for a show in Italy, I took about six months mucking about to realize that in order to enjoy the spontaneity, you've got to understand how it physically works. I had to prop it and work with an infrastructure and understand about leaving it to dry. There's a limit to the kind of free-form expression of those pieces in terms of them being successful objects.

ID: *There were problems firing them?*

MH: Getting them in the kiln was a nightmare. I then had to devise a way of slicing them up into pieces. So enjoying all the spontaneity at the same time as learning how to make these whole objects. The ceramicist was reminding me all the time that I was breaking all their rules because I was coming at it with total ignorance and enthusiasm. So I was cutting corners all the time but I managed to get it together.

ID: *Did you lose any?*

MH: Actually, only one thing blew up to smithereens. The thickness of the clay was an issue; a ceramicist would never have done that, they would have known that the risk was so high.

ID: *That's inspiring.*

MH: It reminded me of my first paintings, of my relationship with paint and how it's beyond brushes and it's a physical performance. And that was like handling the clay, I had a hankering to create a three-dimensional version of that.

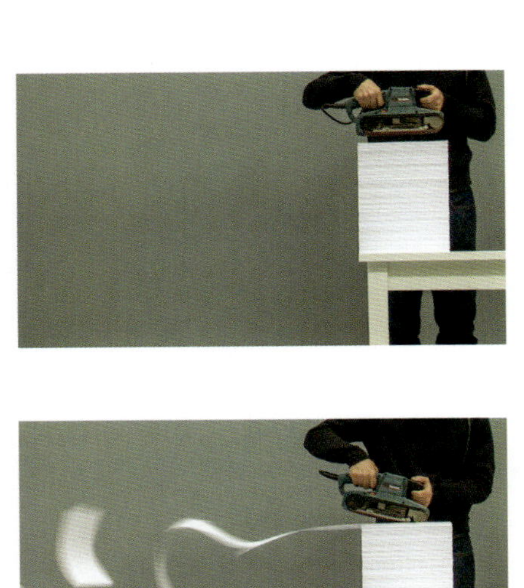
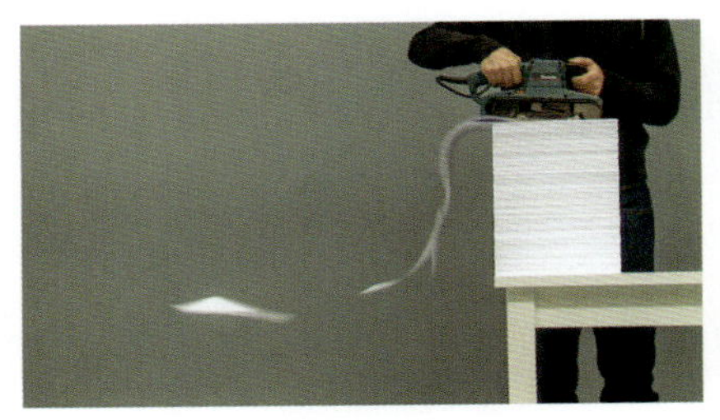
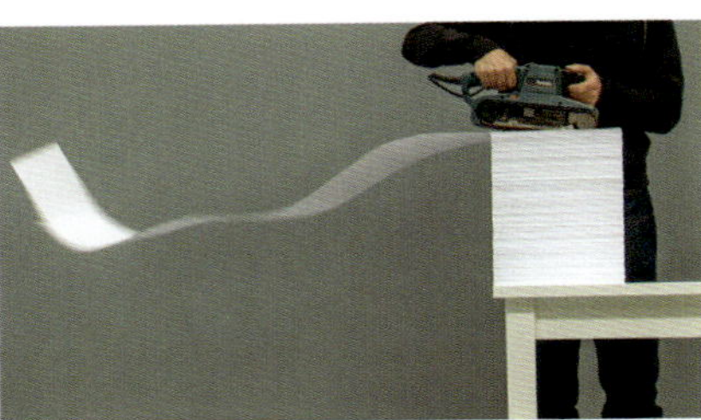
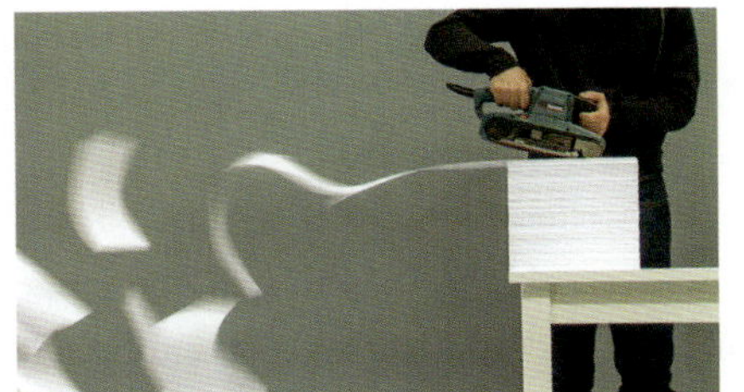
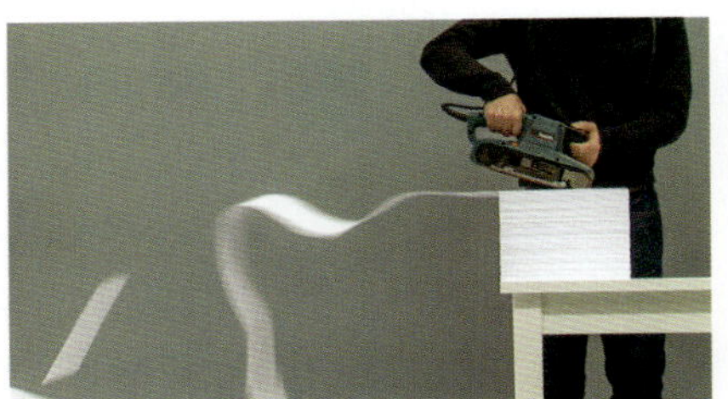
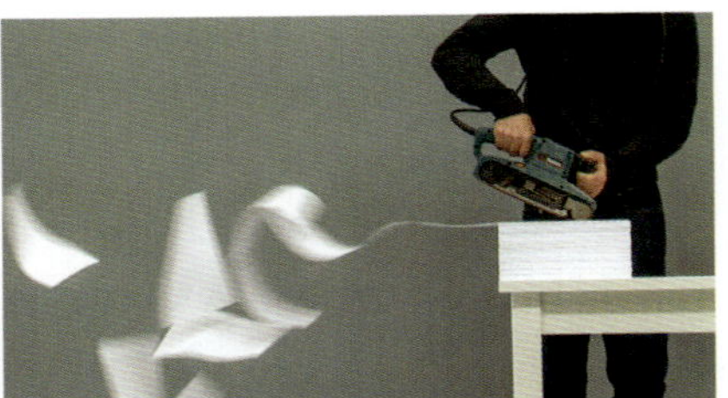
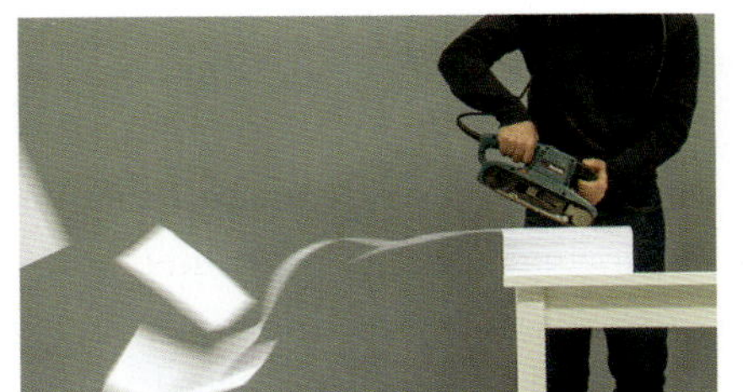
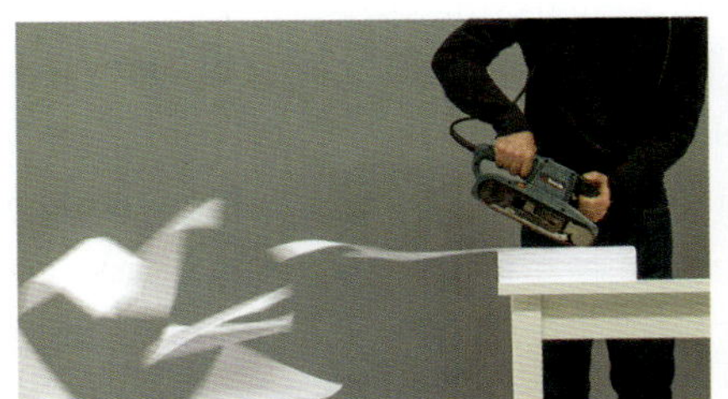
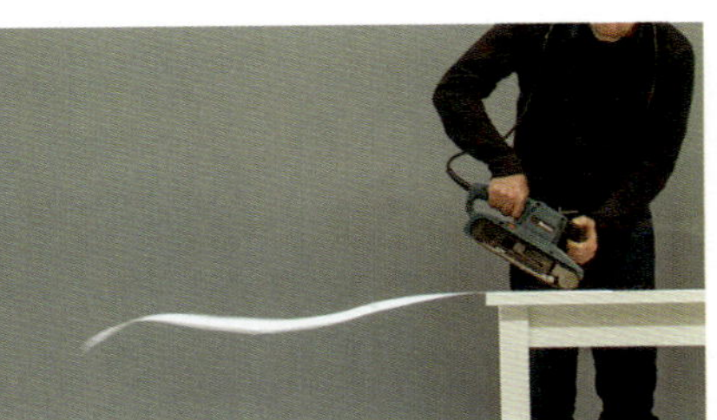

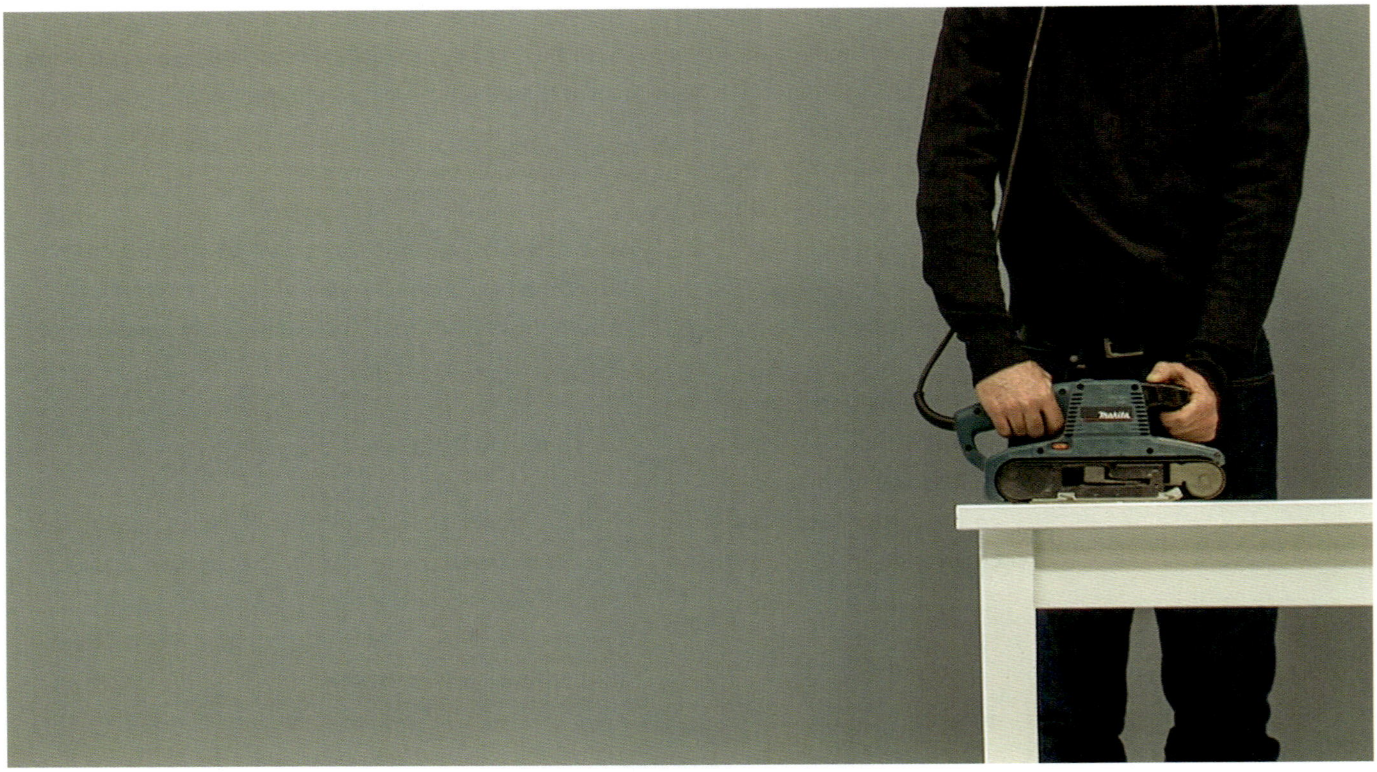

4 Performance

In Switzerland in the 1940s a young Jean Tinguely fixed a high-speed motor onto the ceiling of his apartment and mounted an axle onto it. He began to hang a variety of objects onto this device. He would watch transfixed as the objects, chairs, even his own paintings were flung around, violently dematerializing in a kinetic outburst. In these early comical experiments, Tinguely unmistakably began to explore the equivalence between the static object and the kinetic one, the distinction between the two defined by the relative speed of their demise. These first violent experiments were to later manifest themselves fully in large auto-destructive machines.

The most spectacular and influential of his auto-destructive performances was *Homage to New York*, a vast kinetic construction that engulfed the Sculpture Garden of the Museum of Modern Art on the evening of 17 March 1960. It was one of the world's first happenings of this nature, and was conceived by Tinguely as he crossed the Atlantic by boat.

On his arrival Tinguely began to scour the city's scrap heaps for freshly jettisoned junk, assembling more than sixty bike and pram wheels, tin cans, fans, a piano and bassinet, a washing machine, a cable drum, pulleys, various motors and a meteorological balloon. And using awry engineering methods he began to construct, to make ill-fitting connections so that the entire structure quite deliberately became unpredictable, the antithesis of the accepted logic of a machine. *Homage to New York* incorporated multiple sections: there were two drawing machines, and satellites that were designed to scurry out. Another section was made around a piano; an armature with hammers was rigged to strike its keys periodically. The meteorological balloon was inflated and positioned atop a pole that towered over the structure. The entire machine was set to collapse steadily and there was neither the inclination nor the time, on Tinguely's behalf, to test the piece beforehand. It was hurriedly painted white and the evening of the performance arrived.

It was a bitterly cold evening and the Museum of Modern Art's usual roster of public and art world figures stood shivering: the Governor of New York with Mrs Rockefeller, Mark Rothko, Philip Guston and Rauschenberg. When the machine didn't start on time, the critic David Sylvester left grumpily, saying 'I don't like tuxedo Dada'. And an hour later than advertised, with Tinguely making his final adjustments, the switch was flicked and the destruction phase followed as the machine juddered to life before instantly blowing a fuse. Tinguely got it going again, and although the audience knew something about his work there was an atmosphere of anticipation that it would actually do something functional. Sporadically, and in typical Tinguely fashion, the paper machine rolled itself the wrong way, the machine was whirring and rattling itself into oblivion, after a while the machine began to slump, but the structure defiantly refused to collapse. A fire had broken out from the piano-playing mechanism and was spreading across the piece; reluctantly because of the electronic components the fire-officers finally extinguished the piece. The crowd booed, blaming the firemen. And after only 27 minutes the event was over. *Homage* had famously 'failed to fail'.

OPPOSITE PAGE
John Wood and Paul Harrison *One more kilometer 1* (2009). 2'45", HDV, single channel (16:9).

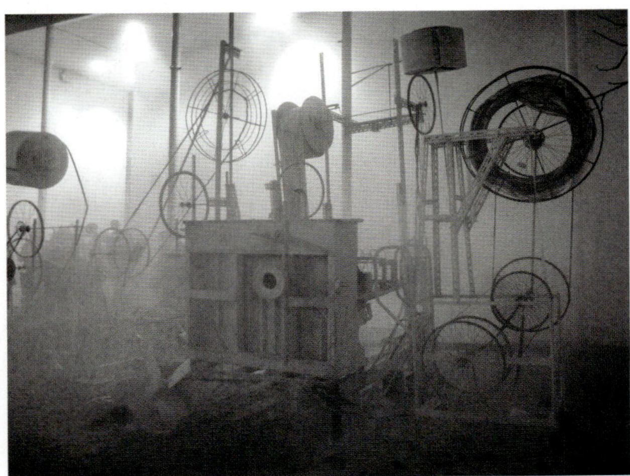

Winchester School of Art students, *Homage to Homage to New York* (2011).

The paradoxical nature of Tinguely's work and its critique of planned obsolescence seemed to sum up a growing feeling perhaps best expressed by Willy Loman in Arthur Miller's *Death of a Salesman* when he exhorts, 'Once in my life I would like to own something outright before it's broken!'

In 2001, inspired by Tinguely's auto-destructive machines, Michael Landy created a different kind of destructive artwork called *Breakdown*. In London, at the western end of Oxford Street in the former C&A storefront over a three-month period Landy proceeded to meticulously log and destroy every single item he possessed. In front of crowds of shoppers, bags in hands, a network of conveyor belts manned by a team of technicians sorted, dismantled and shredded and consigned to landfill all the physical objects accrued by the artist. All 7,227 items of his worldly possessions – his car, his hi-fi, even his passport – trundled down this 'production line of destruction'. And on a cold winter's night in 2011, stirred by Landy's stance and encouraged by his acknowledgement of this work by Tinguely,

> Everything moves continuously. Immobility does not exist. Don't be subject to the influence of out-of-date concepts of time. Forget hours, seconds, and minutes. Accept instability. Live in time. Be static – with movement. For a static of the present moment resist the anxious fear to fix the instantaneous, to kill that which is living. Stop insisting on values that cannot but break down. Be free, live. Stop painting time. Stop building cathedrals and pyramids that are doomed to fall into ruin. Live in the present; live once more in time and by time, for a wonderful and absolute reality.
>
> Jean Tinguely

Winchester School of Art students re-enacted *Homage to New York* on the street in front of the school's lecture theatre, their very own version failing to fail.

It's August 2011 on Rose Hill in the suburbs of Oxford and a JCB is being prepared for work; its pneumatic arm levers out to reveal an extended, savage-looking claw. Made from untreated steel and retaining its dark patina, and looking as though Hannibal Lecter had designed it for a cruel and callous act, the digger is transformed into a mutant, an evolutionary misfit.

To the hum of the diesel engine the talon is lowered and begins to score and scratch at the ground. A line is drawn across the ground, a surprisingly considerate incision, marking a point, a fleeting scratch on the surface of the planet, one final futile gesture, a denouement; one imagines the machine never making another mark again.

This is a performance by James Capper, who, inspired by earth-moving equipment, became inspired to create working machinery himself. I imagine it as a subconscious tribute to another performance that occurred in a nearby Oxford field over a century and a half ago.

On 22 September 1845 a crowd had assembled to observe the inauguration of the Satellite: a multi-function cultivator with arms that would rip, dig, plough and plant seeds across great swathes of land. Fitted with blades for gouging the ground, this prototype was set to prove that it was possible to harness the Earth's natural resources in order to transform it into an abundant paradise. Twelve years earlier the inventor of the Satellite, John Adolphus Etzler, had published his treatise: 'THE PARADISE WITHIN THE REACH OF ALL MEN, WITHOUT LABOR, BY POWERS OF NATURE AND MACHINERY. AN ADDRESS TO ALL INTELLIGENT MEN.' On one level it was a green manifesto, a call to meet humankind's energy needs by using wind, wave and solar power; on another it was a call for

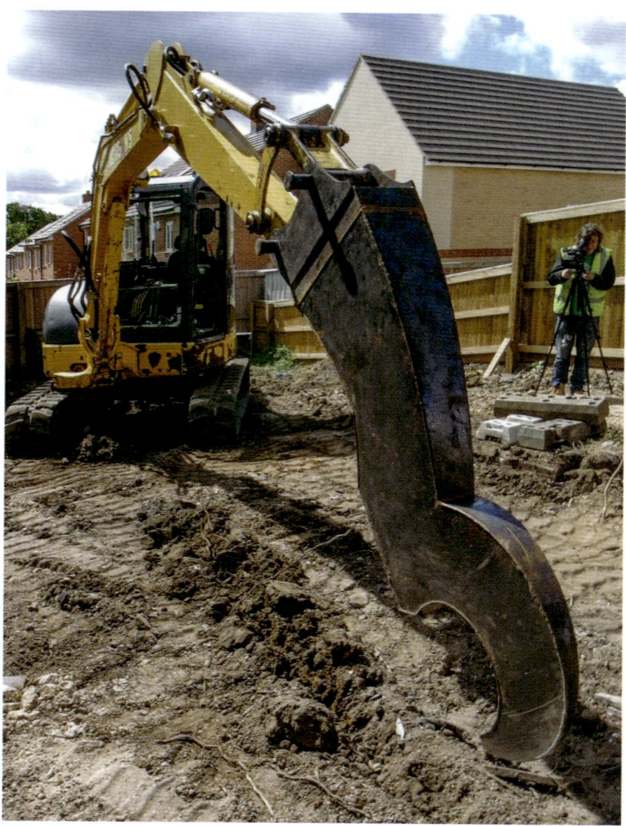

James Capper, *Ripper Teeth* practice.

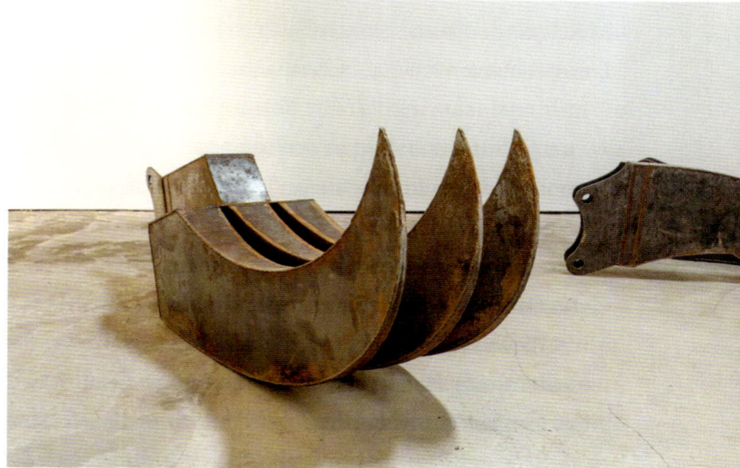

James Capper, *Ripper Teeth* (2011). Steel, acrylic, lights, installation dimensions variable.

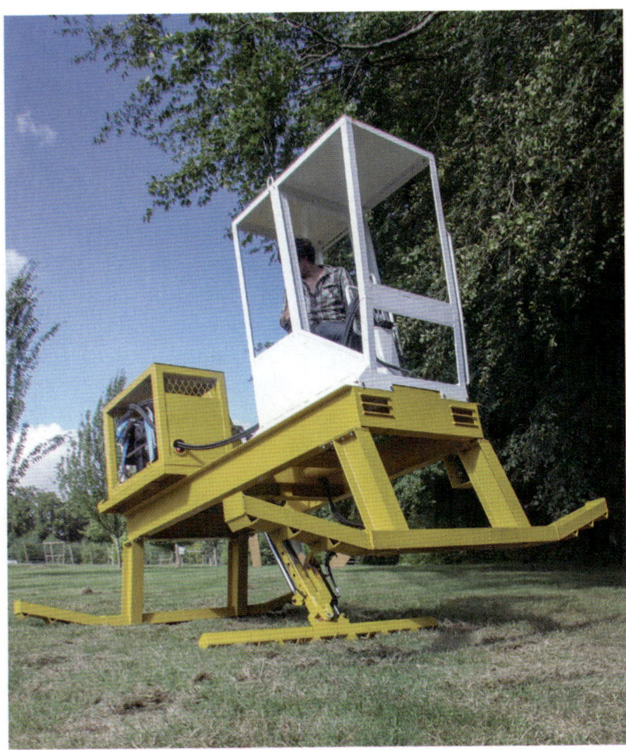

James Capper, *Tread Toe* (2010, The New Art Centre, Roche Court, Wiltshire). Painted steel and hydraulics, 250 × 300 × 250cm.

turned the land into money and began to supercharge an infrastructure-building era that would not exist in those terms again.

And a century after the Satellite creaked into action, thanks to the petro-dollar, R.G. LeTourneau finally manufactured the kind of unsparing machinery Etzler could only dream about. The tree crusher, a blunt machine with huge hexagonal bladed wheels, joined an extraordinary array of earth-moving equipment: self-propelled scrapers, log-stackers, dozer-diggers, disc-ploughs, and self-elevating drilling platforms supplied to carve and shape the landscape.

Fast forward to the present and I arrive at James Capper's studio. It smells of freshly ground steel and is an evocative space. In the courtyard sit two contraptions which Capper calls 'floor-marking machines'. They are constructed with the same vocabulary as an excavator and painted JCB yellow. As these machines function they scrape and crawl, rear up and lumber, scratching and etching markings into the floor in folly.

Capper is absorbed by engineering and its embodiment in those earth-moving vehicles, and the studio is the place he assimilates his interests, looking back to an age of mechanical innovation when pioneers in engineering were wholly in charge of the process. It's a firm gesture of Capper's and fundamental to how his devices are read. 'These machines they have tested my engineering capacities,' he says. The pieces are both successes and failures. 'When I am in a problem-solving zone, when I am going beyond a certain attained level of personal expertise, they don't really ever go wrong – they don't necessarily work they way I want them, but that's different. The hydraulics in *Tread Toe*, for example, exceeded expectation; then with some of the others they just become components again.'

Another object is perched on the roof of the studio: bright orange barrels lashed to a frame.

unprecedented technological and structural expansion. All Etzler required were effective machines, scaled up to maximize the potential; mountains would be levelled, canal systems imposed across continents, and power generation facilities would stretch along whole coastlines.

Then, thirty years later, a colonel returning from the Civil War decides to dump a lump of explosive down a Pennsylvanian oil well. What had been an unsubstantial trickle of oil starts to cough and splutter and splurge. The oil revolution had now begun to bury Etzler's green vision, dismissing its philosophy as the work of a madman. Here was an energy-dense material that was spilling out of the ground for free and there was an instant demand for the stuff too. Whale oil, the traditional fuel for lamps, was becoming ever more scarce; in one bang oil had secured a way of switching the lights on, adding time to the day. It

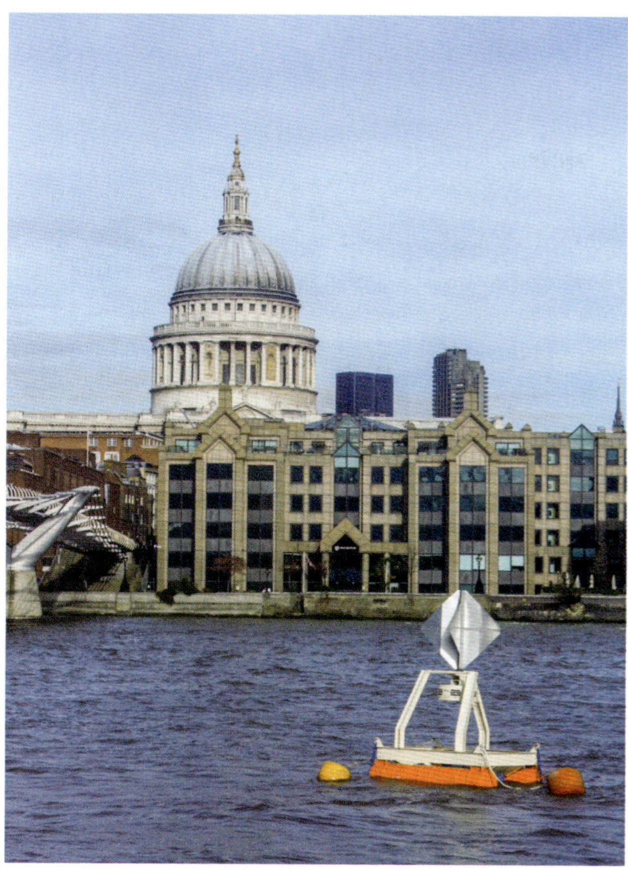

James Capper, *Sea Light* (2010, wind-powered installation, Bankside Pier, London). Steel, light, motor, 400 × 200 × 300cm.

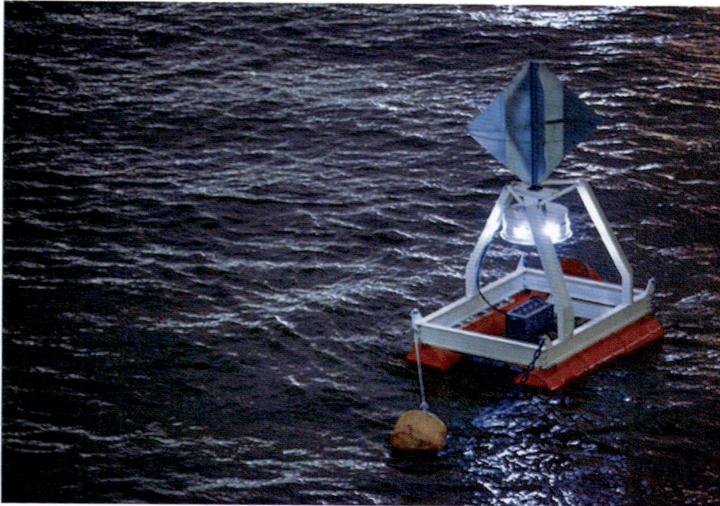

James Capper, *Sea Light*, night (2010, wind-powered installation, Bankside Pier, London). Steel, light, motor, 400 × 200 × 300cm.

That is Sea Light; *it consists of a diamond-shaped fan and a wind turbine, connected to some cells, and lights. The idea is that I could mass produce them and create a floating transformer and have a transportable wind farm. Potentially more useful than the static versions.*

He is going to test this on the Thames.

Capper draws prolifically, with titles like 'walking forks', 'pecker', and 'wacker', which describe a desired action. 'They are drawings for the studio wall, to look at, to think about the best way to use mechanisms like pneumatic cylinders in order to drag something along, or where the cab should be, or how an arm might operate.' Others become more fanciful, exploring the viability of how to modify an agricultural straw baler onto a floating pontoon in order to create an iceberg maker.

Ideas are then worked through into models: 'The maquettes are slightly better physical demonstrations of what the piece is going to be like. It's slightly more understandable than the drawings. Instead of going through pages of different views, most of the questions get answered in the visual.' On a table in the studio he has several versions of a boat fitted with hydraulic legs, permitting itself the freedom to dry-dock independently.

This piece is influenced by LeTourneau's offshore self-raising oil-rigs that he made on the shores of the Mississippi, in response to how get something weighing 96,000 tons lowered into the water. So he devised these platforms with three legs on each corner to lower or lift structures in or out of the water. Literally a walking oil-rig.

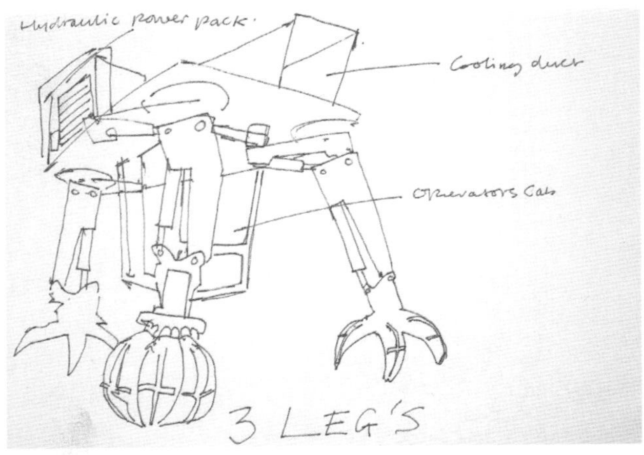

James Capper, *3 Legs*. Drawing.

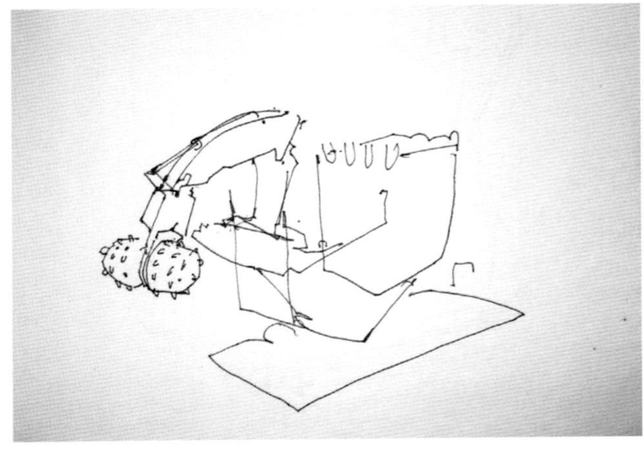

James Capper, *Atlas Concept*. Drawing.

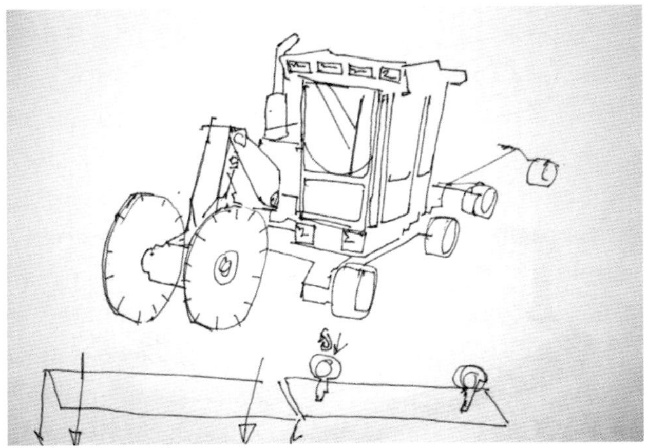

James Capper, *Block Cutter*. Drawing.

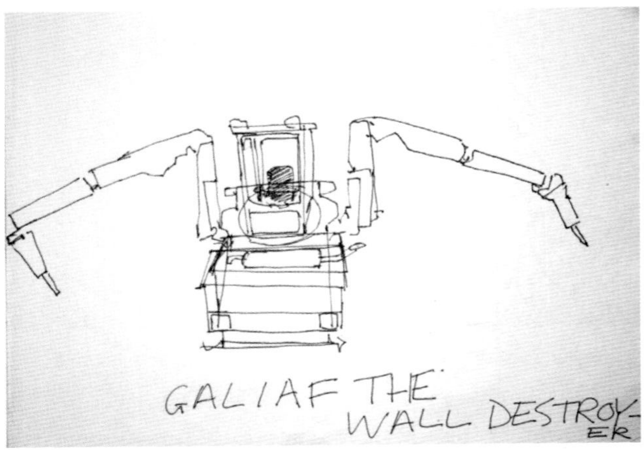

James Capper, *Galiaf the Wall Destroyer*. Drawing.

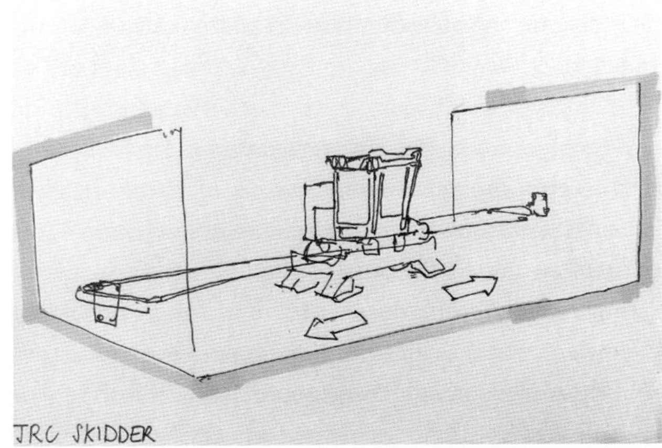

James Capper, *Skidder*. Drawing.

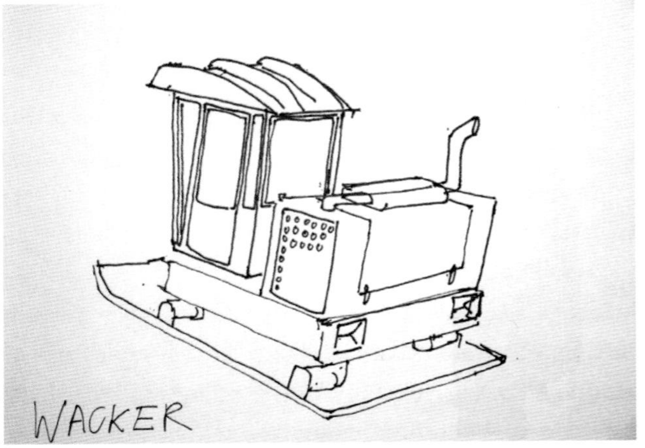

James Capper, *Wacker*. Drawing.

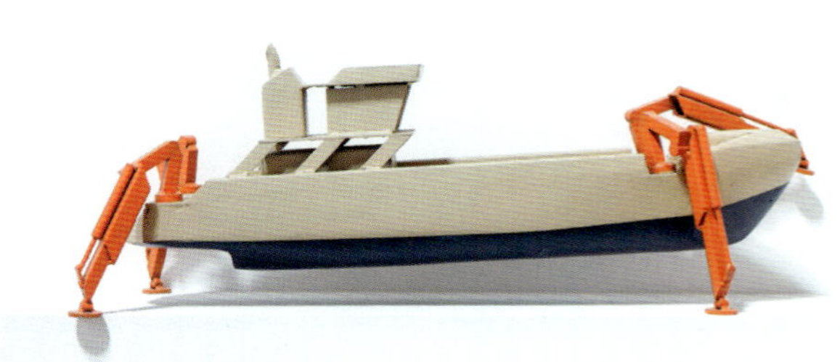

James Capper, maquette 2.

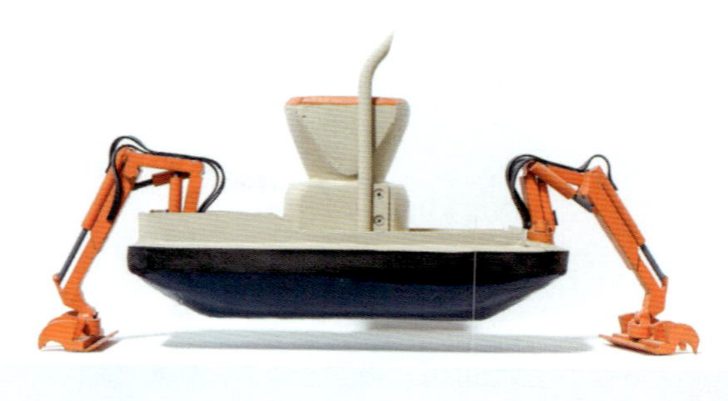

James Capper, maquette 1.

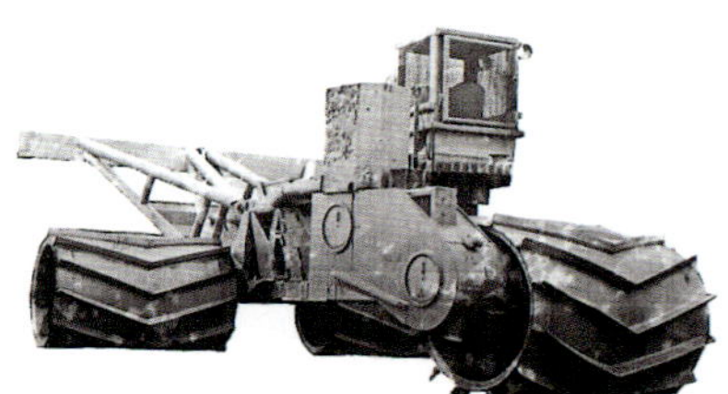

James Capper, *Series G-60 Tree Crusher* (1966).

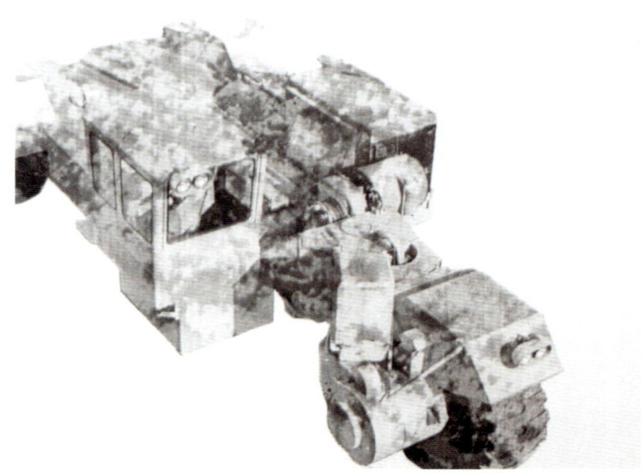

James Capper, *LET2*.

The studio shelves are filled with a mixture of books documenting early earth-moving pioneers and trade magazines from the industry, and these form the basis for his collages, which illustrate his interests in the most straightforward way. Earth-moving vehicles photographed to celebrate their scale, and the feats of their engineering achievements, are cut out and placed on a piece of paper. Shorn of their context they are free to be evaluated and appropriated by Capper.

Capper, who has memories of visiting building sites as a child with his dad, also had a Saturday job as a mechanic, learning about engines and welding.

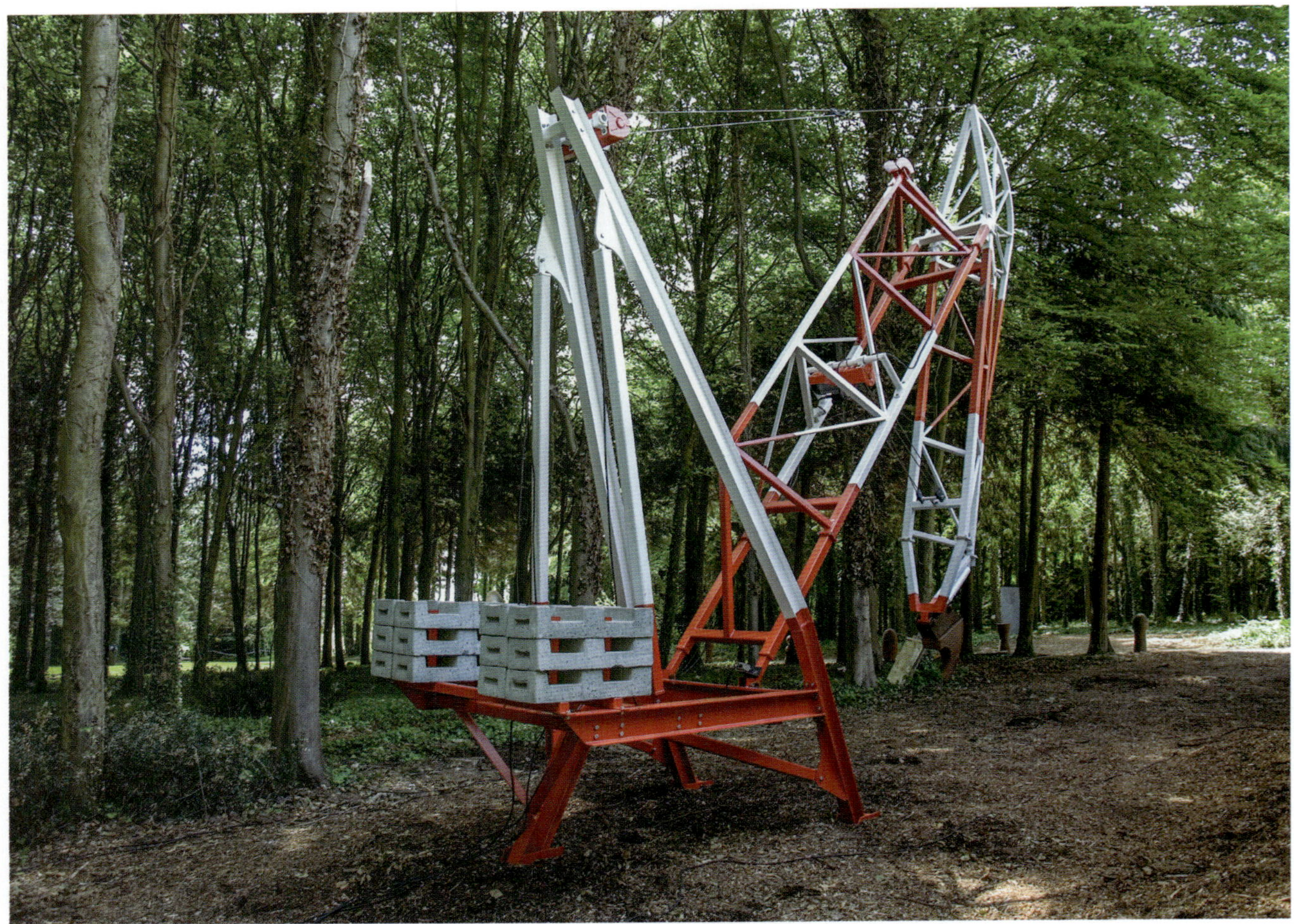

James Capper, *Ripper* (2008). Steel, electric motor, control levers, concrete, cable, 500 × 700 × 200cm.

Art school then became the perfect place to expand on my interests. For example in Ripper I used a tower crane system called a gooseneck, a pivoting jib that has the ability to be lowered and extended at the same time. So it's the growth and maturing of a technical language, the language of sculpture, in an amalgamation with engineering and fabrication – that coded material language learnt from industry.

We return to discuss the performance at Oxford: 'I ended up turning the project into a residency. I really wanted to test the teeth, how they might work in the earth. I was there for the most of the summer; we would drive around leaving these marks in various places.'

I think of Capper's hybrid machines in this way: on the one hand they exist according to the terms of their references, the strategies of the machine; on the other they simultaneously undermine them, creating a mutual relationship between the utilitarian and the functionless, and signify the impossibility of changing a social order without changing a natural order. ■

▶ Francis Thorburn

Francis Thorburn makes primitive vehicles out of
wood and steel, powered by men in underpants.
It is simultaneously a ridiculous and serious
proposition. I arrive at the Bun House, both a pub
and exhibition space that he co-curates. The door
(rather unwelcomingly) has a sign, 'regulars only', taped
across it. I wait rather apprehensively for Thorburn
who is in the middle of preparing for a collaborative
performance with Joel Grey: he is about to drag a
boulder of chalk several miles down the road.

IAN DAWSON: *How did you first get into it?*

FRANCIS THORBURN: I started experimenting with
clichéd body performances, outdoor interventions,
halfway between Chris Burden and Maria Abramovich.
Discovering Throbbing Gristle and Genesis P-Orridge,
it blew my mind along with Viennese Activism. And
a lot of stuff started to come out – rituals, messianic
performance figures – and it all came to a head with a
combination of a sculpture and a performance together
and it put me on to doing what I have been doing since
then.

ID: *What was that?*

FT: I made a big wheel, an 8-foot cylinder that could
roll; I tied myself to it in a cartwheel position on the
side. I was pushed down the road – half crucified, half
cartwheeling – by a bunch of guys in underpants. It
was one of the first times I had used pants as a uniform
to identify performers. Until then my work had been
about durational performance and then this group
street thing really got me going.

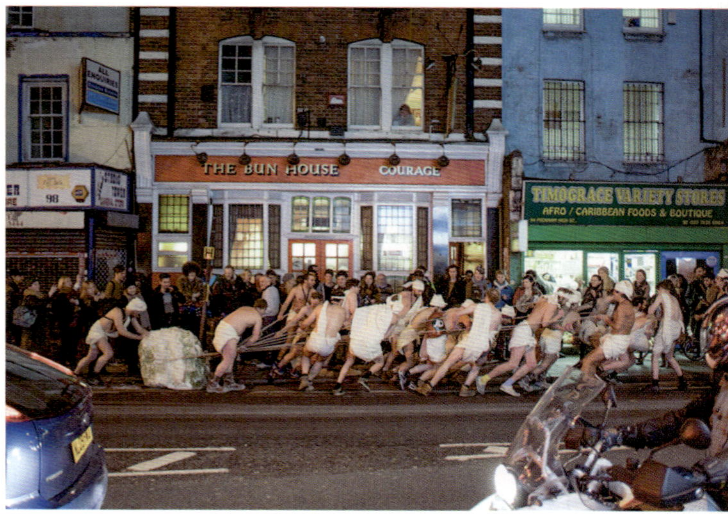
Francis Thorburn, Joel Grey, *Peckham Drag*.

ID: *So you had this pivotal performance?*

FT: I recognized the difference between what I thought
I wanted and what was manifesting itself through what
I was doing. It had a sense of humour. It was also the
first time I had made an object. I suppose from that
point I began looking toward the object first, as a point
of inspiration to what the action was going to be, and
that led me on to do a hamster wheel, which was a
static object with me running in the middle of it.

ID: *You also began to develop a curatorial practice.*

FT: The first show I organized was called SLICS, The
South London Institute for Common Sense. It was a
two-day exhibition including performative lectures,
assuming this role of an absurd institute where
knowledge is passed down through artists to audience
in whatever format anyone decided. There were
anarchic noise band performances, workshops. I think
it was a big failure, to be honest with you.

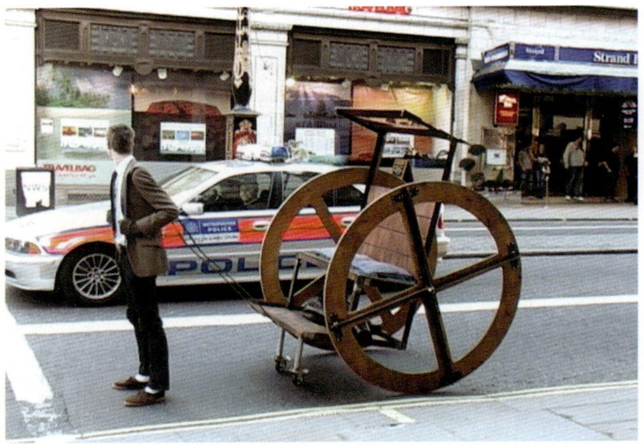

Francis Thorburn, *ATN1* (2009).

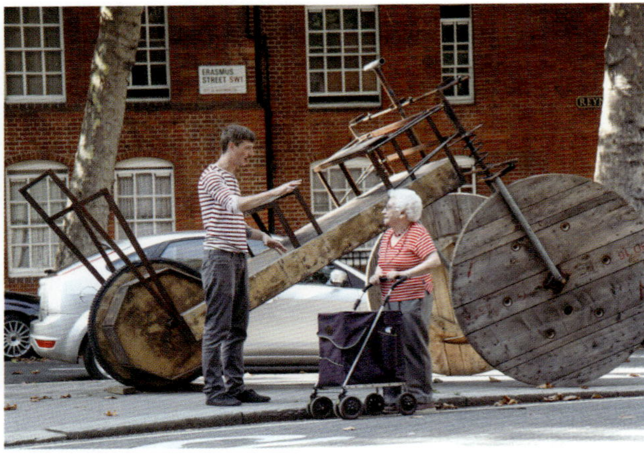

Francis Thorburn, *ATN2* (2009).

ID: *That must have led on to making the performances under a pseudo-title?*

FT: Once I had decided to look at the format of processional performance with the end product being sculptural vehicles, I came up with this absurd role play: I started to call myself the Minister of Alternative Transport and the job is to research the potential for man-power transport in preparation for the day when petrol runs out.

ID: *What is the name?*

FT: *The Alternative Transport Network* is the name of the project. It helps because it's a tangible thing – it's a job that needs to be done, so all of the performers look at it as some kind of choreographed theme; it is more of a task, a job.

ID: *Why is that?*

FT: The task is important, the task produces the energy, you are legitimizing, you are not saying something abstract. You are saying you are moving something from here to here and we are wearing this uniform; it is framed within this absurd proposal. It was a way of enabling me to do what I wanted without having to justify it any more.

ID: *How is this being developed?*

FT: I have an Alternative Transport Network logo. The ATN narrative goes out on press releases, it is an important part of the project that continues to develop beyond each performance. It's the body that archives the project so that it offers an institutional critique. No solutions – just an alternative.

ID: *Who are the performers?*

FT: They are artist friends of mine, there must be fifty or sixty people who have been involved in performances.

ID: *Are they fine about wearing underpants?*

FT: Some people need some persuasion! Part of the beauty of it is that because we know each other it's easy to be comfortable alongside the other ten guys, even in front of a hundred people, and the work begins to encompass this, the idea of unified ambition. There is an energy that builds up within the group, and it is represented by the pants, a symbol of solidarity.

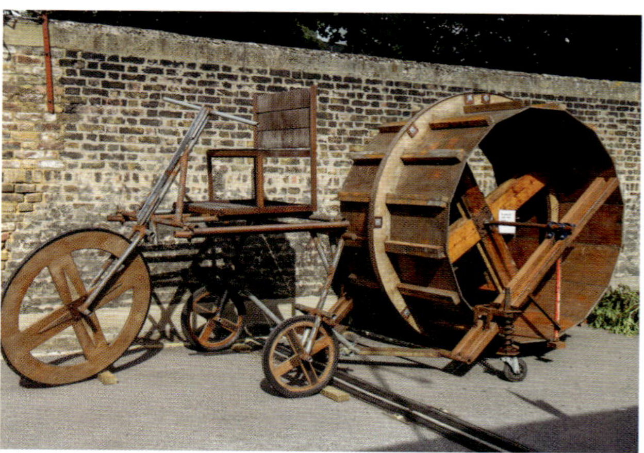

Francis Thorburn, *ATN3* (2009).

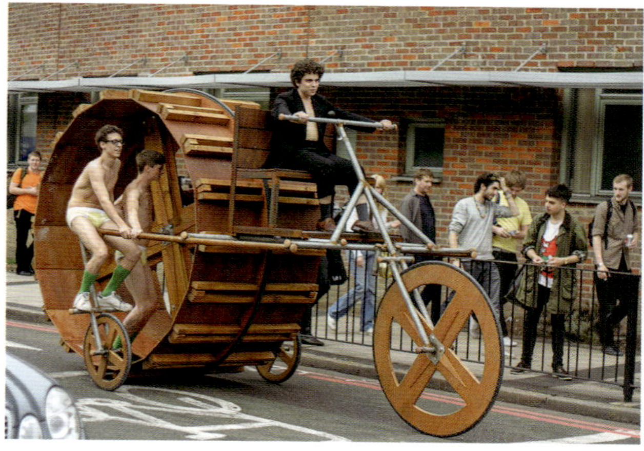

Francis Thorburn, *ATN4* (2009).

ID: *When I first discovered your work you were welding underneath a tarpaulin, in a derelict yard. You were engrossed in the fabrication of these huge vehicles.*

FT: I have been in a cycle where I spend the winter drawing, then choosing from the various designs. Often this might be a combination of three or four ideas into one piece, maybe little thoughts that I want to go with; then with the spring I begin making; then the summer is when you do the events. That has tended to be the cycle. The winter tends to drag – that has got annoying.

ID: *That's interesting, that you are working through a seasonal calendar.*

FT: That's because of the events-based nature of the outputs: the money comes from live events, the kids are out of school, the sculptures are like big toys, so a lot of the funding streams are family-oriented art events. But in my mind the work is much more radical than that and the performative bits, the action, isn't fulfilled successfully within those commissioned works. It's often without the consent of the commissioning body or institution.

ID: *How do you mean?*

FT: The Tate said that the police ban them from doing any kind of processional piece, in this instance because it was on Millbank next to the Conservative Party headquarters. It's not a protest, but it does straddle between protest and celebration. We are a large group of men and we do shout loudly; we are energetic and excited, which might be misinterpreted as aggressive. I think the main concern is that it might cause problems.

ID: *What did you do?*

FT: I did the procession from Peckham to South Kensington past Buckingham Palace to Tate Britain. We arrived on the day and wheeled the piece up. They weren't made aware of the fact it was going to happen so that was fine. Whenever the performance aspect becomes known we are in trouble, so that aspect has been more difficult to maintain.

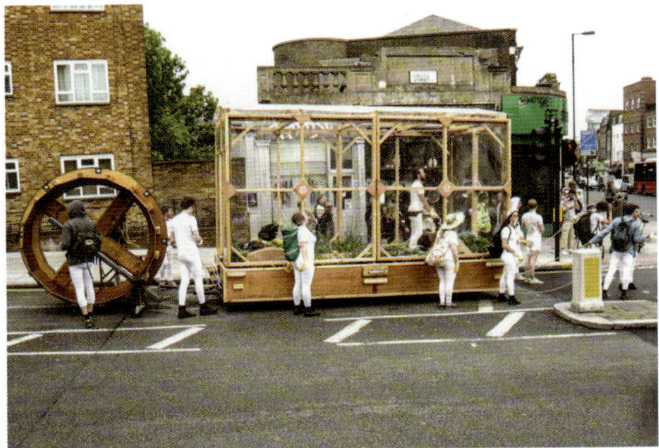

Francis Thorburn, *ATN5* (2009).

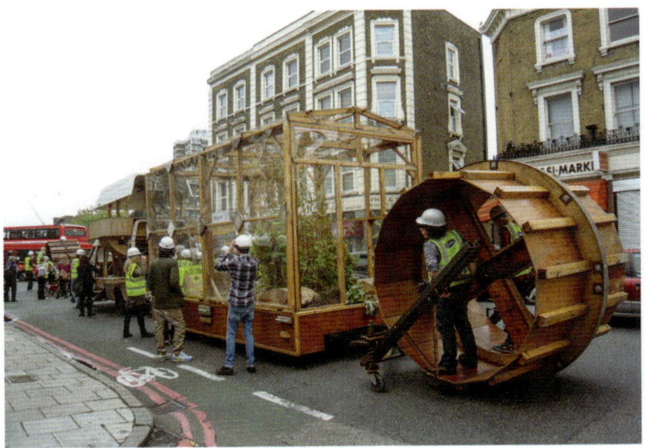

Francis Thorburn, *ATN6* (2009).

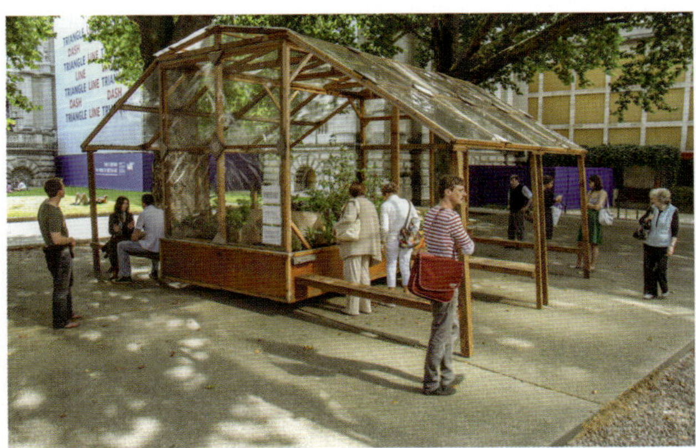

Francis Thorburn, *ATN7* (2009).

ID: *What happens when it becomes known?*

FT: When we had a police escort, that was worse. It was more disorganized, and the police didn't really know what they were there for, other than to follow this piece of work around. They were making more distractions around the whole thing. The Mayor of London's office said that we couldn't use main roads; in a way when you give people information, you are giving them the power to exercise control over it and they do. No one really has a problem with it. It doesn't actually cause any problems, and you can do it in a way that you like it to be done, that's the only way for the performances to be successful.

ID: *Have you ever had any problems?*

FT: No. Every now and again someone shouts out of a car window at us because they've had to wait in a small traffic jam. Once at Elephant and Castle coming back from Tate Modern some police said we should wait and get picked up; we kind of said we would pull over but then just carried on.

ID: *I am amazed that you have been stopped only once.*

FT: I presume that they presume that it's an official event of some description, that it is too overblown not to be something programmed within the grand scheme of London's cultural calendar. A lot of the time what you get is that they pull over in the meat wagon and shout, 'All right boys', or 'We'll race you'. It's always a thumbs up.

FT: If we leave at lunchtime, we are never slowing anyone down much. I've never looked into the highway laws, but I've always told anyone commissioning the work that because it's un-motorized, it's allowed on the roads like a bicycle – providing it's under 8 feet in width.

ID: *That sounds fair enough.*

FT: I make up what I think are the rules. But I think you have just got to disregard the rules anyhow, within reason. We are talking about something that is a positive motion; it is meant to be this futile celebration, that is why I think it doesn't have many problems because there is an enjoyment to it, there is an entertaining feature to it.

ID: *That is the point.*

FT: I want to blur the boundaries between entertainment and art, the framework of the street, its need to be accessible. In this instance we need to give a bit.

ID: *What was the piece at the Folkestone Triennial?*

FT: It was part of the fringe, so on paper we were the only ones responsible for our actions. Yet the curators of the event wanted our presence.

ID: *This particular piece was made in three days?*

FT: Yes, sometimes the low-tech sculptures make a more dynamic performance: they are less cumbersome, lighter, less dangerous, people have more energy to shout and holler, and do not have to be quite as careful.

ID: *There was a great tension to the performance when you started going down the ramp into the harbour – is it going to float or not?*

FT: Everyone thought that.

ID: *And there was this raucous Saturday afternoon summer crowd. They were mocking.*

FT: They wanted to see failure.

ID: *And then you went off and toured the harbour.*

FT: It was the first successful test of an amphibious Alternative Transport Network vehicle. We wanted to attempt a variety of terrain with this piece as well as attempt it in water. To do this we had to maintain hydration so we marked a number of pubs on the high street to call in on.

ID: *Do your other processions call in on pubs?*

FT: A number of times, it's a place that you can go with a big group of people coming together to do an outlandish thing which sparks off a unique atmosphere with the people experiencing the thing.

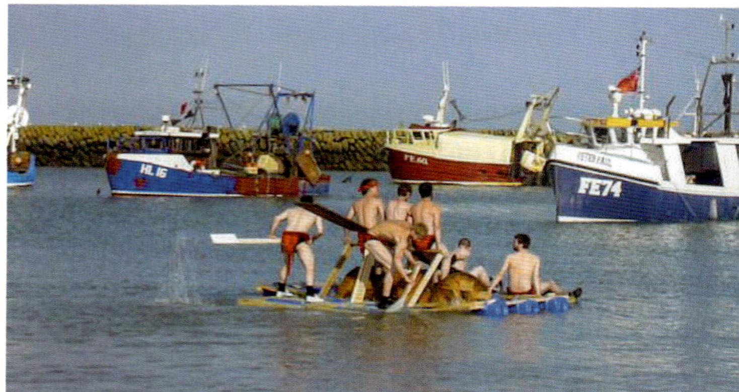

Francis Thorburn, *ATN8* (2009).

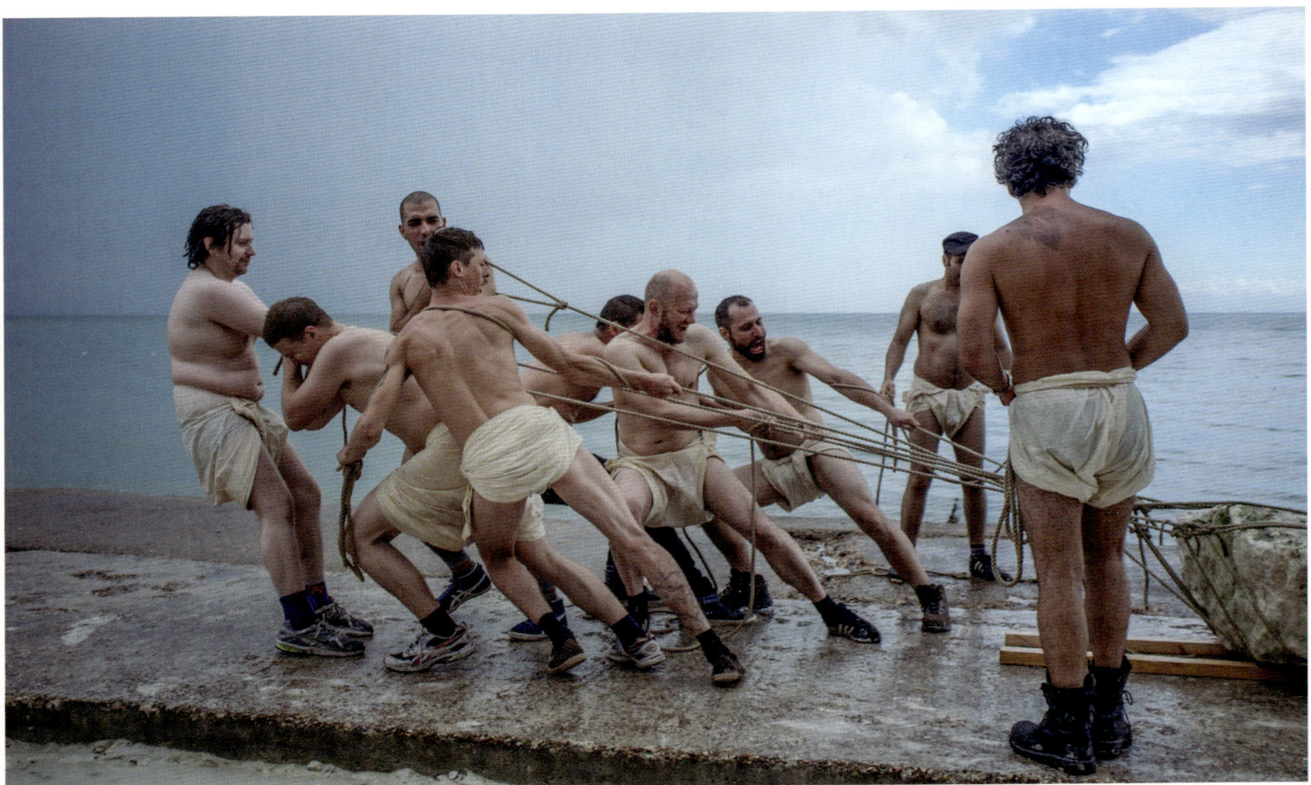

Francis Thorburn, Joel Grey, *Drag.*

ID: *How did that evolve?*

FT: It started with The Peckham Race, an alternative vehicle dash/pub crawl. It worked really nicely as a place where we could reflect on each stage of the race, on who had done what, what vehicle we liked best; it sparked off this strange dynamic. In that event there were quite a few strangers – some with modified skateboards, others with electric moon-buggies – so it was an interesting mix of people who had just come along for the ride and others who had committed to it.

ID: *There is a lads thing, like lads on holiday, when they get into the pant thing?*

FT: When we went into this grotty pub at the bottom of Folkestone. We ran in with our pants, and the pub erupted. It was like a stag night for five minutes, all these big intimidating blokes shouting, 'Get these boys a drink!' and it's a really easy way to access people, just sitting down and having a drink.

ID: *How long do you stay?*

FT: Not more than twenty minutes. It's just a pit stop, it's got to be snappy: in, out, and off to the next one. Part of it is about getting the performance experienced by people. It's sort of a wild animal, different people are involved and I don't tell people what to do, or how to behave. Sometimes it gets raucous and can be considered offensive; sometimes it's a difficult job and you've just got to sweat it out. It's always quite enthralling, enjoying the social experience, having that amount of people about with a unified cause. Enjoying it as well, it radiates what you want to come from the piece. To make something that is entertaining, reclaiming what is entertaining. ■

▶ John Wood and Paul Harrison

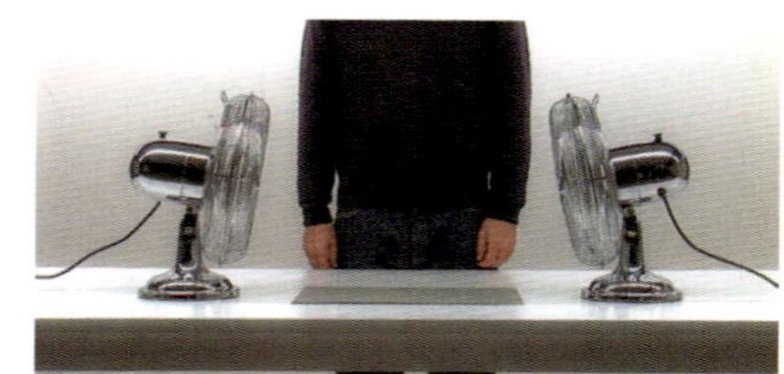

Two chrome desktop fans are sitting on a table, facing inwards toward each other. There is the distinctive hum of the blades blowing air. In the middle of this symmetrical image, separating the two fans lies a single piece of paper, flat on the table. A figure, cropped by the camera, waits behind the table; he stoops and in one single move stands the paper upright, and walks off screen. The paper wobbles but remains upright, held in place by the airflow from both fans. It sways in the turbulence but continues to remain upright in the centre of the screen, dancing, holding the viewer's attention. There is a click, the hum of the blades stop, and the paper keels over, and drops lifelessly onto the table, back to its original inert position. The screen fades to white.

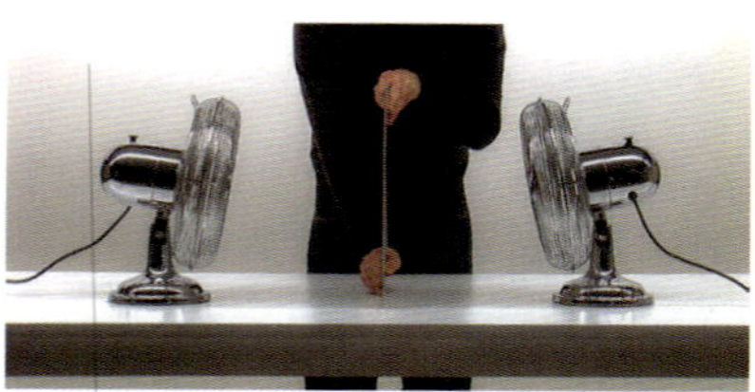

The poetry in this small inquisitive experiment, set against the stark utilitarian environment, is a piece by John Wood and Paul Harrison. They stage strange micro-events that always somehow make sense, no matter how absurd they are, due to the careful timing and choreography.

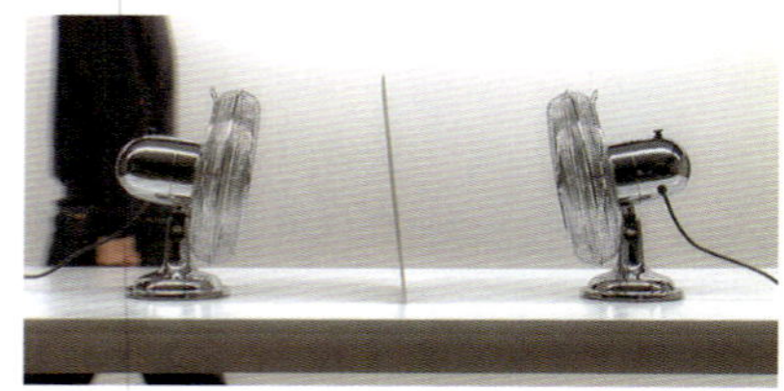

I arrive at John Wood and Paul Harrison's studio. It is located in Bristol's Spike Island, and is next door to one of Aardman Animations' studios, famous for Wallace and Gromit and Morph, a Plasticine figure who along with his alter ego, Chas, would explore and challenge the environment of the animator's desk. Here inside Wood and Harrison's studio is a stage set of an empty office, with its false ceiling, dark grey carpet tiles, a solitary clock and filing cabinet. The open front has a vertical track, a modified ladder; they are attempting to film a sequence of one hundred events as if the camera tracks down the outside of an office block, looking in through the windows.

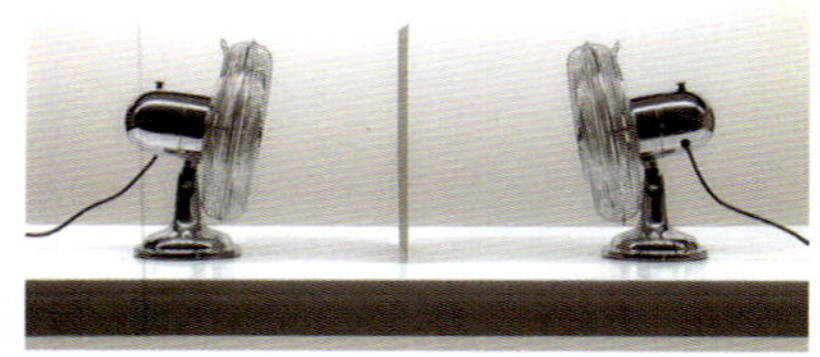

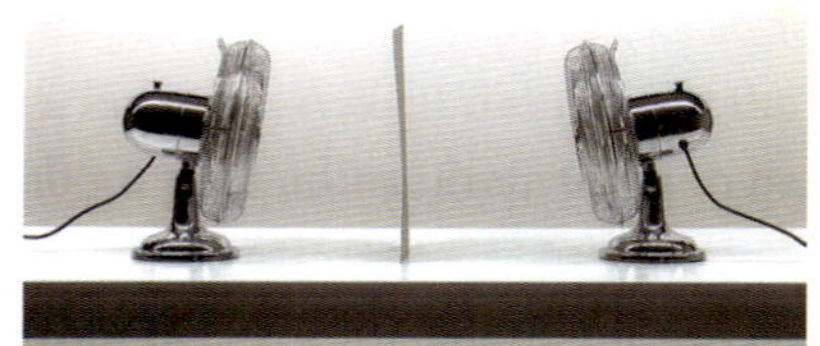

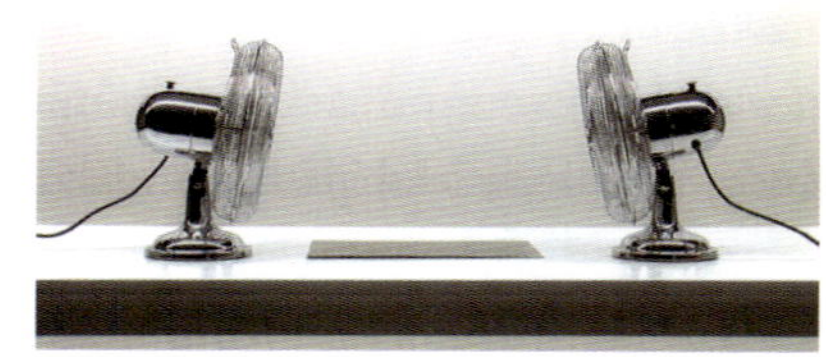

John Wood and Paul Harrison, *Fan/ paper/fan 1–6* (2007). 3'16", HDV, single channel (16:9).

 It's taken us months and months.

JOHN WOOD: Months and months.

IAN DAWSON: *What isn't working?*

JW: Well, we've used the track horizontally before, but when we changed it to vertical it has put loads of different stresses onto it. Initially we couldn't get the speed so we had to change motors. Then it was vibrating a tiny bit, which was being magnified by the camera so we were getting this terrible judder so we had to modify the mechanism. Lew at Aardman's is really brilliant – he's a product engineer and he comes in his lunchtimes to help.

ID: *How often do you both get together to work?*

JW: It depends on what we're working on. It's has changed over the years. If we're in the midst of filming it will be two or three days a week. Now we also get on with stuff separately, Paul from Birmingham and me here in Bristol.

PH: Every day we're on the phone, emails, backwards and forwards. It's a constant conversation about things. John does a lot of the studio-based stuff and the editing and I do more of the travel, installation of the shows and publications. We've ended up splitting the different responsibilities generally along the lines of what we enjoy.

JW: In the past we would post drawings to each other, but technology has changed. People might look at us and say, 'of course you can email', but it's really changed how we work, being able to Skype. For us that's quite amazing, that we're in two different cities and I can show Paul an edit of a piece of work I've just done and

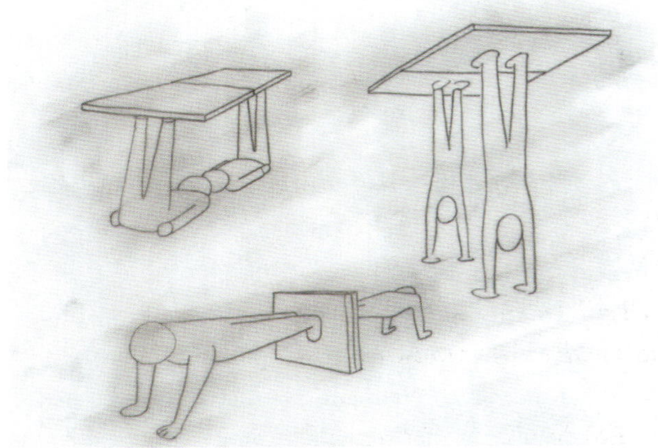

John Wood and Paul Harrison, drawing for *Board 2* (1995). Pencil on tracing paper.

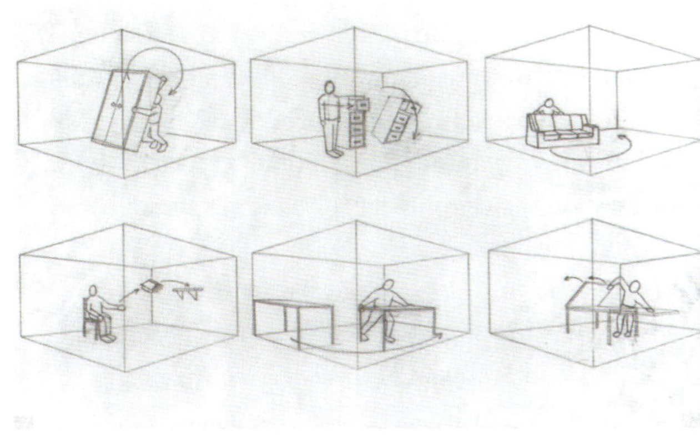

John Wood and Paul Harrison, drawing 2 for *Hundredweight* (2003). Pencil on tracing paper.

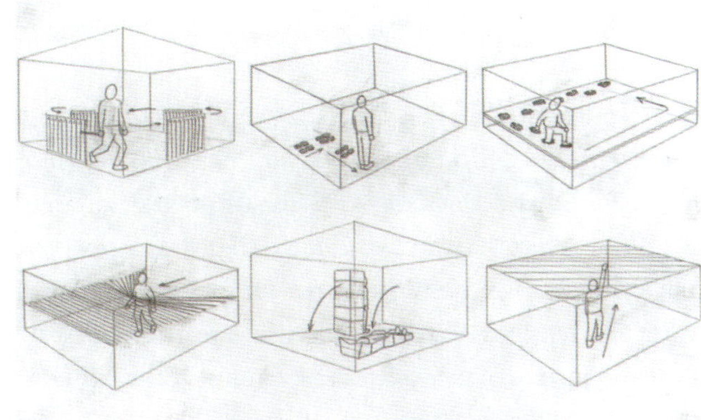

John Wood and Paul Harrison, drawing 1 for *Hundredweight* (2003). Pencil on tracing paper.

he can have a look at that so that we're able to still work on something even if we're not both there.

ID: *I still had that notion that you both would come and meet with all your drawings.*

PH: We do still do that, absolutely! When we're working on a video the first thing we do is come into the room and we lay out all our drawings.

JW: And laugh at them! The ability to be able to work at a distance is the result of twenty years' work. We've got that level of understanding.

PH: In the past we would go into the studio for ten days in a row. We would work out huge amounts in those periods.

ID: *In those blocks I presume you had things you wanted to do and then things that you did for the hell of it.*

JW: We'd come in and get the kettle on and have sandwiches.

PH: Read the paper.

JW: Do the crossword.

PH: We would do long days.

JW: There weren't any emails coming in. There was no one calling us up. We didn't leave art school thinking we were going to sell work, especially with video, and that was quite liberating because our motivation was just to go in and do stuff that we wanted to do.

ID: *You started collaborating at college?*

PH: We were both at college in Bath.

JW: I was one year below.

PH: I had been out a year when I got a residency in a school in Leicestershire. I'd been there about six months when a mutual friend suggested that John should get in touch. So John invited himself along.

ID: *And you started working together from then?*

PH: Yes, we made some work and I sent a VHS tape off to a couple of film festivals just on the off chance and they were selected.

ID: *What happened from then?*

PH: Well the Chisenhale show in 2002 really shifted everything; it was probably the first big show that we were really happy with.

JW: It was the first one that worked as an installation, as opposed to films that we had made.

ID: *What did you go about doing?*

JW: The only thing we set ourselves was to make twenty-six films; we didn't know what they were going to be – we just went into the studio and started making them and they kind of fitted together. It was the first time that it worked as an exhibition as opposed to watching a single screen film, how we started to use the space and how the work related to the space. It changed how the work was viewed.

PH: It was an installation of twenty-six TVs that we got from other projects, and VHS tapes. That was in 2000. I remember I was quoted something like £20,000 for a single DVD to be authored so in the space of a decade it's gone from that to where you churn out twenty DVDs a day for nothing. So the technology has moved on, not just in terms of how you communicate, but also within the work.

JW: The perception of video has changed: up to that point if we had an exhibition often they would ask if it could be played in the foyer – on the foyer screens. So it was important to see it as being a sculptural installation of the work. For a long, long time, we consciously avoided using projection because there was that thing of just exhibiting within a dark room with a single projection separated from other artists' work in the gallery. We didn't want to always end up in a black viewing room as opposed to seeing it in the context of the gallery.

ID: *But you work with projections now.*

JW: As projectors have become more common and less special that's when we started to include them. We liked the 'unsentimental-ness' of monitors, their 'sculpturalness' and the 'domesticness' of it.

PH: Often there isn't a specific way of showing the work and we'll mix it up in very different ways – single-screen versions, multi-screen versions. Just in a way to keep it fresh for us. We haven't got a list of specifications for each piece of work that spaces have to have.

ID: *That's in keeping with the content.*

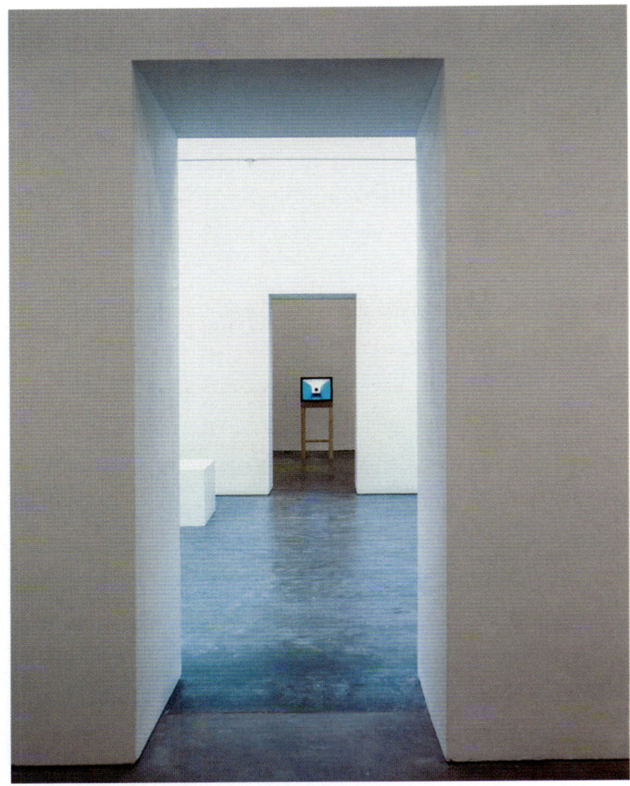

John Wood and Paul Harrison, *Some words, some more words* (2009). Ikon Gallery, Birmingham, England. Work shown: *Blind/ spot* (2007). 0'40", Mini DV, single channel.

JW: There's always been an economy in the work. I like the idea that instead of shooting on film we can shoot it on video, which is inexpensive, then we can spend more time, trying things out and experimenting.

ID: *What did you originally use?*

PH: We just shot straight on VHS.

JW: We will use whatever is affordable to us; it is important to have a camera in the studio all the time.

PH: The bigger pieces can take over a year to make so we need something that's here. We can't afford to hire in a camera. It needs to be one that we can have around all the time.

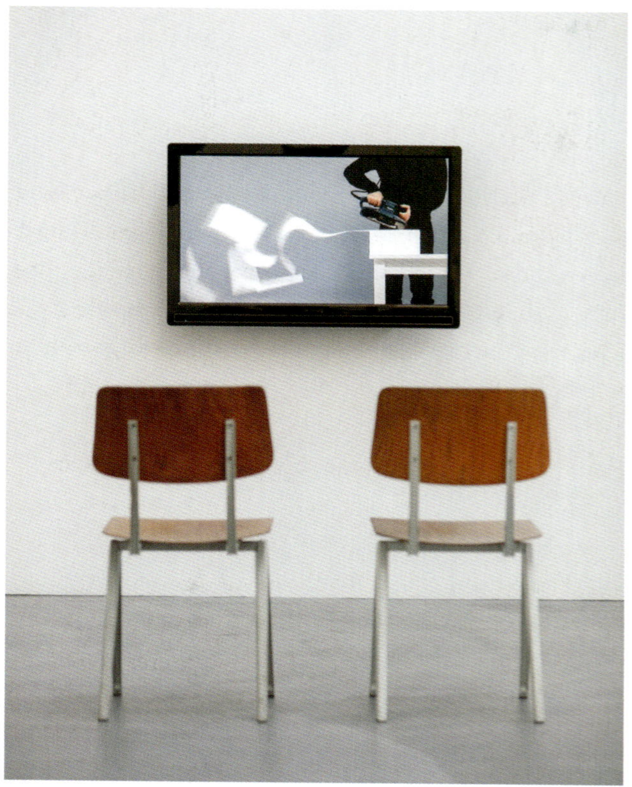

John Wood and Paul Harrison, *There or thereabouts* (2009). Von Bartha Garage, Basel, Switzerland. Work shown: *One more kilometer* (2009). 2'45", HDV.

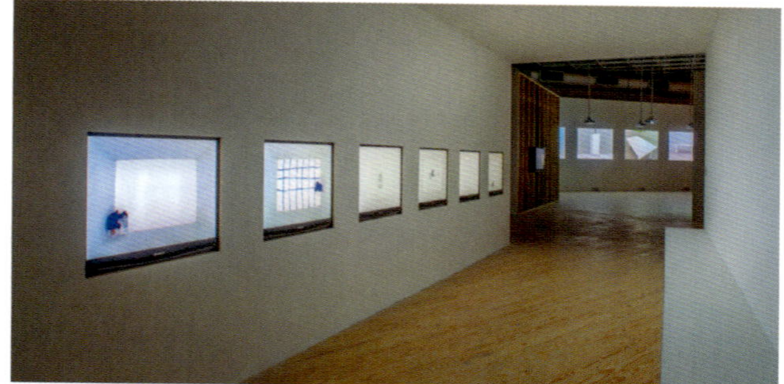

John Wood and Paul Harrison, *Answers to questions* (installation view). Contemporary Arts Museum, Houston, USA (2011).

ID: *I presume that's how you are able to develop your practice?*

JW: It was invaluable in the early days when we were able to just turn the camera on and mess around in front of it, seeing what happened. And I think from that point we began learning about timing, and that's really what it's about for us. The material we use isn't videotape; it's the thing that's in front of the camera and the duration of that. And when we were filming something, we would be doing it again and again to get the take we wanted, adjusting things within it. Getting to know how long the action should last for.

ID: *It often involved lots of takes?*

PH: We joke that we shoot something and on the twenty-first take we get it right. And then we will do it again so we've got another one just in case there's a problem with the take, and we end up shooting it another twenty times before we get another one. Less so now; you get to be more confident. You get that experience of knowing which one is the right take.

JW: Sometimes we'll do something that requires sixty takes. It will be two o'clock in the morning and I genuinely start to think we're never going to get it. And I start to persuade Paul that I like it how it is but you still have this niggling doubt. We then start laughing hysterically and that's followed by a wave of despair. We always get it in the end. You do get there.

PH: I remember making the piece when I lower a belt sander onto a stack of A4 paper and the sheets shoot off in a wave. And I would get so far down into the pile and then a big clump would just go at the same time and I would be thinking 'oh just try and ignore it' but it would ruin the take. And then it was the case of unpacking more paper, stacking it back up, picking up all the thousands of sheets of paper and doing it again and getting all the way down to the bottom and the same thing happening again. It's about trying to make it look easy or simple – but actually behind that there's a lot of really dull, boring work.

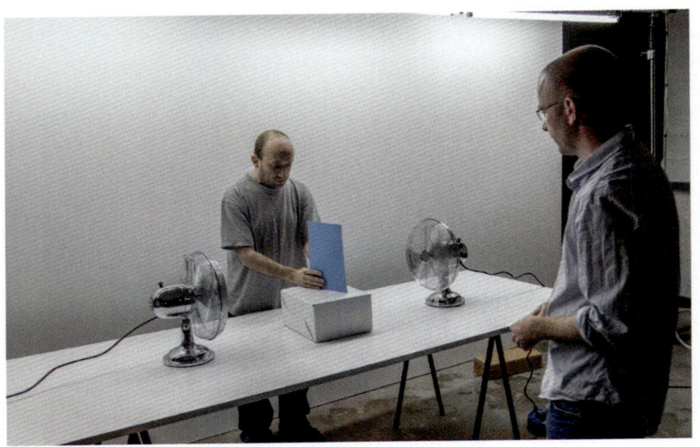

John Wood and Paul Harrison, *Fan/paper/fan* take (2007).

ID: *What possessed you?*

PH: It was a drawing that had been around for a while – one of those drawings that you think: that'll never work. We just set it up with a small pile of paper and it just worked.

JW: After we'd bought various tools, we bought an electric sander – it's one of those things, like a lot of the stuff, we've got in our studio – and you're using it for something, then you think, 'Oh, I could use it for something else,' and certainly in *Notebook* – that was one of our key decision-making factors. Whatever object we chose, we couldn't use it how it was supposed to be used.

ID: *Do you bin ideas after they've been filmed?*

PH: Mostly before. Partly because there are two of us, you've got that other person saying, 'No – hang on.' It doesn't stop us reintroducing those ideas years later.

JW: We operate the three-wall system.

PH: It's very complex.

JW: We would have the 'crap' wall, the 'maybe' wall and the 'definite' wall and we would swap drawings around. We would sit down and discuss: 'Can we move that one over to there?' and every so often one of us would try to sneak drawings back onto the wall without the other one seeing it.

PH: There isn't any pretence between us – we can say: 'This one's shit, this one's okay and this one's a definite.'

JW: The bottom line is that if one of us doesn't want to do it, then we won't do it. But then that makes us very un-precious about ideas. That it's just okay to come up with another one.

ID: *So there aren't any that don't work?*

JW: Not often. Because we've been through such a heavy editing system at the drawing stage, but occasionally it just doesn't work physically. When we bought loads of Hornby train sets for this idea, we were going to have these circular tracks and the trains all started together in sync and then because of the different sizes of the circles they would all go out of sync and then they would all come back into sync. But that didn't take into account that the engines warm up and the trains just go at different speeds.

PH: Once we built this space from huge pieces of Perspex to create a snowstorm with leaf blowers and polystyrene balls. We had spent a lot of time building it, aligning it and getting it all ready. And after about a minute we realized that it wasn't going to work. We just lost it and started laughing at the stupidity of spending so much time on it. So the drawing stage is about the economy of not making stuff that isn't going to work.

JW: Making sure that the idea is robust enough, because what you initially think is a robust idea actually with a bit of repeated looking at and discussing, for whatever reason, you realize that you were seduced by something in the idea and that it isn't strong enough to warrant it being physically made.

ID: *I can appreciate why you need to have somebody like Lew from Aardman's help you with the camera track but it's interesting that you still do the dull and laborious parts like picking up all those reams of paper from the belt sander piece.*

PH: If you are doing something that requires seven or eight hours of continuous filming, lining up something accurately, we know what we want and it's about that level of focus. And contact with the work.

JW: If we are setting up a shoot, we both just know what to do and to get on with it. We don't have to explain anything so we don't have to waste time explaining what to do. Bizarrely, it's easier us doing it.

PH: The studio isn't a precious or magical space. There's no magic! It's just a locked off space, we are quite willing to show the process behind what goes on, partly to prove that we don't use computers.

JW: We're happy to explain our process but actually within the gallery, our aim is to walk a line between the different aspects of the work. Whether it took us sixty takes to do something is unimportant because it isn't about how difficult it was. We want it to look effortless not in a false way, not to trick anyone. We simply want people to be looking at the beauty of how a plastic cup falls off a table. That is the essence we are after.

ID: *The scenes are always pared back too.*

PH: Because what we make originates from a drawing, the use of the sparse white background references the drawing from which the work was developed. There is the fun of explaining something in two dimensions and then working from that in a real three-dimensional space, the factors you have to take into account – gravity, friction – all those kind of things are part of the challenge. And we usually try to get it as close to the drawing as possible.

ID: *And the architectural features?*

PH: In some instances it will be the set of an office. And sometimes just in terms of shot composition, we will just put a light switch in. But it's never very much: a skirting board, or light switch, or plug socket, or a door.

ID: *They are particular items.*

JW: It helps to deliver an 'everyday-ness' within a work.

ID: *From a long period of filming with a static camera, you began working with tracking shots.*

JW: It was quite a big deal to decide to move the camera. We did it first in *The Only Other Point*, then *Night and Day*, and then *Shelf*. With *Shelf* we made what looked like a domestic shelf but tracked past the same section multiple times and edited it together to look like it was 100m long. So the camera travels past objects; it was a progression from *Notebook*, where we compiled 101 different scenes together. But we wanted it to be a kind of single take of objects that you might have on your shelf at home, of toys and bottles of wine, books.

PH: These longer ones, like *Night and Day*, are all made up of short sections. It became this idea of two blokes making a film when they were at work at night, as if we were security guards making our own film in a kind of factory or a studio or something, but they only had a short amount of time to make each bit, so it was filmed each night when they had a bit of time …

ID: *So the longer ones are all compiled by the shorter pieces.*

JW: They're often made up of short sections, and it is something we've always joked about – could we film something longer than three minutes in a single take? It's something that still fascinates us. It's something that we keep looking at; how can you stretch time and the duration of the piece and how long can you engage people for.

PH: We have made longer works, for instance a 63-minute piece where an electric toothbrush is spinning around on a surface, but that has a totally different dynamic. Those works are made more to fit into an exhibition, to complement the multi-sectional works. We showed it in Switzerland and we sited it on a wall where you would see it when you entered the show and again when you left and it would still be doing the same thing.

JW: But the beauty of making pieces that are multi-sectional is that you can see how those sections relate to each other.

PH: And we show them in ways that exploit this. Virtually all of the multi-screen stuff is un-synced so that you've got perhaps four monitors playing twenty-five pieces on each – so the different permutations of what is simultaneously playing are beyond our control.

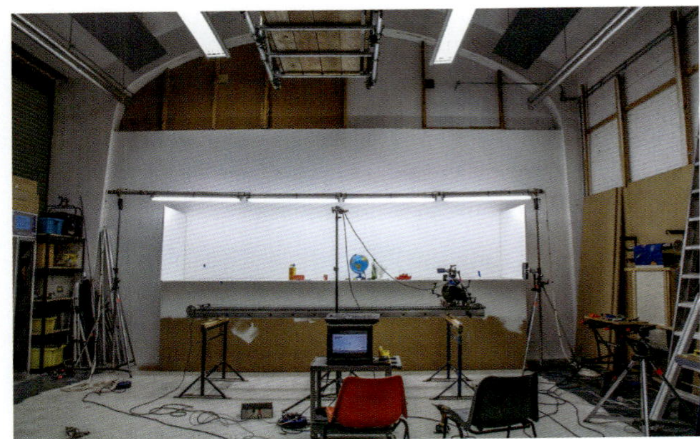

John Wood and Paul Harrison, *Shelf* in progress 1.

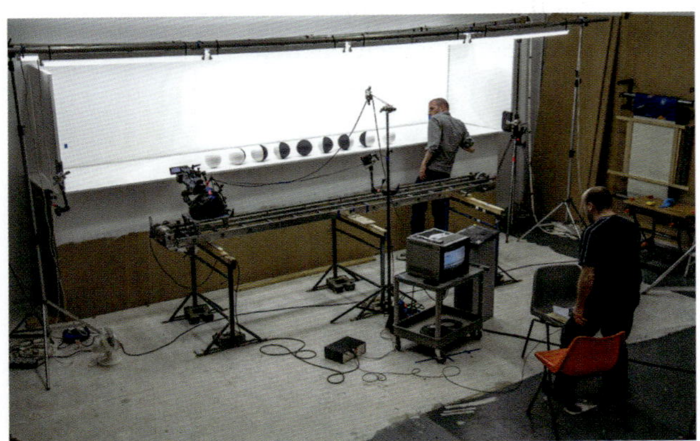

John Wood and Paul Harrison, *Shelf* in progress 2.

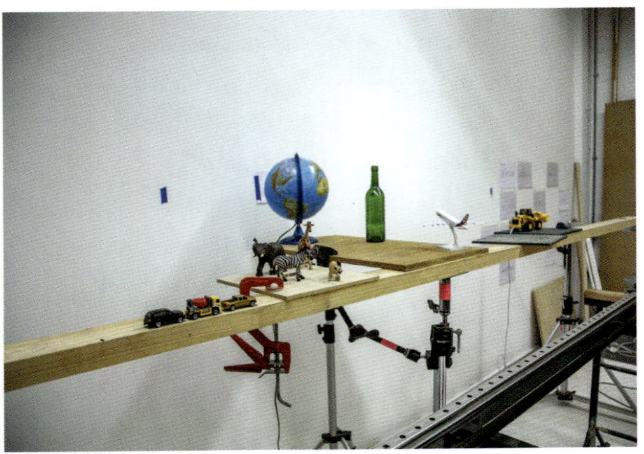

John Wood and Paul Harrison, *Shelf* in progress 3.

JW: It's anti-beginning, middle and end.

PH: I think we are always actively looking to engage an audience: we don't expect people to enter a dark, awkward space halfway through a lengthy film and for them to get it. We quite like the idea of making shows that people can come in and engage with in all sorts of ways. Get some kind of experience, pleasure or something from it.

ID: *You cite Laurel and Hardy as an influence?*

PH: I think that there's so much stuff that we bring in to it, that there's not a direct line from anything. We're quite happy to mix in *You've Been Framed* with …

JW: I would cite Morecambe and Wise as being fairly important.

PH: Simon and Garfunkel, Spike Milligan, Woody Allen …

JW: Equally Ken Loach, looking at the duration, one could talk about the mechanics, not of gaps, but of time and looking at the relationship between Morecombe and Wise sketch and how long Ken Loach leaves a tape running at the end of a bit of dialogue. So I guess in terms of comedy it's looking at timing.

PH: People tend to go for the high-end reference like Buster Keaton, whereas we'll say Laurel and Hardy – because they used to be on TV when we got back from school.

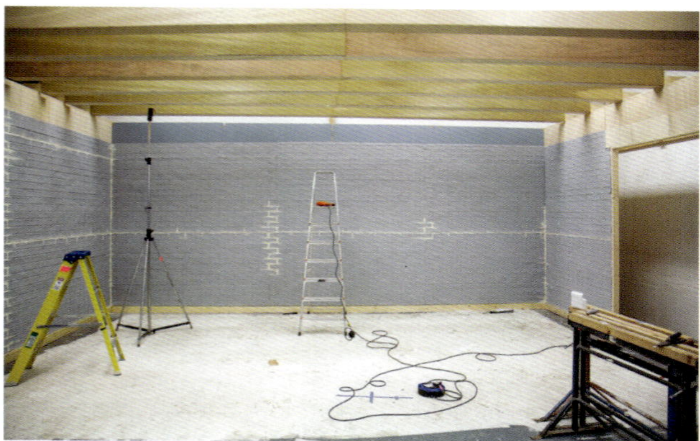

John Wood and Paul Harrison, *Night and day 23*.

ID: *It always looks a lot of fun when you make something.*

PH: I think we deliberately try to keep a sense of enjoyment of making something out of next to nothing for not much money.

JW: It comes back to that thing – what do you do with your time? Us making the work is about that: what do you choose to do with your time?

PH: We're increasingly finding out that about 80 per cent of the time is spent doing all the other stuff around making the work. We have about 20 per cent of our time in the studio when you can actually do what you always wanted to do. And that studio bit is the reward that then drives you through to carry on doing all the other stuff which isn't always as rewarding, but it's what you have to do to be able to be in the studio and make the work. ∎

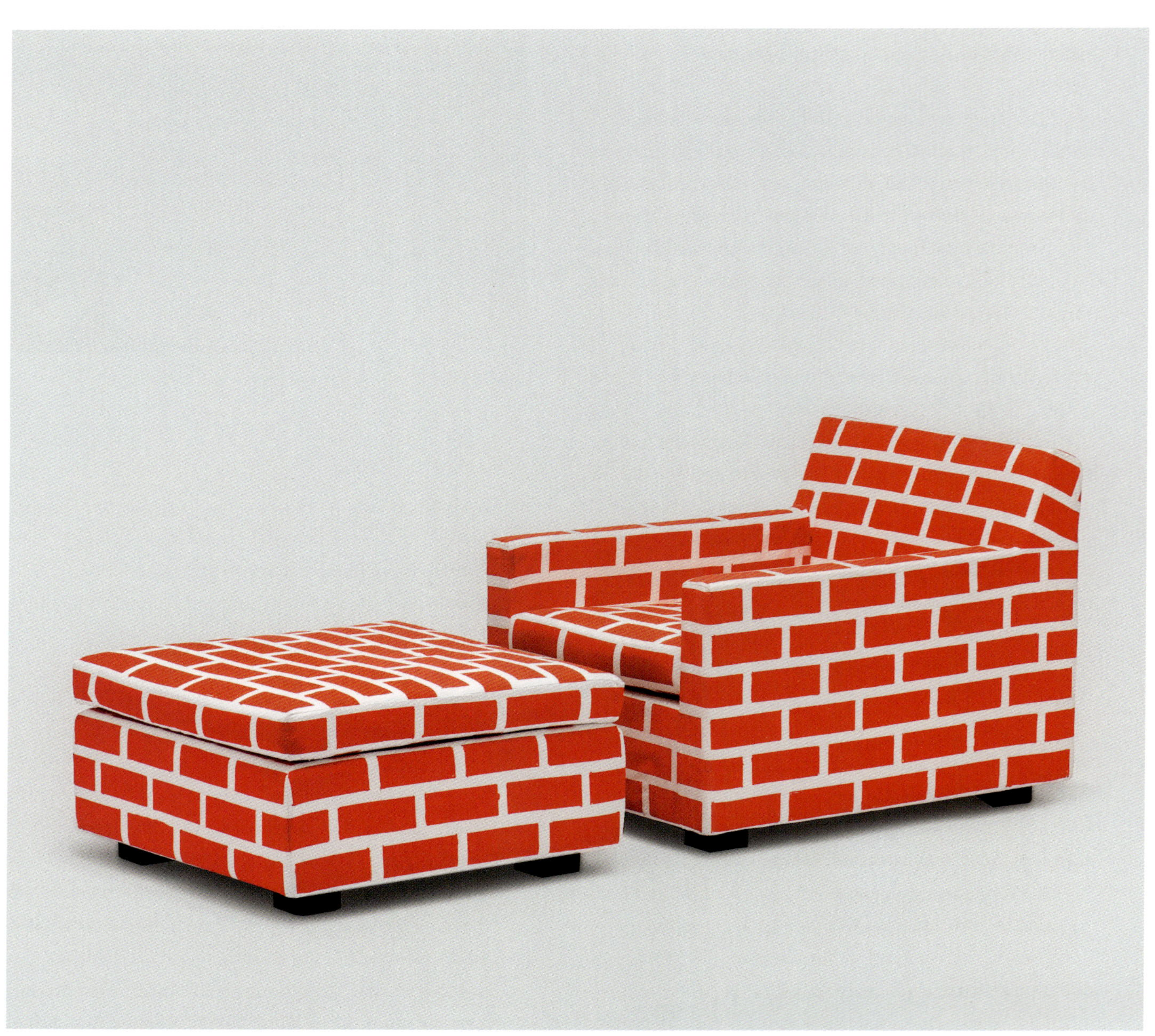

Richard Woods, *Bricks & Mortar* (2009). In collaboration with
Sebastian Wrong and Established & Sons, presented at the Salone
Internazionale de Mobile 2009, Milan.

5 Intervention and Collaboration

In 1977 the American sculptor Richard Serra arrived at a Ruhr Valley steel mill to be greeted by striking steelworkers and a trade unionist, Clara Weyergraf (who later became Serra's wife). Serra was in Germany to make a sculpture for the National Gallery in Berlin. Producing his powerful free-standing rolled and forged steel obelisks and lumps required the full cooperation of an industrial steel mill. At the gates Weyergraf had a lengthy discussion about her perception of Serra's position as a privileged American about to forge something purely for the *intelligentsia* of Berlin. She asked him not to disregard the current situation of the region, and they agreed to film an extended residency by Serra in the mill. Weyergraf and Serra's joint film, *Steelmill*, became a documentary about both the history of steel making in the region as well as the workers' relationship to producing a work of art.

Serra stated: 'It ends for me being one of the more social conscious things I've done. I don't say it in a way that I am trying to sell somebody a bill of goods; I took time to really understand people that bring my work into the world, and the pride and responsibility they take in doing it.'

Throughout the Seventies the traditional relationship between artist and audience had been changing. Martha Rosler, for example, had been creating 'real' yet orchestrated garage sales. Assortments of goods and fake belongings were haggled over and bought, Rosler assuming the persona of a Californian mother with her conflicting materialistic attitude of owning and then selling her possessions.

> All artists are alike. They dream of doing something that's more social, more collaborative, and more real than art.
>
> Dan Graham

Experimentation with an audience, a group of people who not only attended but participated, continued during the recession of the early 1990s; artists were afforded the unusual opportunity of developing experimental projects within galleries that weren't selling work anyway. In 1992 Rikrit Tiravanija cooked and served Thai curry to visitors for the duration of his exhibition at 303 Gallery in New York. Whilst the visitors participated by feasting on the food, they could observe the normally private workings of the gallery as Tiravanija relocated the backroom offices into the showing space.

Since then, collaborative pursuits – activities that engage the audience – have spread and are ever more likely to take the form of social events, workshops and performances. Artists are choosing to operate in urban and public spaces as much as in art institutions. With a tendency to see little difference between a museum, classroom or a site on the street, these places are simply part of a larger scheme. Equally, artists are likely to bypass a dilemma between material and immaterial by refusing to set one against the other.

▶ Alex Schady

The Frieze Art Fair is England's annual autumn trade fair. A massive marquee is erected in Regent's Park, nearly two hundred galleries set up their pitches to display their wares, and the collectors descend to buy what's hot from the dealers and to shun what's not. But Frieze Art Fair had become more than this, it's now a cultural occasion; it operates lecture programmes and commissions site-specific interventions, and its education department runs school workshops when the road-show is in town, demonstrating the extent to which institutions compete for audience participation.

It comes as no surprise that art is being made from this parallel arena and I speak to Alex Schady about his work.

IAN DAWSON: *Where did it all start?*

ALEX SCHADY: It started out of gallery education. I had started teaching in galleries and within communities, doing gallery projects with groups of people, and I started to get really interested in the politics of that, because what you are asked to do is often quite problematic.

ID: *What was problematic?*

AS: I was aware that I was working within this area where an artist is brought into a situation, and is expected through the transcendent power of art to make it better. Yet art doesn't do that; that isn't the role of art, it doesn't transform in that way. A lot of work emerging out of socially engaged practice was just an ego trip for the artist and institution. The artist goes in and pretends to make a housing estate better, and then leaves.

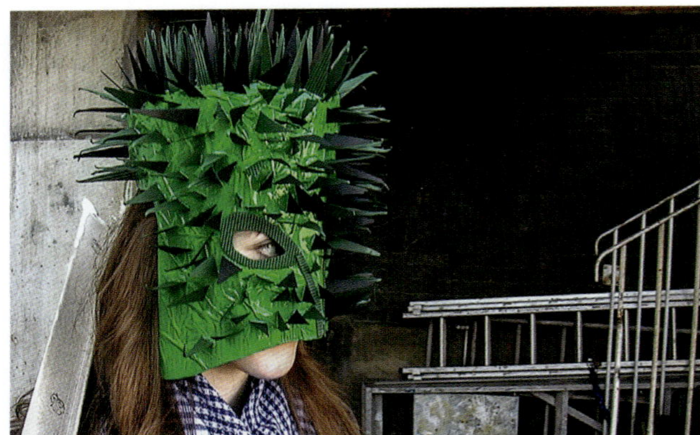

Alex Schady, *The Rulers*. Film still.

ID: *How did you deal with that?*

AS: I decided that instead of being benevolent, I would do the opposite, to make it clear: 'I am not trying to save you, art isn't good for you, it is bad for you, but we are going to do it anyway so if you are going to do it, you are going to accept that.'

ID: *And this was how you began to develop the work?*

AS: Initially I had to get to grips with the politics of collaborative practice and it being quite separate from my studio practice but over time it began to converge, and suddenly I found that there wasn't a separation between the two things, that my education projects were part of my practice and vice versa.

ID: *What were the differences?*

AS: My work in the studio wasn't directly political or politicized, but the work dealing with other people was very much considering the power relationships between the facilitator and the participant in the context of where it is displayed.

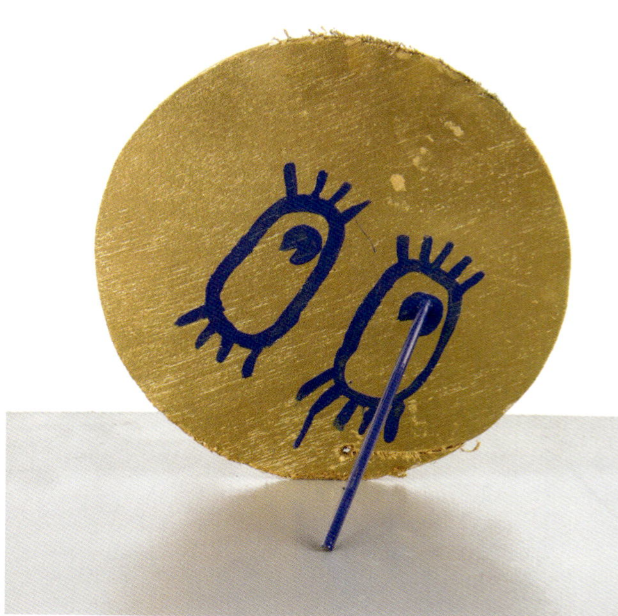

Alex Schady, *Untitled*.

ID: *How do the un-benevolent scenarios play out?*

AS: For example in the Bethnal Green Library workshop the students are all dressed up with gimp masks and I am a demonic, cultish figure. There is no talking or interaction but I am giving them instructions to make a sculpture out of black balloons covered in black tape. The end result is this giant black cloud of helium balloons that becomes a dark brooding shadow across the ceiling of the library. It doesn't stay in the ceiling long because with all that tape it is quite heavy, so it's up there for a couple of hours, it sinks and recedes to nothing. All this effort and time and you have just made a big black shadow that rises and falls again.

ID: *You control the parameters of the project quite tightly.*

AS: If you tell people that they are free and it isn't questioned then you are not exploring that sense of freedom. I find it more interesting to control, and tell them that you are controlling, and let certain things open up from there.

ID: *How do you achieve that?*

AS: I sometimes provide a script to ensure a rigid structure, three pages that everyone has to follow, with limited resources – and, paradoxically, the tighter those restrictions the more likely you are to get unexpected results.

ID: *That seems to subvert an idea about creative workshops.*

AS: The result of saying anything is possible, of having empowering meetings and claiming the artist is just an enabler, is often banal. The danger when you open things up too much is that you revert back to cliché. I am more interested in being dictatorial; it's counter to what I saw as the prevalent ethos within socially engaged practice.

ID: *Have you ever met with any negativity?*

AS: A recent piece discussed the power imbalance that is in any shared artistic endeavour. It's a bunch of kids dressed up just wearing masks; it's useful for them to wear masks because I don't have to get clearance for them to be in the video. I asked them all to draw my face on the masks. Then different groups of kids just stand up and point at the camera and say, 'He made me do it' and it goes on, this constant set of shots of these masked kids standing up and sitting down, pointing at the camera saying, 'He made me do it'.

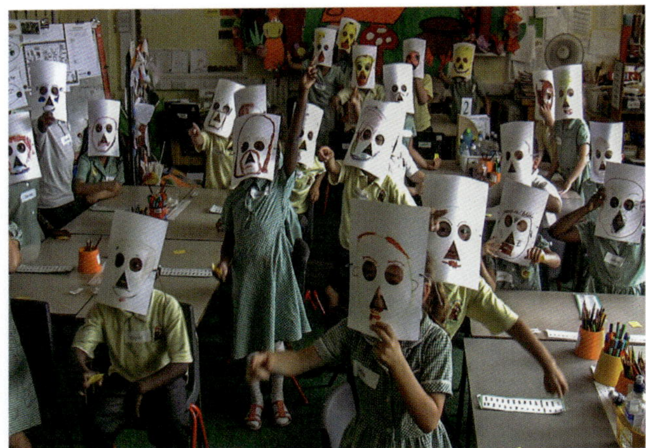

Alex Schady, *He made me do it*. Film still 1.

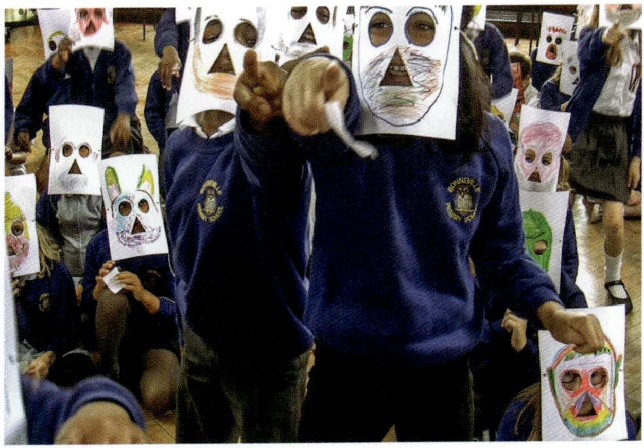

Alex Schady, *He made me do it*. Film still 2.

 What were your reasons?

AS: It was a critique as well as a dramatization of the project itself: of course I had made them do it, I am the artist who is behind the scenes who doesn't reveal himself.

ID: *What happened?*

AS: A parent became concerned that I had used their child as material in my own work. Of course they were right – I was, but I imagine there wouldn't have been a problem if I had followed an anodyne narrative.

ID: *So you are always trying to subvert the situation?*

AS: Afterwards I had thought about how I could push this. Could I shackle the children to the table, how much of an abuse of power could happen in something and it still be a critique of it or when does it just become an abuse?

ID: *It's very cult-like.*

AS: That issue of who has the power, who is in control and to what extent are people participating because they want to or because they have been coerced, it really starts to matter for me. I also became interested in the idea of protest for these reasons.

ID: *You created a protest piece in Sandness, Norway.*

AS: I had just started to make a boulder with Hadas Kedar when we discovered a line from Muriel Spark's *The Prime of Miss Jean Brody* – 'no more petrification'. She discusses petrification as the worst thing that can happen. And we found it funny that we were making this big fake stone boulder and talking about petrification.

ID: *That was the beginning of the project.*

AS: We arrived in Norway and gave the students this phrase, and asked them to think about what they could ban and made a series of banners and placards that had those slogans on them. At the same time we made the giant boulder from bits of tape and tubing and expanding foam, crudely assembled and painted grey.

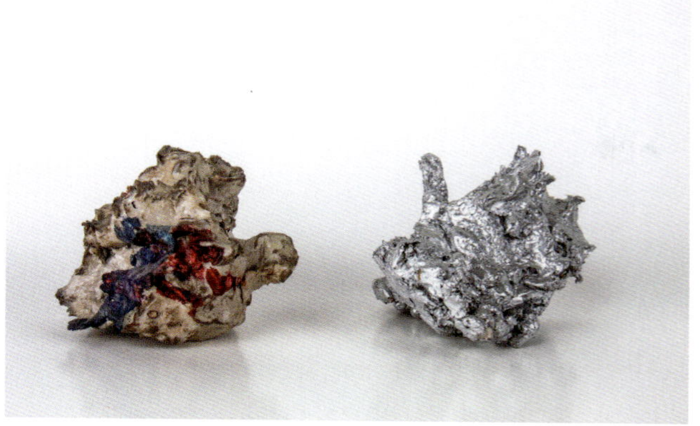

Alex Schady, *Untitled* (2).

ID: *And the march itself?*

AS: The procession begins at the science museum; all week a large screen outside the museum had been announcing the boulder's arrival.

ID: *Where did it go from there?*

AS: We rolled the boulder down the narrow high street of the town. It was a Saturday. We had embedded cans of Pepsi in the boulder and every so often we would stop and ceremoniously open a can with a splurt and a dribble.

ID: *A surreal procession.*

AS: It was a completely absurd and fabricated ritual that on the one hand appeared mythical (it might have happened in this town for the last three hundred years) but also contemporary, with a politicized group of students who are protesting, yet what they are protesting for is very ambivalent, obscure and tangential.

ID: *What was on the placards?*

AS: Things like: 'It's better to take a step in the wrong direction than not to move at all' or 'no more change', 'defy gravity', 'don't get stuck', 'be unique', 'be rebellious'.

ID: *How did you go about making the boulder?*

AS: We had very little time to do the whole thing – we made the boulder and the placards over three days, there were about twenty participants. It was important that the boulder was rough and made quickly.

ID: *Why?*

AS: The boulder is only superficially suggesting a big lump of stone. And during the 45-minute procession the boulder became ever more dishevelled. By the end it had collapsed in on itself, it had no weight, its volume was shifting all the time and it had imploded. All those attributes that a sculpture should have, this boulder had failed those qualities.

ID: *You are all wearing uniform?*

AS: We wanted some way of unifying the group, making it clear that this group of protestors were one entity, were a united group – they are just plastic boiler suits. None of the participants are allowed to talk during a performance, and I instruct by signalling and marshalling. Hadas and I are the cult leaders. So there is a sense of an uncomfortable power relationship.

ID: *What was the response from the public?*

AS: The high street is very narrow and the boulder almost spanned the width of the street. It was busy with shoppers, we were blocking traffic, not talking or stopping to explain. And it ended up being like a Pied Piper thing where everyone started to follow us.

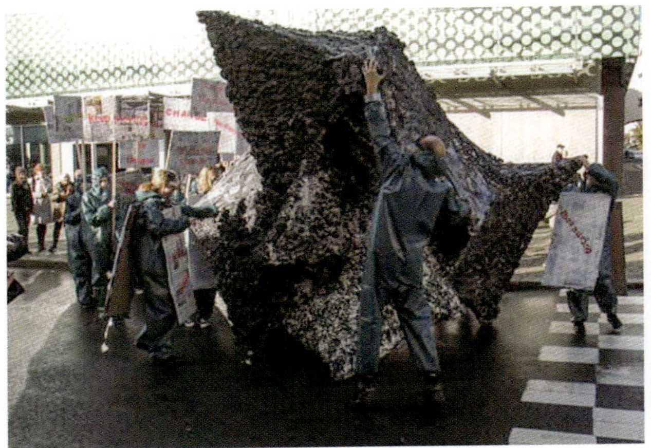

Alex Schady, *Petrification*. Film still.

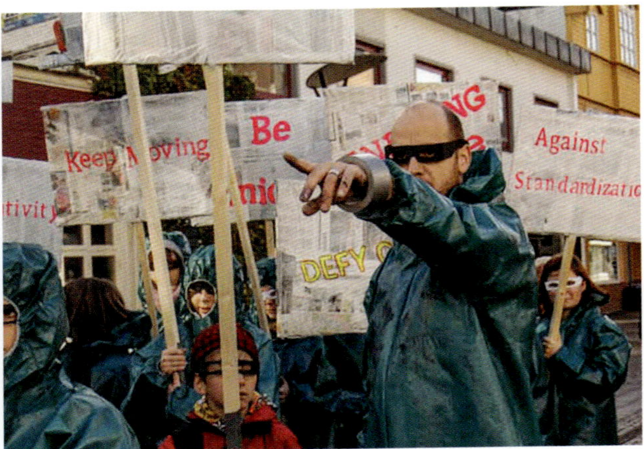

Alex Schady, *Petrification*. Film still 2.

ID: *Had you collaborated with Hadas Kedar before?*

AS: We began by making a series of accidental works. With a map of London we randomly choose a location, and randomly choose a material. Then we would go to that spot on any given day and do something with that material.

ID: *Like what?*

AS: They are often installations. Put carpet on a traffic island. Make a string drawing across a building. They are pieces that can be left but are very quickly done. We didn't consider them finished pieces of work but a way of developing a process between the two of us, to start to understand the collaborative dynamic.

ID: *The masks appear important.*

AS: It's an example of how my practice has developed; all the masks that are made for this Camden project were all using ways of making that I figured out in the studio through making sculpture. And then, because someone else is now making them I often discover something that I then bring back into the studio. Interestingly, I always wear a sculpture in some way to check if it's finished. I grab the sculpture, put it on my head and I look at myself in the mirror. There is something about wearing a sculpture that gives me an idea about whether it's finished or not. I enjoy the comparison with hats: they are sort of frivolous, the icing on the cake, the decoration not the structure, they are plonked on top – so the idea that a sculpture can be a 'plonked-on-top' thing and not the primary structure seems quite interesting to me.

ID: *You must have developed a method of working where you can achieve results in a short amount of time.*

AS: It depends on the task. Sometimes the amount of time spent on a task ends up imbuing it with an importance, such as the text on banners. It's not that I am after craft or a beautiful letter but it somehow has to have the right level of time on it to engage the audience. With the placards I insist on a font; it ensures that all the text from any given project has a unity.

ID: *And other times?*

AS: Working quickly is something that I enjoy within the practice. I will only have a couple of days to get a shot, or have only got an afternoon to do something else, and maybe in the long term that is not sustainable but that time pressure is good. To squeeze something in; to fit in an activity is important. ■

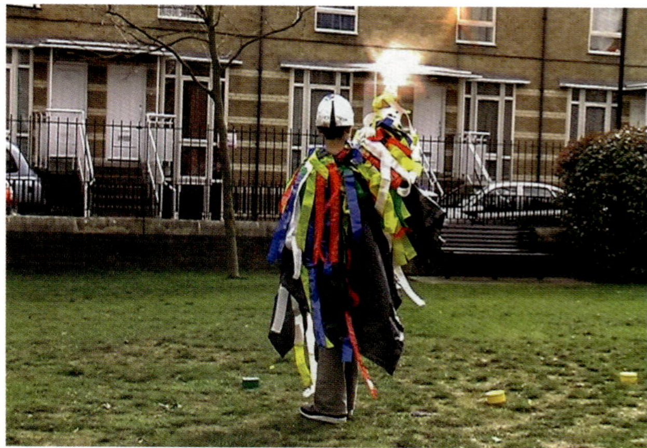

Alex Schady, *Everything must go*. Film still 2.

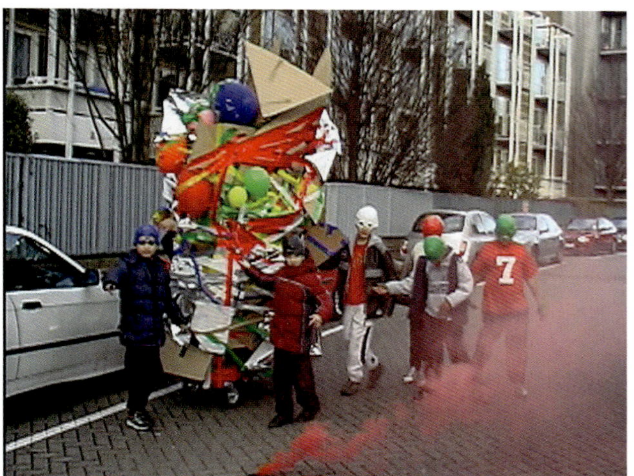

Alex Schady, *Everything must go*. Video still 1.

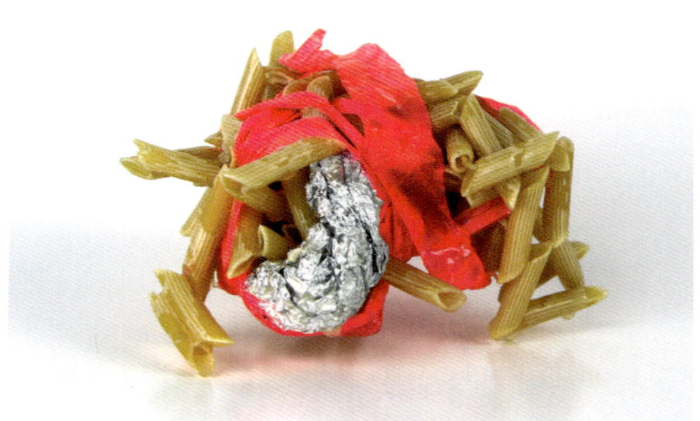

Alex Schady, *Untitled* (3).

▶ Jessica Voorsanger

Audience involvement, once confined to either a heckle or a cheer, is now a part of the distant past as each generation is involved in the changing mechanisms that supply the cult of personality to their followers. This is Jessica Voorsanger's territory. Her interests span the characters who populate the world of the stage, the world of celebrity: it might be Blondie, the Beatles or Zoe Ball; Charlton Heston, Amy Winehouse or Woody Allen; the Brady Bunch or Alan Sugar or William Shatner. The players.

Voorsanger has also periodically made work about football supporters, the epitome of fandom, obsessed and submerged in the world of their team. One such piece saw her secretly install floor tiles imprinted with the footprints of the Blackpool football team into a supporter's garden. This same supporter (who had earlier utterly dismissed, tabloid style, Carl André's bricks at the Tate) arrived back to be overwhelmed by this gesture, celebrating and cherishing it as art.

Here I interview Voorsanger about her work.

IAN DAWSON: *Do you want to describe your practice?*

JESSICA VOORSANGER: Celebrity and popular culture have been the main themes for well over twenty years and that stems from my fascination with how fans relate to their idols.

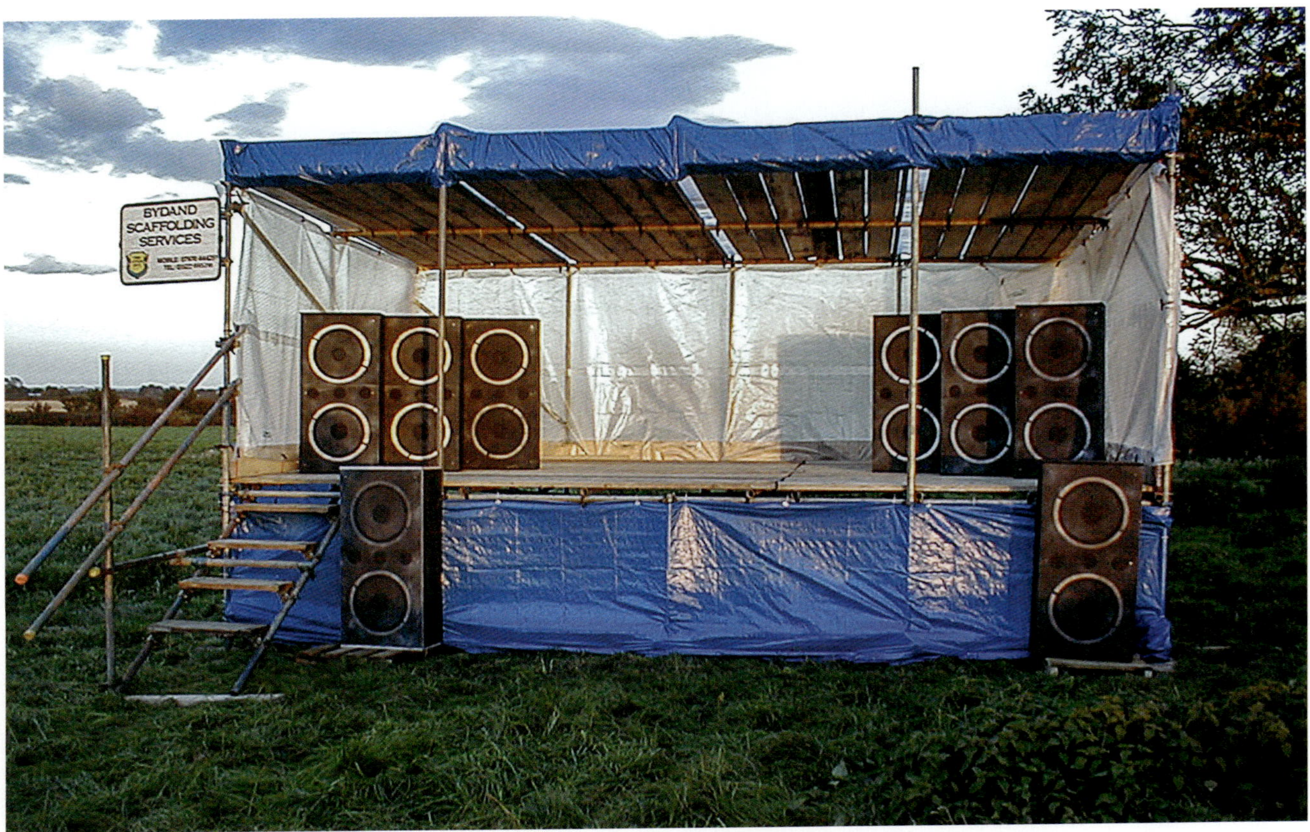

Jessica Voorsanger, *Stage* (Beacon, 2004).

ID: *Were you a fan?*

JV: I fell in love with David Cassidy when I was six years old – he was my first love! I found it really interesting that as I got older I never threw David Cassidy aside when I went through different phases; he was always sort of there.

ID: *When did you start making work about celebrities?*

JV: I first began making work about romantic fiction, with its levels of fantasy and escapism, the formulaic structure always culminating in the resolution of a conflict. The problem always solved.

ID: *You then began a series of mail art projects.*

JV: I had started making work from home. It was a solution to having less space. I did lots of interactive mail art pieces where I wrote letters, huge mail-outs. Very theme based. And the thing that would be brilliant about these mail art pieces was I could make them here, send them off; what came back would fit into a box, yet when installed they would became large installations.

ID: *And your performances?*

JV: It really came down to what triggered one idea and how to manifest it. Or it was coming across something and taking advantage of that moment, like realising that I was in possession of Bob Geldof's rubbish, nicking it and putting it in a show.

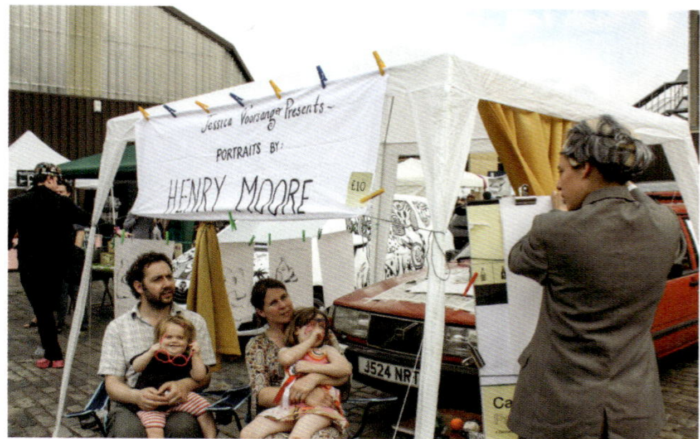

Jessica Voorsanger, *The Imposters: Henry Moore 1* (2009). Art Car Boot Fair.

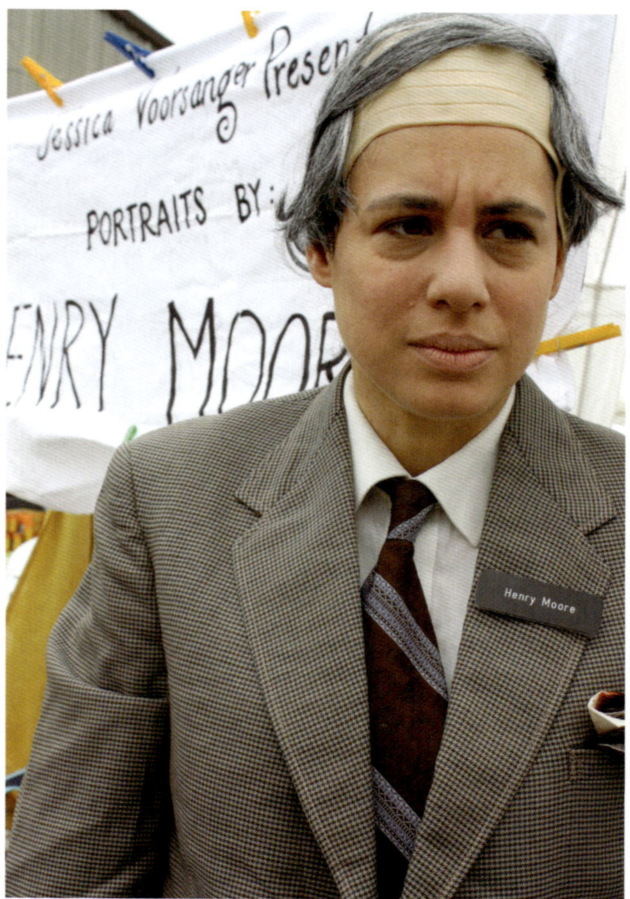

Jessica Voorsanger, *The Imposters: Henry Moore 2* (2009). Art Car Boot Fair.

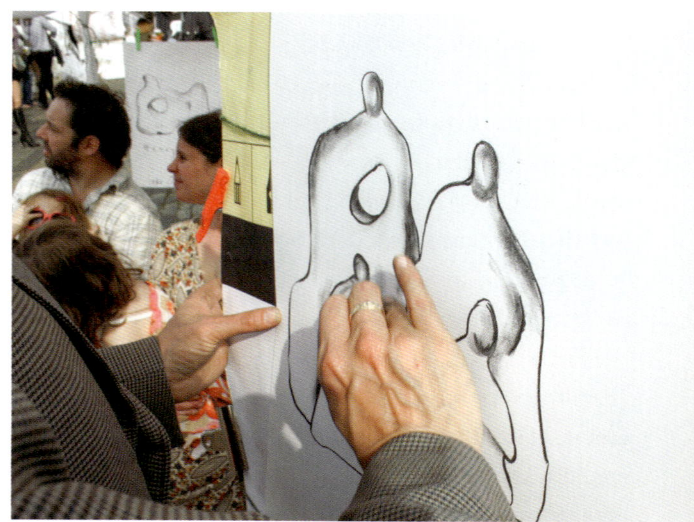

Jessica Voorsanger, *The Imposters: Henry Moore 3* (2009). Art Car Boot Fair.

ID: *After that?*

JV: I finally went and got David Cassidy's autograph as a piece of work and filmed that, then in 1995 I had made my first costume piece, *Partridge Wear*. I watched sixty-three consecutive episodes of *The Partridge Family* and then copied and recreated all the costumes from the programme. Each costume had a swing-tag label attached with a synopsis and a featured song identifying it to an episode.

ID: *The work moved into a more socially engaged arena, creating installations for an audience to participate. How did that develop?*

JV: I first began a series called *The Imposters* where I dressed up as notable people and made appearances. At the Art Car Boot Fair, I dressed as Henry Moore and made portraits.

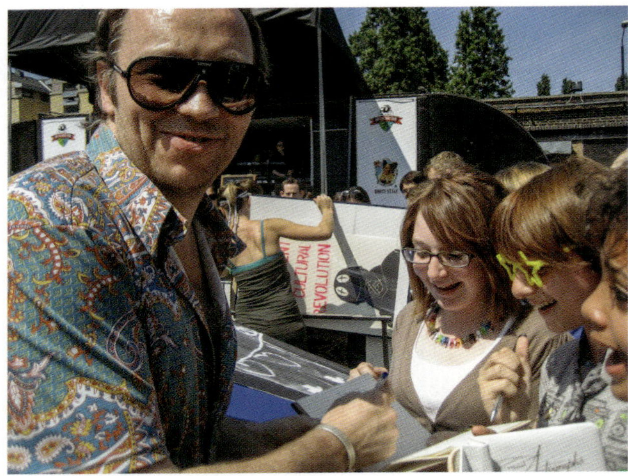

Jessica Voorsanger, *Fan-a-Grams* (2007). Art Car Boot Fair.

ID: *Those were your first experiments with live participation?*

JV: It was apparent earlier when I was making mail-art pieces, writing to people and asking for responses to different things, and then I did a book signing with a huge stack of Mills and Boons that I signed with a 'p.p.' suffix on behalf of the author. It was much more successful than I thought it would be, and I really engaged with the people who had been waiting to get a signed copy.

ID: *How did that develop?*

JV: The *Fan-a-grams* came from this. It was an instant fan club based on the idea of a telegram, It was interesting because it engaged with the audience in a way that I took no responsibility for whatsoever.

ID: *How did it work?*

JV: Any member of the public could come to my stall and nominate somebody to receive a *Fan-a-gram*. They would fill in a certificate as if it was a gift, from them to their nominated person. A large group of girls between the ages of twelve and eighteen would then search the nominated person out and would start screaming, 'Oh my God, it's Joe Bloggs – ahhhh!' Once the recipient had been identified, the fans would chase and harangue them until they got their autograph. Screaming, *I love you!* and *I can't believe it's really you!* That sort of thing.

ID: *Where did you perform the* Fan-a-grams?

JV: Always in a very crowded place, an art fair, a gallery or museum event, somewhere that allowed for an instant audience. A fascinating aspect of what happens is that the minute the girls start screaming, everybody turns to look who it is, to attempt to identify the celebrity. But as the performance progresses through the event, they realize quite obviously that it is repeating and it's not celebrities, that they are just unwitting people.

ID: *And what happens?*

JV: From the initial excitement of everybody turning to look it progressively becomes about people withdrawing because they don't want it to be them. It was interesting to put the intensity of having a fan base on people who wouldn't necessarily have it.

ID: *Sounds intimidating.*

JV: It is uncomfortable. It isn't always a surprise, people guess that a friend might do it to them, but they aren't necessarily willing participants. At the Art Car Boot Fair Gavin Turk was selected but he legged it, he really legged it. And the girls had to chase him round the block, but they got him. In terms of socially engaged practice the point is that it's not always voluntary.

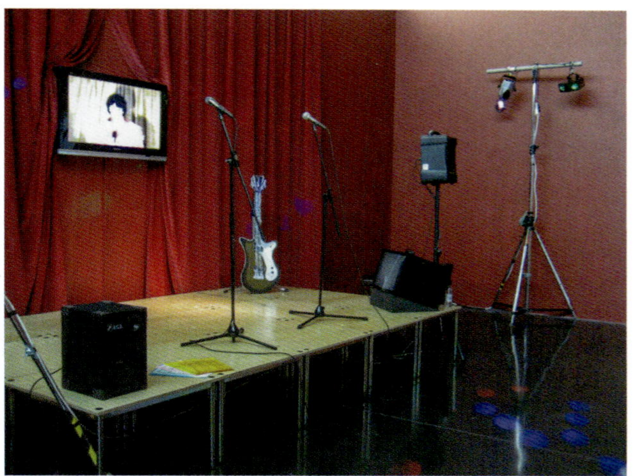

Jessica Voorsanger, *Stage Struck 1* (2008). New Art Gallery, Walsall.

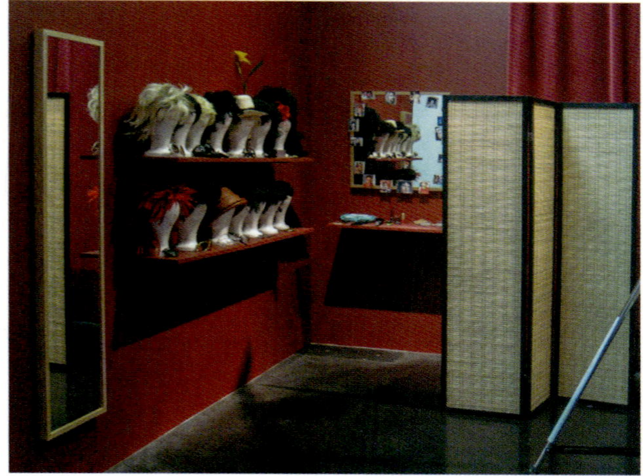

Jessica Voorsanger, *Stage Struck 2* (2008). New Art Gallery, Walsall.

 But you don't force anybody to get on stage and sing karaoke?

JV: Those are voluntary. It started with a piece called *Stage Struck* at the New Art Gallery, Walsall in 2008. I created a karaoke-style environment with a large stage, a karaoke system with disco lights, which was a response to changing values.

ID: *What was that?*

JV: I always believed that it was meant to be special and exciting, to be a fan. Something about the world of the fan meeting the world of the celebrity, either through watching their TV shows or seeing them in the street. I had become disillusioned with melding between reality and fantasy. I identified with a sentimental feeling that celebrity had stopped being something that was special and exciting, that gave you butterflies in your stomach, and it had turned into something tawdry.

ID: *What did you do?*

JV: I chose people who I thought deserved to be celebrities and made it so that we could pretend to be them. Playing on the Warhol 'fifteen minutes of fame' maxim, everyone has their opportunity so I chose a mix of celebrities – Kurt Cobain, George Harrison, Billy Idol, Michael Jackson from his 'Thriller' phase, David Hockney because I just love David Hockney, Morrissey, Amy Winehouse, Cher, Elvis, David Bowie, Siouxsie Sioux, Paul Weller.

ID: *So there were costumes to get dressed up in?*

JV: I had also painted portraits of them. I realized that if I was giving people costumes and allowing them to become somebody, I really had to give them something to do, and that was where the karaoke really played a part. Karaoke allows people who can't sing (like me) to perform; it's fun and when you've got a costume on you're not yourself anymore. There was also a film playing of people performing with interchangeable characters; for example, Elvis sings the Black Eyed Peas, and Amy Winehouse is singing the Monkees.

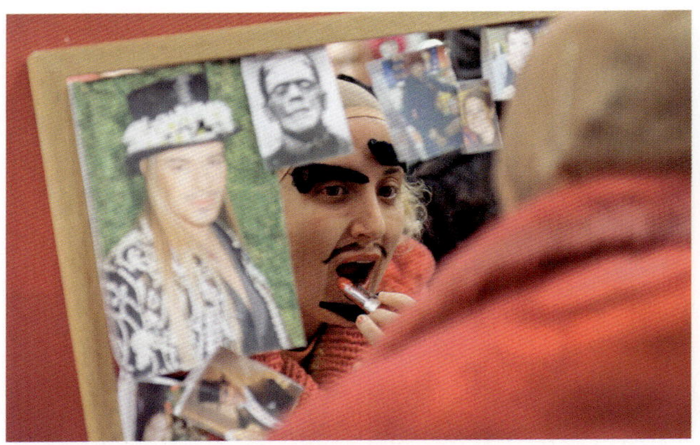

Jessica Voorsanger, *Peckham Heroes 1* (2011). Art Space.

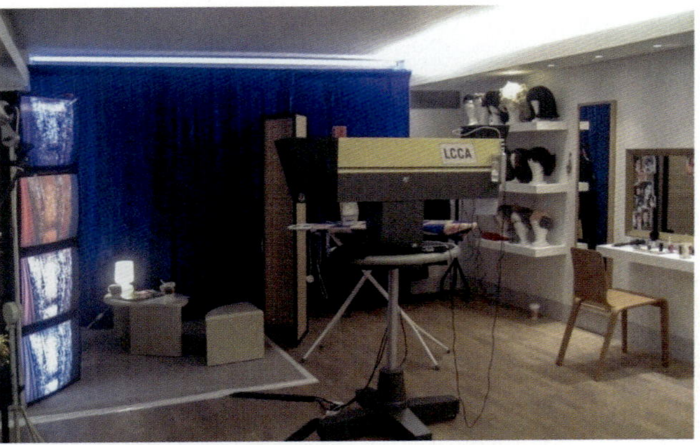

Jessica Voorsanger, *Eastenders 1* (2009). Whitechapel.

ID: *It seems to have become a total experience now.*

JV: It solidified all the different aspects of my practice, that one show – the painting, the costumes, the performance, the installation and the interactivity. When all of these things culminated into one piece, I realized, 'This is it!' Seeing the different school groups come to the show and seeing them, all running and putting the costumes on and taking pictures of one another on their phones was just brilliant.

ID: *You've continued with this.*

JV: In the Peckham space I embraced the actual nightclub setting, having a bar and tables as well as a stage and then at the Whitechapel I created a television studio as an environment for the audience to interact with.

ID: *How did that work?*

JV: It was done in the style of a television studio, so the viewer first walks past the portraits before the make-up section with the walls covered with costumes and accessories, wigs, glasses, earrings, necklaces. The penultimate area is the green room where participants wait to go on stage. Monitors were situated throughout the space broadcasting what was happening on stage, like in any TV studio.

ID: *These were local celebrities?*

JV: All from the London's East End: Honor Blackman, Dudley Moore, Alan Sugar, Barbara Windsor, David Beckham, Sandie Shaw. I selected theme songs. Alfred Hitchcock's was 'Psycho Killer', the Kray twins' was 'Stand and Deliver' by Adam and the Ants.

ID: *You enjoy the ethos of stand-up?*

JV: Funny you should say that, Bob and Roberta Smith and I were the lead artists for a show called *Hearing Voices Seeing Things*, exploring mental health at The Serpentine. I devised comedy sessions for the Day Centres where one in four people suffers from mental health issues. My exhibition became a stand-up show called *What's So Funny*. People would write jokes like: 'I went to the library the other day and I asked the librarian if he had any books on suicide and the librarian said no, because people used to borrow them and never return them.'

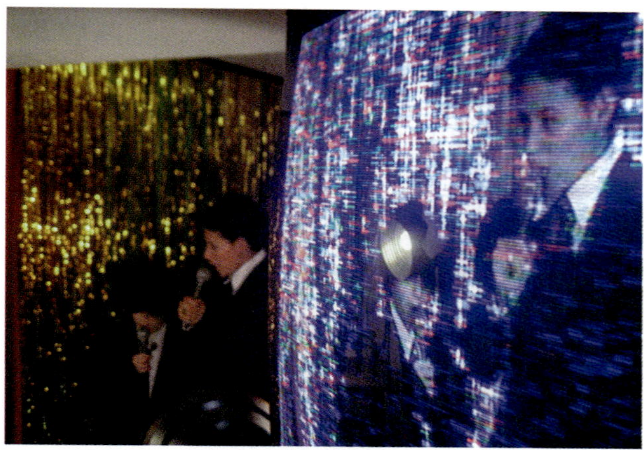

Jessica Voorsanger, *Eastenders 2* (2009). Whitechapel.

ID: *There is also always a humorous angle to the work.*

JV: Humour in artwork is interesting. It often provides a level of lightness that invites the audience to engage with it on a very different level. Using humour within my practice is a powerful tool, equally with intervention and interactivity. Especially when a family comes to an exhibition with disinterested kids. And they can't believe that they can get on stage and play and go through all this make-up and then the parents are enjoying their kids enjoying themselves in a place where they didn't expect to because they thought it would be serious. ∎

▶ Richard Woods

Richard Woods' work appears quickly, and is un-missable, transforming buildings and spaces into incongruous, alter-ego versions of themselves.

These interventions might even be considered parasitic; they piggyback on pre-existing structures, his printed patterned veneers clinging to buildings like second skin. Like any parasite they are aware of the importance of the host. Woods will often impose a contradictory style: cladding an exaggerated crazy paving pattern across a Venetian piazza or covering a historic Oxford building with a red brick façade.

These juxtapositions have both a hand-made and cartoon quality, asserting their difference to the existing environment, ensuring they remain ideologically separate entities. Woods, who also collaborates with furniture designer Sebastian Wong, in order that his surfaces are able to ride on smaller structures, is creating an ever-expanding series of floors. Called *Logo*, they are striking wood-patterned flooring, which, by becoming ever more ubiquitous, continue to excite Woods in the way that they visually democratize a host of different spaces.

I speak to Richard in the paint-splattered surrounding of his studio.

IAN DAWSON: *So I'm interested in how you make your work.*

RICHARD WOODS: My working methods are based on a kind of pragmatism, of trying to find the cheapest and easiest way to cover something. So the way I work in the studio is just an extension of that really. All of the stuff that goes on in the studio is about finding the most efficient and simplest way to achieve something.

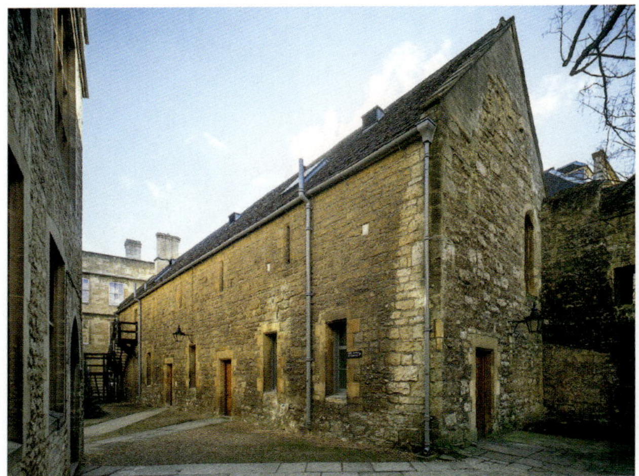

Richard Woods, The Long Room, New College, Oxford – *New Build* (before).

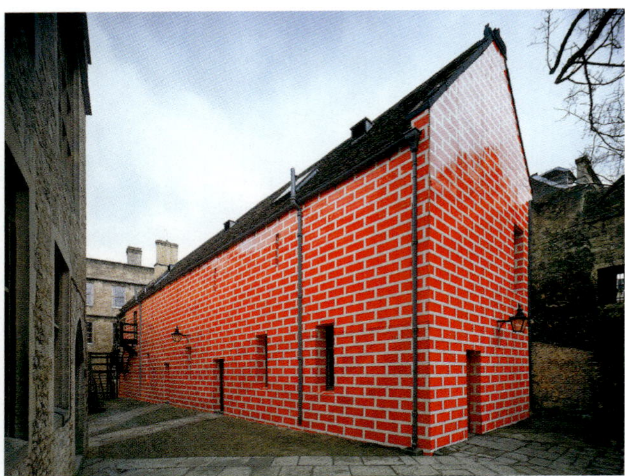

Richard Woods, *New Build* (2005). New College, Oxford, commissioned in association with the Ruskin School of Drawing and Fine Art, University of Oxford.

 This economy is the key thing?

RW: Definitely. I suppose for me there is a kind of poetry to that. I like to keep everything here as opposed to getting other producers or manufacturers to make it. And then with it all being here, I like the idea that I find the simplest way to make the work.

ID: *What is important about maintaining those in-house qualities?*

RW: Well, all art has a practical side at one end and a conceptual side at the other, and the only thing that varies is how far along that line they meet. So for me what's really interesting is how that object can change because of the practical constraints that go with it. For some artists the making aspect can be a kind of hindrance to realizing their idea. But when I set out to make a piece of work, I want to make it here in the studio, precisely so that sometimes it comes out looking really different to the original idea. Because I work with the limitations of a small studio, for example, this ensures that the solutions I arrive at have an intrinsic bearing on the work.

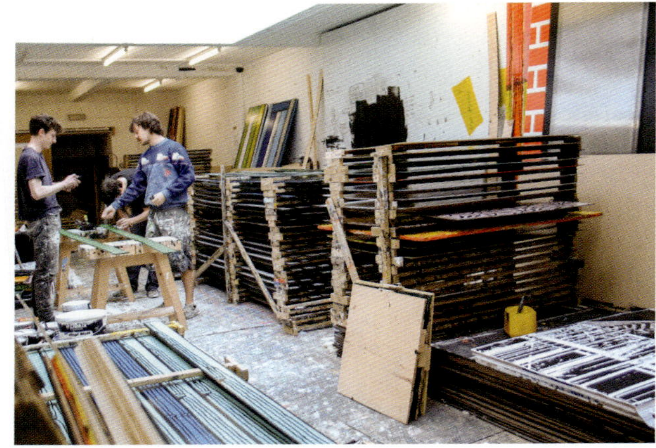

Richard Woods' studio.

ID: *So how is the studio set up?*

RW: I have a wood shop, then an office and a print studio and that's it basically. I find it easier that the ideas happen in here [the office] and you kind of make them in there [the studio]. I didn't always do that; I used to have it all in one but I found that was too confusing – a little bit what we're talking about. That the objects are the way they are because they're a meeting point between the idea and the practical way that they can be realized. Doing it this way, it keeps it kind of cleaner.

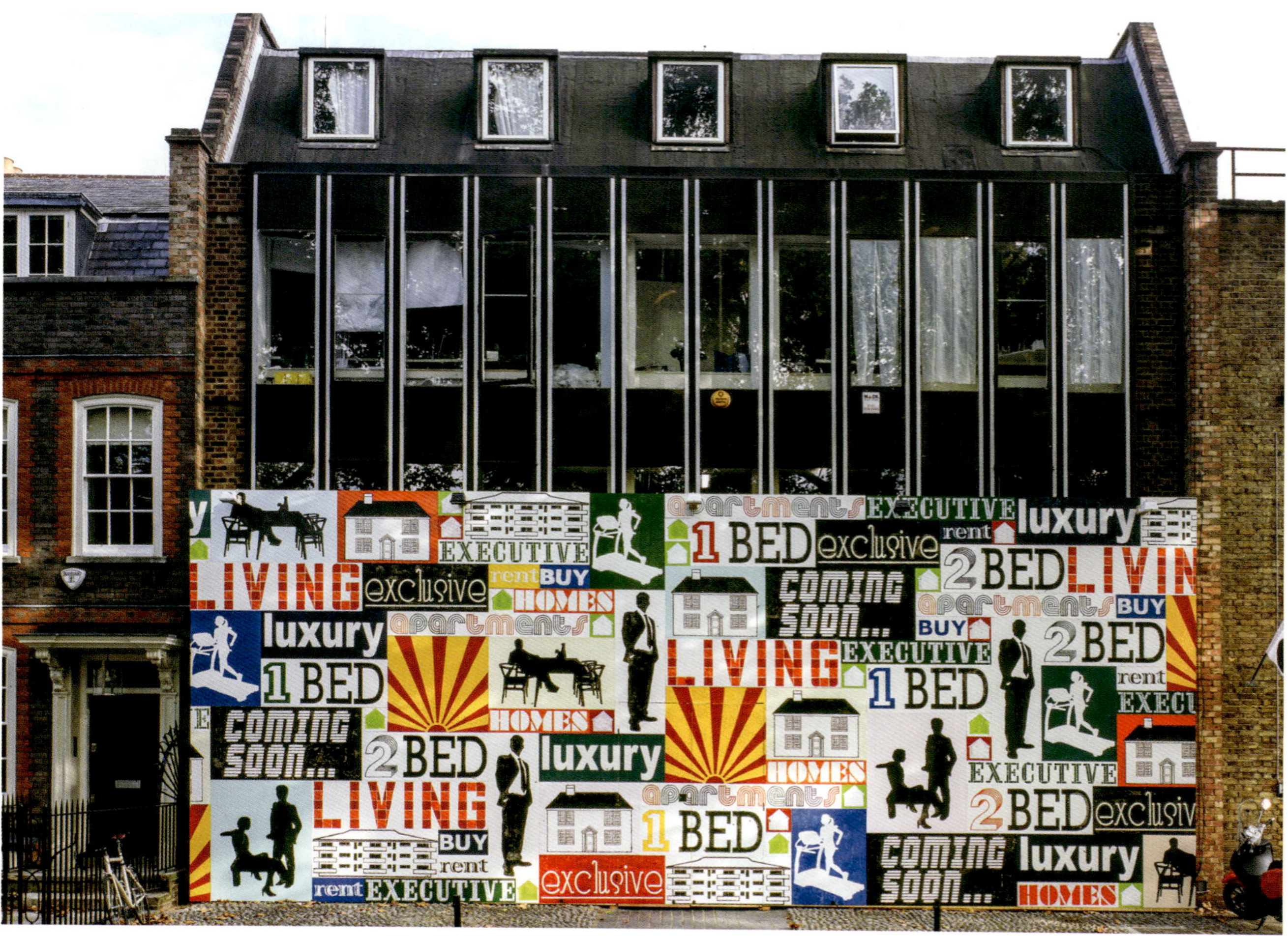

Richard Woods, *Exclusive Luxury Living.*

ID: *It's like a cottage industry.*

RW: I think it's about keeping something where you've still got control over it. I like the idea that you do these enormous things and people come here and think, 'Is this it?' Because they imagine that you'd have some massive base on an industrial estate.

ID: *You could almost go back to using your garage at home!*

RW: Definitely – that would be brilliant if I could do that. You could just literally make a skyscraper-sized piece of work with just a roller. I can't quite do that, but it's not far off.

ID: *I imagine these large projects are quite a feat.*

RW: I'm really interested in that notion, the romance of doing a big project. There has always been an element of that throughout art history and I think that it's a shame that maybe that's perceived with some negativity now. I think the idea of somebody undertaking a big, outrageously physical act is really interesting for an artist.

As an extension to that I try to ensure that the exterior cladding goes up really fast so that somebody is wandering down the street on one day and there's nothing there and suddenly they come by again and this whole building has been transformed. And that it disappears equally as quickly, so it behaves like a little bit of guerrilla activity.

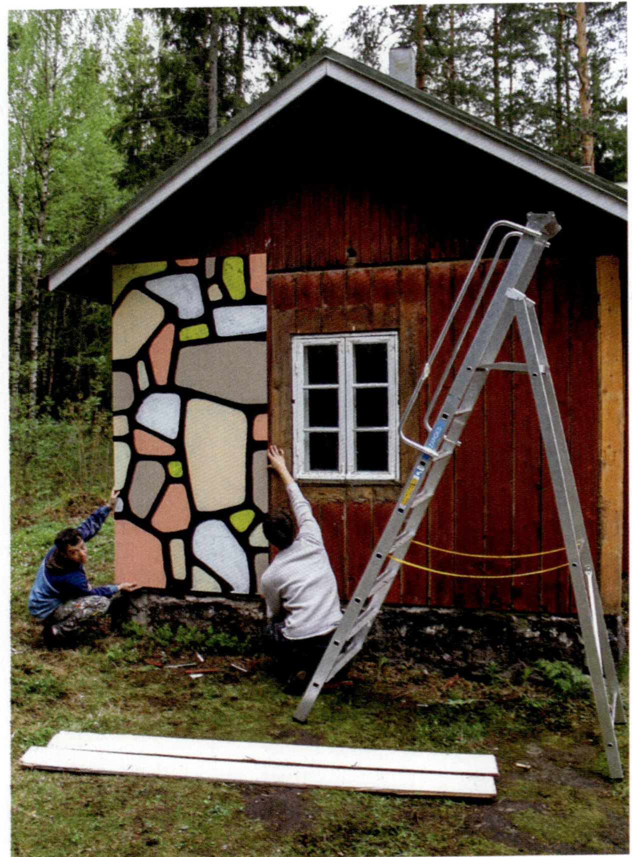

Richard Woods, *Stone-clad Cottage* installation 1.

libraries and shops and in bars and in cafés, because it is like a kind of democracy. I really like the fact that one might be in an ice-cream shop and another in a collector's house. Some people might have a problem with that, but I think it's really interesting.

ID: *How did you begin to develop this way of printing and cladding?*

RW: I've always been interested in stuff that borders on the practical, and about twelve years ago I started painting on lino and on carpet and I found that I was painting on them because it was a way of re-playing with the surface of those objects. And I got to a point where I thought, actually, the lino is more interesting than what I was doing to it, so I suppose I thought, 'How do I make my own lino?'

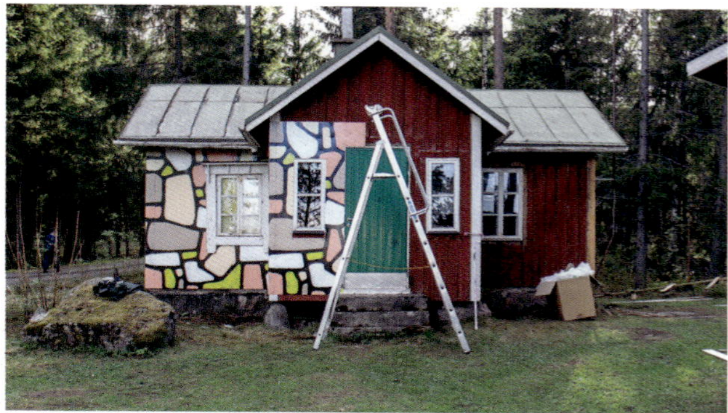

Richard Woods, *Stone-clad Cottage* installation 2.

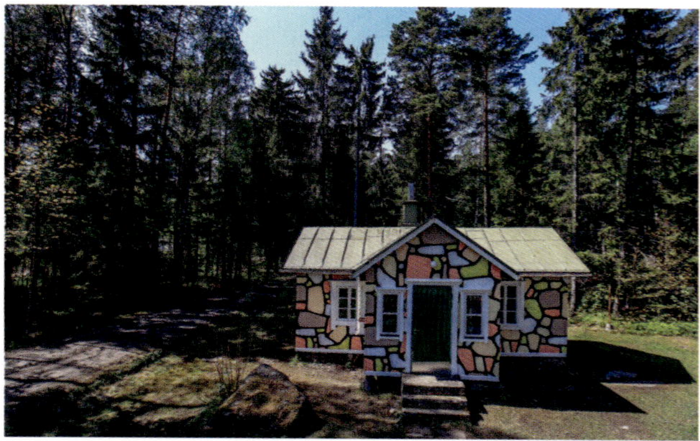

Richard Woods, *Stone-clad Cottage* (2008).

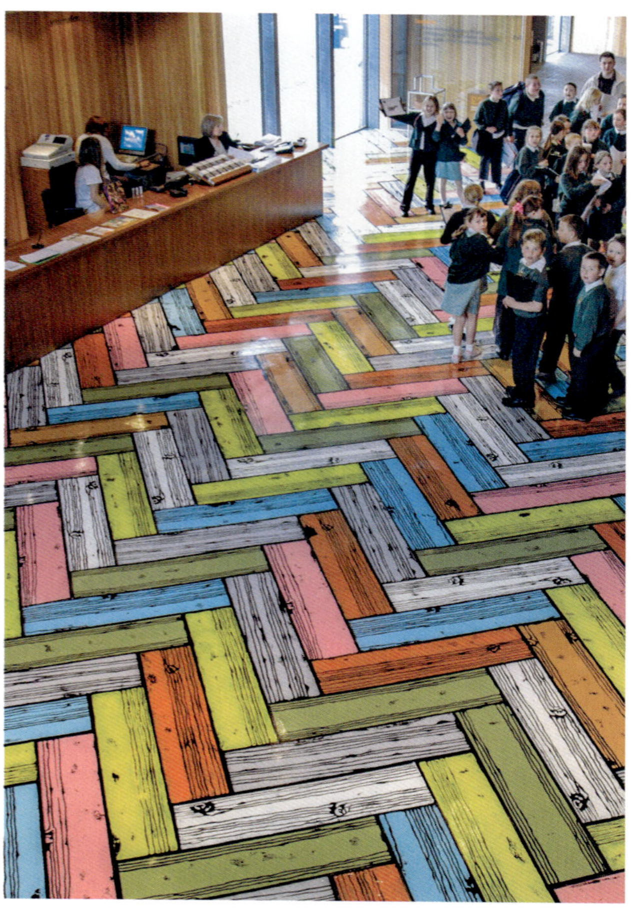

Richard Woods, *Logo No. 14*, The New Art Gallery, Walsall.

RW: I felt much more comfortable when the process became more industrial again, a way of making my own flooring. I have said that it would be great if I could get the wooden floors (*Logos*) into B&Q, just sell them literally as real floors.

ID: *Yet the stuff remains so obviously handmade.*

RW: I want it to have a very craft-based reference; I don't necessarily need it to be made by me but the aesthetic is very particular. I also find the concept of DIY interesting – it's people's way of relating to the places where they live. So it is an artistic outlet isn't it? And that's fascinating. It's like cave-painting, people just wanting to put a mark on their habitat, so this has been a spectacle for a lot longer than people have wanted to hang pictures in galleries. So it's an interesting fascination, for me, that in a very sort of basic way we all share a need to make the place that we live reflect what we are. DIY, like art, reflects our aspirations but with different social pressures attached.

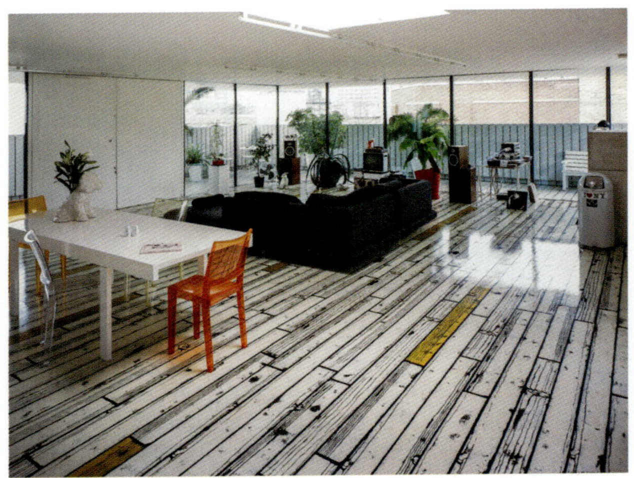

Richard Woods, *Logo No. 10* (2004). Commissioned by Tim Noble and Sue Webster for Dirty House, London.

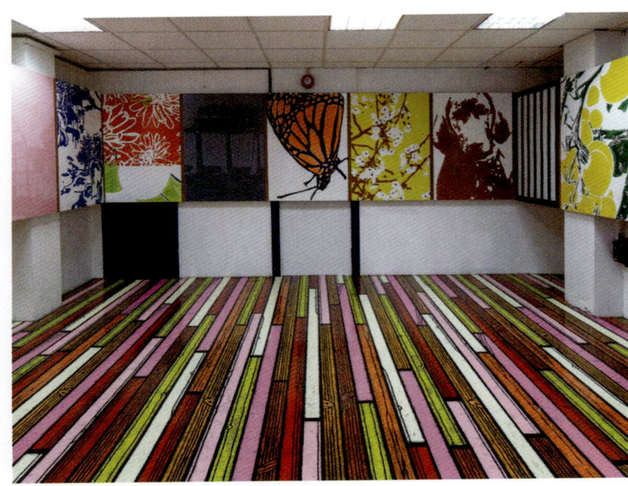

Richard Woods, *Logo No. 91, Nice Life 3* (Dover Street 2009).

RW: I'm really interested in these things being kind of ubiquitous. I've always had a problem with the relationship the art world has with design. The reality is that it is mostly a market-led thing – most galleries don't like design because it's cheaper than art so they don't make as much money out of it. But I really like the idea that you can have an artwork that exists in that way. History will dictate whether it was of any interest or not. The notion we have of where art should sit is only really a hundred years old. It's a tiny, little blip in time, it's only since 1910 that art galleries have had white walls – this orthodoxy didn't exist before then. Where art goes into the real world, I find that really interesting.

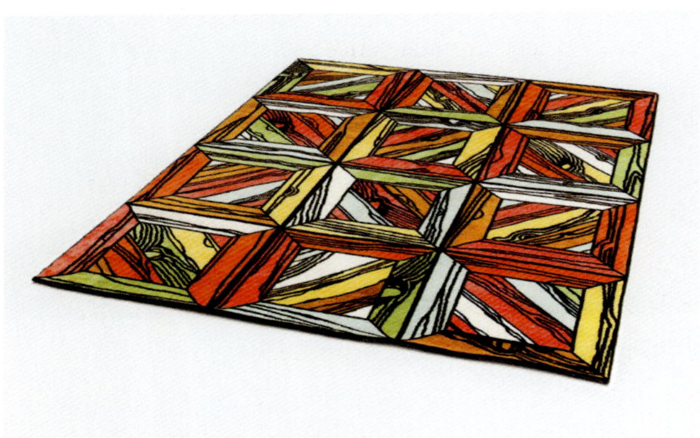

Richard Woods, *Wood Rug* (2010). In collaboration with Established & Sons.

ID: *And the future?*

RW: The art that people make is a result of the economic situation of that particular time, so the kind of thing that's happened over the last thirty years is to do with the stock market. So even in twenty or thirty years' time, the model of what artists do will change dramatically – I don't know how it will change, but it will. As I say, it's only been in the last hundred years or so that we have had art galleries. Before that people made stuff in churches. So it's not beyond the bounds of possibility that current art practice will be looked at as part of an economic blip and art will just go back to being public. What is crazy is the perception that the model that's developed in the last hundred years is the model that will always exist – that's kind of absurd.

ID: *Your interest in design seems to also be apparent with the imagery that you choose to print with.*

RW: I think all of the work is embedded in a kind of local vernacular for me. So some of it is memory-led from childhood; some is just stuff that I kind of pick up along the way. There is very little that anyone will find alien – I like to print stuff that is already common or already exists and just reflect it back.

ID: *Are there ever any issues with planning?*

RW: As long as something doesn't exist for more than three months, you don't have any really – you just do it. So most of the things I do, I don't have to have planning. In my experience, it's best not to apply for planning; you just do it and if people get really upset you just tell them it's only for three months. And then if people are okay about it, you can always extend it. I mean it's not a permanent thing is it?

ID: *I guess you're just decorating something.*

RW: Quite often these things are the things that the planners might refuse, but once they're in reality, once they're existing, then people seem quite happy about it. I can't really make art via countless planning stages; I would never be able to do anything. There has to be an element of arrogance involved in it, otherwise whatever you wanted to do would be vetted by other people's taste and I think for all of this stuff, it's important that it's not.

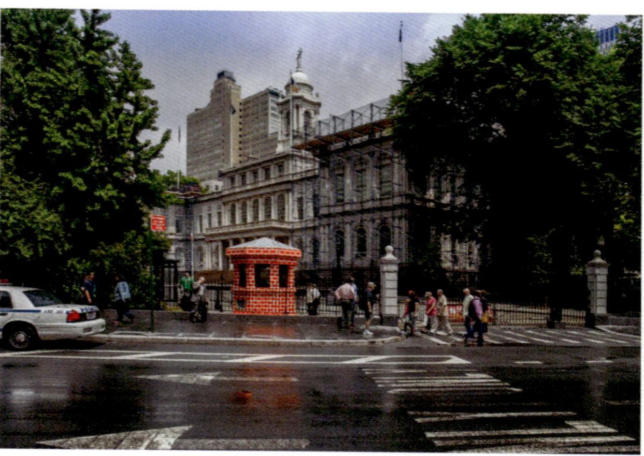

Richard Woods, *Wall And Door And Roof* (2009). City Hall Park, New York.

ID: *Have there ever been any times when things haven't gone right?*

RW: Well it's weird isn't it – whenever you do anything in public, it's always horrifying and terrifying for various reasons; whenever you build you never really know how visually successful it's going to be until you do it. It's quite an aggressive act in lots of ways, to do it and to make something that's so huge, that's so public and so visible; often it's quite uncomfortable. The piece at NY City Hall (2009) became embroiled in a political argument over public funding and we ended up attracting outrage, and the piece became a visual tag in the media for specific issues at the time. And that was purely because it appeared at a certain time, and that's the interesting thing about art in public – the way somebody will perceive it on one day, if the weather is good or they've had a bad day or it's raining, or there's a political storm – you can't control that. So I made this thing, I came up with this idea sitting here in one kind of world that I exist in and then it was installed in New York six months later in a very different political climate; something happens and suddenly this piece became enmeshed in this completely different situation.

ID: *That is interesting, that the timing of a public intervention is so powerful.*

RW: If you do something on the street, it's completely laying itself open to not only politics, but the political climate at that time. So it's kind of the way that everything is read goes through a filter of what's in the newspaper that day. The *Angel of the North* wasn't of much interest to anybody until somebody put a football shirt on it, and then suddenly the context of it changed, and people became really comfortable with it and it's become the symbol of what's great about public art. But it could've really easily been everything that we think is really bad about public art – if it had been installed now, everyone might well have hated it. And that's interesting.

ID: *Do you ever have leeway when you're installing?*

RW: It's always pretty much what it is. I don't really allow much. I suppose I can change bits, but often when we're completely cladding a building you think it would be interesting to leave it a bit unfinished – that's a different thing; I like to follow through and do the building as the drawing was. A different aesthetic consideration would happen and it's best if I don't let that take over.

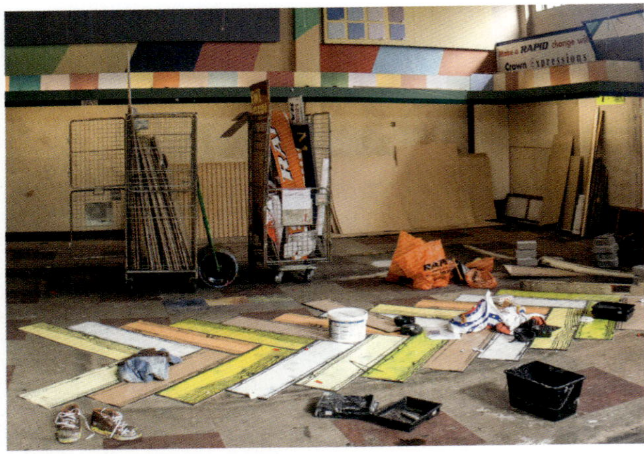

Richard Woods, installation shot 1.

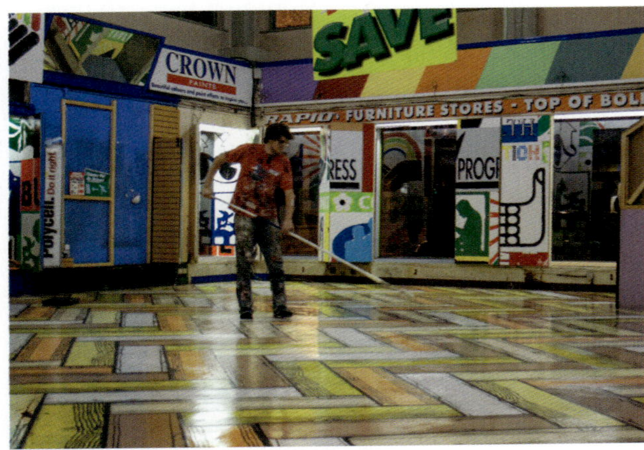

Richard Woods, installation shot 2.

ID: *Sometimes there is an urge to do that?*

RW: Definitely – there's a kind of an art aesthetic thing that I'm kind of wary of. Of finding this bit or that bit interesting, and saying I'll leave that – but the idea of the piece of work is a different thing, so it's not that one's right and one's wrong, it's just that I don't ever have an idea where I'm going to leave half of it with the bit sticking out. So it's back to that notion first discussed: the difference between the object and the idea – and I want these things to be the way I've most efficiently done the idea.

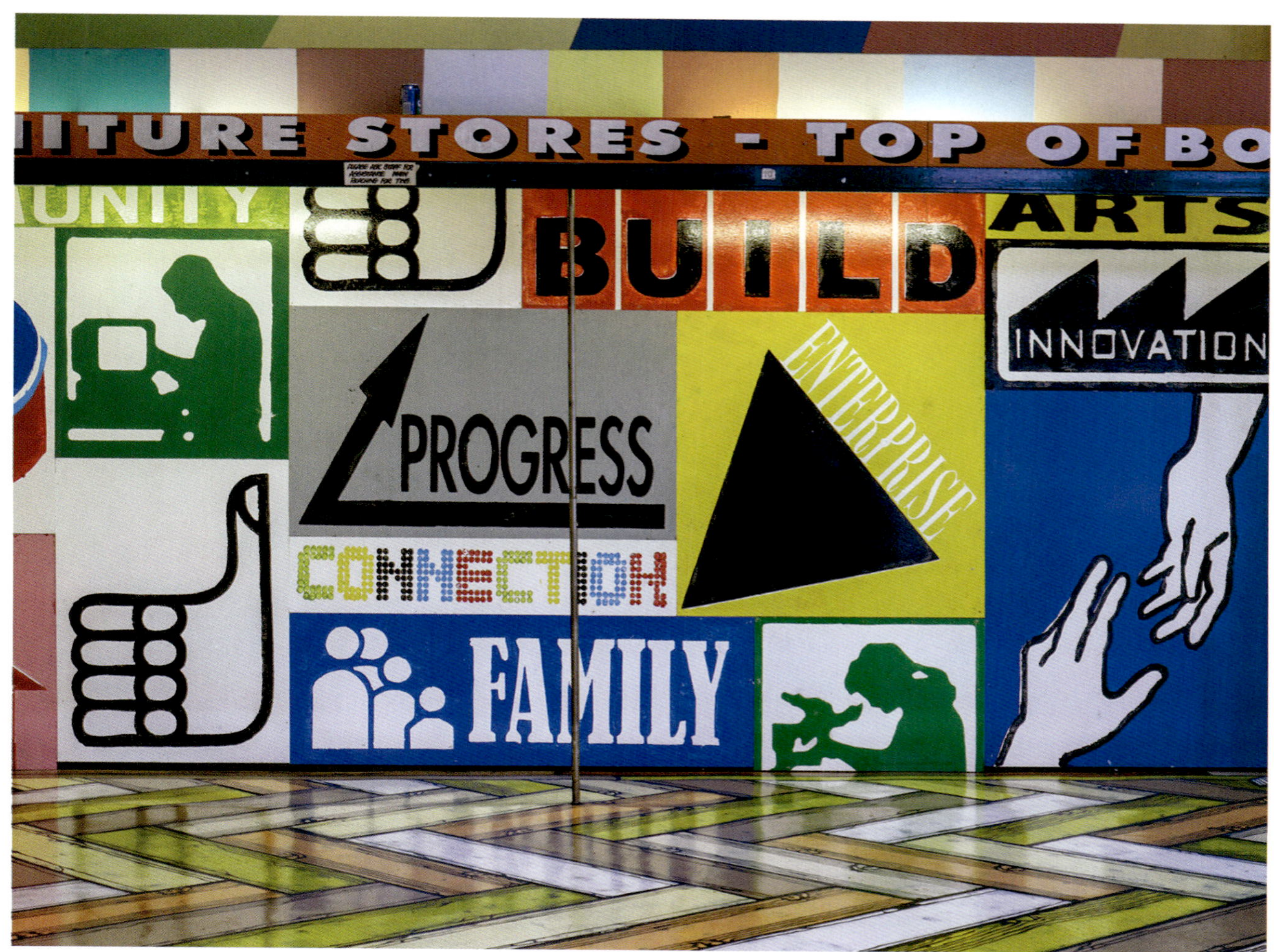

Richard Woods, *Innovation–investment–progress* (2008). The Old Paint Shop, Liverpool, commissioned by Liverpool Biennal International '08.

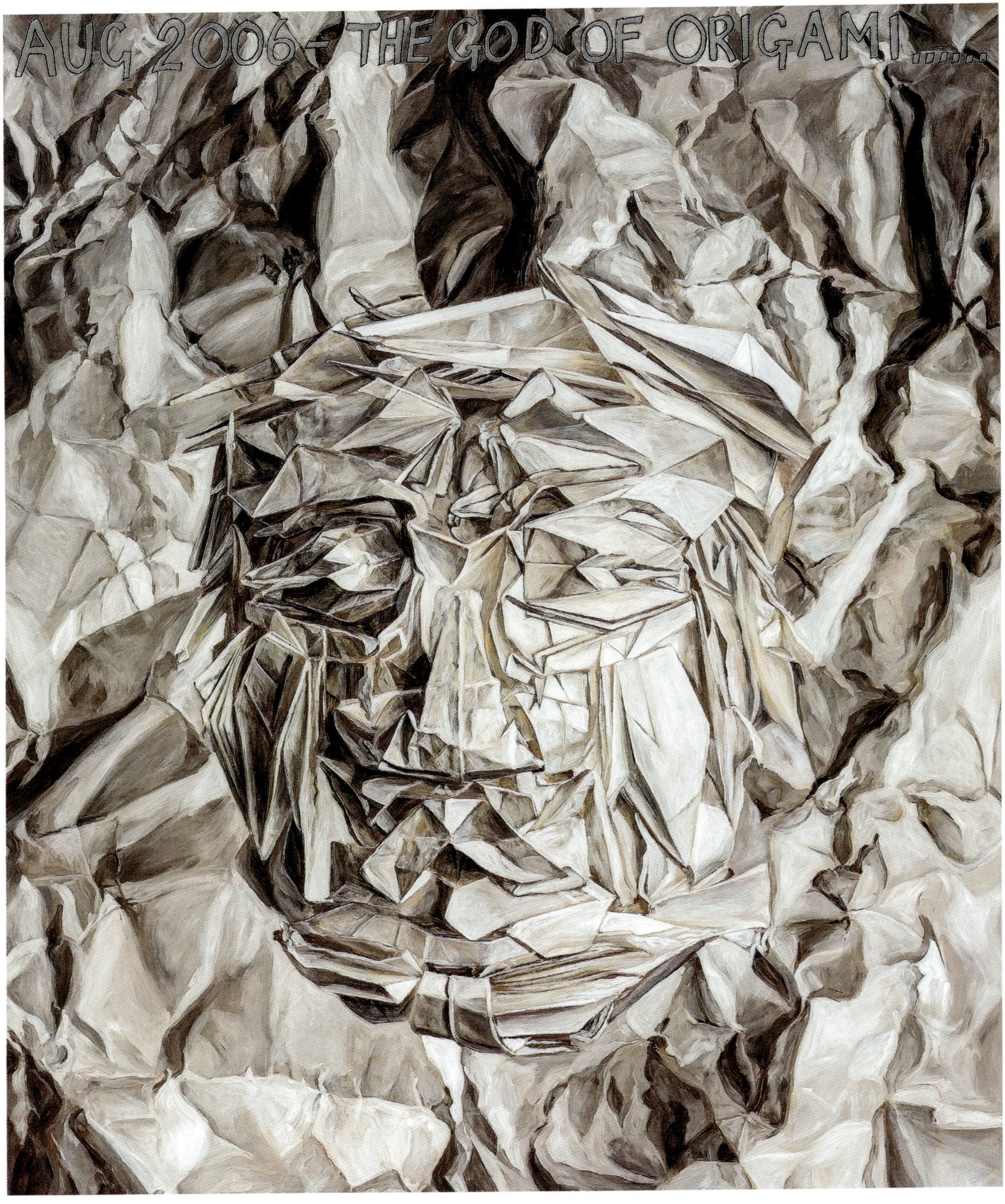
AUG 2006 - THE GOD OF ORIGAMI......

6 The Plan

Take a newspaper.
Take some scissors.
Choose an article of the length you wish your poem
to have.
Cut out the article.
Then cut out carefully each of the words in the
article and put them in a bag.
Shake gently.
Then pull out each cutting one after the other.
Copy them down conscientiously in the order in
which they left the bag.
The poem will resemble you.
And you will be the writer of infinite originality and
of charming sensitivity, although incomprehensible
to the masses.

In 1920 Tristan Tzara read out his plan for making poetry at Francis Picabia's Paris Exhibition. It describes the extent to which artists had embraced the accident within their work. Constructing an image that appeared coincidental had occurred in paintings depicting the hubbub of a peasant crowd or of a teeming tavern scene, for example; then cubism began to depict accidental relationships as subject matter; and the next step was to use the accident as an actual principle.

Working unpredictably allowed for a gap to exist between intention and outcome, and has been a crucial feature in making art. By allowing the unintended into their work, artists have destroyed old aesthetic habits and created new patterns of perception. There has been a receptive attitude towards the use of chance which has resonated with changing views of the world; in physics Heisenberg's uncertainty principle broke the deterministic hypothesis of the physical universe, and in psychology Jung's theory of synchronicity brought an interest in grouping simultaneous yet accidental events together.

The use of chance became a way to access an order beyond the ideas advanced by causal and logical thought.

Take infinite masses.
Conscientiously of a cutting
Then bag.
After the take of incomprehensible
Have words one newspaper.
Gently. Originality
Although the order which then charming
Carefully choose sensitivity,
Writer be copy them
them will wish poem
An you shake will your down
Poem to other.
Of the article a bag
The in the each pull article.
To in and the cut the and in length scissors.
You.
Resemble of and out some they put in
Left out you the each the out the article.

OPPOSITE PAGE
Keith Tyson, studio wall drawing: *The God of Origami*
(August 2006).

In 1991 Keith Tyson constructed the Artmachine; it comprised an expanding set of flow charts and diagrams, and these algorithms presented him with a complex set of instructions by which to make his work. This apparatus would formulate all the decisions: medium, scale, style, composition, title, even the time required to make the piece.

Over the next decade Tyson was the fabricator of the iterations thrown up by this mechanism. Many remain as yet unmade: proposals such as the 'Scubasculpture' coded AMCHII.XXXVI – a steel and iron sculpture destined for a sixteen-year gestation period on the sea bed, before being raised and renovated. In 1996 the Artmachine's painting algorithm directed him to make *An Emergency Meeting of the Doughnut Assembly* and forced Tyson to depict the scene described in the title. In this piece a bizarre congress of cast rubber rings on stands (the doughnuts) surround a central wall-mounted effigy (the guest speaker), whilst paint spews down tubes and along wooden conveyors (the dumping ballot), the proceedings illuminated from the side by a configuration of fluorescent lights (the sugar fucker). This was the Artmachine at its most utterly diverse and aesthetically unrestricted.

Here I interview Tyson about his practice.

IAN DAWSON: *How does the work happen?*

KEITH TYSON: I think that's the correct way of talking about it. I've always thought of myself as on the peripheries of invention and discovery; I discover systems from the world in order to have a dialogue with it through the work.

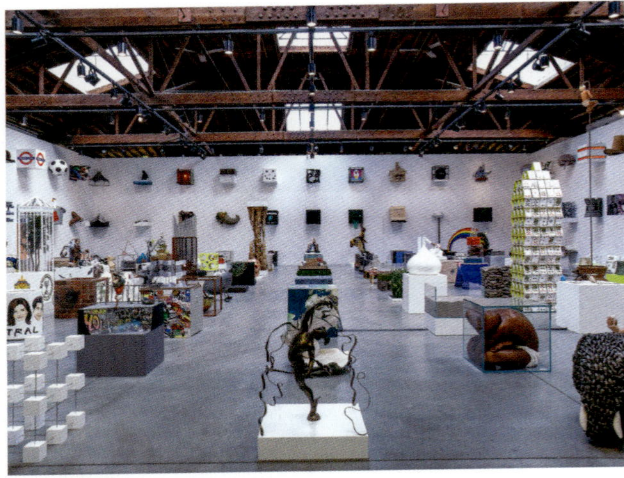

Keith Tyson, *Large Field Array* installation shot.

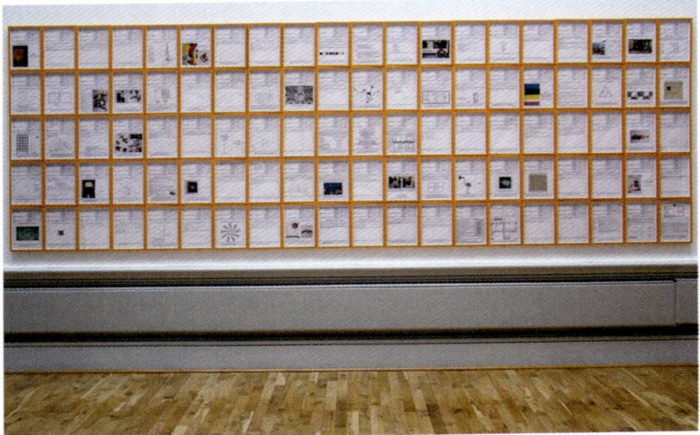

Keith Tyson, 100 original *Artmachine Iteration* sheets (1994).

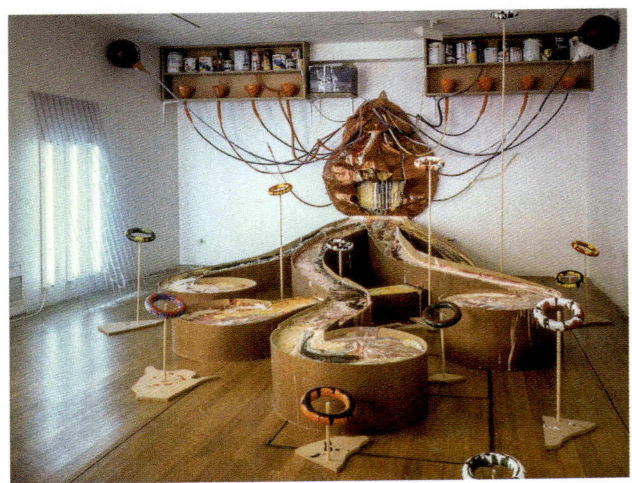

Keith Tyson, *Artmachine Iteration: Emergency meeting at the doughnut assembly* (1997).

ID: *How does that manifest itself?*

KT: Normally I have a system in play where the work sort of makes itself; it describes what it wants to be according to initial rules and I think my role is often about setting those parentheses on what something can be. Those rules can be very loose: just 'express the last fifty nightmares you remember'. Something else might be extremely precise, like 'take Conway's cellular automata (a mathematical kind of game) and generate x number of iterations that will form sculptures', and that would be a very strict way with no human interaction and interpretation. And I just play around in those spaces and try and create something as a whole body of work that will eventually represent something of what it is like to be an artist of this time in a time flooded with images, a complex, multifaceted world.

ID: *I noticed the number of encyclopaedias and books you have around the studio that you must plunder from.*

KT: Well, we're sitting in a room filled with catalogues, but it is more like a subconscious backdrop because who knows how an idea comes into being. You could argue that I think something up but thought is a bit like sweat. When you go on a run your brain starts thinking stuff like, 'you should stop, this hurts, this is stupid, what are you on this run for', and it is all just like emotional sweat, and I think that the brain, the mind, some might say the soul, has a lot more wisdom than that and it understands something in a really non-linear way, and the thoughts that come up are just a kind of narrative, it surfaces like sweat on the top. So you think I'm going to do something, this is my thought but who knows the machinations that have been going on underneath, subconsciously. So I have always taken the approach of putting myself in an environment that is highly stimulating, to take it all

in. And when you put yourself in that place something happens, and you know when it's right, and that's the bit that is mysterious about being an artist: you just know when it's right and it's like a seam of clarity through all this mess and you think, 'That's what I'm going to do.' And then you get this rush because all that potential energy gets focused into a process of making something. And even the process of making it, those rules that are there, they're not really expressed either, *it's* just got a rightness about it. That's it done. And then you feel totally depressed; you sit around waiting for the next sparkling thing to hit you.

ID: *How often does this happen? I imagine a sparkling thought hits you quite often.*

KT: Very few amazing thoughts; I have a lot of thoughts a day. I have lots of things going on which may or may not turn into something good. For instance at the moment I am fascinated with the idea of a matrix, a grid of so many by so many, and how they fit together and how the compound conglomeration of those individual images will work and compose itself in terms of the overall structure. But I don't know where that's going, so at the moment I just have some small paintings of images that I think will start the process. And then at some point I might realize that image (A) actually doesn't fit with what I want it to do anymore, and actually I want a lot tighter rule on it, and eventually the rule itself will manifest itself and I will know what it is.

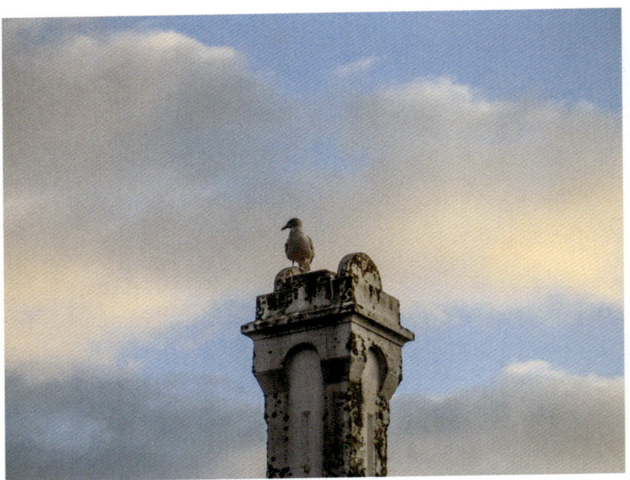

Seagull.

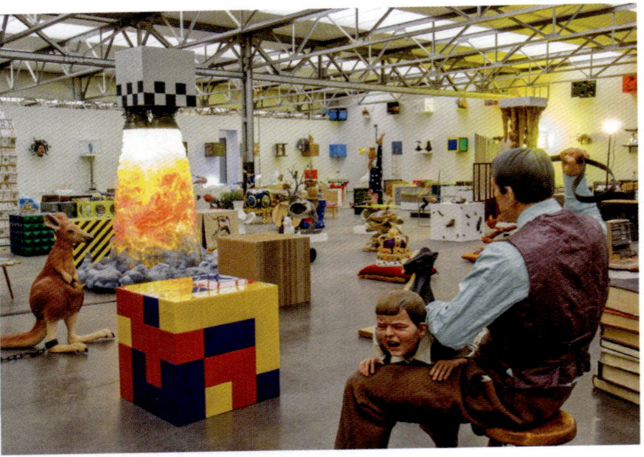

Keith Tyson, *Large Field Array* (detail).

ID: *Is that what happened with the* Large Field Array?

KT: When I made that I knew it was going to be about mass and complexity, and I had all these ideas of what I wanted of the complexity and the subtlety of what I wanted to put into this piece. But everything has to start with a single step, so I had to start with something. I looked out of my window and there was a seagull on top of a chimney pot and I thought, 'That's kind of a cube. I will make a cube out of brick with a chimney pot on it with a stuffed seagull on top and a satellite dish and we will see where we go from there.' And the next one came along, and all of a sudden you recognize that there are associations to satellite imagery and slowly the internal logic of the thing begins to portray itself.

ID: *How many pieces were you thinking of introducing?*

KT: Originally I thought I was going to make 1,200 objects. That would have been insane, in terms of production, but that's what I set off thinking. I was thinking about pixels on an image, I was thinking like a solid static object lies about itself because it kind of has a sense of what it is. It's not embodied: it's disembodied as an object. Or at least that was what modernism tried to proclaim, but I wanted to put some of the dynamism into sculpture, in a way – how do you make sculpture into film and there are things you can do with multiple objects that you can't do with one object. So as soon as you put two things together they begin to define themselves by their difference. So *Large Field Array* was really about creating space and relationships.

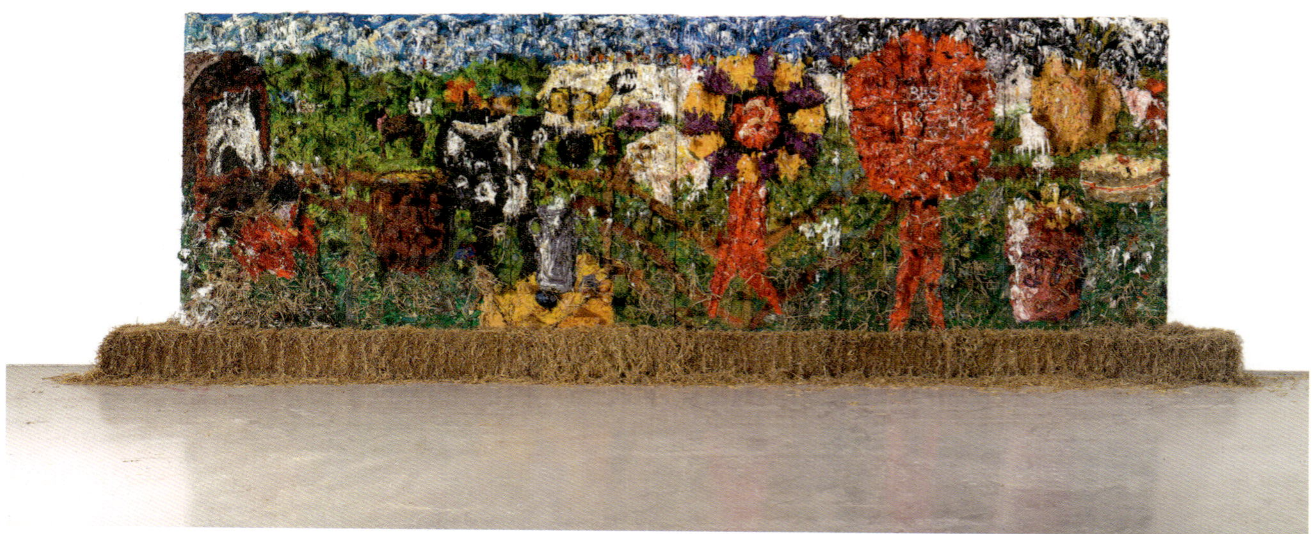

Keith Tyson, *Artmachine Iteration: Country Fair with Prize Tent.*

ID: *And there were 300 objects, all 2 feet apart.*

KT: What I liked was that firstly the work was bigger than you. I don't mean just like an installation and you just entered it; I mean it was bigger than you because the human mind can think about so many elements at once. It was bigger than you, bigger than me, I couldn't hold on to it in my mind. I think my breaking point was about 160 objects, and it kind of cracked and I could no longer hold onto it. Even with 160 objects I still had a sense of balancing it. But then it developed its own dynamic and that moment – the breaking point when something just un-tethers itself from your control and becomes a dialogue with you – that is the magical bit. You are doing it for that moment, this magical moment when you think the work is wanting this and you are wanting it, and you are in dynamic flow. That is the bit you live for: the process, and it's relatively short lived, but it's that moment when it suddenly becomes bigger than you and it's telling you what it wants to be and you are kind of following orders from something you have thought up. I imagine it is like the Buddhist who talks about breathing: are you controlling the breathing or is the breathing controlling you?

ID: *How long did the project take?*

KT: Ages in terms of thinking up the idea, maybe five years before I even started it, and then when I started actually physically producing it, it was relatively quick – I got a lot of people involved. At certain points I had up to a hundred people working on it in different places. It took about two years to make. I think if one person had done it would have taken a hundred years, in terms of man-hours. I tend to think about things in man-hours; whether it is myself or someone else, it is how many man-hours have gone into it. So it took two years, or in man-hours, a hundred years. I guess the truth is somewhere between those two.

KT: The Artmachine was the most clumsy and literal version of what I am saying. I hadn't worked out that the world was a machine, but really I was looking for the philosophical understanding of how you produce something. I was at an art school dominated by post-structuralism, and the death of the author. And I am a stubborn sod. So I thought, if that's the case, if the text generates everything and there are no authors, then I will just invent a machine that uses text and information from the world to create artworks, then we can all sit around and look at them. I wasn't saying it was good, I wasn't saying it was bad, I wasn't championing technology or offering a critique; for me it was just a philosophical experiment. I just said, if I create a device that can come up with ideas – seemingly the most precious human part of making art – if I can automate that, create a ready-made for the idea and choice, how will people view those things?

ID: *You made works from this device.*

KT: It was kind of interesting because I would get these instructions and they would be almost good. It would ask for something and it would be almost a beautiful idea, but then it would require, for example, that a motorway cone be stuck in the middle of a piece and that would just spoil it. So part of me felt upset that I was rigidly adhering to these rules, but for me it was a philosophical experiment. Even though I did Artmachine pieces for a few years I kind of see it as one piece of work. You have to remember that the Internet hadn't fully developed then either.

ID: *And its similarity to the Internet?*

KT: I guess if I was an art student today, I could go to Google, and construct an arbitrary sort of system for creating really diverse work. It is not far from what the Artmachine was; at the time I used dictionaries, books, and I had algorithms written out as flow charts – stuff that I followed meticulously and I made the stuff. But everybody wanted to see the machine and I thought, they've missed the point really. Who cares if you see the machine, what will that achieve? I still have it, though.

ID: *It must have been liberating to be freed from the angst of decision-making.*

KT: It seemed that way, but you were still making decisions. You sat there going, 'OK, I've made three thousand proposals, now which ones am I going to build?' And of course if it says make the Eiffel Tower out of jelly, life-size, it's like, a) physically it can't be done, and b) it's very expensive, and c) does the world need it? So then it tests your commitment to this philosophical argument. I also didn't want to set myself a conceptual strategy and pursue it till I'm dead. The idea of controlling the future and how I might feel and sticking to one thing; although that might be simple and help people who need that, it had run its course. And I thought, I'm not learning anything anymore from this, and if I'm not learning anything how is anyone else going to? I had started thinking about the mind being something similar really.

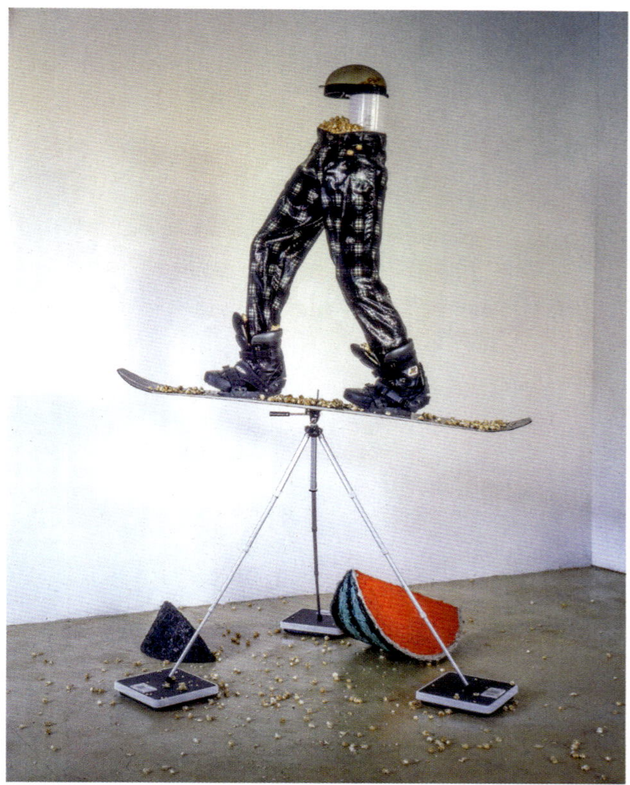

Keith Tyson, *Artmachine Iteration: Bay City Pop Colossus, Bulimic Still Life with Melons*.

ID: *Are you still building a lexicon?*

KT: No I don't think I'm doing that. The work is emerging. That might sound really slight, but it took me ages to be able to say that. It's emerging from something really complex, and that's the collision of my autobiographical history, of my desires, of art history and with process and rules, and I find that endlessly fascinating. I did a painting the other day of the moon on the back of a playing card. And the question I always ask is, 'How did this painting come into being?' So that moon pictured on the back of that card for it to look the way it looks, a designer somewhere decided on that photograph being on the back of that playing card; not only that, but when my paint moves in an arc to represent a crater on the moon, a piece of rock had to have hit the moon 40 million years ago at a precise speed and that's the reason my brush has moved that

way on the canvas as much as all my conceptual ideas and everything else.

I think human beings have a myopic focus: they focus all the time on objects and things and the artist's job has often been to widen that perspective. The world to me is a network of amazingly intricate, beautiful interdependent systems, and that's what I am trying to represent and if I were going to make just one thing didactically, then I wouldn't be representing it. The way I make work is the same as what I am trying to depict. That's why I have lots of different systems, and lots of different types of work and the style changes. It's not to be facetious or clever or say, 'I'm the guy who doesn't have a style'. It's because that's what I'm interested in. 'Interested' is too small a word, that's what I find wondrous about living in the world.

ID: *So in a way you are trying to describe the implausibility of life.*

KT: Any child will tell you, when you give them a pack of new pens and a white piece of paper, the excitement of potential – they could create anything on this, it could be anything. And then all that excitement and risk during the process of making an artwork changes and suddenly you have certitude and less risk, you have lost the potential. There is ultimately the disappointment that it is whatever it is, because no matter how beautiful it is, it's still one thing instead of anything. And that's the transition every artist experiences and I want to leave a little bit of the smell of the potential in whatever gets resolved, so that somehow you know it could have turned out different, whether it is because there is a rule or it is something random, so you think that this could have looked different. And I am trying to keep some of this excitement in the result. Not all art should be like this but mine should be.

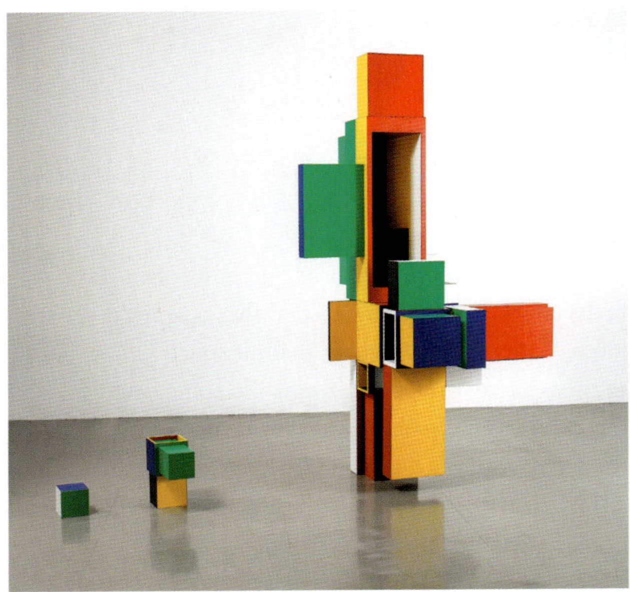

Keith Tyson, *Fractal Die – First Roll* (2005–08). Aluminium and plastic, 1756 × 1000 × 2804mm.

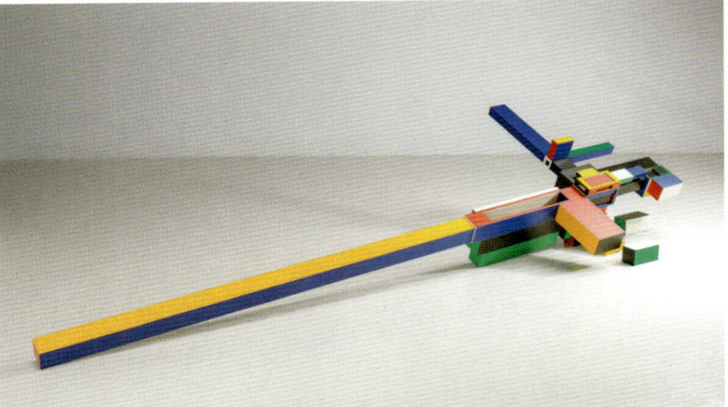

Keith Tyson, *Fractal Die – Third Roll* (2005–08). Aluminium and plastic, 610 × 2959 × 1092mm.

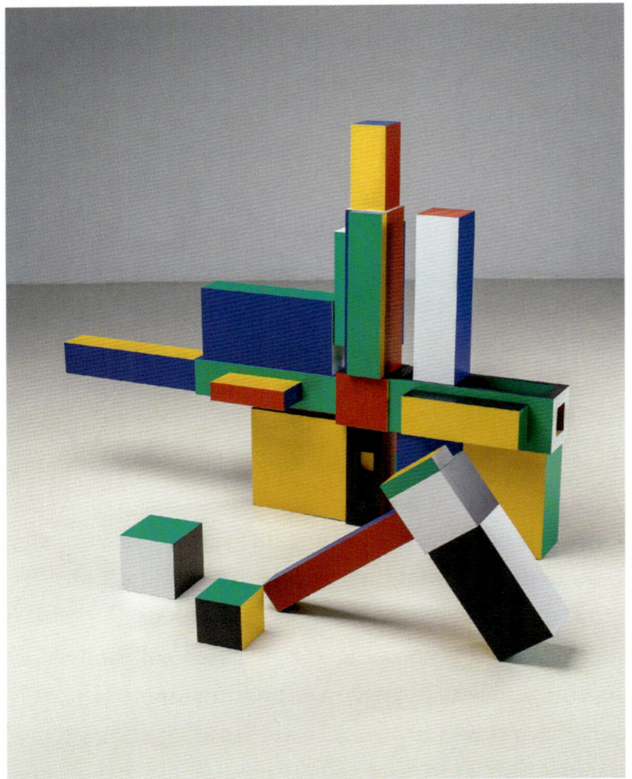

Keith Tyson, *Fractal Die – Seventh Roll* (2005–08). Aluminium and plastic, 749 × 1130 × 810mm.

ID: *What were the parentheses behind Fractal Die?*

KT: Well that was a very specific and tight rule. I had been asked by Pace Gallery, New York, to do an exhibition and I was really interested in the idea of just sending an equation to a gallery, which was going to be my total contribution to the show.

ID: *What did you send?*

KT: The idea is that you rolled a die and it expanded into a really primary sculpture based on how it fell and what colours it picked during its fall through space. So you had to roll a given number of dice and each face of that dice would expand or contract or change the colours, and each face of that expansion would expand to make a complex form. It was actually very difficult to construct as it turned out. The next time I was involved was when I turned up at the show and it was all there installed.

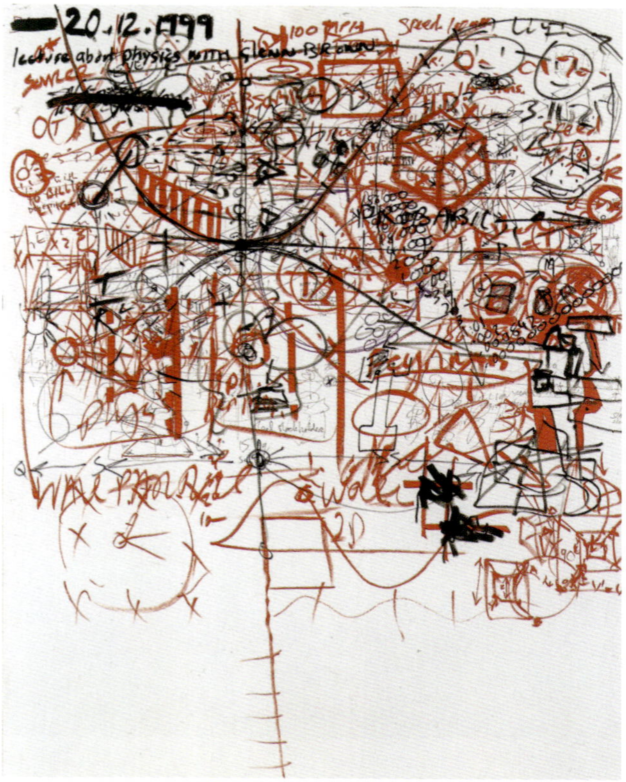

Keith Tyson, studio wall drawing: *An impromptu lecture about astrophysics with Glenn Brown.*

ID: *That's quite an extreme form of rules.*

KT: My studio wall drawings would be the other end of the spectrum: the only rule there is that I go up to a piece of paper and I put something on it and I date it on the day it's begun, sometimes on the day it has ended. Sometimes it's my emotional state; sometimes it's a world event; sometimes it's just me working out how big a piece should be.

ID: *The studio wall drawings have remained consistent.*

KT: Yes, that's something I do because they are like place holders for me. They allow me to think about something and come back to it maybe three, five, ten years later. It's a way of freezing it, with minimal infrastructure commitment, in a state halfway between a thought, an idea and a work, and there is something there.

ID: *How do they take shape?*

KT: It might be an essence of something. It might just be about a sculpture that I've seen – and it's not the sculpture, it's something else. It's about its attitude to gravity or something, and you might just want to represent that attitude to gravity somehow on that piece of paper. And you don't really know what that's about or what it will be, but you just place it down and you write some title, 'An attitude to gravity', and you put a date on it. And then it goes, perhaps somebody buys it, but at least I have them all on record, and now and again I will find myself looking through and maybe I will think, 'You know what? That's ready to be a body of work.' I am receptive to that idea now, whereas earlier maybe I was on some other trip; I might have been doing something precise and I couldn't allow myself to be in that state of mind.

It's a practical way of managing the schizophrenia of that. Otherwise it would get confusing. If you make a lot of work and different bodies of work you have to find a practical system for managing all that information otherwise you would go bonkers.

ID: *You worked on the Barrow Shipyards, building the nuclear submarines before you went to art school. What was that like?*

KT: Tough. It was inane work where you went and made 25,000 washers, or a component for a missile tube. You are making something for destroying mankind so philosophically I couldn't get to grips with that, yet I met a lot of passionate and bright people in there. I'm really glad I did it because when I got to

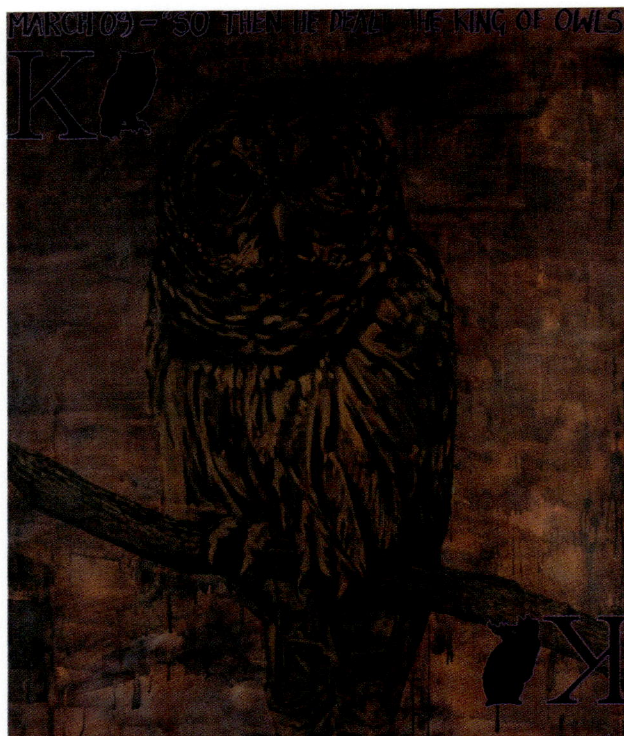

Keith Tyson, studio wall drawing: *So then he dealt the Kings of Owls and instantly the game seemed pointless* (March 2009).

college it just seemed like a walk in the park. They said, 'Go do an essay'; I would think, 'I'll happily do that all day, beats getting up at 5 o'clock in the morning and going to make washers all day.'

ID: *Was there anything about the work itself?*

KT: I saw how massive projects are broken up into little steps. Because you go in and think, 'Wow – look at that huge submarine! How the hell do they build that?' and then you realize that it's just loads and loads of tiny little practical steps that all fit together to make this massively complex thing, but each individual step isn't complex. I remember working on the shaft that linked the engine to the propeller. It was a solid piece of steel, 5.5 feet in diameter, perhaps 30 feet long, and the job was to take 2 millimetres off the whole thing. So you have it on this enormous lathe and you think this massive thing is going to have a massive cutting tool, but it doesn't; it has the same sized cutting tool as if you were making something as big as your thumb. It just takes a long time; you just set off at one end, get it spinning at the right speed, you get the coolant on, but if you stop halfway you ruin it, so you have got to make sure the tool is going to last for the entire job. So you set off cutting and it's going to run for 36 hours, one cut across the whole thing. So it sets off and you work shifts and this thing just cuts the entire thing and you have to keep it at the right height and keep checking it. Things like that were amazing. So now if I have a massive project I'm not fazed by it: I just go all shipyard on it!

ID: *But you're not working with a plan like the shipyard.*

KT: I have a plan in the sense that there is an outcome, it's a plan and a system that works and I have to have faith in it, but it would be very hard to explain it. You could ask a great poker player, 'How do you play?' and they could tell you every single play – you play aces before you flop in an early position and you do this and you do that. But at the highest level it becomes intuition, and you can explain it all day long but it doesn't matter unless you are at the scene of the action and you just know the guy is holding a pair of sevens. You can ask, 'How does he know he was holding a pair of sevens?' and he can explain it all, but he never thought all that in his head. He just knew it and that's kind of like the process in the studio. You could explain exactly, and that is the trouble with interviews, that you get caught in the trap of explaining it and people think that's what you actually did, but it happens so quickly and it's all blurred from one thought that then becomes a feeling in your stomach. So you come in and go, 'We are going to paint an elephant on this canvas today', and someone could ask, 'Why?' and you could go through it all and explain it, but it wouldn't be the truth. You just get the gut feeling to paint an elephant.

That doesn't mean that I don't have a plan; it doesn't mean there is no rule, no system; it just means you have allowed it to be extremely lateral instead of very acutely linear. So you come in and you are open and the more open wide you are the harder it is to apply precise definitions. It's like in the uncertainty principle: you can tell how fast something is going but you can't tell where it's going. Or you know its destination but you can't tell how fast it is going – you can't know it all. You can't be totally open and precise about everything.

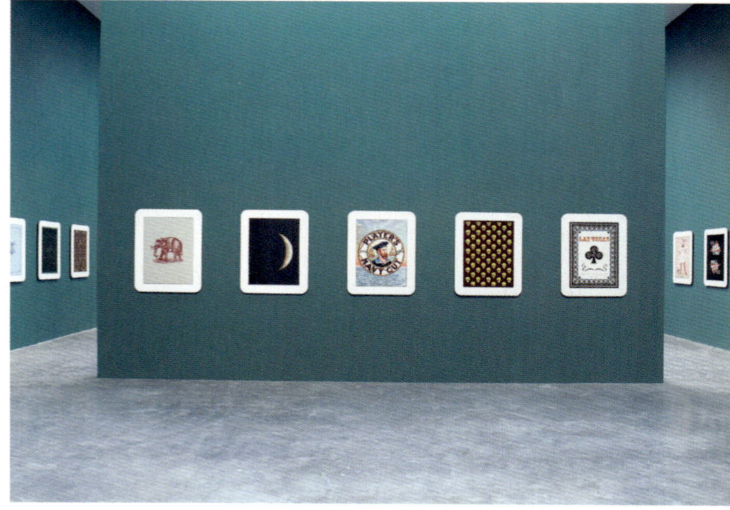

Keith Tyson, *52 Variables* installation (2010).

ID: *You work frequently with principles?*

KT: Principles hold true through everything. Principles will stand you good despite your feelings. For example, with the principle of entropy, everything disintegrates. Everything is working towards its own demise unless you put equal or more energy into stopping that rot, so you are either getting poorer or richer, fatter or thinner; there is no stasis in this world, none. You could take that principle into the studio, you are either improving your work or it is dying a death, and that keeps you hungry to keep working on it because everything is subject to it.

ID: *Your interest in science is deep rooted.*

KT: When I am using equations I'm not interested in science. I'm not a boffin, I'm not a mad scientist, these are fundamental materials like paint and clay. And rules: they are just materials that make things happen. We are living in an information age, we're not in the Industrial Revolution anymore where we understand ourselves through the focus of objects and production and work being done thermodynamically. We are in an information age where ideas cause change; we see things in terms of the amount of information. Even scientists don't understand things in terms of mass anymore, they think about a black hole in terms of quanta of information. The electron is a probabilistic mathematical object – it's not a solid thing, it's potentially there – and so you don't live in a world like that anymore, so it seems totally natural to me, as Michelangelo painted his cosmology of God and fire and brimstone, I paint mine which is this interdependent flow of information.

ID: *Thank you for offering an insight into how you think.*

KT: Well like I said at the start, I don't trust what I think very much anyway. What comes out of your mouth is an approximation of what is really going on. I cannot tell you how I make work, not because I don't want to, not because I am not articulate, it's because it's impossible because no system can describe a system that is more complex than it. And my speech and language is less complicated than the system that is creating the art. So I can't; I get a feeling of how I can describe the experience of making work but I definitely can't tell you why. I can say, 'I do this and do that' and, 'I feel this', but there is stuff going on that is way out of my control. But I am cool with that. I've learnt that it's OK, in fact it's brilliant, otherwise it would be tedious. ∎

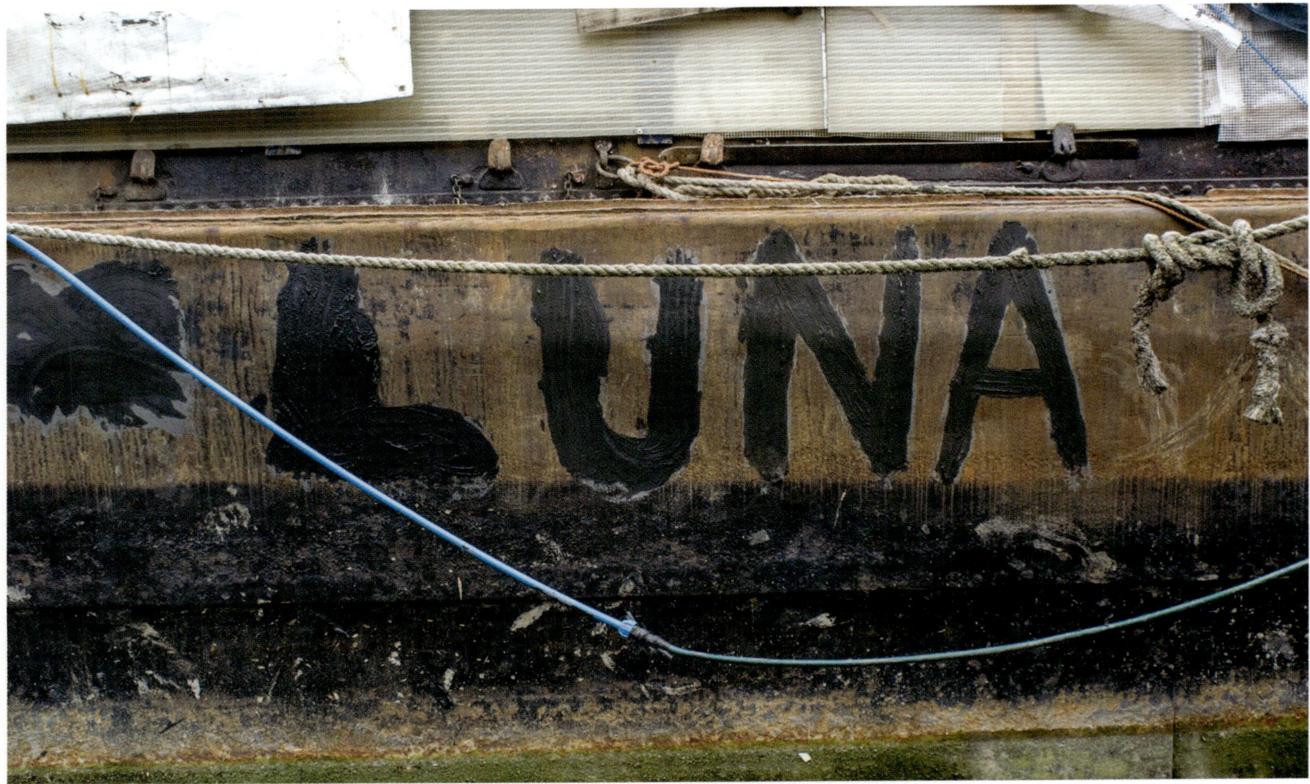

Jack Livesey, *Luna* 1 (2011).

▶ JACK LIVESEY

In 1969 Buckminster Fuller published *Utopia or Oblivion: The Prospects for Humanity*, in which he proposes that in order for there to be any fulfilment in the future, there should be an alliance and accord upon the answers to these forty strategic questions:

It is my working assumption that the following forty questions must be definitely answered before we may realistically discuss our respective philosophies and grand strategies.

1.   What do we mean by universe?
2.   Has man a function in universe?
3.   What is thinking?
4.   What are experiences?
5.   What are experiments?
6.   What is subjective?
7.   What is objective?
8.   What is apprehension?
9.   What is comprehension?
10.   What is positive? Why?
11.   What is negative? Why?
12.   What is physical?
13.   What is metaphysical?
14.   What is synergy?
15.   What is energy?
16.   What is brain?
17.   What is intellect?
18.   What is science?
19.   What is a system?
20.   What is consciousness?
21.   What is subconsciousness?
22.   What is teleology?
23.   What is automation?
24.   What is a tool?
25.   What is industry?

26. *What is animate?*

27. *What is inanimate?*

28. *What are metabolics?*

29. *What is wealth?*

30. *What is intuition?*

31. *What are aesthetics?*

32. *What is harmonic?*

33. *What is prosaic?*

34. *What are the senses?*

35. *What are mathematics?*

36. *What is structure?*

37. *What is differentiation?*

38. *What is integration?*

39. *What is integrity?*

40. *What is 'truth'?*

This was a typical strategy from Fuller, a modernist thinker, designer, inventor and architect who had made popular the notion of ecology through terminology such as 'spaceship earth', describing the planet as a well-stocked but limited vessel in a vast universe. In 1961, influenced by Fuller's teaching at Black Mountain College where he had built his first geodesic dome, a group of students were determined to break art out of the confines of museums and galleries and integrate it with everyday life. Overwhelmed by the Vietnam War, they wanted to build something themselves, to collect and utilize detritus that surrounded them and to make something out of it. It wasn't primarily intellectual; it was a personal positive statement, getting satisfaction out of being inventive. In May 1965 they founded Drop City in Colorado and began to build and live in geodesic domes built from old car parts. Drop City was one of the first communes of the Sixties, the first to be grounded in art practice. This was a short-lived experiment and by 1969 the founding residents had left and by 1973 Drop City was a geodesic ghost town.

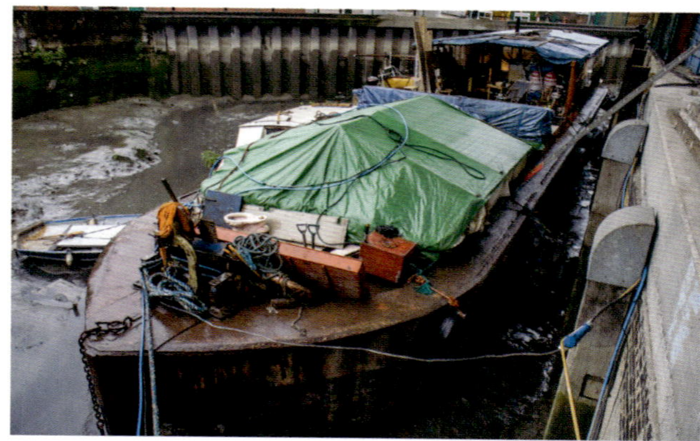

Jack Livesey, *Luna* 2 (2011).

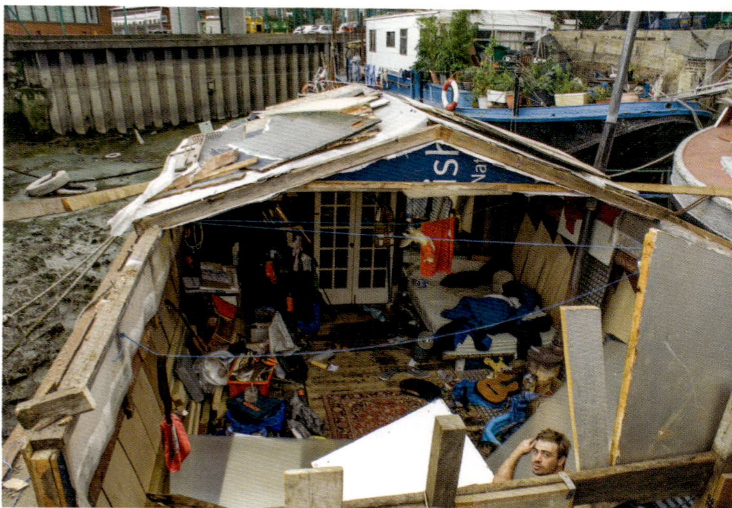

Jack Livesey, *Luna* 3 (2011).

Certain themes developed during this first wave of counterculture are being re-evaluated with ever more frequency: Heather and Ivan Morrison's conversion of a Green Goddess into a mobile sci-fi archive tapping into Roger D. Beck's west-coast house-trucks; Alex Hartley inspired by the Drop City commune; and Gavin Wade inviting artists to respond to Fuller's forty strategic questions.

Jack Livesey is also driven to explore sculpture and the environment. Earlier work, like Richard Long's, had explored possibilities by the most simple of acts, of walking across a landscape. This continues with Livesey who has become unconcerned with the visual but with the simply effective, and with a simple premise of wanting to make something better.

Livesey has had a residency of sorts, on a dredger called *Luna*, situated on a stretch of mud- and silt-filled causeways carved into the landscape south of the Thames. Opposite the glass towers of Docklands, here is a boat community, an odd and eccentric collection of individuals. These are not narrowboats and barges; they are large-scale dredgers that are chopped and modified, and then fitted. Here, amongst a small community who value isolation, a loose group of artists began a project to make habitable and live on this dredger.

Livesey's experiments, as documented on *Luna*, speak of an ambition to experience and document a journey of how to override assumptions about the way the world works, and to attempt to exorcize that human trait of inventing illusion. By focusing on the here and now, Livesey reminds us of a way of physically experiencing and thinking about our constructed surroundings. An earlier piece, tellingly entitled *Making Life Easier*, is where he first established this dialogue.

IAN DAWSON: *What was* Making Life Easier?

JACK LIVESEY: It was a collaborative project. Nick Davies and I built a canoe in Hackney and then paddled it to Llangollen in North Wales and then back to Reading.

ID: *How long did that take you?*

JL: Thirty-six days of paddling.

ID: *Why?*

JL: We had been on some long-distance walks with tents and sleeping bags and cooking gear and video cameras. On one of those we ended up on Salisbury Plains trying to make a film with some huge black balloons filled with helium. The balloons were supposed to be carrying our backpacks and tents and camping gear but instead they were bobbling along like a flock of sheep and we ended up making a film out of it. So we just wanted to take that a bit further and decided to make a canoe so we could go longer distances whilst being able to carry on filming.

ID: *Where did you build the boat?*

JL: Part of it in a studio in Hackney, and then we walked it down to a warehouse on the canal to finish it off. We built it using a stitch and tape method. We used blueprints from the Internet to create templates. We then drilled sets of corresponding holes in the profiles before zip-tying them together. The sides then peeled up once we started tightening the ties. We glued the space between the zip-ties and then the whole thing holds itself together.

ID: *What a beautiful method.*

JL: We posted the whole material list on the website. So it was like an instruction manual and a reference book. We used four sheets of 5.5mm plywood and one sheet of 9mm plywood for fitting out the gunwales.

ID: *The first boat you had made?*

JL: Yes, and we also made everything else: a cooking tripod, the paddles, wheels (so we could wheel the boat over land), and a herb garden for the side of it so we could cook with herbs. We were filming with mini DV camcorders with half a pair of binoculars stuck onto the lens.

ID: *Where did you set off from?*

JL: We finally built a large ramp to launch it into the Regent's Canal, and had a bit of a party. It got doused in gin by a neighbour as a send-off. We planned to paddle from there to Aberystwyth on the west coast of Wales. We both have family there and thought that would be a good journey.

ID: *Did you have a route in mind?*

JL: To follow the canal system to Llangollen, then on to the river Dee upstream to Lake Bala, and then across the side of the mountains to the river Ystwyth, which goes to Aberystwyth.

ID: *What happened?*

JL: We were fine to Llangollen but then we ran into trouble. It was salmon season. Using the river at the same time as the fishermen wasn't going to happen. We went back down the canal system. We were navigating with a road atlas that hadn't got the waterways marked, and we stumbled across the River Perry; we offloaded from the aqueduct and onto this little river. We paddled through Shropshire and it was like being in *Swallows and Amazons* or something, punting through reeds, chopping logs out of our way. I don't think we saw anybody for three days.

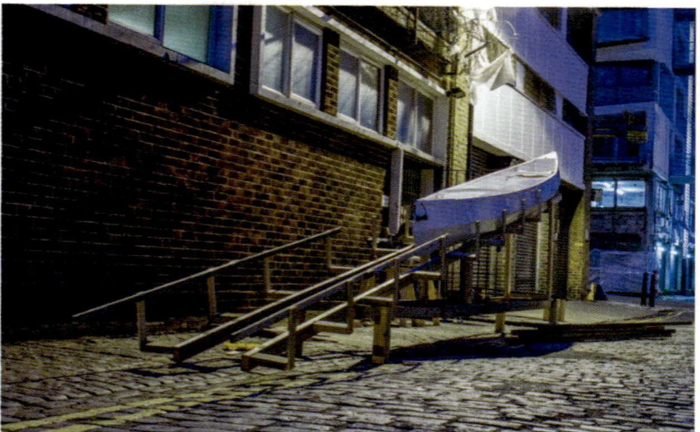

Jack Livesey and Nick Davies, *Making life easier* 1 (2009).

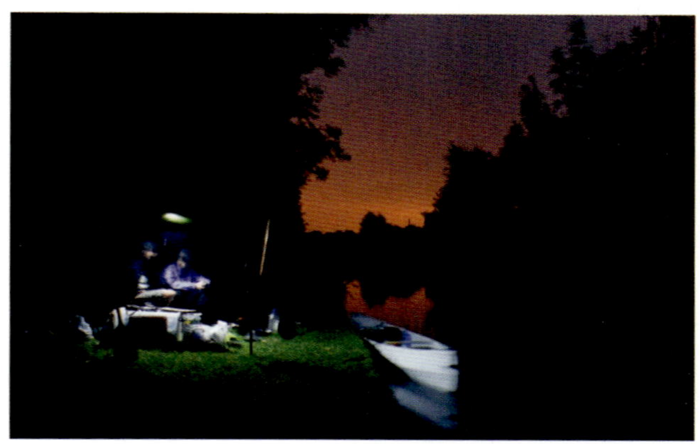

Jack Livesey and Nick Davies, *Making life easier* 2 (2009).

ID: *That sounds idyllic.*

JL: We came out onto the River Severn. That was amazing too: a canal is flat and still, and we were always paddling, whereas on the river we could just relax and glide down on the current. The view is also quite different: because a canal is man-made we could be paddling along halfway up a hill enjoying the vista; on the river we were always on the bottom, always looking up, out of it.

ID: *Did it all go wrong?*

JL: We were just outside Telford and we capsized going through a rapid. A big standing wave loomed, the river appeared like an egg-timer, we hit this wave side on. Everything was thrown out of the boat and was floating around with us. I had lost my glasses and couldn't see anything and we had lost the tent. The next day, after sleeping on the riverbank, we caught a bus to Telford. We had grown accustomed to doing 6 miles an hour on the canoe, and I got on this bus; I couldn't see a thing and it was going 50 miles an hour down the dual carriageway. I was hanging on to the coach seats, completely freaked out at the speed of it, going, 'Fucking hell, what's going on?' It was the most surreal thing. We got the bus to an indoor shopping mall and we looked like we had been in a canoe for a month. I was squinting, waddling around this shopping mall, looking at blurry signs and everyone was looking at us. I got a free eye test and new glasses after telling them our story. We went to Millets and got a discount after telling them our story. People liked our story.

ID: *Did you continue?*

JL: I had my new spectacles, we got back to the canoe and we decided to head for Gloucester and the Bristol Channel. We started going down there and past huge merchant tug boats, hulking engines going up and down collecting gravel, past big hoppers dropping gravel. The tugs were going past us really slowly, looking at us like, 'Who are these two jokers in this canoe? What are they doing?' And we kind of got round them and we just got too sketched out, after capsizing. So we ended up getting a lift back to Lechlade at the head of the Thames, got back in the Thames and rowed back to Reading.

ID: *And the film?*

JL: We had lost one of our cameras and tapes when we capsized. It took a while to edit the film; we didn't quite know what to do with it. The remaining tapes had also got wet in the river, the cameras had also been out for a long time, the tape had started to degrade and the footage was splattered with interference. We finally put two video channels next to one another, binocular like, the footage playing across from one channel to another. It was like two eyes having a conversation with one another. It was surprisingly watchable because of the framing.

What made it interesting was that due to the degradation of the tape, each time we captured the footage from the camera onto the computer it came out totally different. So the exact same video would play differently, stuttering in different places each time.

ID: *You then collaborated on another boat in Deptford?*

JL: David, an old college friend, had bought a dredger called *Luna* and it was approaching wintertime and he really needed help.

ID: *What were you going to do?*

JL: I was trying to find a studio, but everything was too expensive, so this came along. It became an experiment. To go somewhere with the potential to build something to live in was an exciting proposition.

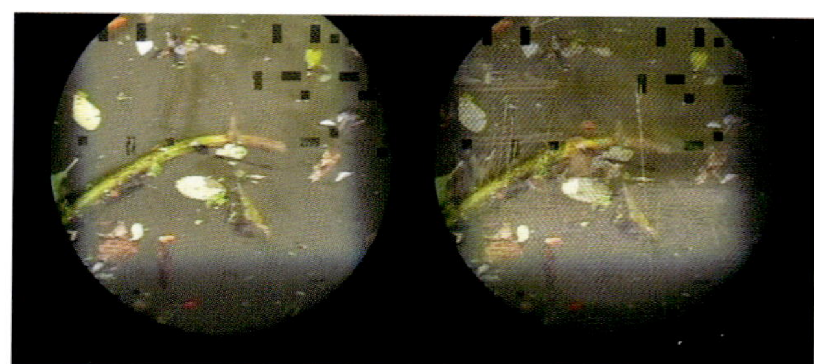

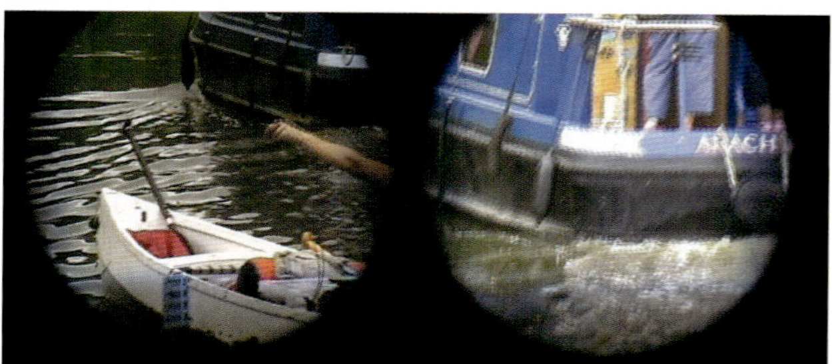

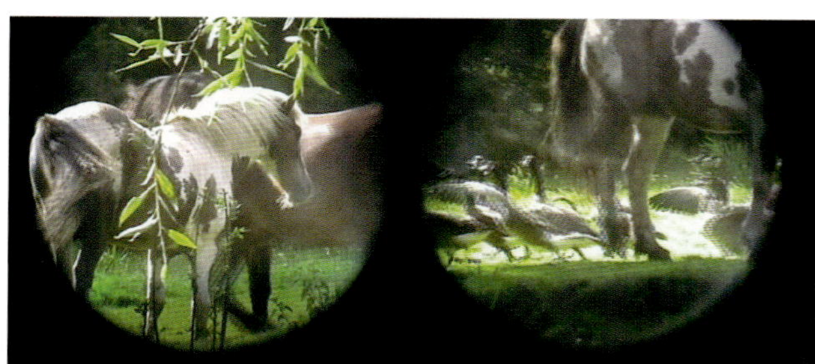

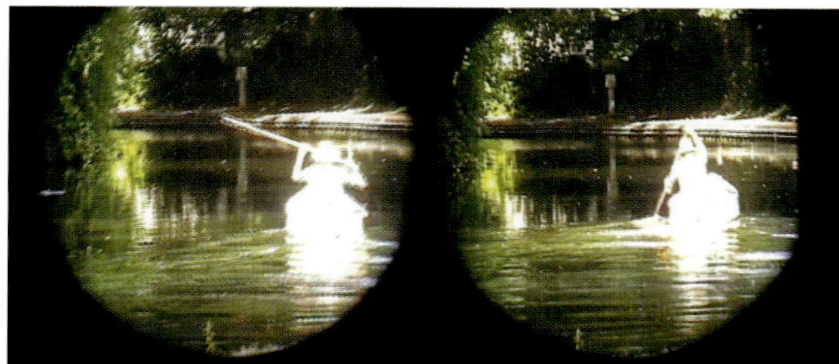

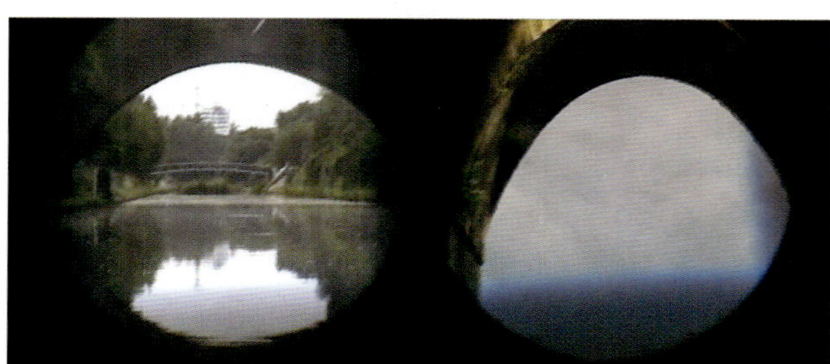

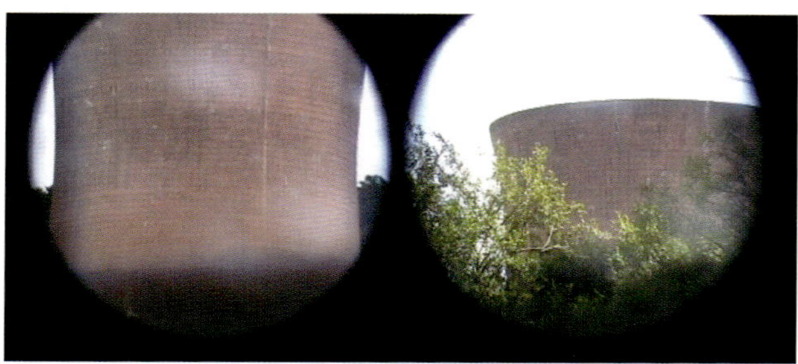

ID: *What needed doing?*

JL: The first thing we did was to waterproof the roof and build a bathroom. There was no way to heat it, no way to cook anything and no place to wash or shower. There was a toilet and a 27-inch iMac. That sums up the beginning; making the ladder safe so no-one fell off into the quagmire of the creek. There were five of us choosing to live there, and a list was drawn up with what people wanted – stuff like a sink that didn't block, a light in the kitchen – and I worked through the list. I was like a maintenance man; people would come to me with a grievance and I would have to deal with it. There was no budget.

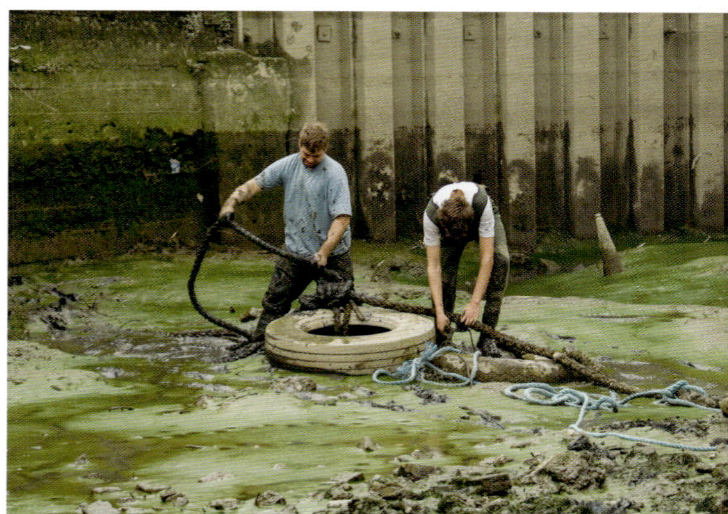

Jack Livesey and David in the creek.

Jack Livesey and Nick Davies, *Making life easier,* film still 01–06 (2009).

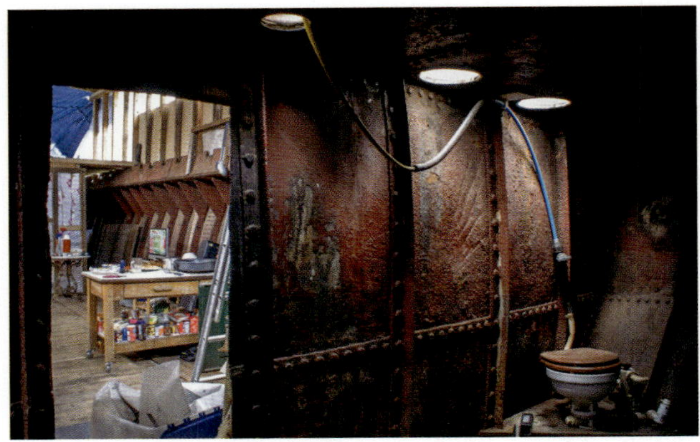

Jack Livesey, *Luna* 4 (2011).

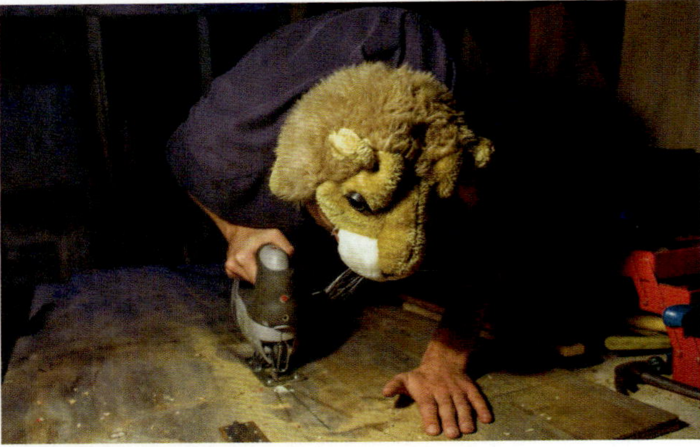

Jack Livesey, *Luna* 5 (2011).

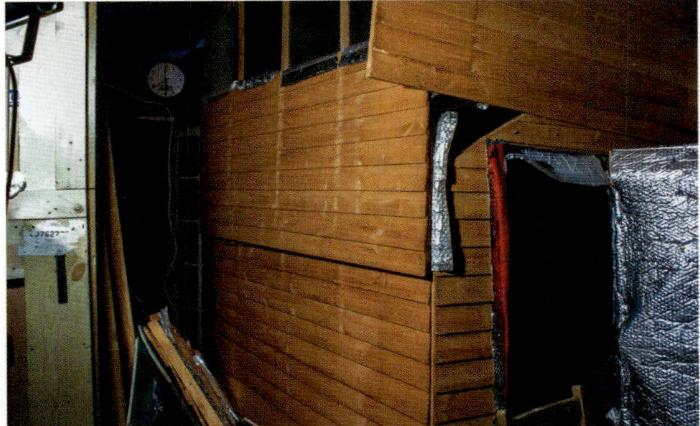

Jack Livesey, *Luna* 6 (2011).

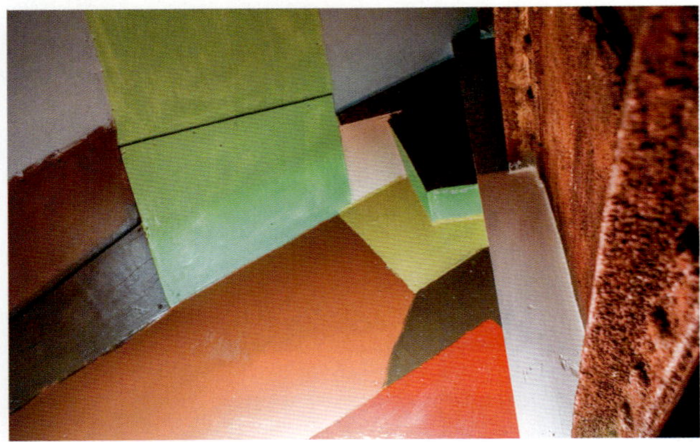

Jack Livesey, *Luna* 7 (2011).

ID: *How were you getting materials?*

JL: Mostly scavenged. There were inventive moments, like making a buoyancy crane using plastic bottles to lift and move lumps of concrete around the creek. Dealing with the phenomena of the tide. If something needed to get done I had to work it out myself: nobody else was going to do it. It was also seasonal, always on the eye out for wood, always browsing the flea-market for odd things that will be useful.

I would end up chatting to people. When you are rummaging for scrap wood for the burner, there is something so basic about getting something that you can heat your home with that seems universal for people; everyone can appreciate having a warm space to live in.

ID: *Were there any defining stages?*

JL: During the winter it got a bit sad – there wasn't much light. Looking back I don't know how we stayed there. I think we all stayed because everyone stayed. Not one of us left. We stuck it out. Then getting the hot water working in the spring was a good point.

ID: *What stage is it at now?*

JL: It's hard to say if there are stages. We don't know how long things are going to last. The boat is constantly moving, and with the high moisture content, there are already bits that need replacing. So it needs constant investment of time, like the Forth Bridge analogy.

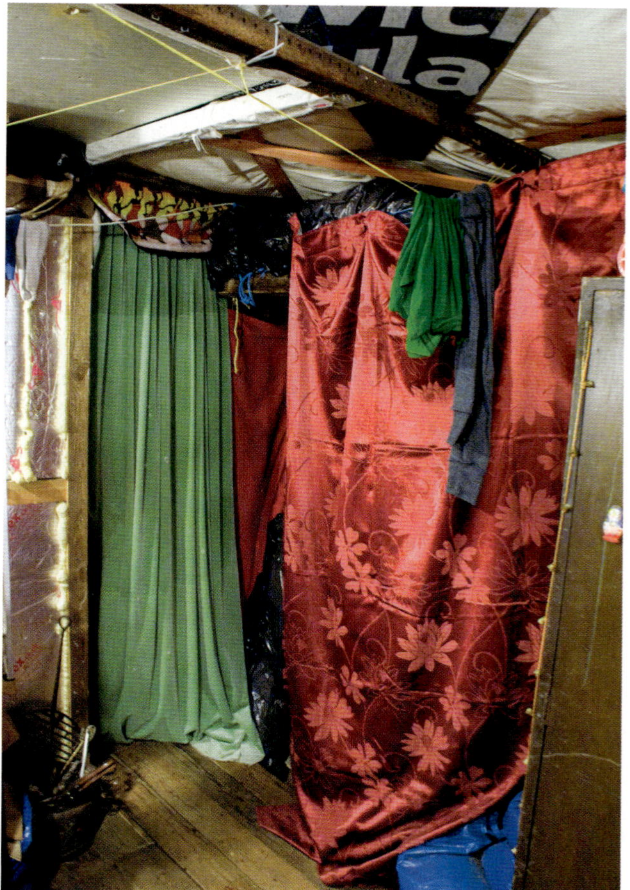

Jack Livesey, *Luna* 8 (2011).

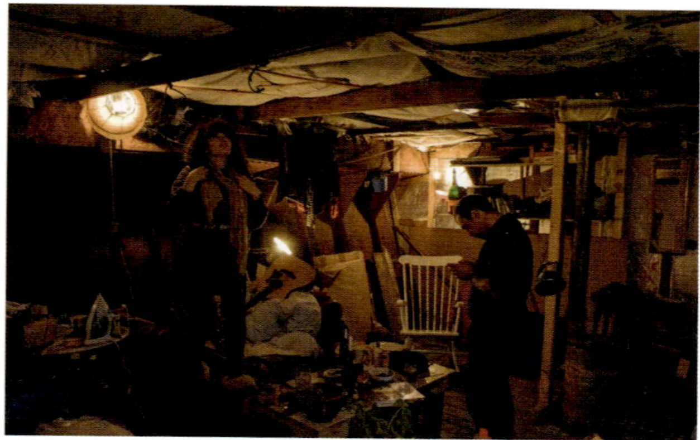

Jack Livesey, *Luna* 9 (2011).

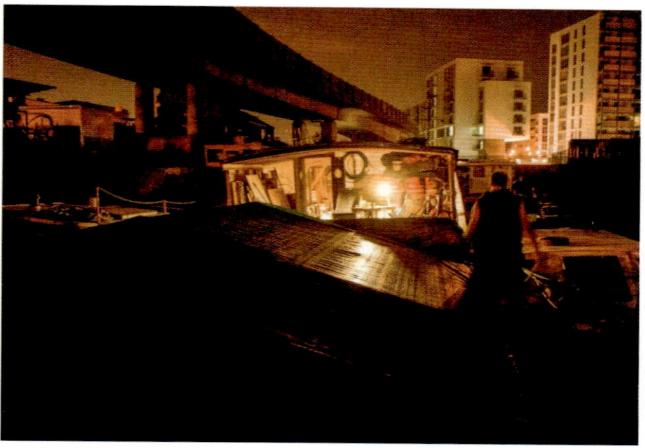

Jack Livesey, *Luna* 10 (2011).

ID: *How does the experience add to your practice as a sculptor?*

JL: It's about understanding what I am living in. It's a way of learning about how and what stuff is. Similar to the canoe trip, which turned out to be a tool rather than a home, but then with *Luna* it's down to understanding my relationship to stuff.

For example at Deptford Market at the end of a day, the stallholders pack away their boxes into vans. There are always two or three of the big bins filled up with stuff that they are not taking away with them, that they haven't sold; I don't know how they make the decision to get rid of it that day. It's a massive pile of stuff that's run its course before it has even been sold.

So I was able to take some of that stuff and rework it into something useful to live with. And having to deal with the weather and the elements, and having to deal with influences, the tide and the changing centre of gravity – it was so rich with everything that had to be thought about. It made me think. It wasn't about what it looked look like because we were making it up as we went along. It was freestyle architecture.

ID: *Did you ever work with a plan?*

JL: I recently found a working drawing on a scrap of paper. It was made of about twenty lines, sketching the hull and where a bunch of walls were going to be. So when we got to the detail of how to fix things to the hull, I just problem-solved. ◾

There is a common assumption that making a successful and effective decision is based on weighing up all the facts; that a measured choice will be arrived at by the rigorous application of all the evidence. I was recently drawn to some research that contradicted that supposition. A team of scholars from the University of Amsterdam had published evidence that proved the opposite and for a brief moment national newspapers and journals ran the story under headlines such as, 'Trust your instincts', and, 'Why you should go with your gut'.

The Dutch research team had conducted a number of experiments such as asking groups of people to make product choices from a long list of attributes. The information consisted of a range of statements from positive but irrelevant qualities to important but negative characteristics. And in this instance a group of people who were distracted, who weren't consciously focused on the specific subject, chose the better option.

The research added to a growing debate over whether conscious thought has any effect on behaviour at all. The idea of it as an epiphenomenon began a century earlier when the evolutionary biologist Thomas Huxley contended that 'consciousness had no more influence on our actions than a steam whistle had on a locomotive train'.

I was reminded of this when reviewing Richard Wilson's *20:50*, a room submerged to waist height in sump oil, the surface of this pitch black liquid acting as a perfect mirror reflecting the space downwards, turning the floor into an elevated walkway. I had an initial assumption that a piece that was so assured in its masterful transformation of space had doubtless occurred through a conscious strategy; that it couldn't have developed tangential origins and its physical repercussions were probably predicted. How wrong I was.

In 1987 Richard Wilson was floating in a swimming pool in the Algarve. Five years earlier he had begun to forge a method of working that had extended his work outside of the studio, making casts *in situ* so that the building had become part of the work, enlisted as part of the piece. He was due to start work on his second show at Matt's Gallery in London. Casting within the gallery space was still on his mind but outside of that he was struggling for an idea. He kept diving down to the bottom of the pool for another bottle of beer and bobbing around on the surface of the water, the horizontal plane of the pool slowly beginning to play on his mind. Then one day it hit him: 'I know! I'll flood the place!' he said, continuing:

I was so excited I just had to make this maquette. I went into town, it was a Sunday afternoon and nothing was open but there was a white shoebox in the gutter and that shoebox became the first maquette for 20:50. It was the only material I had so I had to be economical about the use of it.

What material to flood it in? Wilson had had a drum of oil sitting in the studio, from an earlier project, waiting to be thrown out.

The drum hadn't a lid on it, and all sorts of rubbish had accumulated around it. I had always loved the way that in amongst all these bits of wood and junk, there was this void, this perfect reflection. I thought, 'If I am going to transform the space, let's use a material that has been through its own transformation. Let's take something that is medieval like oil, millions of years old, absolutely toxic, gooey and horrible, the sort of thing you don't make art from. Let's put it in the gallery in the white space.'

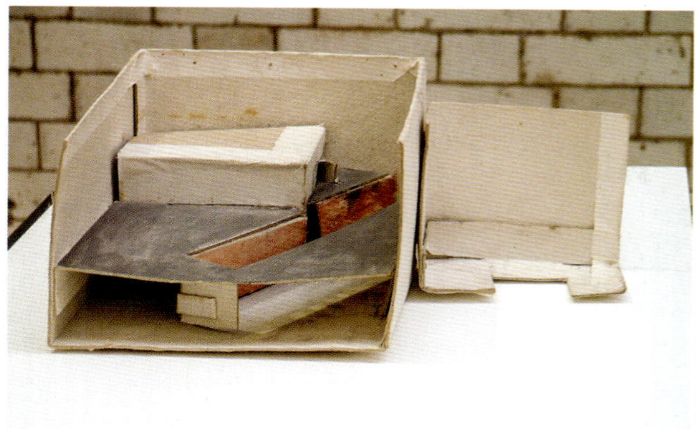

Richard Wilson, *20:50* model (1997).

From these impulsive and intuitive origins *20:50* was created, and Wilson recollects a nervous Robin Klasnik (owner of Matt's Gallery) waiting for Wilson to find a pump and enough oil for the piece. 'And then we looked at it and we were really astounded. We thought it would be good – but it was incredible.'

IAN DAWSON: *So you plan the work using a variety of media including collage?*

RICHARD WILSON: There's an immediacy to collage. If I want to talk about how a sculpture will go together, I will draw a sense of it in a space. But rather than draw a projector, I'll just get a Jessop's catalogue and cut it out and stick it down. Put a yellow line onto that object I've built and it says everything for me. It says light, done in yellow pencil. It says projector because it's been cut out from a Jessop's catalogue; it might not be the projector I use, but you can see immediately what it is.

ID: *That's a very instant physical approach.*

RW: And it's like sculpture. You've 'built' the drawing, as opposed to trying to use your technical facility as a draughtsman or illustrator. You've kind of built the thing. You get a sense of how things get placed in the set-up. The space of the gallery is the white sheet of paper and you are laying out things on it. And you can also push things around. You know if the projector needs to be a bit higher up, then you can move it.

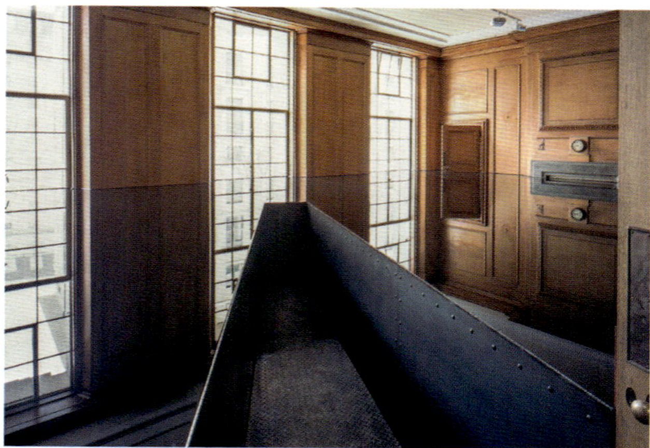

Richard Wilson, *20:50* (1987–2003, installed at County Hall, London 2003). Used sump oil, steel, wood, valve tap. Dimensions variable.

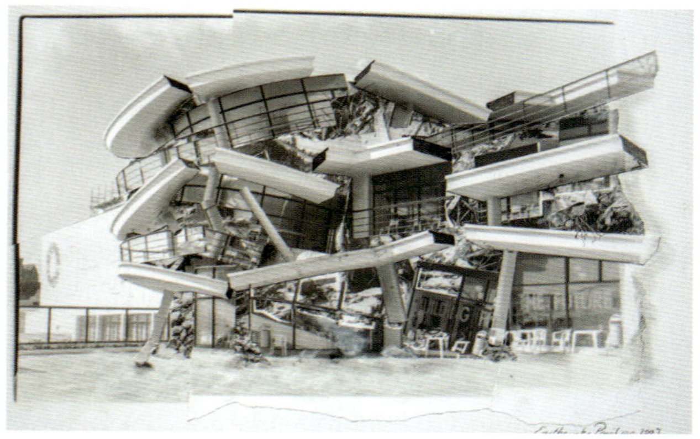

Richard Wilson, *Earthquake Pavilion* (2004). Photo collage and paint on paper.

ID: *You also draw as well?*

RW: I work in various stages of drawing. I constantly work with a sketchbook. I'm a great believer in the sketchbook. I probably use a pencil and a sketchbook at least an hour every day. But that's not continuous: it's just that I'm constantly firing on an idea or how an idea might get made. I may come back from a meeting where I've resolved three technical problems and I have had to let someone else know about that. So I have scribbled and scanned them off to various people who needed to know.

ID: *So it's mostly practical exercise?*

RW: No, my sketchbooks have always been used as a form of mental gymnastics. Some people go down the gym; I don't do that, but what I do instead is get the sketchbook out. That's my gym. That's what I use. I work out and get myself and my notions all set, then I've got the day ready and I can go off and do this, that and the other. And so the sketchbook is vital so you can be very free, in that it's not precious. Three lines and I may then tear it out and carry on.

ID: *What happens next?*

RW: Then I get to a point where I like to convert those sketches into things that are drawings, either in their own right as ideas (which probably won't be realized yet, but they're on the backburner and held), or they're drawings that I know are the next stage to convincing someone that I want to do the project.

So at the moment, I've done all the sketches for a proposal for the De La Warr Pavilion. But the next stage is to know how to get it to work; I've got to go bigger. It's not enough to work everything out small, that's not my scale. My scale's quite large so I will go to A2 size of paper which will then afford me ways in which I can really work things out.

ID: *So you are beginning to create a body of work in order to understand physically what you might want to achieve.*

RW: What's great is that they do then become drawings in their own right as things that people are also interested in. And I kind of pride myself on that. I do a fair few drawings for each project and they're exhibited as work too. I enjoy drawing on a large scale and from that, those drawings get converted into a sculpture.

So those are the stages to get to the idea: sketchbook, drawing, maquette and then to making the final thing. That's the process.

ID: *What's your relationship with the work when it enters the latter stages?*

RW: I am really hands-on. And the best situation would be to do it myself, or with my team. Like the *Beach Huts* for the Folkestone Triennial, which were cut from an existing crazy golf course. We went to Folkestone seafront, chose the sections based on the drawings and photographs, and once they were all cut, we got a crane driver in. I built all the jigs to lift them out and then, with a team, we put them all together. We converted them all and we built everything.

ID: *That sounds very direct and economical.*

RW: When there are restrictions like a limited budget and yet it's a good idea that you want to realize, you have to do that. When it gets monumental (for example, the ship, or *Turning The Place Over*, those big pieces), you have to go to the outside world. It's the only way to do it; I don't have the team or the expertise or the kit for that scale. So in that respect it would have to be done by outside professionals.

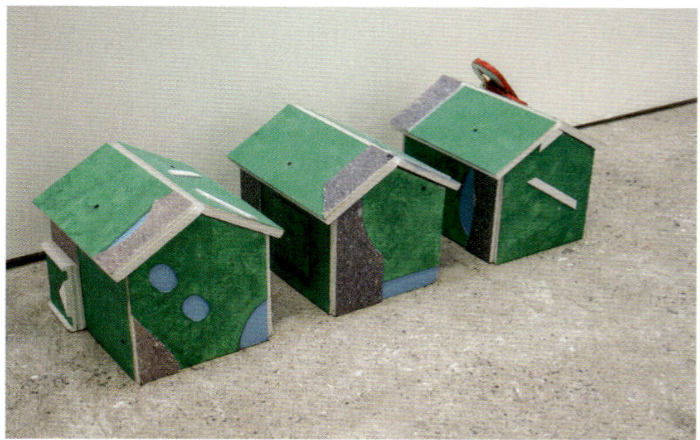

Richard Wilson, *18 Holes* maquette (2008).

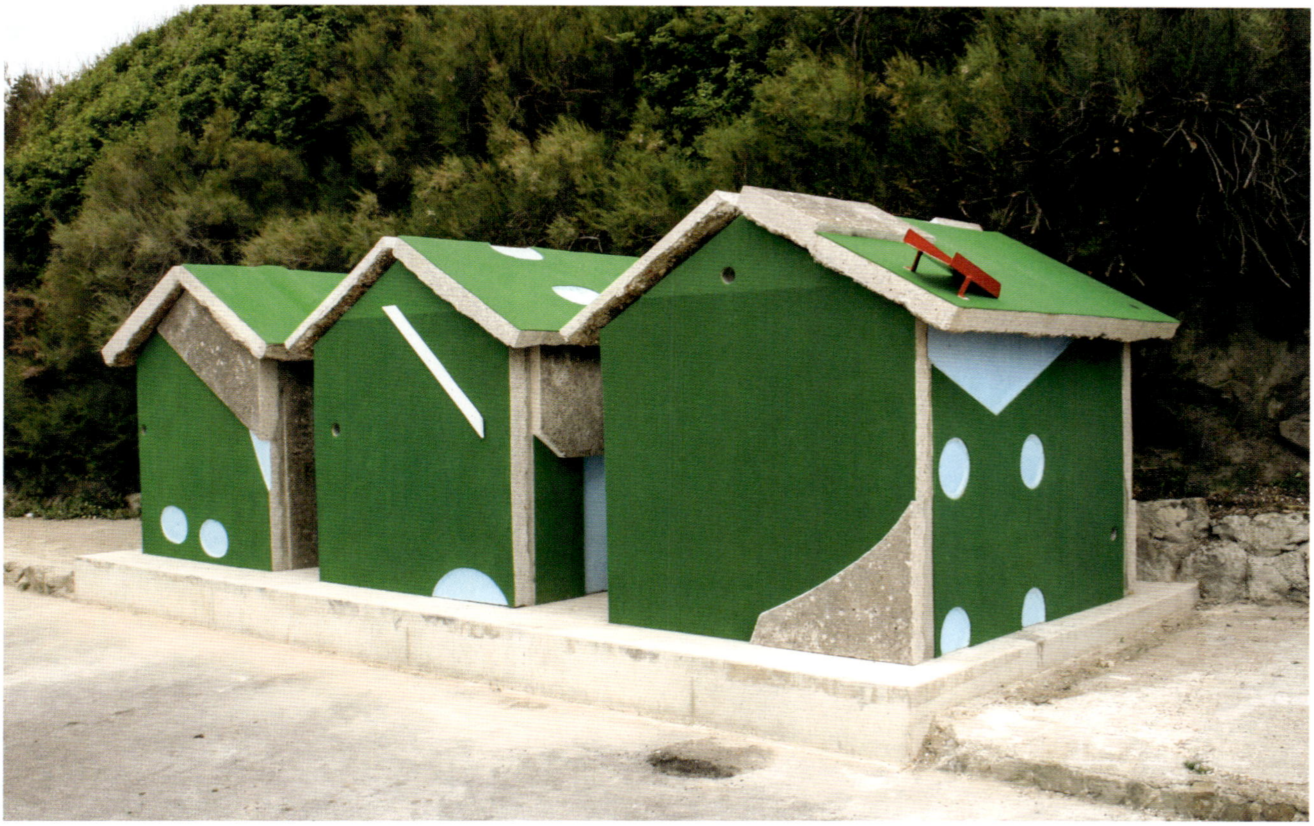

Richard Wilson, *18 Holes*. (Folkstone Triennial, 2008). Concrete, steel, paint.

ID: *How do you manage that?*

RW: I make sure I'm involved and I make sure I visit the work all the time. So with the ship, it was being cut up north; they needed instructions on what needed cutting and needed painting, so I would go up there two days a week. Firstly I would make sure I know them all by first name – that's always such a big breakthrough, just getting to know them by their names. Then you just deal with the manufacture of the sculpture by being around. Showing that interest in them and their skills is important because you develop respect from them as well.

ID: *It sounds like you are at ease with overseeing the projects.*

RW: I like to run a team. I remember reading about Gordon Matta-Clarke when he said that he would never delegate anything where it was just a subservient delegation. That holds true, so I always try and delegate only because I need to learn how to do it myself or because I know someone is better than me at a task. It's never because a job is too dirty; I won't do that, I don't delegate because of that reason.

It's also important to be there so it's not a 'them and me' thing: it's a team. We're all equal, that team spirit needs to be kept when working with a group of people. And through that the work gains a respect. I've noticed with people who aren't versed in an art-grammar will really appreciate the work that they've put in to your piece if you're around. Whereas if you arrive and you are being a little bit aloof about things, you know your worker will have been uninspired by the work at the end of the day. I've seen that happen.

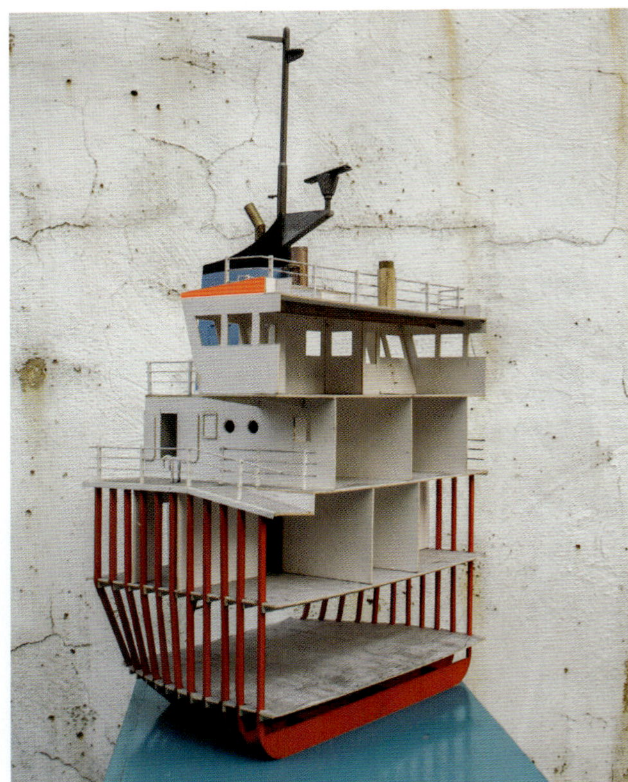

Richard Wilson, *Slice of Reality* maquette (1999).

ID: *That's a mutually beneficial relationship.*

RW: It's really a case of it being a really respectful situation, showing respect for the team, you're not any better than them. They're skilled people. And I like learning from watching workers, it's also important to keep a check on the aesthetic because if you delegate, there is decision-making outside of your control. But the aesthetic you've got to hold on to. Now sometimes you'll get a happy accident where you will arrive on site and someone will say, 'I didn't know what you wanted to do here so I decided to do this,' and you go, 'Jesus that's all right, I like that, keep it in!' Sometimes you'll get in and you'll be like, 'Why have you done that? Can we undo that and do it this way?' So it's important to be around. If you don't actively oversee the project you'll get it back and you've got a sculpture that you doubt, that you've got to put into the outside world. How do you deal with that? That can be a problem.

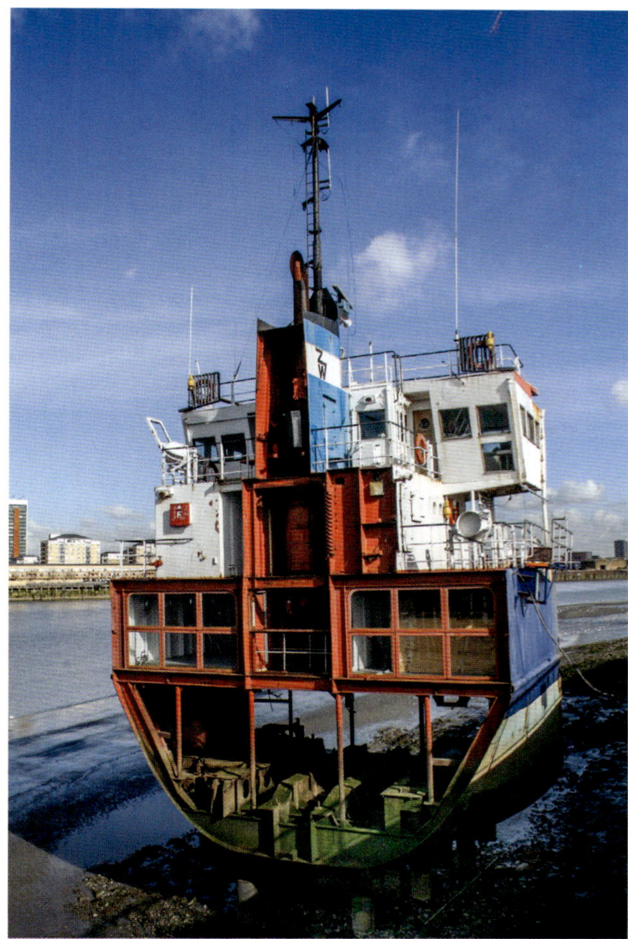

Richard Wilson, *Slice of Reality* (2000). Section of 700-ton sand dredger on six piles on the river Thames, Greenwich, London. 2100 × 975 × 790cm.

ID: *The piece is only finished when it's finished and every stage has decision-making that is affected by you.*

RW: Absolutely. And what happens is I'll still be making maquettes when they're finishing off. Because there is something I'm not sure about, maybe a section of it needs moving; do we take it apart or do we need to put a lifting mechanism on? So it might be a technical model, looking at where it can be lifted from, or it might be that we've sussed everything out but there's been a change in the way it's been sited (because you know they're going to put paving stones down for the work rather than something else and you think, 'Well, I

don't want it to be stuck lower than the paving stones, we've got to find a way of it sitting as though it's just lowered onto it'). It's a technical thing at that stage – it won't be directly about the aesthetic but somehow the aesthetic is embroidered into it, the way something touches the ground.

ID: *So making technical and aesthetic decisions might be one and the same in order to maintain the simplicity of the piece. The effectiveness of the piece on this scale has a lot to do with its apparent simplicity.*

RW: Yeah. B.B. King – *Keep It Simple, Keep it Going*. So, I always think that. I think if I had to criticize myself as a sculptor I can be over-complex with solutions and I think that sometimes starts to cloud the clarity of an idea. To have an idea you need to put it into the world in the simplest way possible. By simple I mean the most simply effective way possible. So usually that's to do with taking an idea on a journey through the drawings, sketches and maquettes and bringing it back when it's gone too far, pruning it back to where the work sits best within the idea. What's interesting for me is that there are two main principles of an idea: one is finding an idea; then once you've got that idea, finding the best way that it can sit in the world. So it's a bit like, yeah I want to turn a building, I can do it like this, like that. But what part do I need to turn? How much of the mechanism do I want to reveal and what sort of impact would the speed have moving faster as opposed to slower? So you see, you can have an idea, but you've got to fine-tune that idea. So that's where the drawings get you to the idea and then another set of drawings gets you to how the idea might be best realized. So it's all small details being challenged and that's usually done at the maquette stage – the drawings find the idea and then the maquettes fine-tune it.

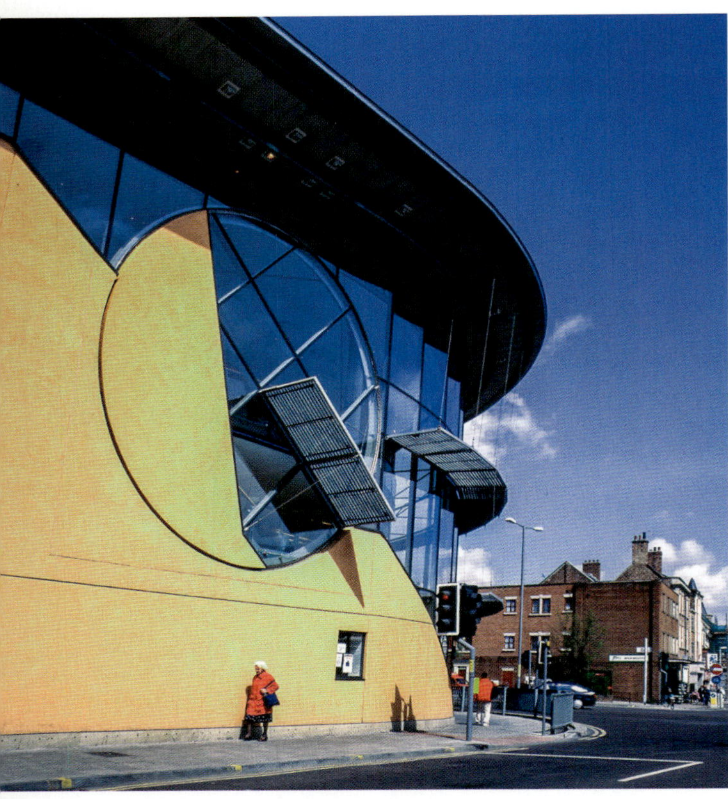

Richard Wilson, *Over Easy* (1998). The Arc, Stockton-Upon-Tees.

ID: *How do you find the ideas through drawing?*

RW: Like I said, the sketchbook generates a lot of ideas: certain things get done for observation; others get done to clarify a method to get something made. But some things are done just to generate an idea. I see something and I think that I must remember that. For example I once saw on my travels someone had used the back of a lorry as part of an extension to a building – 'What a great idea. You know, I'll just draw it.' I remember looking at a building being pulled down and I made a tiny sketch and it just said 'climbing centre'; the way it had been pulled down, the rubble looked like a side of a mountain and I thought, 'Wouldn't it be great to make a building that was climbable; people traversing up and down the façade. Buildings are for functional use, so why not climb one, then? You get these guys, that French guy always getting arrested for climbing up buildings, a no-go zone, but what about making a

building just designed for climbing on – so these guys can climb up and bungee jump from?' So you get these crazy little moments but they do lead on to a more determined research towards a direct issue or idea. But they always start in the world as a little scribble, and like putting stuff down in a messy workshop, I know where all these ideas are within the masses of books that I have; I can fill a book in a month.

ID: *That's a wonderfully fluid and open development to the work, where the drawings, sketches and maquettes are instrumental in developing all aspects of your thinking.*

RW: I would make drawings every time I went up North to the *Slice of Reality* project. They were job lists and I lost a lot of them because I left them up there, and they were great because you'd find one lying around the Dock… in the wheelhouse and they'd be covered in old coffee cup rings. They'd obviously been examining it, then, slam with the coffee mug, and they're off again! I liked the way that my precious work had been embroidered by their marks, their fingerprints. It meant that they were used things, rather like referencing a cookbook while baking.

ID: *Are there timescales, not necessarily for the production of the work but for the development of the ideas?*

RW: I tend to work to demand; however, some of my ideas will go off on a tangent – you think, 'Well, that's not possible for this particular project but it's something that's very interesting.' So I will be running two trains of thought. So you're keeping another set of drawings on the go that might be used one day. That's what happened with *Turning the Place Over*.

In the late Nineties I worked on a piece called *Over Easy* which was a bearing that oscillated the façade of a building. It was through a happy accident on

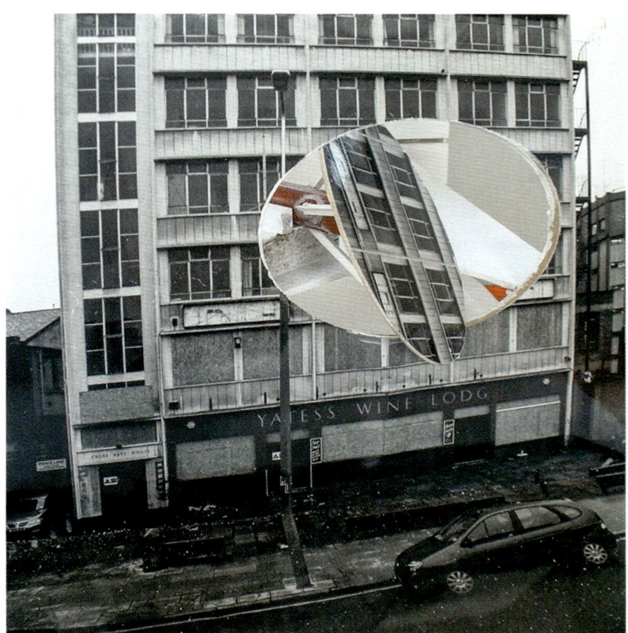

Richard Wilson, *Turning the Place Over* (2006). Collage.

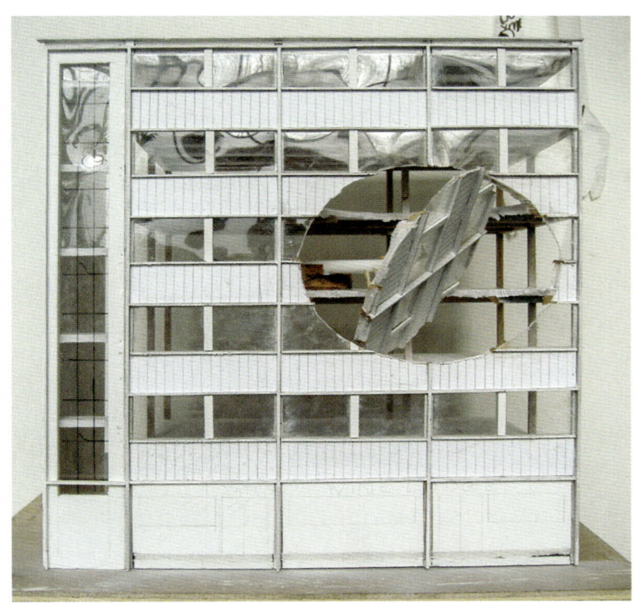

Richard Wilson, *Turning the Place Over* maquette (2006) .

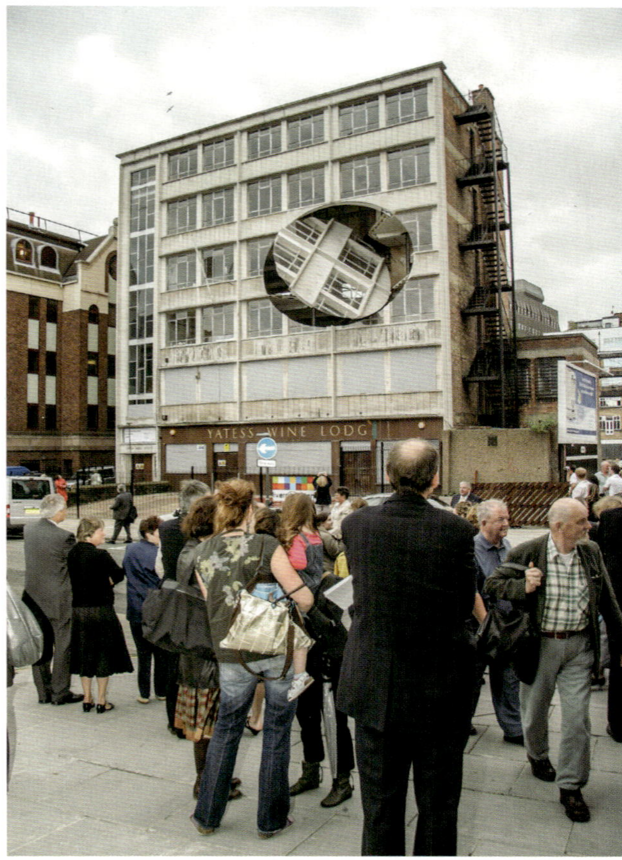

Richard Wilson, *Turning the Place Over* (2007). Yates's Wine Lodge building, Moorfields, Liverpool. Rotating 8m-diameter wall and window disc.

that project research that I could get to *Turning the Place Over*. I kept a whole train of drawings going for nine years and I made about eight maquettes, which eventually became the piece used for the Liverpool European Capital of Culture. I tried for nine years to find someone to do it, to find both the money and the property. One time I got the money but no property, and another time there was some property but no one came forward with the cash. It was nine years later that it all fell into position and we could do it. It was something I knew had to be made.

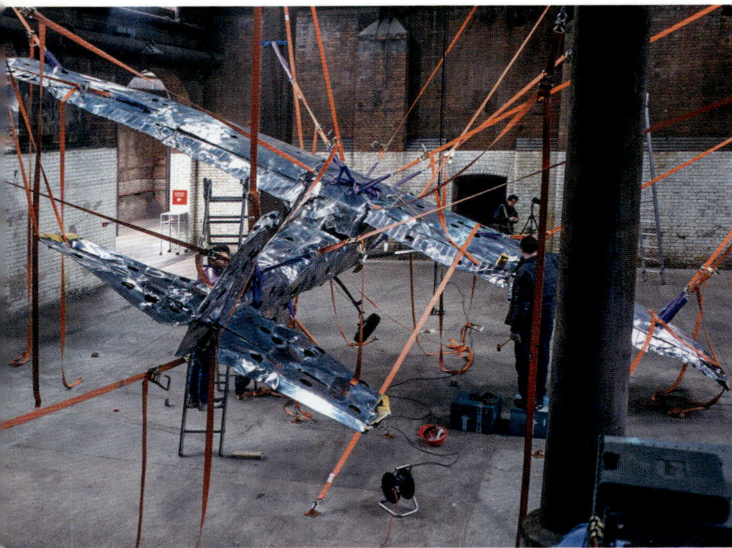

Richard Wilson, *Butterfly* (work in progress, 2003). Crushed Cessna light aircraft, hawsters, strops, ratchet straps. Wapping Project Space, London.

ID: *You also work with sound and performance as well.*

RW: I've always made it absolutely clear that I make sculpture. Some people don't think it is. Some people also ask if I'm an architect or an engineer. But what I've always said is that my sculptural practice is all-inclusive and has incorporated film and sound. If you can take a form and place it there and you can put a feather up there for example, why not do that with sound as well? Why isn't powder to shadow to a sound to a smell defined as material for sculpture as much as bronze, wood and steel? It's just being open to the full spectrum or vocabulary of a sculptor's possibilities. I think that's quite interesting.

I've worked with ideas that incorporate film as a way of bringing time or process into the work. An example of that would be the *Butterfly* piece where I took an aeroplane, cleaned it all up, crushed it and hung it in the Wapping Project Space as a crushed object. Over a period of about three weeks with students of the University of East London, we hauled it out and unfurled it back to be an aeroplane again as a process. While we were doing that I had cameras filming from a bird's-eye view and I realized halfway through the process that it wasn't the aeroplane, it was the compression of time that I was interested in. So with these photographs we edited a three-minute film where this thing undergoes a metamorphosis.

ID: *Bow Gamelan Ensemble would have been an early departure into collaborative projects.*

RW: That was founded in 1983 with Anne Bean and the late Paul Burwell. It began as playful experimentation with discarded stuff to generate sound. Paul and I would build a drum kit that would be wired to a switch mechanism, a car battery and a load of lights. We housed it on a rowing boat that I had and we would row out in the darkness under Tower Bridge and play, things like that. Just playful experimentation that was all an extension out of the freedom of being able to, as a sculptor, set up a situation.

This developed over the years into big performances. We would go to scrapyards and everything we hauled out was made into this mammoth orchestra. And depending on what you'd find in the scrapyard, that would become the show. For example, when we did a touring show in Japan we went to one scrap-yard; it was full of metal ladders so the whole show was up in the air. At a different place it was all farming equipment so you could get these enormous feed silos and they all became great big spring gongs and marimbas and drums, but they also became the megaphones on the instruments – so you had these extraordinary situations that were built up out of what was available at that time. It felt a bit schizophrenic as I was also continuing to make my own work through that period and it was like, 'How does that relate to what I'm doing?' But it was liberating, I didn't feel tied to one 'ism'; I didn't feel like I had to conform and I could do whatever I wanted to do.

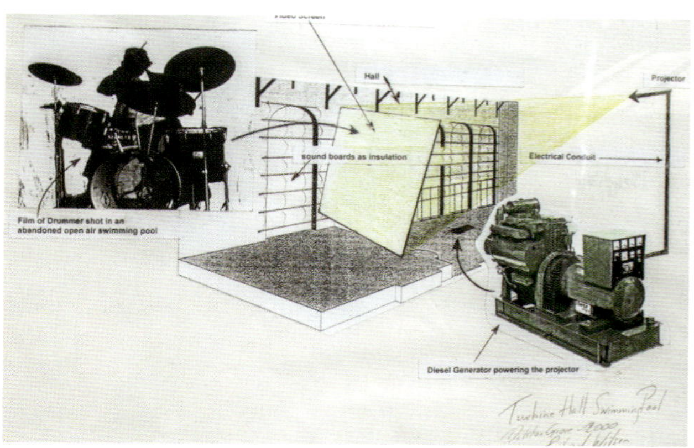

Richard Wilson, *Turbine Hall Swimming Pool* (1999). Collage.

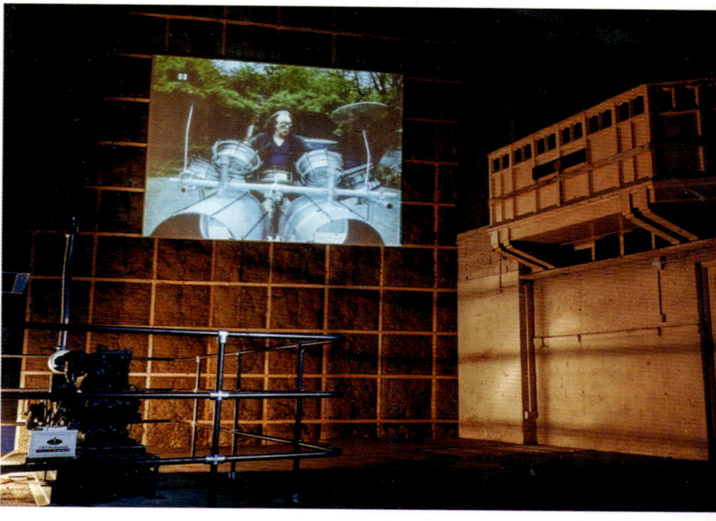

Richard Wilson, *Turbine Hall Swimming Pool* (2000). Diesel generator, DVD, amplifier speakers, wood, rockwool, steel fittings, bar-fire elements, lighting. Dimensions variable.

ID: *With* 20:50 *you filled a room with oil; with* One Piece at a Time *it is suspended car parts, and then at Dilston Grove you used generators in a church – there is some kind of narrative about energy and industry.*

RW: The Dilston Grove piece was called *Turbine Hall Swimming Pool*; in this piece a diesel generator is powering a projection of Paul Burwell playing on a moving homemade drum kit that we filmed in a disused swimming pool. And he's playing to the sound of the generator – he found five different rhythmic patterns while he listened to it – he's just going apeshit on the kit!

ID: *Where was the site?*

RW: A disused church, and the disused swimming pool next to the church, were both in Southwark Park. The piece was a dialogue on change and dereliction between the two sites. Why do they become obsolete spaces for communities? What causes property to breakdown? Unlike the new awaiting Tate Modern down the road that was ripping out its generators, I turned Dilston Grove into a generating station installing a diesel generator that powered the film of Paul drumming. I wanted to think about what happens when the engine gets turned off. Both the drumming and the engine were metaphors for energy and change.

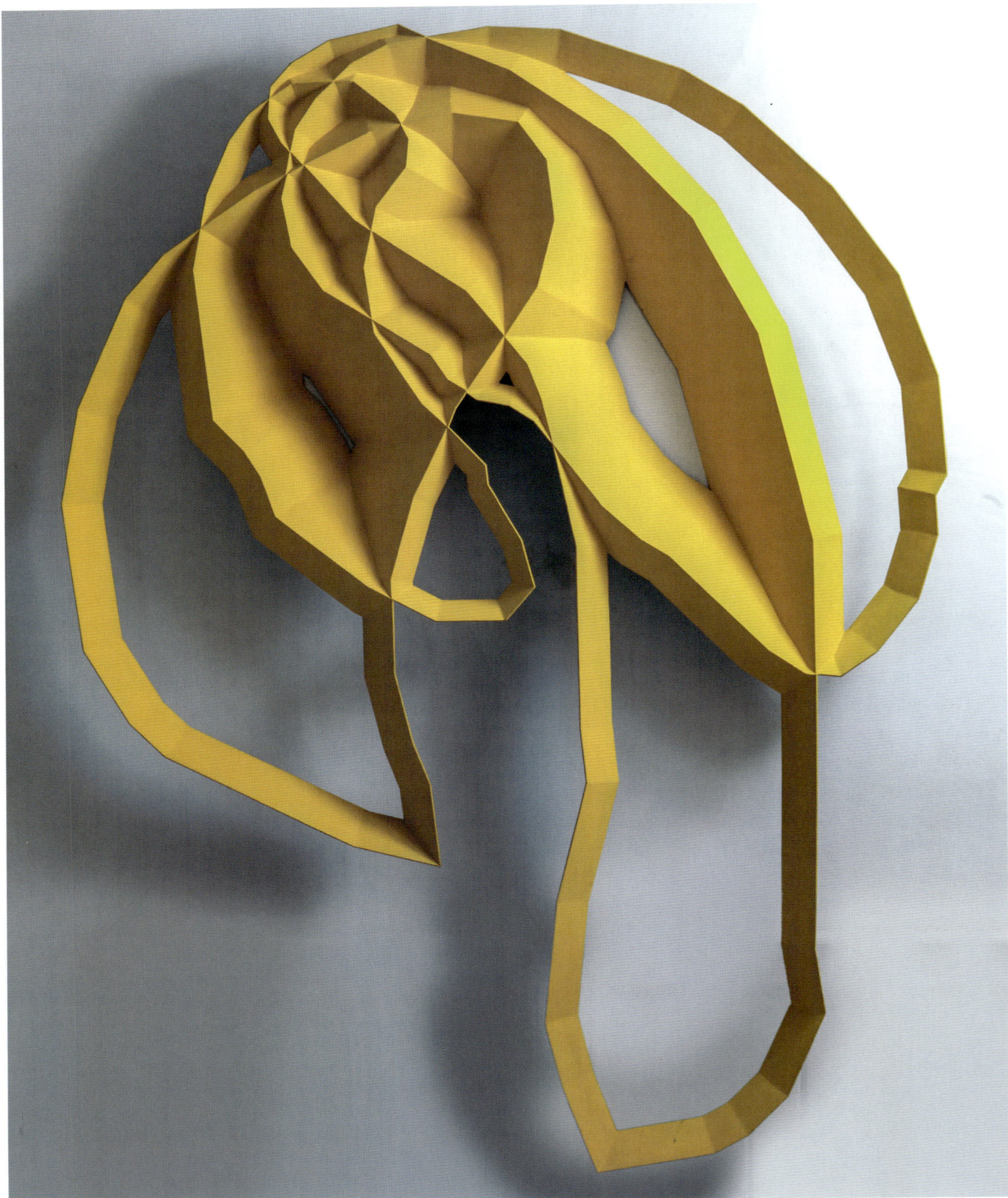

7 Formal Concerns

In 1963 Anthony Caro exhibited a bright red sculpture; it was made from a combination of salvaged steel and aluminium and was painted in bold gloss paint. It was a masterpiece of spatial beauty. Crucially, the work purported to have no external connotations; it was a sculpture without representation. This was the brief moment when sculpture progressed and crossed a threshold into an essential discipline. The idea of its meaning was delivered only through the object; by its form, its structure and its substance. Any context and external content was superfluous. This was a sculpture about sculpture.

Since the end of the nineteenth century specific discussions over form and content have besieged artistic practice. In 1890 the post-Impressionist painter Maurice Denis wrote, 'Remember that a picture, before it is a picture of a horse, a nude woman, or some story, is essentially a flat surface covered in colours arranged in a certain order.' And during different periods, preoccupation with formal qualities – of becoming immersed in the way that something has been constructed – has either been acclaimed or scorned, with a notable polarization of beliefs during the Cold War.

The Soviet Union, directly after the 1917 Revolution, had initially embraced formal experimentation, for example Tatlin's Tower, the iconic spiral (never built) that unequivocally signalled a new era. It was a period that witnessed Kazimir Malevich paint a white off-set square on white canvas, which challenged previous conventions of painting with a bravado to rival any painter in Paris. The fusion of attitudes with a greater European avant-garde was short lived and by the 1930s, artists such as Malevich were ostracized and their work was labelled 'debauched'. Art was expected to take an ideological and moral stance and the Communist state singularly supported Socialist Realism, a style that espoused romantic portrayals of heroic proletarian imagery. Any earlier patronage of formally experimental, non-traditional practices disappeared; it was classed as cultural elitism, was condemned, and the term 'formalism' was universally used to disparage.

There was, however, a very different attitude being expressed in North America. An influx of European artists into New York such as Josef Albers, Max Ernst and Piet Mondrian helped create a scene of accelerated stylistic development. A new generation of American artists was both moved and then motivated by the idea of making work with an experimental and original aesthetic. The dominant manner was labelled Abstract Expressionism, as artists such as Jackson Pollock made formal innovations. The easel disappeared, then the stretcher, and with Pollock, finally the brush in his giant immersive canvases, painting in its totality. Critics such as Michael Fried championed and celebrated the work with the belief that great art was about *how* not *what*. It was subsequently revealed that the state had financially and politically supported this movement; a substantiation of the creativity and intellectual freedom inherent within its own ideological system.

On the one hand was the idea of art for art's sake as a valid, essential proposition; and on the other an elite activity, a bourgeois language. This contradiction changed with Postmodernism, with collapsing distinctions between high culture and mass- or popular

OPPOSITE PAGE
Almuth Tebbenhoff, *Yellow* (1996). Fabricated steel, painted, 195 × 150 × 12cm.

culture. Media specificity was no longer important, and consideration towards formal decision-making was a modernist conceit.

New artists emerged, effacing the boundary between art and life, and in 1992 Damien Hirst placed a severed cow's head on to the floor of a gallery. A pool of blood seeped across the immaculate floor, its putrefaction forming maggots, then flies, framed within a glass vitrine. A fog of dancing spots, charged particles in Brownian motion, dancing to their death as the hanging insect-o-cutor deposited these dots back down to earth. Hirst titled the piece *One Thousand Years* and much was discussed about the 'aesthetics of revulsion' and the 'micro-drama of survival' – life and death. But what were his motivations to enclose and frame the flies in this way? He explains: 'Formally, I wanted an empty space with moving points within it, moving like stars, a solution to the problem of how to suspend things without strings or wires and have them constantly change pattern in space.' A formal concern.

▶ Sir Anthony Caro

I am on my way to visit an artist whose work elevated sculpture into a new modern era, an era where the hierarchical plane between painting and its craft- and process-laden cousin began to level.

In 1959 Tony Caro had just returned from his first trip to America. He was ready for changes, he had trained first at the (then) outmoded Royal Academy Schools before working for Henry Moore, and Caro was restless; his figures had become ever more abstract, yet they were still figures. Though one from 1959 hinted at what was to come: an expressive, highly worked abstracted figure had been sat on a slice of metal girder, this girder acting as a simple, sparse sculptural motif.

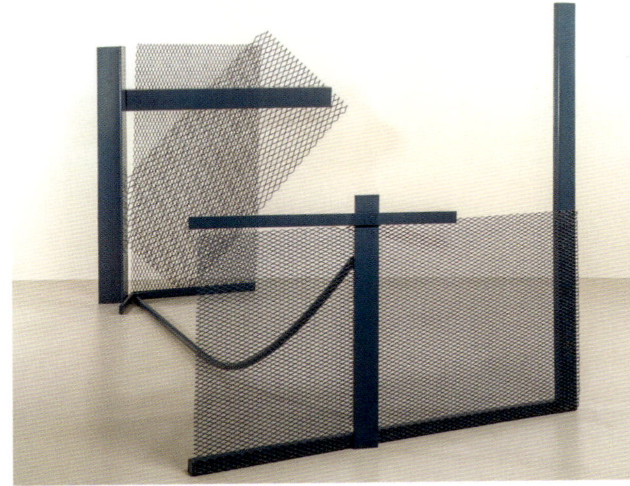

Sir Anthony Caro, *Carriage* (1966). Steel, painted blue, 195.5 × 203.5 × 396.5cm.

Caro's trip to America was an introduction to painters such as Robert Motherwell, Jasper Johns and Kenneth Noland. He also met with Clement Greenberg, the influential critic who was championing Jackson Pollock. Greenberg's advice was simple: 'If you want to change your art, change your habits.'

On his return an invigorated Caro went down to the docks and bought some scrap steel, which was delivered and dropped off onto the cobbled yard of his studio by the driver reversing furiously before slamming on his brakes.

It was a complete deviation: Caro, who initially didn't know how to weld and began by blowing a hole through the metal, soon got the hang of it. With just a gas-torch and welder and using basic construction methods, he began to work in an instantaneous way, free of the more complex traditional techniques. Because of the immediacy of the medium Caro was able to develop work in series, a method predominantly used by painters, and a body of work evolved that was of itself. The work existed off the plinth and in real space, it was open and expansive, using flat colour to ensure a feeling of weightlessness.

The influence of American painting (and of his

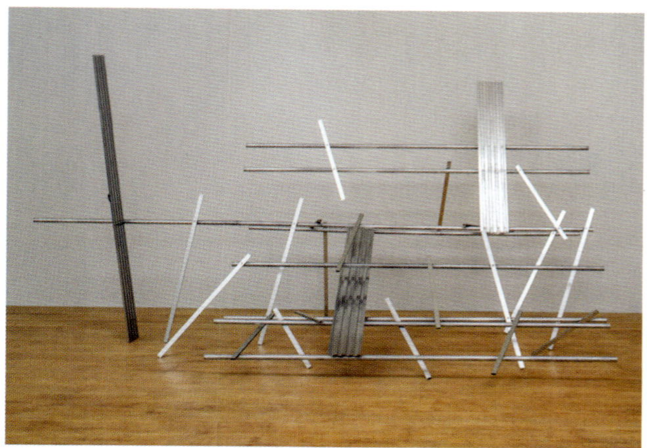

Sir Anthony Caro, *Hopscotch* (1962). Aluminium.

friendship with Kenneth Noland) was immense. Commercial air flight had opened this avenue of influence. Ideas about practice were shared and just as Noland would paint horizontally on canvases, Caro would work to the limitations of the garage that was his studio, both acknowledging to each other that the appearance of the work was not an essential aspect to its evolution. In fact it had the potential to hinder the kind of breakthrough that Caro was after.

This was a journey of discovery and the deliberate exploitation of his studio space was apparent in the creation of *Early One Morning*. The horizontal box section was already fully across the available space in the garage. It had been like that for a while with Caro not knowing where it would go from there. Eventually he opened the studio doors, bolted on an additional length, and extended the sculpture into the courtyard; it now became emphatically about horizontality.

As soon as it was finished Caro pulled the whole piece into the yard and left it there; it was originally painted green but didn't look right. The next morning the painter Sheila Girling, Tony's wife, suggested he 'try it red'. He did, and the piece was complete.

IAN DAWSON: *I want to ask about the moment when you eradicated likeness.*

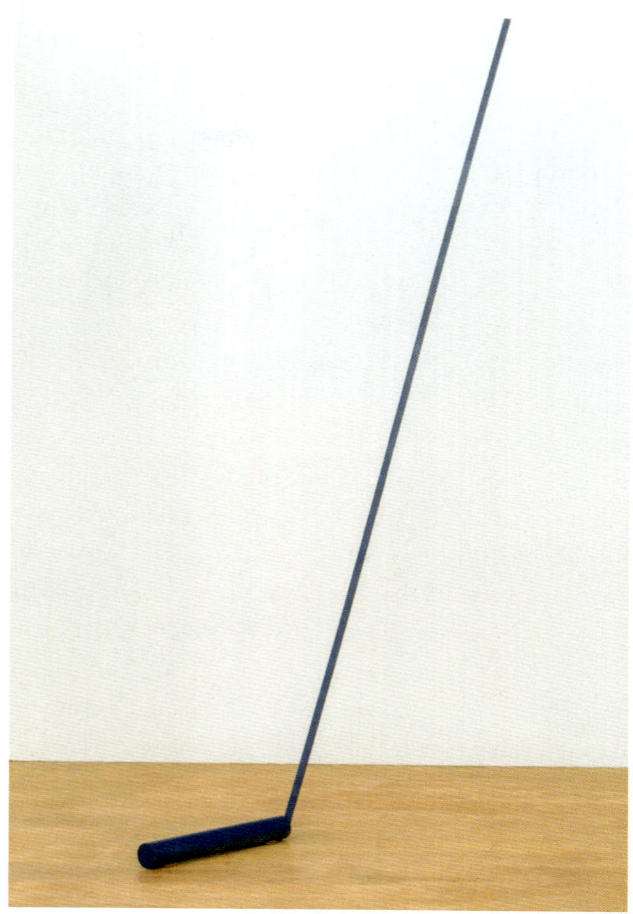

Sir Anthony Caro, *Sight* (1965). Steel, paint.

ANTHONY CARO: I didn't want my sculpture to be about pretending. Pretending to be a person. It can be that, but that wasn't what I wanted. I was getting away from figuration; I felt that it was coming between me as a viewer and what I was making – the sculpture. There are certain times when you need figuration: the Greeks got more figurative. However, this is where we are historically, and about the whole of sculpture. It's about where we happened to be in the 1960s. I felt that I must find a way to make the object that I make count for itself as a piece of sculpture. That's why I put it on the floor – to make it as immediate and as real as talking to you now, or rather talking to you without this microphone here!

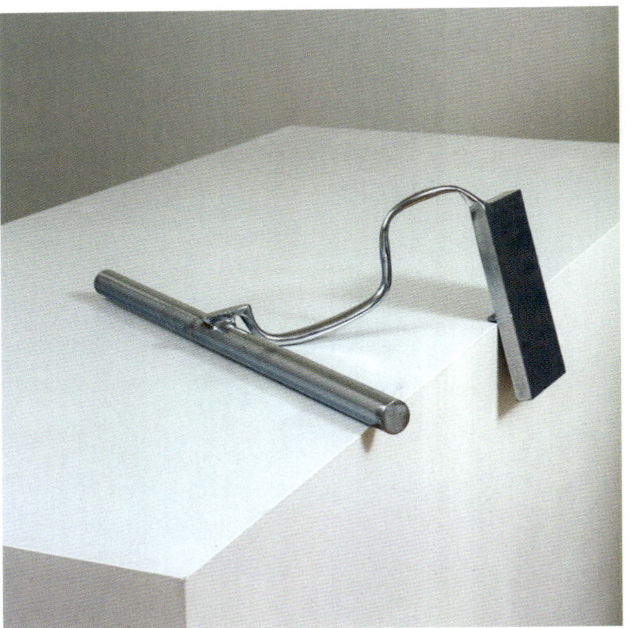

Sir Anthony Caro, *Table Piece XVIII* (1966). Steel.

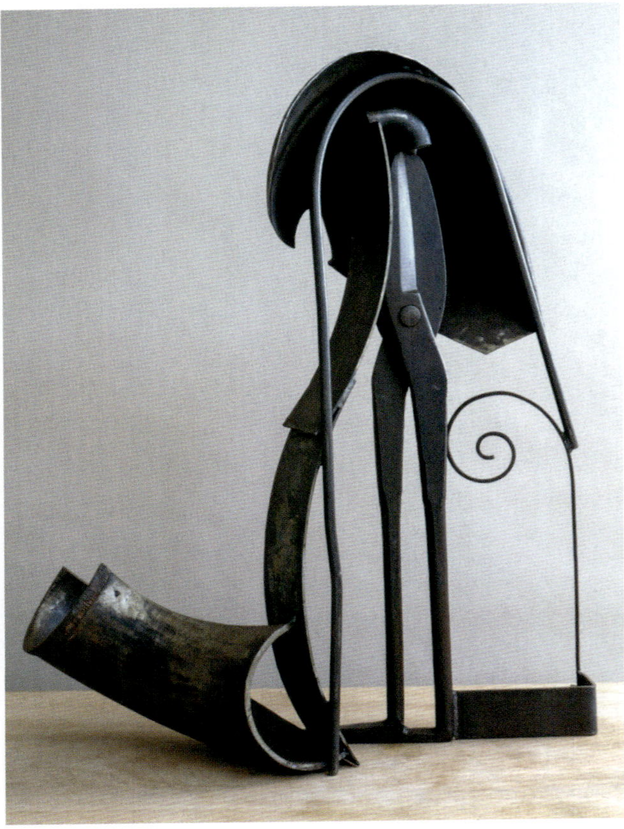

Sir Anthony Caro, *Catalan Cowl* (1987–88). Steel, waxed, 105.5 × 94 × 48cm.

ID: *How do you feel about this legacy?*

AC: It's a different set of problems now than it was then.

ID: *You began to share aspirations with some American painters during your visits to Bennington.*

AC: I remember Jules Olitski saying that he was trying to make a painting as naked as possible. That was the way I was going too. Seeing how close to the edge I could go and still call it a sculpture. I made a piece that was a block on the floor with a pole standing up. It was nearly just an upright pole but not quite. And in the end, having made those pieces, it struck me that I could put parts of those together, and make more complicated works. So I developed, from one sort of outrageous position into a more complicated and complex situation.

ID: *When did you return to the plinth with your table sculptures?*

AC: Snaking things across the floor became the fashion, one I had made myself. However, I got fed up with seeing it. I thought, 'How do I make a small sculpture?' I was thinking about handles, how they attract you to holding. And I would have to deal with putting it on another level. What is different about a table from the floor? It's got an edge, so in the first one I just made the piece go over the edge and put a handle on it, and that was it. And it develops from there. After a while, I can lose things. Maybe it doesn't have a handle, or maybe it doesn't go over the edge of the table. But it's no longer a maquette; small sculptures used to be maquettes – a little thing in its own world – and I didn't want it to be that.

ID: *At a certain point they inform the larger sculptures?*

AC: They've always played against each other. I am trying to give sculpture the same sort of respect and emphasis that painting had. Painting was something you look at and have to address; sculpture was something you bumped into. The idea of making casts, making editions makes it less unique, more like a lithograph, less 'one off', like a painting. So I said, 'No, I won't do that.' All my sculptures feed into this same story of mine.

ID: *So within the studio set-up, do you work with the small ones and big ones simultaneously?*

AC: Up to a while ago I was working on little ones at weekends and at home in my garage. Welding them up, tacking them, putting them outside, then bringing them down to the studio. Then I don't look at them for three or four months and then address them again, see them afresh because I want to keep the spontaneity.

ID: *I find the small pieces fascinating.*

AC: I go back into them again and again. I see them at every stage. That's what I think is important; I'm very keen to keep my work fresh. I don't work and work until I'm blue in the face because that way it's going to lose its life. I have a shot, get it as right as I can, give it to Pat [Cunningham, Caro's assistant] to weld it up, don't look at it, and then later look at it again. Each time I try and keep that freshness, always. It's quite nice to have a studio away from home, and after a night's sleep, to come in and see it and it's a new thing. It says 'hello' to you. 'Do I like it or do I hate it?' Or 'What's wrong with it?'

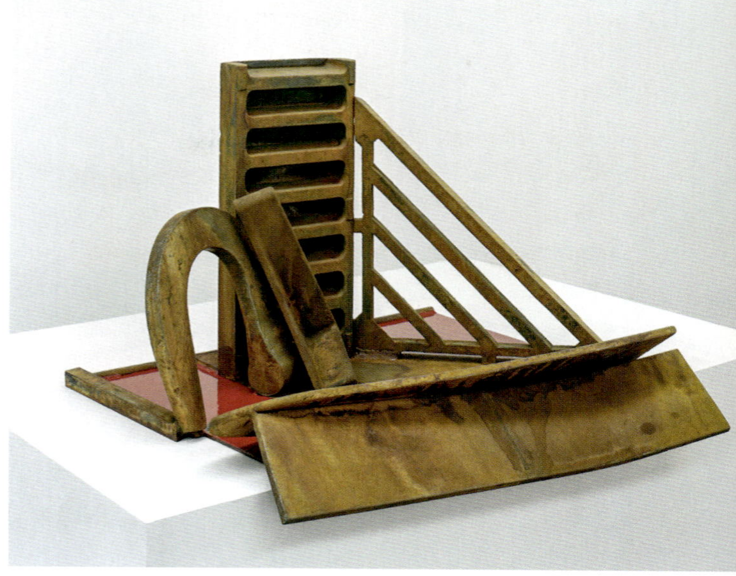

Sir Anthony Caro, *Slope* (2010). Steel, rusted, and part-painted cast iron, 54 × 82 × 66cm.

ID: *There was a period when you put a figurative element back into the pieces.*

AC: Chillida and Tapies had both said to me, 'You should go and work with Hans Spinner.' He had done things with them and they had both enjoyed working with him. I had done some clay things before, but with other people. I went to Hans in the south of France and when we started, he said, 'Tony, start away. What are you going to do?' and I said, 'I haven't a clue. I have no idea what I'm going to do. Hans, why don't you start?' And he said, 'Nobody's ever said that to me before.' Then he lifted up this block of clay (he called them *breads*) and he slammed it down on the floor. I said, 'Okay, now I know where I'm going.'

When I work with somebody else, I am not just working with a material: I'm also working with their approach to that material. When Hans threw this lump of clay down on the floor, I could see that his was a very physical approach. He's very strong, he knows exactly where he's going, but he's kind of rough. I understood the way that he was thinking. The material and him were all part of the same thing. Once I could see how

he was approaching the block of clay I would play
with all sorts of variations, sticking things in, making
indentations, adding, subtracting.

I also discovered that you can't mess with clay. You
can't work on it like you work with steel, which you can
cut and change. It's either right or wrong, that's the end
of it. It's not a thing to work into. So, the pieces would
be quite quickly made; we would make a lot of stuff
and put it on the table. And I'd say, 'Let it dry. Fire it in
Hans's kiln and let me see them when they come back.'
When they were done, they came back to the studio
and Pat undid them and left them on the floor and I
realized that they were heads – you can't escape it. They
were warriors and I saw it as the Trojan War. And that
was how I started and I thought, 'What am I doing?
I'm going into figuration. But all the same I don't care!
That's the way it's going and I'm going to follow it!'

ID: *That's a wonderful description of an intuitive
approach.*

AC: A lot of what we're talking about is how you
respond to your feelings. Do you fight them or do you
go with them? You do both, at different times. This was
a case when I simply went with what it looked like, how
it felt right. In the end I put some of them with wood,
some of them with steel and they became figurative, a
group of figures.

ID: *Was this also a response to abstraction?*

AC: If abstraction becomes decoration, it gets really
boring. There is a tendency to bring some figuration
back in, whenever abstraction becomes taken for
granted.

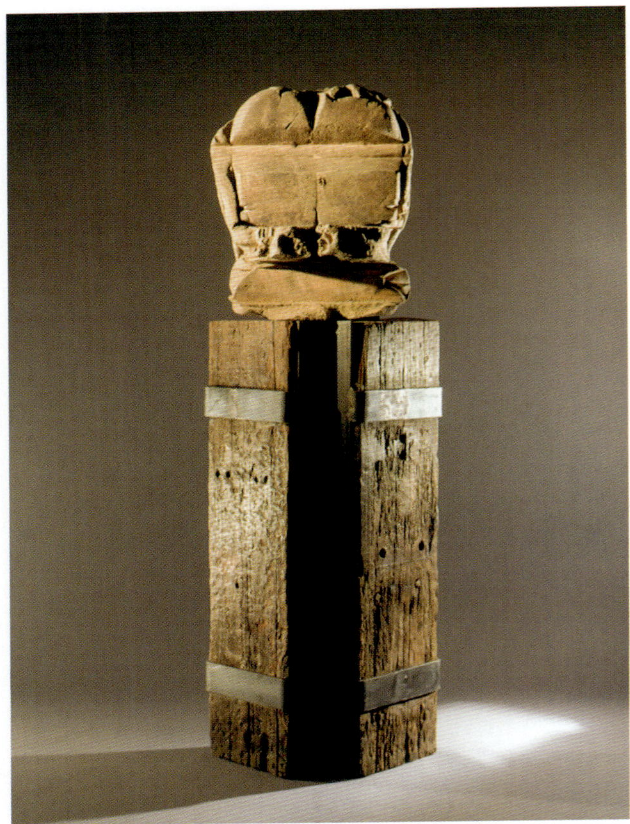

Sir Anthony Caro, *Agamemnon* (1965). Ceramic, wood and
steel.

ID: *I was thinking here about the workshops that
you have done. And I was thinking that the human
interaction during making has been important to you.*

AC: Very much so; I like having people around. I like
working in the studio with a small pool of people.
For me, sculpture is not an utterly private activity – I
need a bit of ping-pong, ideas coming backwards
and forwards. That's the way I've always thought
and always taught. We never had enough space at St
Martin's, everybody was tripping over each other and
I thought that was excellent. To go to a place where
there are no other artists around and make art would
be quite a challenge and far more difficult than being
overwhelmed with other people.

ID: *That's probably the way that good art gets made.*

AC: Sculpture and probably architecture, yes. Painting, no. I think painting is a more solitary occupation.

ID: *You are still influenced by painting?*

AC: Sculpture either goes towards painting or architecture. I would look at paintings much more than anything else in the early days, but now I think about architecture quite a lot.

ID: *Modernist architecture?*

AC: I don't mean specific architecture, but the idea of inwardness and the idea of inside/outside. I don't take up everything about architecture and I don't try and make a building. I think we have got terribly involved in the idea that sculpture since Michelangelo had to be in the round. Yes, but if you look at Donatello, you've got a back and a front, and even if the back doesn't need to be as important as the front, that's like a building. That was very different from the way that we were taught, that you always were expected to be walking round your piece, that you didn't really work with views, you always had to see everything in the round.

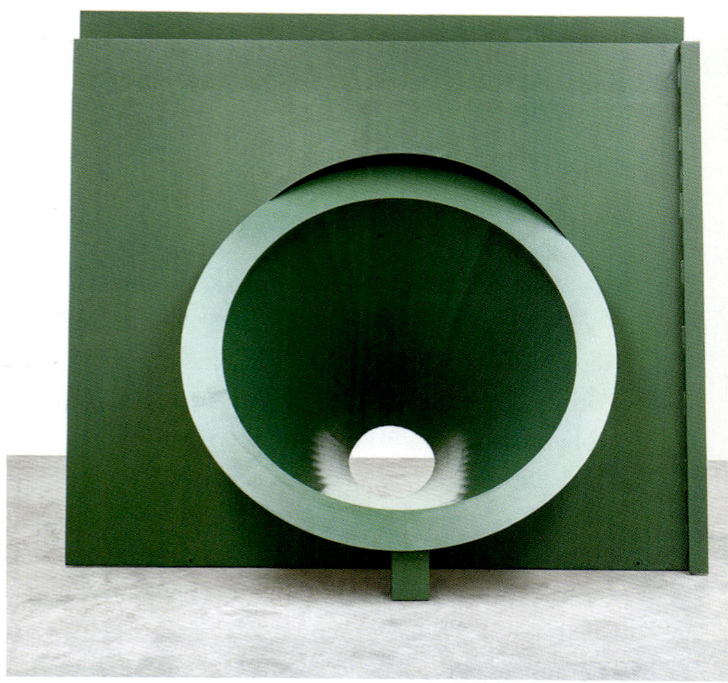

Sir Anthony Caro, *Up Front* (2010). Steel, painted, 237.5 × 259 × 173cm.

ID: *Fascinating.*

AC: With Michelangelo, you're pulled around like a corkscrew. That's what I mean when I say that there is more to sculpture than one approach: whether having a rule or breaking it, there's more than that. And it's no good to be too conceptual, too theoretical; it's got to be real. I like the fact that we take stuff that is used in everyday life and try and give it some emotional content. However much we talk, and have all these thoughts, we're making things with stuff. It's marvellous that it's hard stuff or soft stuff; whatever it is, it's stuff. Our activity is very real, that's what we're playing with. ∎

▶ Almuth Tebbenhoff

Almuth Tebbenhoff's studio is teeming with material and equipment, kilns and clay, metal and welders, band saws, hoists, stone and carving equipment. I was first drawn to Tebbenhoff's floating forms of deeply pigmented colour that undulate with a geometric rhythm. Sited on the wall, *Yellow 1996* glows corona-like: both in and apart from the world. I went to meet Tebbenhoff, thinking of this sense of the supernatural through a geometric vocabulary. It came as a surprise that she first trained as a ceramicist.

ALMUTH TEBBENHOFF: In 1972 I started making pots. First at the Chelsea Pottery just off the King's Road. I don't know if it still exists, but it was very cool to be on the King's Road in platform boots and hot pants and all that sort of thing making pots! I was twenty-three and it was something I'd always wanted to do and so I started getting into art that way. And then towards the end of the Seventies, I met Eduardo Paolozzi who saw some of the ceramic pieces that I'd made. At that stage I was already frustrated with everything being round when you work on a wheel; I'd sort of distorted pieces and tried doing things with them because I wanted to push through the materials to somewhere else, and he said, 'You're not a potter, don't be stupid.' And he invited me to come to the Royal College: 'Just help yourself,' he said, 'and if anybody asks you, say Paolozzi sent you.' And that was brilliant. Because it opened my mind towards other methods and ways, and I realized it didn't have to be clay, it could be anything. That opened things up for me tremendously. I was like a stowaway.

IAN DAWSON: *And now in your studio you're working with ceramics again?*

AT: Yes, it's a joy working with ceramics again, because they're old friends. I know the materials; I just feel very comfortable. When I work with a material, I have to love the whole thing, the smell of it even. You know, you might say it's strange with steel but I love the smell of the coolant and the greases and all that – the smell of metal, even the welding – delicious! There is also something about the sound of a hammer on metal, bashing around on an anvil beating something; it's very satisfying. And then you've got the clay – the mouldy, earthy smell. And also it's so receptive. You put a fingerprint into it and it's there. And now with the marble, when you've got the right stone, the right resistance, a strong but workable stone, and you start taking the chisel into it, you can really get a sense of the structure of that material. You get an understanding of the way it shears off as you get under it and lift layer after layer until you get to the bit that you want and that releases strange smells. Sometimes you get a whiff of sulphur and all sorts of other things. So making work is an interplay between the senses and the intellect. And I think that it's a huge privilege to use your senses – all of them, touch, sight, hearing – everything making a piece of work. And maybe that informs it and it might be why I actually work with it rather than just ringing up the marble studio and saying, 'Guys, make me one of those.' I think I'd be missing out.

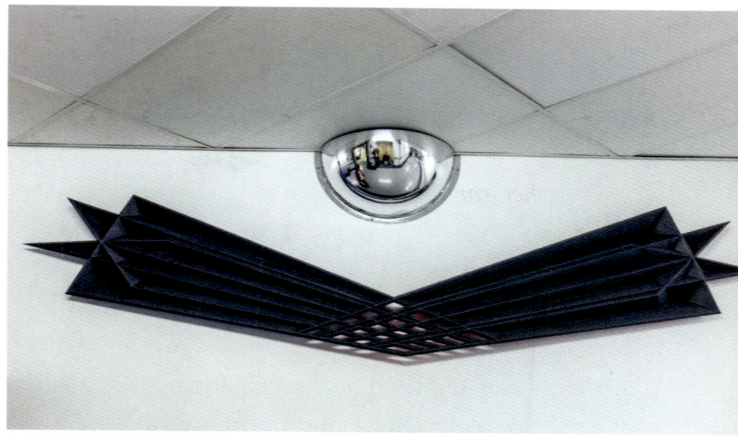

Almuth Tebbenhoff, *Cosmic Event* (1993). Fabricated steel, painted, 290 × 110 × 15cm.

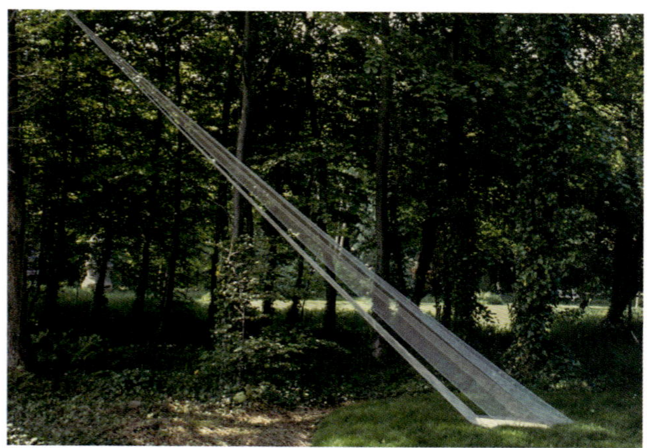

Almuth Tebbenhoff, *Beam* (1998–99). Fabricated stainless steel, mesh, gold leaf, 500 × 500 × 120cm.

ID: *You are very grounded in processes; can you trace that back?*

AT: I have an agricultural background. My parents had a large farm. It was a tremendous way of growing up, when you're so close to the soil, to the earth, to crops growing and failing and animals being born, slaughtered and dying. Something that is very real; there was no sense of time for embellishment. There is a resourcefulness required living on a farm, and my father would invent strange pieces of machinery. If anything were ever needed to help plant the potatoes he would work something out. Make an apparatus of machinery that would do something to make life that bit easier. So he invented all the time. And he had this wonderful blacksmith working with him in the forge, so that made a deep impression. But culturally there were no references to art, it was totally removed from anything other than the function. It was pure function. There wasn't any value added! And when he died I got his little welder and I started making metal pieces.

ID: *There was another side too?*

AT: My father was also sort of very astronomically influenced. He spent hours looking at the stars through his telescope, so that opened my mind towards that direction.

ID: *I read that your father took you outside one night onto the 52nd degree of latitude with the telescope to observe* Sputnik *travelling across the night sky; that poetic moment is very evident in these first pieces.*

AT: Black holes, unimaginable distances were all in my mind at the time. I was out in space, I remember: at the time I wasn't really all that grounded. I'd had a dream of being watched from outer space by two eyes.

ID: *The illusionary space of the wall was a physical plane that you were utilizing with these first pieces.*

AT: For years the wall was my support system against which I could fantasize about deep space. Use it as an aid to defy gravity, because I would like my sculptures to lift, to fly or to hover. The wall allowed me to play with that illusion.

ID: *You then came back down to earth. The sculpture*
Beam *literally describes your change in focus. From*
gazing upwards at the cosmos you have looked
downwards onto the ground.

AT: I was looking for something else, recognizing that
there was something missing, like yeast in a dense
material. A spiritual dimension that, like yeast, livens
it, makes it grow. I felt like there was this yeast that I
needed. I went back to meditation and for three days
every week I would be in deepest meditation. I was
trying to understand why I was around, who I was, why
I was alive, why I'd been given this gift of life and what
I had to do for it. At the same time, I began making
all the steel *flowers*, which was a response to being
overwhelmed by what I thought was the most beautiful
thing I could make.

ID: *The simplicity of them belies the intricacy of the*
making process.

AT: They're very complex things that I drew on paper
– these huge overlapping curves and then every little
angle; where to cut them, because I wanted diamond-
like facets. So I would have a curved drawn line, and
I would work out how many angles I would need in
order to achieve a flow. But these steel flowers just
happened out of my desire to make something so
beautiful that it touches your heart and what the
meditation gave me was the strength to wrestle with
them.

ID: *And you were working on the pieces flat?*

AT: I actually welded on top of the sheets of paper, on
the drawings. I worked out all the hundreds of angles;
it had to be very accurate. I measured an angle, I'd split

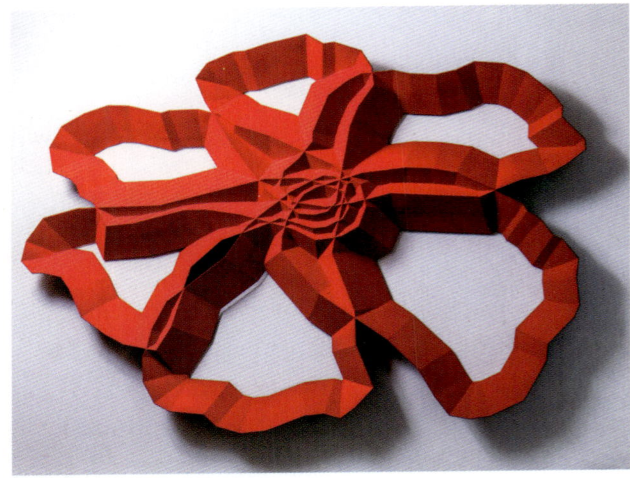

Almuth Tebbenhoff, *Red Flower* (1995). Fabricated steel,
painted, 180 × 130 × 12cm.

it in half and set the setting on the saw to cut it, so it
was unbelievably tedious work and I think I needed
to have that meditative frame of mind in order to be
able to do it, otherwise you'd go crazy. But for me, at
the time, it actually satisfied something: it became like
a sort of votive offering. I'd seen something beautiful
and I wanted to show the world. Which is what an
artist does. And the series grew and I made ones in a
spectrum of colours. I could have carried on but I also
needed to move on.

ID: *It is almost like you then focused out.*

AT: I wanted to make work in a landscape, bigger
in scope and in the mind, more expansive. Creating
volumes became another concern, and again to try and
overcome the weight of the material and give it that
lightness. And then I just arrived at the free-standing
pieces. And then perhaps because this angle-iron is
containing and describing a volume that doesn't exist,
maybe that's why Helaine Blumenfeld, of the RBSS,
said, 'Have you ever thought of working with stone?'
She then told me about the scholarship at Studio Sem
in Pietrasanta that offered to teach sculptors to carve
marble.

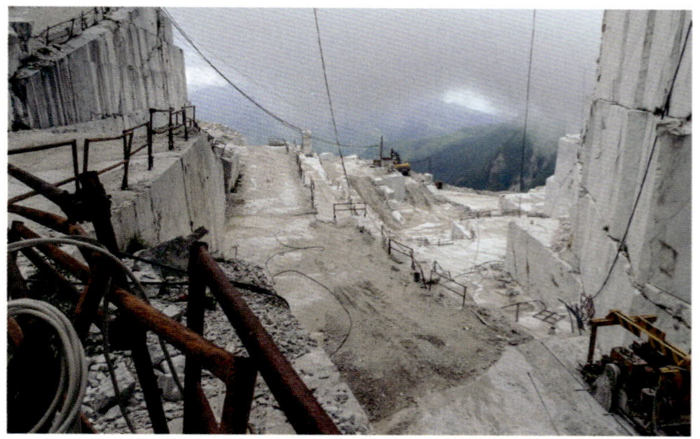

Almuth Tebbenhoff, *Marble Quarry*.

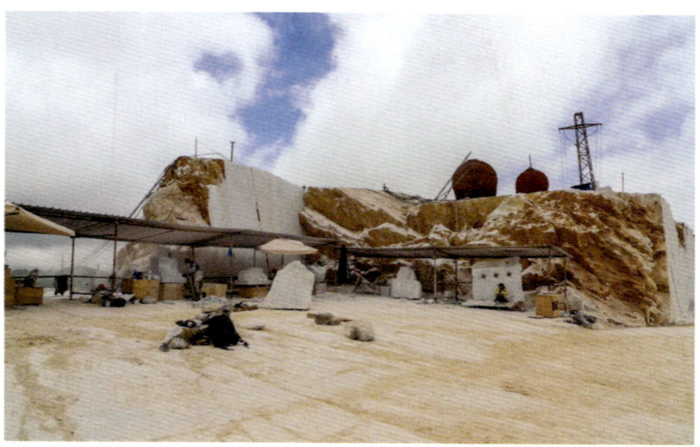

Almuth Tebbenhoff, *Marble Quarry*.

ID: *And you did?*

AT: It was such a tremendous challenge. I thought that it was a sensible thing for an artist to go and work with stone at some stage in their life because it is such a commitment and you have to be so clear and grown-up. It's hard to make such a dense material light.

ID: *And how did it go?*

AT: Well, I think the first piece I made was leaning very heavily on what I'd been making before in clay, because I had no language and I had no understanding of the material. So I just thought, 'I've got to find a way in', so I picked up a hammer and a chisel and there was a lump and I just sort of worked into it from a previous image that I had in my head, just to get familiar with the material a bit. And then over the years, every time I make a new piece I feel, 'Yes, I'm getting closer and closer into the stone', but at first it was very frightening – the confrontation with something heavier than myself.

ID: *You go to carve in Italy?*

AT: I don't have any clutter with me there. Life is light. So I can make things there without the restrictions of here. It's essential for me to have something like that, to have that sort of freedom. But it was quite something on my first trip to suddenly start from scratch. It is an environment where people don't have respect for what you've done in the past; they have respect for what you're doing now. And the place is always flooded with artists so you only impress if you do something really good. So it's humbling in that way and I found that incredibly refreshing. I thought I was somebody and to have that support system pulled from under me – it was horrible but also very liberating.

ID: *You then picked up carving techniques.*

AT: Learning the scaling-up process was important, using the compass and points the way it was used in Michelangelo's time. You use this method of circles, a line and a tangent forming a triangle and lots of strategic points on the model. You can then find the points in the stone with several compasses of different sizes, transferring the measurements from the model to the block. It's accurate when the *artigiani* do it, and I find it looks quite poetic, whirling these long metal callipers about, but I am a bit slower than them.

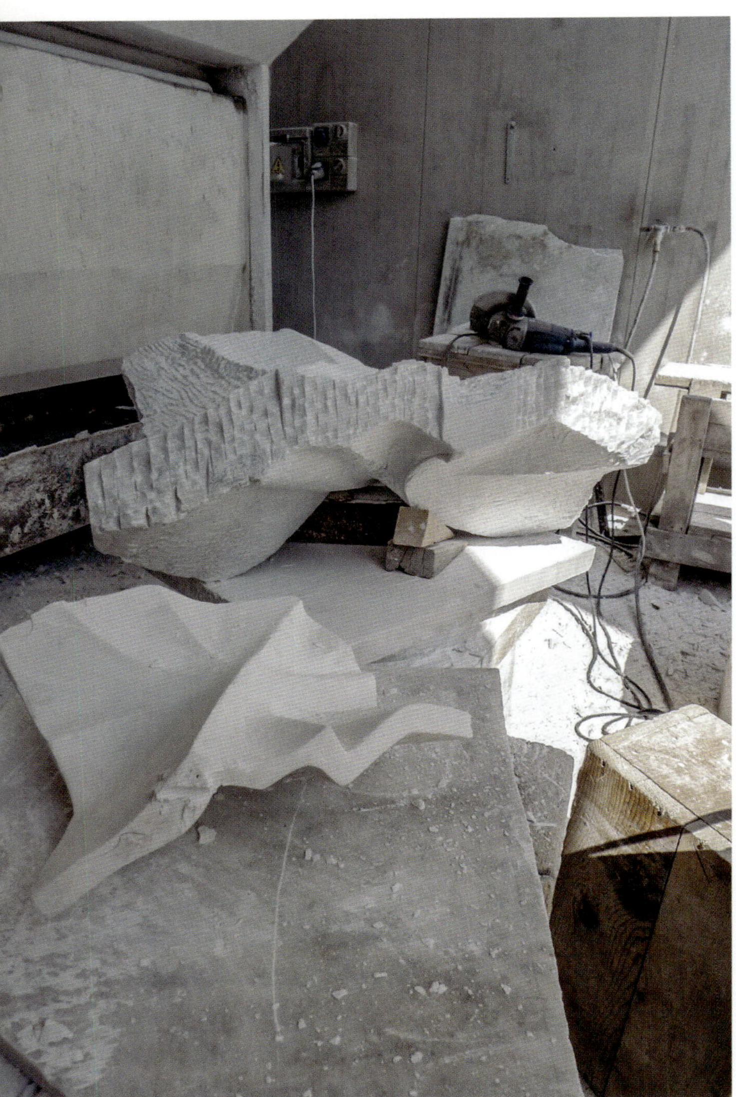

Almuth Tebbenhoff, carving in progress.

block in the sculpture. That may be a beauty in itself, but they're very cuboid and they don't have this kind of total freedom of a form, you know. I feel they're dense. And that didn't interest me so much. I wanted to learn how to get really into the heart of the stone, where I wanted to be. Rather than accepting limitations just because it's a long way in.

ID: I guess it helps with allowing you to utilize the models that you make.

AT: I prepare some of the models here, take them with me and then scale them up in the studio in Italy. But in the process they change. You can't just expand it and expect it to work. Big pieces work in a different way to small pieces; they need to grow consciously so you need to be fully there when you're scaling up. Rather than just mechanistically scaling it up, you need to be present and creative with it.

ID: What happens when you are not happy with something? You said that you have some pieces in the kiln that you weren't happy with.

ID: It sounds like you relished the process. It has similarities to plotting the orbit of a satellite and equally how you became absorbed in the fabrication of the curved steel line. How did it help you?

AT: In some ways the work I'm not happy with can be the most important work. It isn't just about showing me where I'm going wrong; that is important, but sometimes what I have thought of as a mistake is some part of me that I'm rejecting for old psychological reasons that are no longer relevant and this can help me to reclaim something that's a legitimate part of me. Sometimes my hands that create something know better than the head. I don't know how clear this is.

AT: It gives me the security to tackle more complex shapes. Because if you just work your way into a block from the outside without a model it ends up looking all blocky. I think that's something I noticed about English sculptors from the twentieth century: you can see the

AT: It's healthy to bin stuff; in some pieces, it could be that something is overstated or it's tedious or boring or banal or whatever. Life's too short to pursue something that doesn't have a real power. So I chuck those at a certain stage. But sometimes the things that I think are horrible are not. They may be powerful and close to the core; they may reveal something to me that is uncomfortable, and that may be why I think they're horrible. Those are the things that I look at a couple of years later and suddenly think: 'Wow', because I don't judge it anymore – it's grown away from me or I've grown away from it far enough to really see it, and then you can really see the power in it.

ID: *How do you deal with that?*

AT: That's why I am firing the small ceramics, particularly because they are done with spontaneity and have an immediacy about them.

ID: *How do you find the difference between the spontaneity of the little ones, and then the rigour of the process you have to apply when you enlarge them?*

AT: That's a growing-up process. It's a maturing process, that you make choices, informed choices, and hopefully the right choices. So I have this process going on all the time, of having an idea and making it and thinking, 'Actually that's not what I wanted'. So you've got lots and lots of things, but then every now and then, I hit upon something and I think, 'That's so good', and, 'That needs to be made big', and, 'That could be amazing', and then all the other aspects kick in. ■

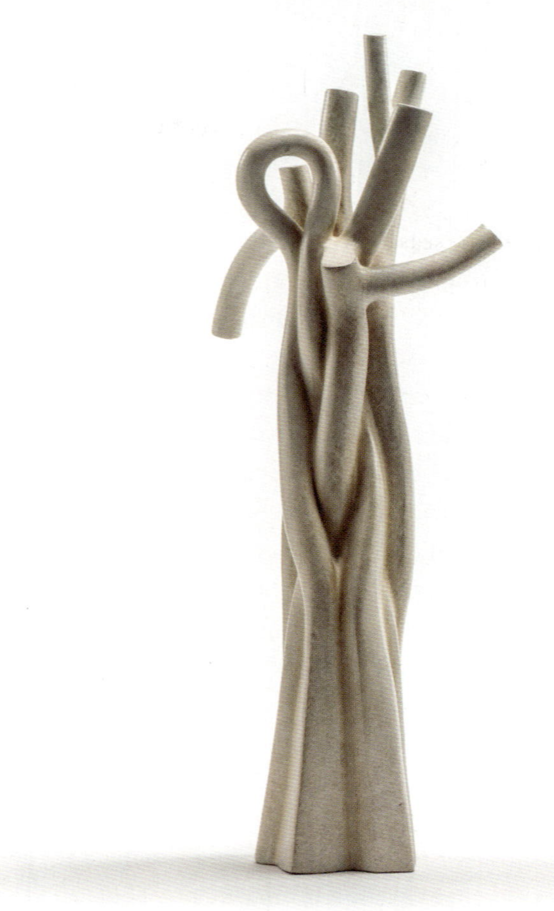

Almuth Tebbenhoff, *September waking* (2006). Honey-coloured onyx, height 84cm.

▶ Shell-Collecting Shells

In temperate seas, on continental shelves and on the slopes of tropical oceans, in shallow waters and in murky depths there lives a small, curious group of molluscs. This family of twenty-two species of sea snail has one very particular trait: they adorn detritus from their habitat onto their shells. Symptomatically these creatures cover themselves with other shells, shell fragments, coral, worm tubes, stones, pebbles, wood, aluminium ring pulls, corroded plastic, glass fragments and rusted steel remnants. They use their feet, proboscis and tentacles periodically to find, clean and place these foreign objects onto the growing edge of their shells. They then cement them in place with a secretion of calcium carbonate, lying idle whilst it sets.

Each species has a preferred style. Some members of the family place a narrow range of small shells in regular intervals, some use a greater variety of sea-floor debris in more dynamic arrangements. These are the family Xenophoridae, from the Greek *xenos* (foreign) and *phora* (carrying), and are commonly known as 'carrier snails' or, even more poetically, as 'shell-collecting shells'.

Who are they? What are their motives? To peculiarly burden their own casing with additional forms and extend their armour with ludicrous-looking prosthetic limbs? Most are driven by the need to disguise, to avoid discovery by predators. So they adorn, cover and camouflage, to blend in with the seabed debris.

However, some of the clan live in deeper, darker waters, where there are different imperatives. Their appendages are necessitated by a desire not to be sucked into the dense and profuse muck in which they live. The additions and extensions to their shells help spread their surface area, assisting them in averting their descent into the mire. In some instances these

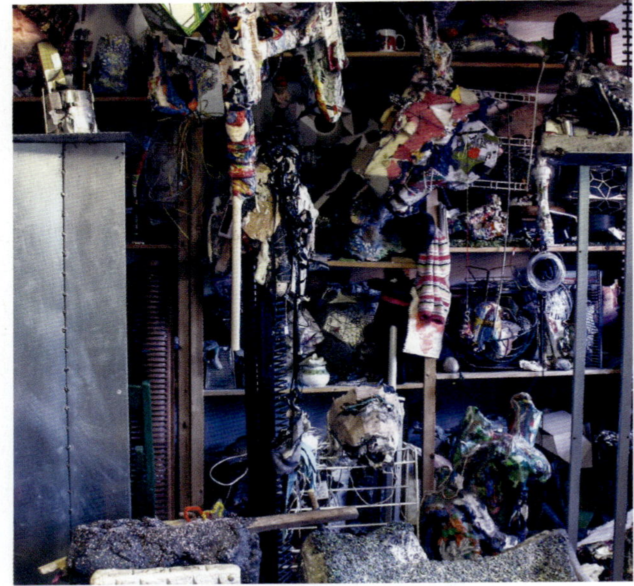

Ian Dawson, studio wall (2008).

extra wings help raise the molluscs from the ocean floor, granting better feeding conditions.

The tale of these *Xenophora* inspired me. I had been collecting broken objects without knowing what I was going to do with them, becoming ever more sensitized towards all this stuff that surrounded me, at home as well as on the street. The studio became the sea bed and the objects within it attempted to survive a crowded situation; I grabbed onto things – domestic detritus, broken ornaments, pound shop tat, and started to affix them, akin to the *Xenophora*. It was a way of working that formalized my material compulsiveness. Fortified with a tube of Gripfil (the construction worker's universal adhesive of choice), cement, bitumen, PVA and papier-mâché, objects would be added in the turmoil of the studio. Most objects didn't make it; some survived; some attached themselves via an extended arm to drawings.

One gesture, then another in response to that first mark, and then another in response to the first two. Of work being constructed, that the next cycle delivers something of benefit. Object-carrying objects. ■

OPPOSITE PAGE:
Collection of *Xenophora pallidula* with various objects.

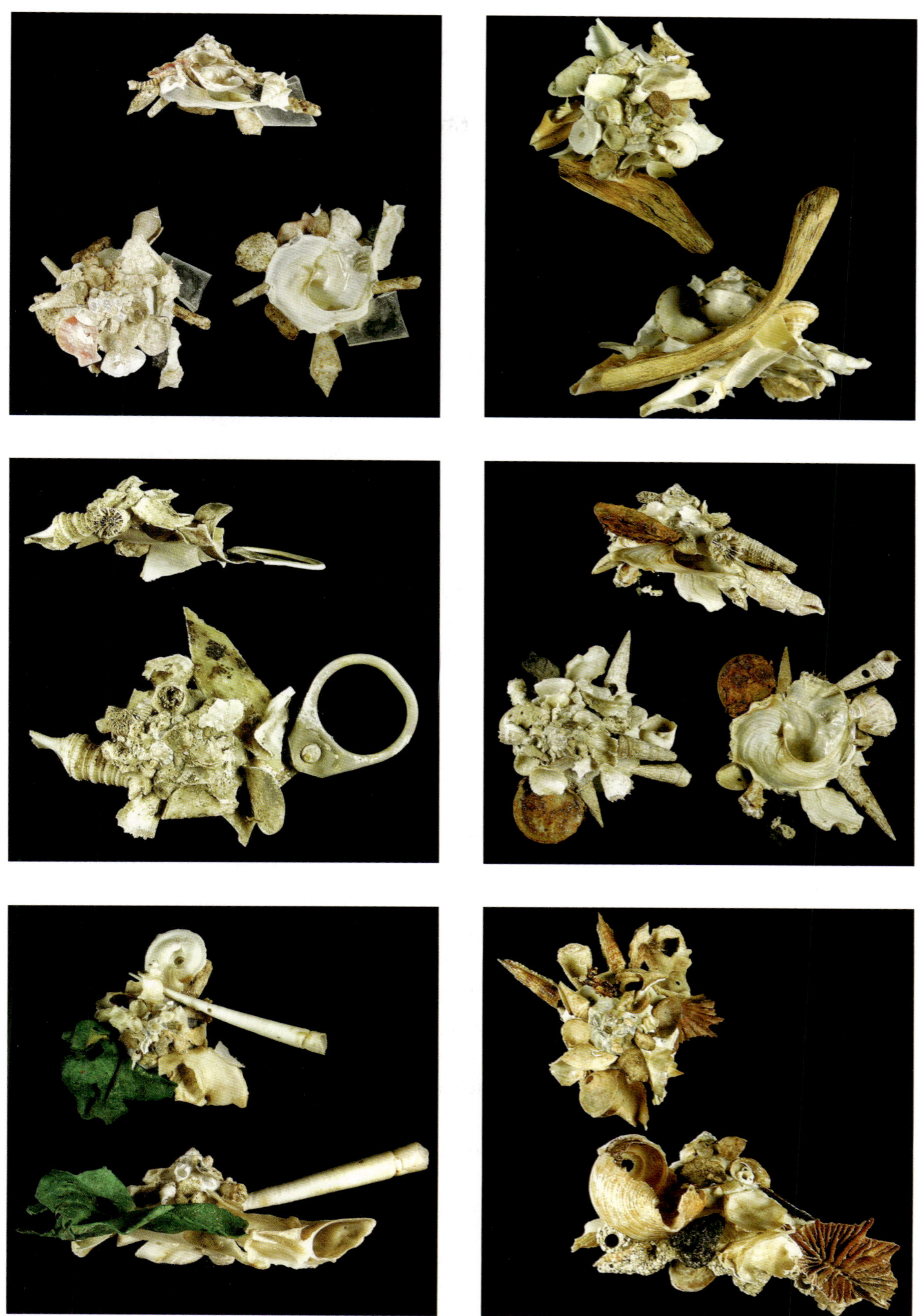

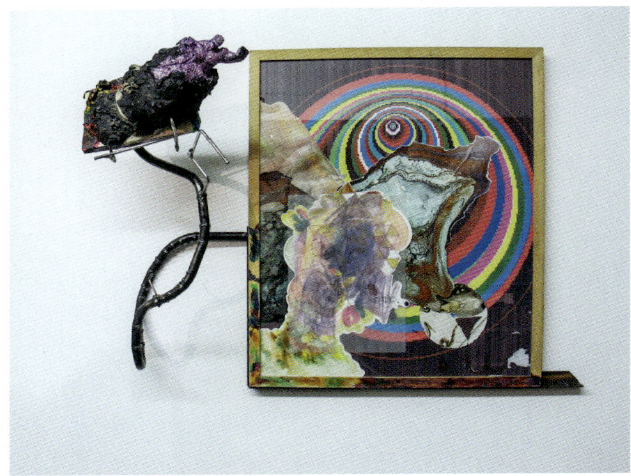

Ian Dawson, *Superman* (2009). Frame, drawing, model of the hulk, book by Nietzsche, bitumen, glitter, steel, assorted mixed media items, 52 × 48 × 15cm.

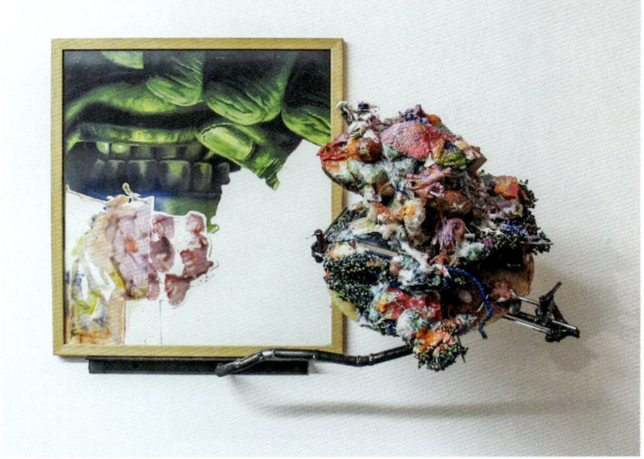

Ian Dawson, *There is a collar for the wild dog II* (2009). Drawing, frame, ceramic frog, rubber, paint, glitter, pipe cleaners, wooden tray, steel, assorted mixed media items, 53 × 48 × 16cm.

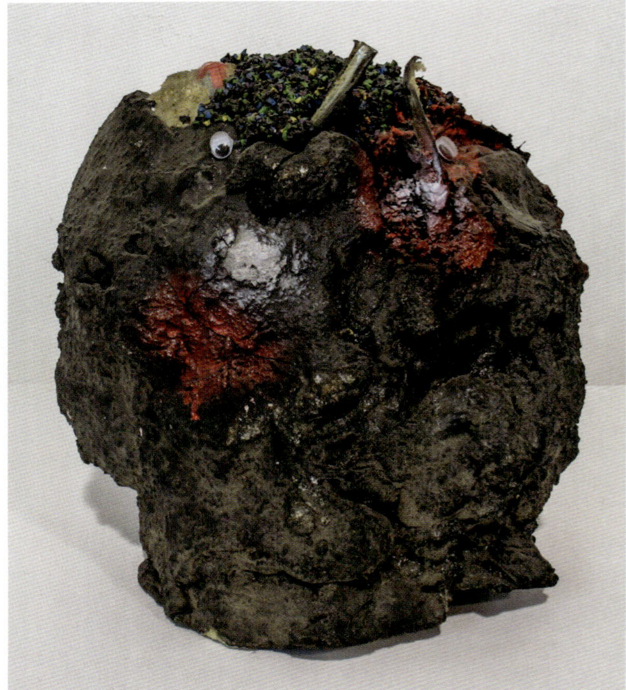

Ian Dawson, *Exhibit E (Tarman)* (2008). Rubber granules, foam, galvanized metal, plastic, paint, bitumen, 35 × 37 × 33cm.

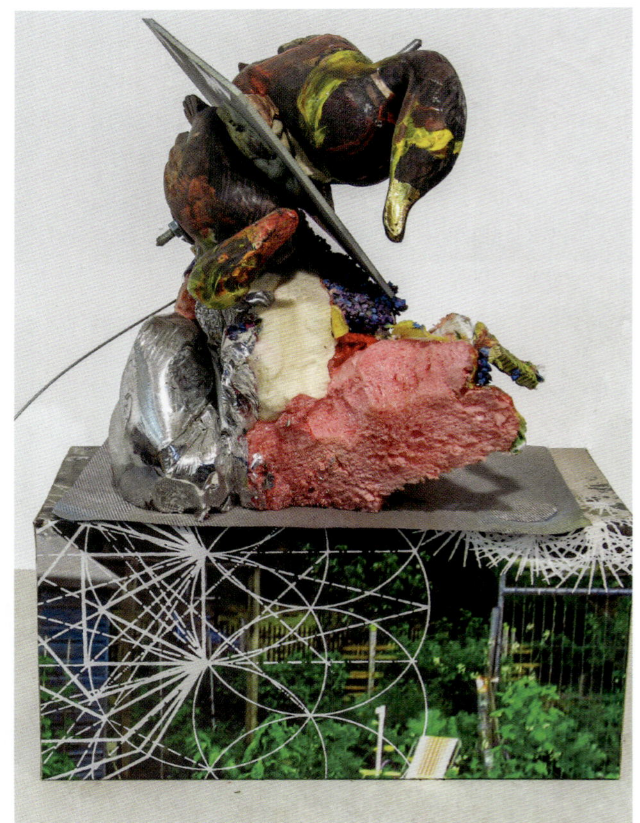

Ian Dawson, *Exhibit B (Indiscriminate anger)* (2008). Card, photograph, silkscreen aluminium, foil, perspex wood, paint, paper, 41 × 23 × 47cm.

▶ Matt Calderwood

ID: *There was a pivotal moment for your sculptures.*

MC: At the time I was working at Momart (the art moving company) and I was just messing about in the warehouse with a shovel and broom and I did this thing – a really nice bit of balance. At some point I took a couple of pictures of it and had them around in the studio. At some point someone was talking about doing a show and it came to mind, and I thought, 'Actually, maybe that is a bit of work.'

ID: *What happened then?*

MC: I had to liberate the brush and shovel from Momart Warehouse 2 (you can see, if you look closely, the broom has WH2 written on it). A few years later it was amusing when Momart came to pick the piece up to take it to Basle, for an exhibition, to see the guys come and pick up their own broom and shovel! The piece is called *Some Things Just Work* because, well, this just works. They now have a kind of celebrity lifestyle – they don't have to work anymore.

ID: *It led on to more extreme balancing acts.*

MC: Yes, shortly after I was in an exhibition called *Ad-Hoc*, I took various objects from the gallery cupboard – stuff that was hanging around the place – and started to make arrangements of objects within gaps. So that all those individual objects had to work together to physically span a space, and if you removed any single part of it the whole system would collapse.

ID: *How many glasses do you break?*

MC: I don't really.

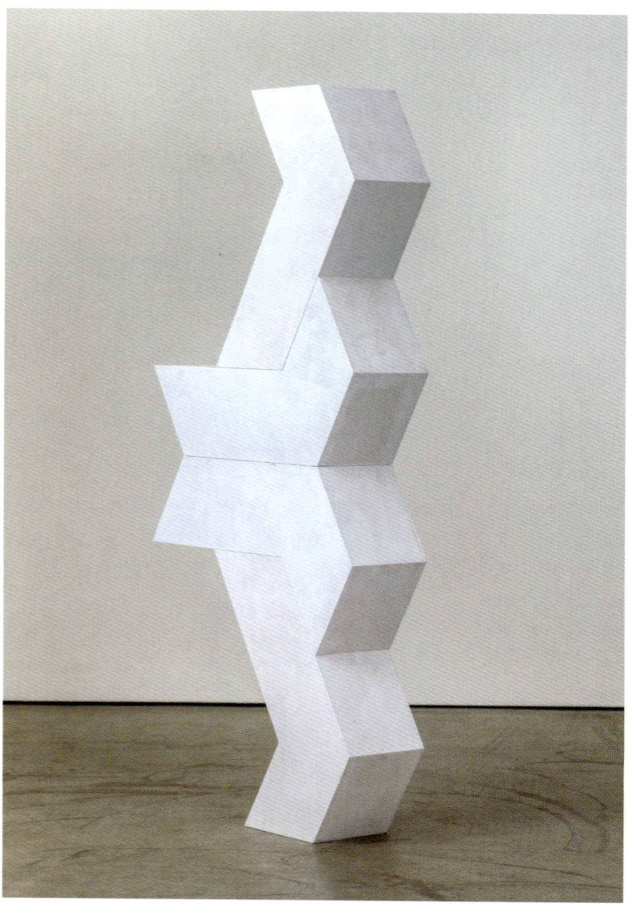

Matt Calderwood, *Untitled* (2011). 126.5 × 98 × 28.5cm.

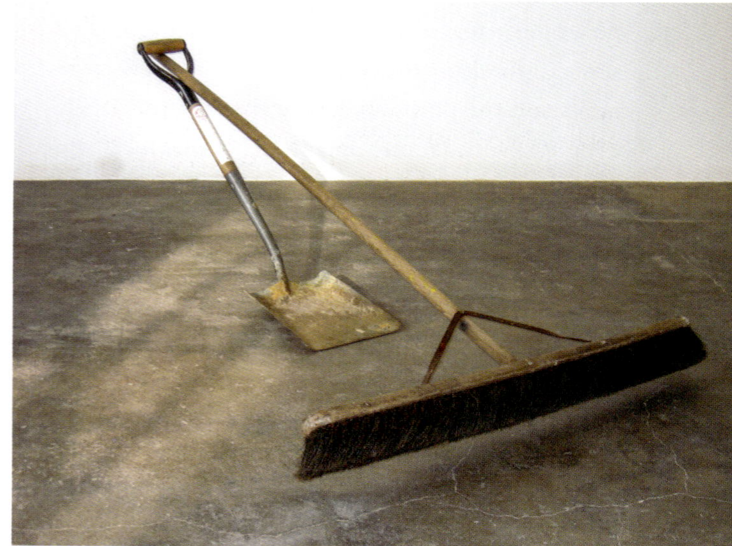

Matt Calderwood, *Some Things Just Work* (2004). Shovel, broom.

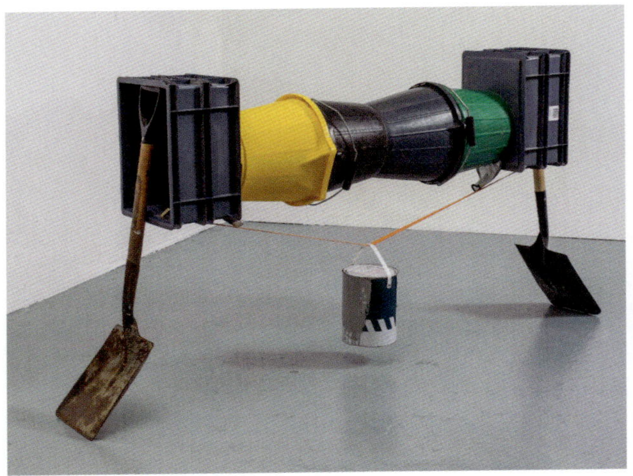

Matt Calderwood, *Span* (2009). Buckets, shovels, crates, gloves, nylon strap, paint tin.

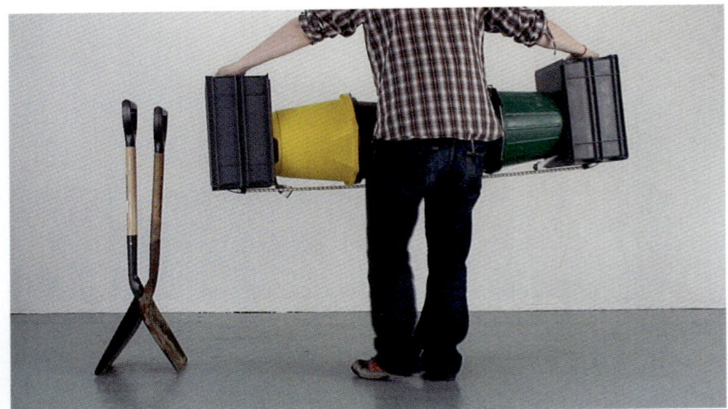

Matt Calderwood, *Suspension* (2009). Film still.

ID: *I find that surprising.*

MC: I really don't. I mean, I break more in normal life, doing the washing up. It's all pretty controlled. It's quite interesting and strange that things don't tend to explode or collapse that much.

ID: *I imagine that there is such precision that if you just miss it that slight bit it would go ping!*

MC: I think it would, but I suppose I'm quite precise when I am setting them up. The hardest bits to put up are the early segments and it becomes progressively easier. And you go along until at the very end, it becomes a very delicate operation, until you just let go.

ID: *Do you ever need help when installing in a space?*

MC: No. There is a certain amount of force and energy needed to keep the construction in the air. And if anybody helps or puts their hand on anything it's almost like they've earthed it and I can't feel it any more. The only time I've had a real collapse was when I had help. It was almost as if the instant they put their hand on it, it fell. It's about getting around the problems of, 'How do you put a dozen objects in the air when you've only got two hands?' I like the help I get

from the objects that I'm using, and that extends into the work, this cooperation between all the objects to a single end, to maintaining a status quo of sorts within a given space. I find it interesting that the process both extends beyond and precedes the work, that the same kind of mentality in the work produces the work.

ID: *All the formal concerns are based in you being in the middle, balancing the thing together.*

MC: I find it quite interesting how many variations you could do – there are so many different ways of filling that particular space with roughly those objects. Some ways are going to be easier than others, and I like to make it as hard as I can for myself, by placing the crowbar in the middle, for example. I mean, there are tonnes and tonnes of stuff you can do, but at some point it's a sculpture and at some point it's not. I find that really interesting: when you make a sculpture, you know when something works and when it doesn't.

ID: *So you are feeling relationships?*

MC: It's like, if I pass you a glass at some point I know you've got it and I don't need to hold it any more, and it's like the same here. I suddenly hand over the control of the piece to a wine glass or a glove or something. I find that curious, where the power and control shifts from one thing to the other.

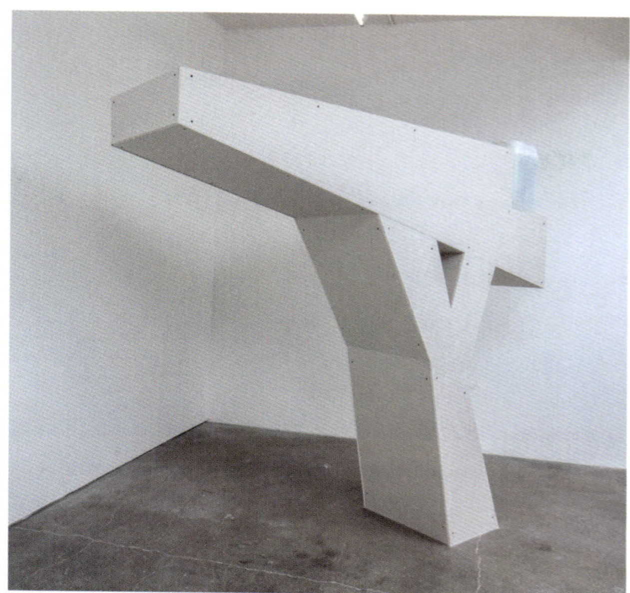

Matt Calderwood, *Unfinished Structure #1* (2007). Plasterboard, wood, plastic containers, water.

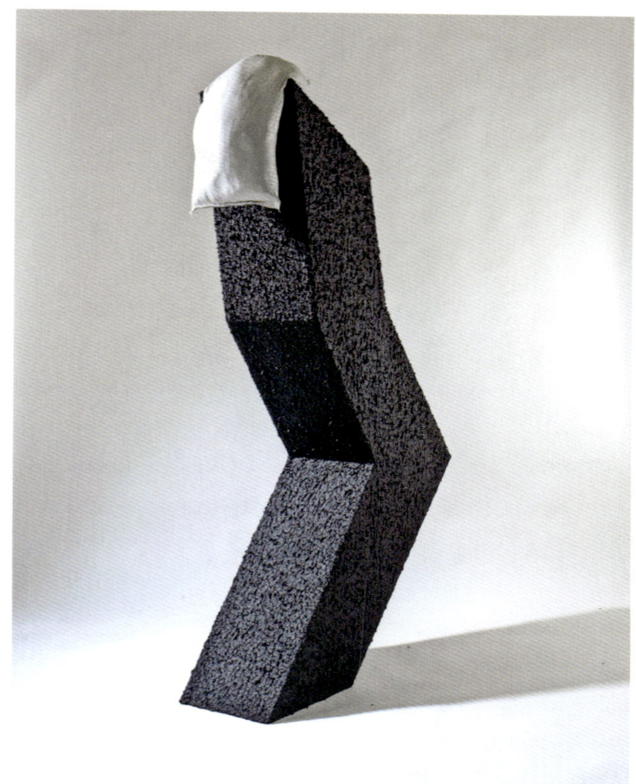

Matt Calderwood, *DAM4* (2008). Plywood, anti fly poster coating, polypropylene sack, sand.

ID: *Do you practise in the studio?*

MC: I do studio tests. I might recreate a span in the studio so that I can just play around with it and see what might be possible. But I never really want to make these things absolutely perfect in advance. For the piece at Kettle's Yard, I made an equivalent gap in the studio to generally get a feel of how much material I required to fill the gap. Then I took certain bits from here – two or three crates and a bucket – and I went to the gallery and found the rest of the bits there. I only had a morning to install it so I needed to take some stuff to have some insurance, but I still wanted a bit of risk in it and I wanted it to be fresh for me.

ID: *Your choice of materials?*

MC: The glasses are important because they give you a transparency to the system – literally proof that there is no bolt running through the thing. And the tennis balls: they're Slazenger Ultra-Viz and just the idea that they are these kind of high visibility objects within the sculpture, that is their function. It's important that they are common objects and very understandable, that everyone knows what they do and their physical properties. I guess they all just have qualities that I appreciate and want in the works. And they serve purposes: they have the tone that I want for them. They perform really well.

ID: *You explore balance in other sculptures too?*

MC: I built a series of *Unfinished Structures* made from plasterboard and deliberately off-balance, which required a counterbalance. 25-kilo barrels of water would act as counterweights. The final object had a tension between the barrels of water and the structure. It was partly inspired from seeing engineered motorway structures, objects that are pre-stressed for a particular load. They don't hold themselves up if they don't have the load.

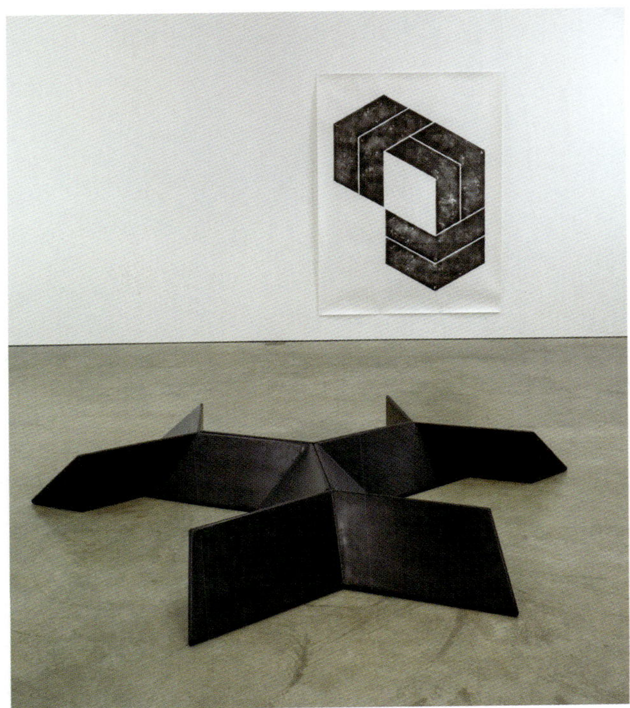

Matt Calderwood, Wilkinson Gallery installation 2.

ID: They appear to have led into these new sculptures that are made and then printed from.

MC: Originally I had made some rubber sculptures for their material quality, grip and friction, so they could be stacked and tessellated, and they needed to be rubber so they wouldn't slip off each other.

ID: The materiality of them is important?

MC: I made some smaller ones the size of those rubber lifesaving diving bricks, the ones that they chuck in the swimming pool and you've got to dive down and get. I was interested in the curves, the quality of that piece of rubber. They have a weight to them; they're dense and indestructible. I imagine you can throw them out of a ten-storey window and they would be fine. I was interested in something that gets better the more it's handled – a surface that becomes more even. A non-precious and non-fragile object that benefits from being handled, developing a patina of wear.

ID: The rubber pieces appear manufactured.

MC: In this instance I wanted a factory finish. Some people assume that I had ordered them from a catalogue.

ID: Why don't you?

MC: I have pretty much gone off the idea of people making my work. It is very easy to communicate the first 98 per cent of what I might want someone to do, but it's the last 2 per cent where it goes slightly against a manufacturer's normal practice where it all gets messed up. I could learn from that and communicate better, but there is so much to be taken from the experience of making things myself and of the problems thrown up by that, that it would be a real shame to lose that by having someone else make the work.

ID: How did you arrive at the idea of printing from the sculptures?

MC: I had photographed them and the photographs were very graphic. I was excited about them as images and I was trying to work out how these might become an image, running through ideas of putting the sculpture on the wall. And at some point I realized that those rubber sculptures were basically printing blocks – they had flat surfaces and were made with a similar material – and it occurred to me that if I were to ink them up and put them flat on the floor and apply some pressure I would hopefully get a decent image from it.

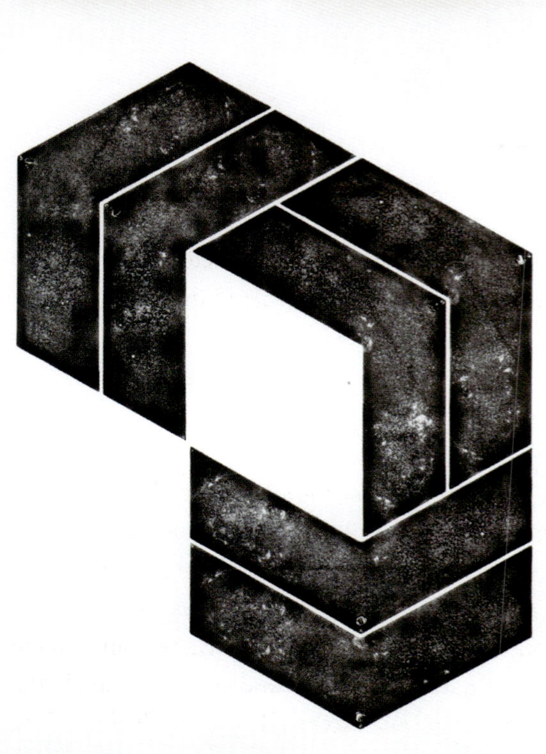

Matt Calderwood, print.

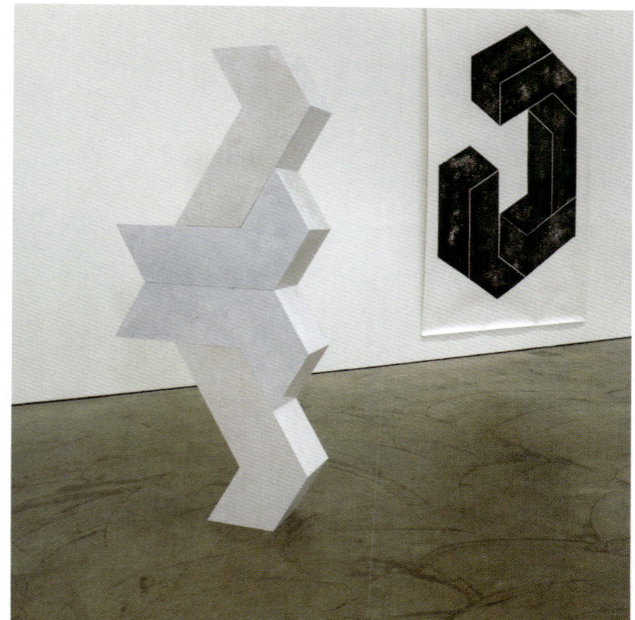

Matt Calderwood, Wilkinson Gallery installation 3.

ID: *Was it successful?*

MC: Earlier I had imagined what it might be like to put these sculptures onto a photocopier, so when I lifted that first sculpture off the paper and the print was right there in front of me I realized that because of the scale and method it appeared coincidentally like a photocopy.

ID: *The shift between the three-dimensional geometry and the two-dimensional illusion is subtle, yet pronounced.*

MC: There was a very particular shape to the sculptures that allowed them to function stacked on top of each other in reality and because they are constructed around an isometric geometry, the printed image then has a quality of a forced and false perspective.

ID: *You don't really see it when you look at the object on the floor but you see it immediately in the print.*

MC: We have all seen images like this before, but it's strange that an image taken from a sculpture can suggest a sculpture quite different from the one that it is taken from.

ID: *How did you manage to print them?*

MC: It was an interesting process, and there were various stages and problems. I think it's important that you view the relationship between the work on the wall and the work on the floor without a precise explanation of the methods.

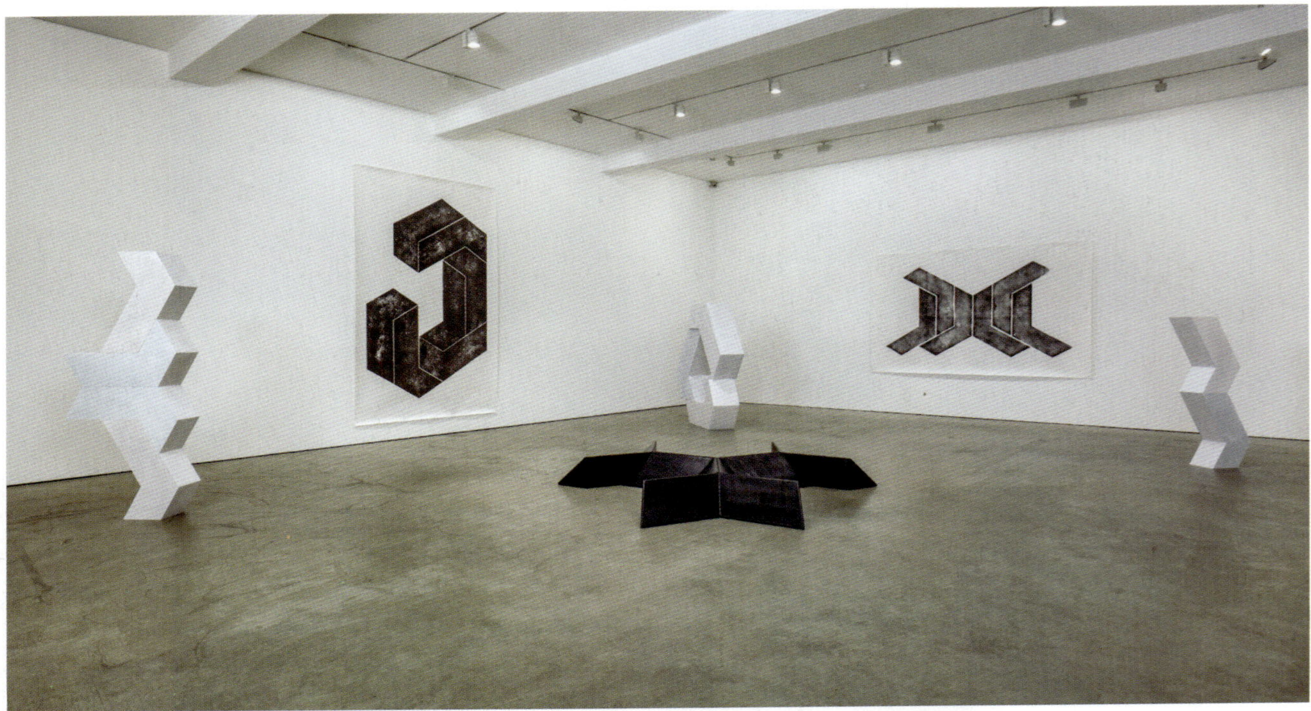

Matt Calderwood, Wilkinson Gallery installation 1.

ID: *It is just that you mentioned earlier that you had a physical relationship with the objects by laying it on the floor.*

MC: I am printing a large surface area and it needs a considerable amount of pressure. The simplest way is to get on top of the objects and to stamp on them, which in a funny way has been a recurrent theme in my work, from the first video I ever made called *Ground Experiment 1*, when I jumped onto a concrete slab suspended by wine glasses.

ID: *How long did the work take you to produce?*

MC: I don't want to say how long the work takes me to produce; I don't want any work that I've produced to give you an accurate impression of how much time it has taken. I wouldn't want you to know for certain if it has taken me longer to make the print or the sculpture. I have a problem with the fetishization of labour; building a full-sized caravan out of tooth picks would be an instantly dull art work because it is instantly about the effort.

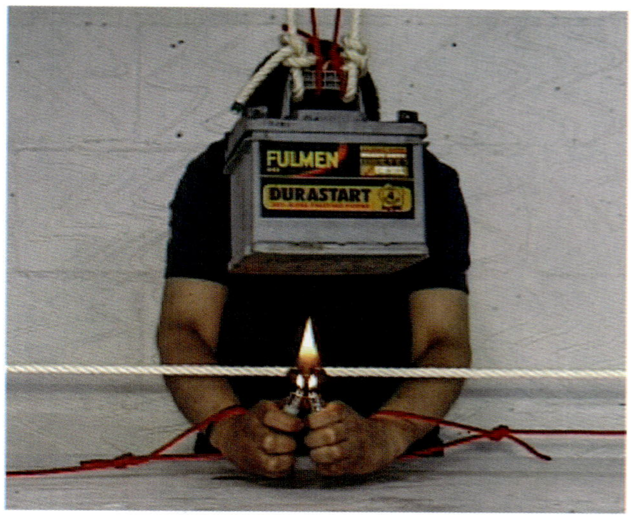

Matt Calderwood, *Battery* (2003). Film still.

ID: *OK, but how long between having the idea and making the work?*

MC: When I realized that I wanted to print directly from the sculpture, the timescale from that realization was until the next morning, until I got into the studio. I did it immediately, that day I got really excited about it and I started testing with bits of rubber and printing from other objects. I got into it straight away; I couldn't hold back. It was a very brief gestation.

ID: *In the exhibition there are four prints – how many are in the series?*

MC: There were five or six others. I brought the whole series to the space to give myself as much chance as I could.

ID: *How do you edit?*

MC: When I started printing I really enjoyed it and I thought every one was great. They had a quality that seduced me immediately and I absolutely loved it. But the more I tested it and the more I worked (and you look at what you've got in front of you so I had about fifteen works), it was just natural development to ask, 'What are the five best?' and then, 'What are the two best?' and maybe in the end you just focus on those two. And once you have focused on those two and you reappraise the fifteen that you started with, most of them might become unacceptable. Some of them that you thought were good, with another tier of refinement you realize that they are wrong for whatever reason. There is nothing uncommon about this. The great thing about art is that it is infinitely open in terms of what you can do and it is about a constant reduction and reduction.

ID: *Your work is a good example of this.*

MC: If you look at my video works there was never anything in the frame that wasn't essential. Like *Battery*, for example, where there is a system of ropes and a car battery suspended above my hands. I burn the rope and the battery falls. But the system that holds the battery is also attached to my hands, so when I burn the rope the battery falls as if to hit my hands but also throws my hands away. It's perfectly clear to anyone that there is a system of pulleys outside of the frame that allows that to happen, but if I had pulled the frame back and shown you the system it would have added nothing to what you understand it as. Your understanding that there are pulleys is all you need to know and the action is what you need to focus on. ■

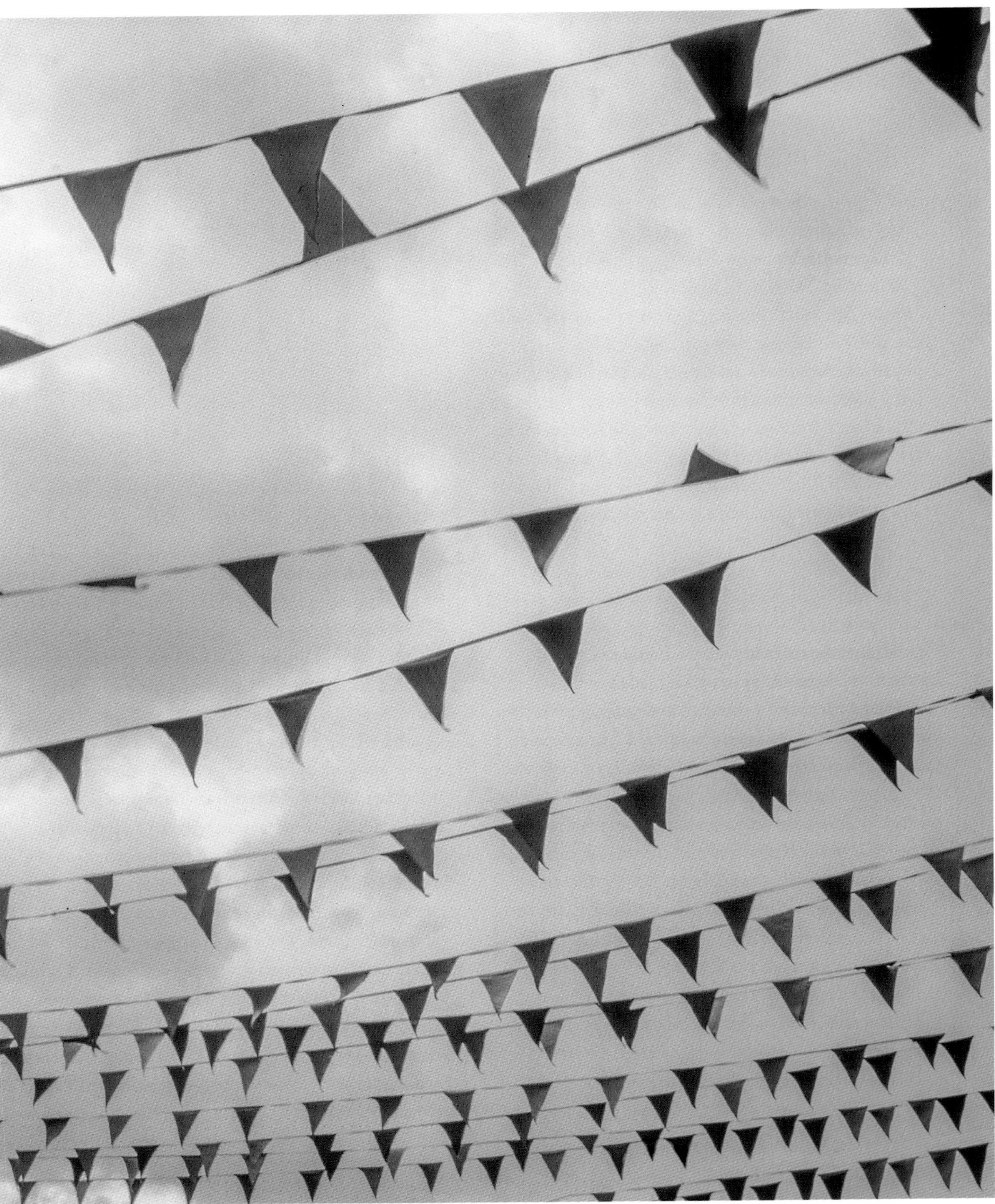

8 Space

I t's the summer of 1991, and the annual degree show calendar is about to get into full swing again. All the art schools across the country paint out their studios as bucket loads of white emulsion gets slopped onto scuffed and pitted walls, grey gloss paint sloshed across shabby floors. Every year these spaces shrink a fraction of an inch as another coat of whitewash covers over the cracks. This was, and still is, the customary preparation for final-year students in order to exhibit their work, gain their degree and showcase themselves to the wider world.

It was the last ever show within the dishevelled sheds of the Royal College of Art, a quaint sort of space tucked behind the Natural History Museum, before the department moved from this notable building. The space had accommodated waves of British sculptors: Paolozzi, Wentworth, Cragg, Wilding, Deacon; one could always tell which of their works was made there due to the particularity of the undulating wooden floor-boards.

In one of those spaces that year, a young graduating student mounted a blue ceramic English Heritage plaque on the wall. It read 'Borough of Kensington. Gavin Turk, Sculptor, worked here 1989–1991'. This was the only statement by Turk in an otherwise uninhabited space.

By simultaneously commemorating an event, by declaring the gesture of his demise to have historical importance was somehow commenting on what Francis Fukuyama had pronounced the year that

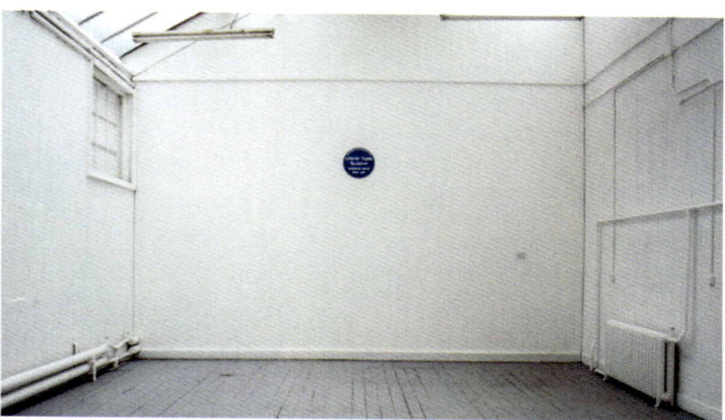

Gavin Turk, *Cave* (1991). Ceramic laid on concrete, 49 x 5 x 49cm.

Turk had begun his study: that it was, 'The End of History'. That the grand narratives were concluded and the world would now be made up from lots of little stories, lots of little lives and deaths, adding up and interconnecting to create a homogenous timeline.

The work created a storm. Graduation exhibitions are the public face of art schools, and the Royal College of Art had recently appointed a reactionary figurehead. The new incoming professor of sculpture, Glynn Williams, was about to give his inaugural lecture – 'Kicking out the Cuckoo', a call for the practice of sculpture to return to more customary values, a bid to rid the discipline of the brood parasites, video, installation and performance. And the vacant space of the Turk sculpture was perfect fodder for the conservative Rector Jocelyn Stevens and the RCA Examinations Board to flex their muscles. The body of professors, who pass judgment with the authority of connoisseurs, famously failed to award Turk his Masters degree. It was the most fitting denouement imaginable, ensuring that the piece assumed the historical significance that it was fabricated to have.

OPPOSITE PAGE
Fiona Banner, *Black Bunting* (2001). Fabric, dimensions variable. Installation view, South Bank, London.

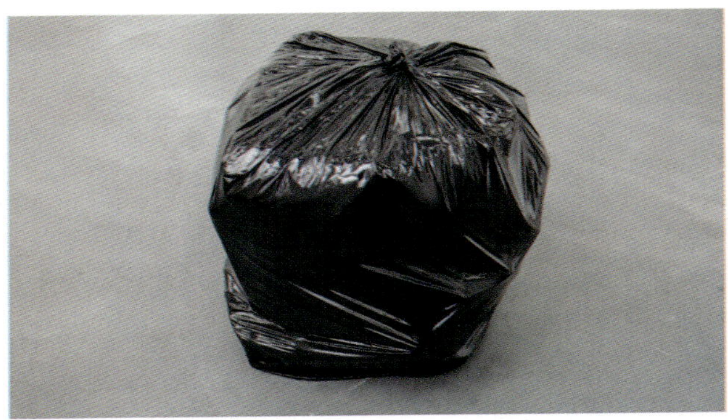

Gavin Turk, *Waste* (2007). Edition of eight, painted bronze, 46 × 48 × 52cm.

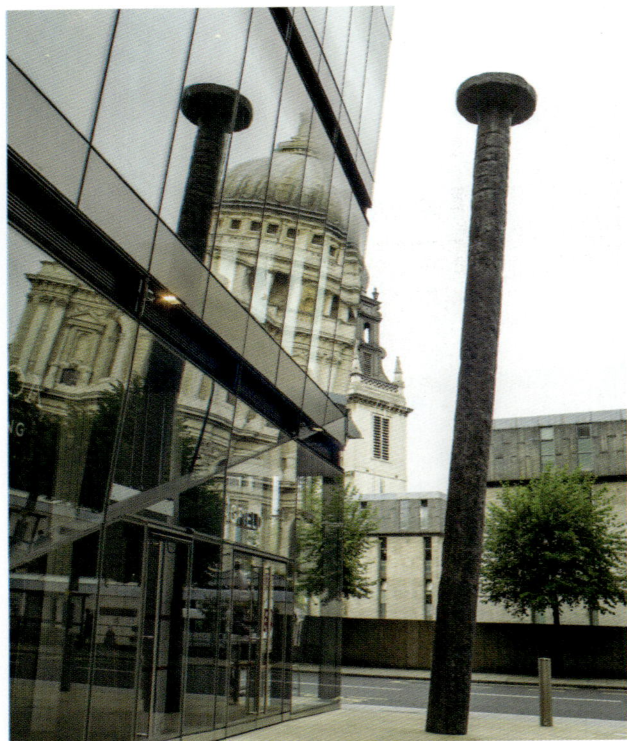

Gavin Turk, *Nail* (2011). Permanent public sculpture, One New Change, City of London.

Turk titled the work *Cave*, an allusion to Plato's allegorical tale of not being able to comprehend any reality beyond one's immediate surroundings. It was a complete sculptural statement: seventy-six years after Duchamp exhibited a ready-made, here was a piece that declared the beauty of absence with similar wit and deftness.

Ruminations on space continue in Turk's work, he casts a series of bulging bin liners in bronze and paints them black; these are impenetrably dense objects carefully sited to the side of empty spaces. These are the black holes of the everyday; it's the morning after the party, everything has been cleared up and everyone has gone home, all other matter is sucked up and condensed into these lumps.

Twenty years since his first foray, Turk has created another spatial play, on the edge of the City of London's financial district, in shouting distance of St Paul's Cathedral: a 20m-tall bronze impression of a rusty nail has been staked into the ground. Leaning on a slight tilt, is it pinning the pavement down? It alludes to empty space, to absence – a single nail left after the removal of whatever it was used to attach. It has freed the space that surrounds it, like the comedian who understands the ultimate value of the pause, that it's not merely the void between the matter: that it is all. As Frank Lloyd Wright said, 'Space is the breath of art.'

▶ Keith Wilson

In 1998 Keith Wilson made a proposal to site a sculpture in the market square in front of the Harris Museum in Preston. It was a simple plan: workmen were to uplift a quartet of paving slabs, remove a small amount of ballast and replace them in such a way that if it were to rain it would create a puddle.

This piece of site-specific sculpture, prosaically entitled *Puddle*, was eventually denied its existence by Preston City Council. Even though it had satisfied all other requirements, no single councillor was prepared to sign off the project; the idea of a nonentity was too difficult a political statement. This is Wilson's work; it exists through amusing adoptions of space, of twisting the symbolic codes that define it. They often include slapstick oppositions between street furniture and farmyard fencing, cattle pens and modular compartments.

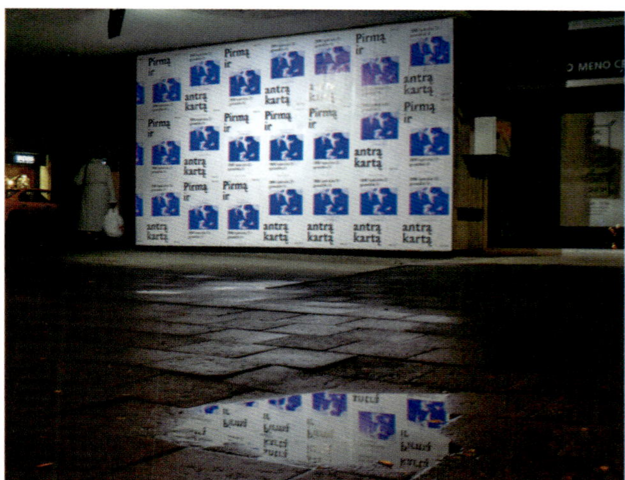

Keith Wilson, *Puddle* (2008).

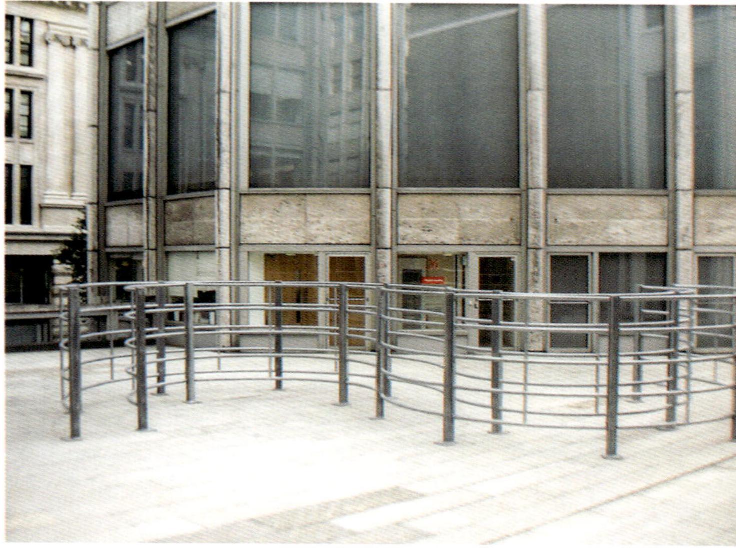

Keith Wilson, *Double-Blind S-Bend* (2005), Economist Plaza.

Puddle existed for a time as folklore; it was first rumoured to have been bought by a collector, and then commissioned by a town in Holland and renamed *De Droom Van Een Fontein* ('The Dream of a Fountain'). It has since been exhibited, installed on the streets of Malmo and Lithuania but rejected in Warwick and Sunderland.

I interview Keith Wilson about his expanding practice of placing the viewer as a central part of the spectacle that it is both mundane and particular, that mischievously examines attitudes toward sculpture and space. Wilson had also recently co-curated Modern British Sculpture at the Royal Academy.

IAN DAWSON: *I'm interested in how you began to develop the work that utilized spatial structures.*

KEITH WILSON: Really it was just that I like utilitarian architecture and structures. If you see a gate and a fence, you understand both the history of what it does in terms of demarking a space but you also know what it can do structurally, such as to be hinged to swing in a particular direction.

ID: *And the particular language of the farming structures?*

KW: It's funny: my family are all farmers but I grew up in Birmingham so it's not really my thing, but every summer I would end up spending time on a farm and pretend to dip a sheep. There was such a sense of comedy to it – the suburban boy dipping sheep – that was just all wrong!

ID: *And this same comic juxtaposition has seen you now supplanting farmyard devices back into the urban setting?*

KW: Putting it in the wrong place. Just pulling a simple walkway designed for cows and putting it for example at the Economist Plaza, connecting the space between two buildings. You would come out onto the plaza and you could either walk straight to the other building or you could walk through this slightly wiggly chute; it was just funny. People carrying stacks of papers, they'd come out and they'd have to make a decision: 'Shall I go the wobbly way or shall I go the straight way?' And for me that was a bit of slapstick.

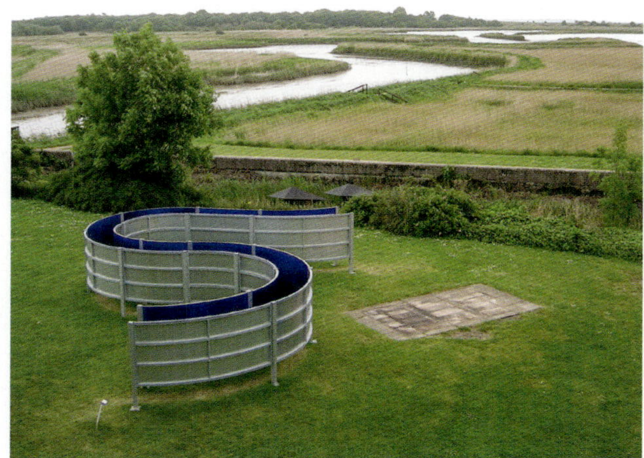

Keith Wilson, *Boat Race* (2008). Galvanized steel (hot-dipped and cold-rolled) with blue lacquered interior, 12 × 9 × 2m.

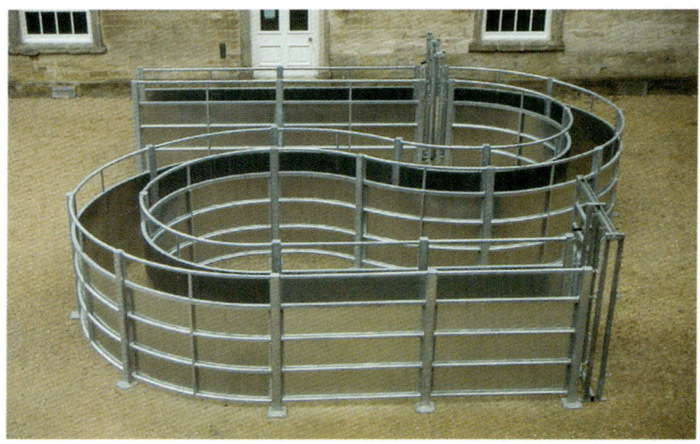

Keith Wilson, *Double-Blind S-Bend* (2003). Galvanized steel, 48 × 7.48 × 1.75m.

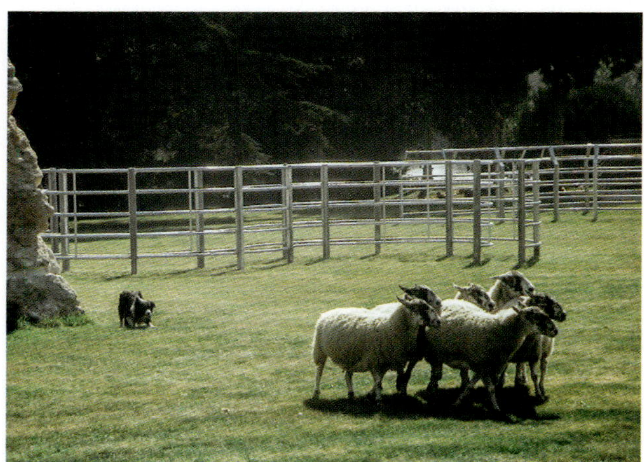

Keith Wilson, *Double-Blind S-Bend* at Compton Verney (with sheep).

ID: *And your choice of the blue perspex?*

KW: Originally they were in clear lacquer so you could still see the galvanized steel, but I thought that was getting a bit stylized, and apparently it is best practice to paint them blue on the interior, which I can't believe can really be to do with the cow. There are numerous theories about how to keep animals calm; another theory is if they're walking around curves rather than a straight line, they'll not panic. So it's about the efficiency of killing them of course – again this humorous idea that this little walk is a therapeutic journey.

ID: *And the curves solely relate to this?*

KW: I married that idea with the cod psycho-geography of cities. Many cities get built on the late stages of a river, on the meander, so with this idea that there's a form of meander, it doesn't really matter if that form is London, Paris or Rome: it's the same kind of walk. So, actually, let's just make it as a slaughterhouse route. So I did the Tiber and Putney to Barnes on the Thames, and in a way it's this idea that you over-interpret the significance of the local, because our patterns of behaviour are kind of primary. And so in a way this just brings in that elemental nature to the physical organization of social space.

ID: *And at Compton Verney you played with boundaries again.*

KW: Playing with the grand estate; crossing the ha-ha. Very often, the merchant would have made his money from the land and then the ha-ha was built on the estate to separate the gardens from the actual farmland. It's very literally the sort of boundary that the animals can't cross. Placing the furniture of agriculture back

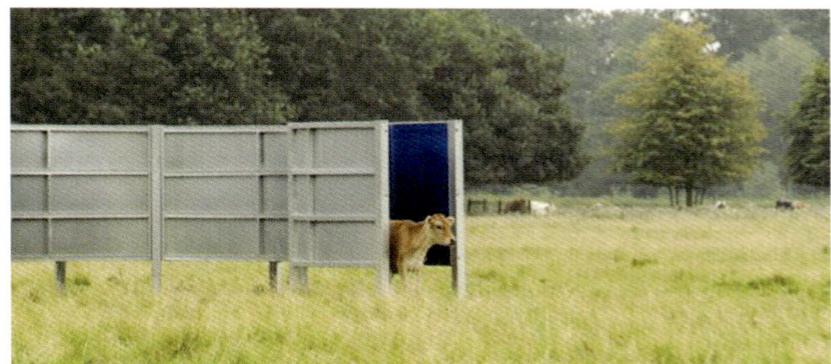

Keith Wilson, *Double-Blind S-Bend* (cow shot).

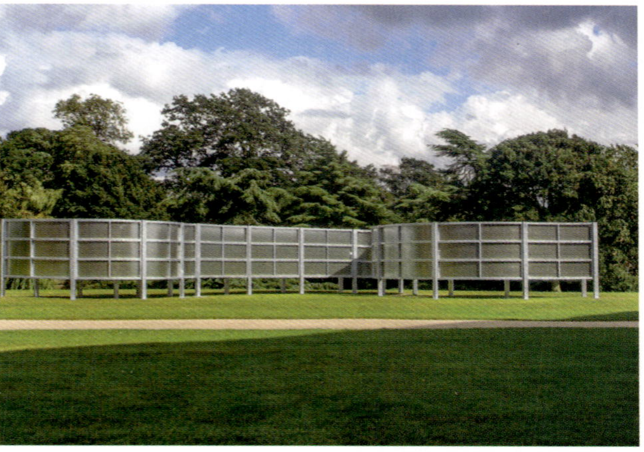

Keith Wilson, *Roma* (2008). Galvanized steel, PU elastomer.

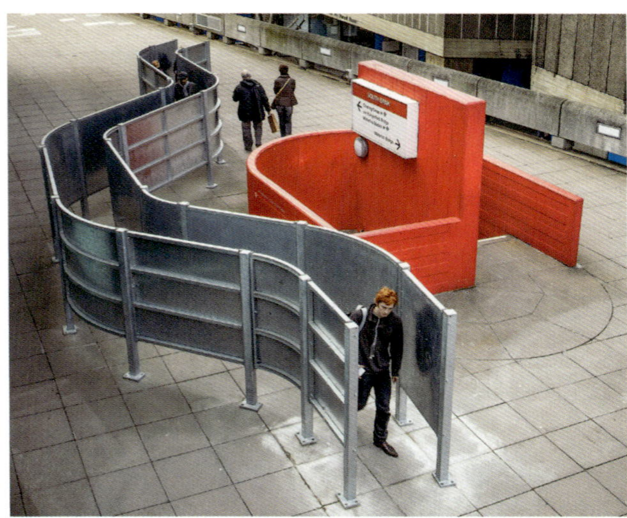

Keith Wilson, *Zone 1*. Hayward Gallery, 19 × 8 × 2m.

onto the land of the estate was a bit of amusement about which side of the fence you're on. I had an opening there for sheep before I had an opening for the people – I thought that was important. They seemed pretty unimpressed; the dogs were managing their visit so it probably wasn't an ideal viewing situation – they didn't seem very relaxed.

ID: *Where do you manufacture the objects?*

KW: The fabricator is in Staffordshire. It's a large-scale industrial agricultural factory that does a lot of fencing. Once I get into a body of work, I tend to use one factory. I've got one factory for the cow walkways, I've got one factory for the blue panels, and that's it. I really like the factories and getting them to do almost exactly what they already do, but I've got my own purposes; I'm there because they're the right place. There is a humour affixed to misunderstanding, so I'm in a studio in London imagining how big a cow is, or a bull or a pig, and then I'm making the work that would house it at market, or transport it in the slaughterhouse or calm it down whilst it waits to be snipped or whatever. So it's partly the thought that in some way it's a mini version of what the organization of the wider social world is. It's also just a pigpen or a sheep chute, fabricated by the people who make the ordinary ones. They often say, 'You know it won't work, it's a bit wrong', and I would reply, 'Don't worry about that, just make it.' At first I think they thought I was just an eccentric bad farmer, but they rumbled me on the sculpture for London Underground.

ID: *Are you meant to interact with and walk down all of these works?*

KW: I think sculpture is very good at making you stand up straight to address certain minimal forms, like the Cenotaph, and then whether you comply with the form or not becomes an act of will. So it then becomes a test of your perversity of mind. I very much doubt that I would ever walk down one of my sculptures. Yet other people come and have a phenomenological experience! And I really like the fact that there's no right answer to that. It is blue and it bendy. That's fine if that's your

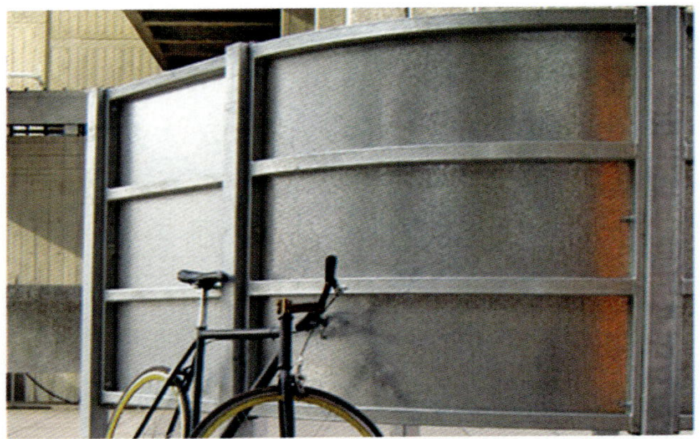

Keith Wilson, *Zone 1*, Hayward Gallery (detail).

thing, or you could stand there and say, 'No, I will not walk that extra bit, simply because someone has determined that I would.'

ID: *I've leant on one of your rails and surveyed a landscape.*

KW: You do tend to lean on them; it's pretty irresistible and some of the posts I make are like spindles. I tend to make at a height where you can rather flamboyantly lean on them, especially when they're blue or big bright yellow. You can just place an arm while you have a coffee and discuss matters of importance.

ID: *Do they get used in other ways?*

KW: The kids love them, the BMX-ers love them. I gather it's a real challenge to get the speed through one with double blind corners and stuff like that. I mean, the one at the Hayward Gallery instantly became a bicycle rack, which might have troubled sculptors a generation ago but it completely doesn't trouble me. It's just the mind-set's changed and in a way, it's more ordinary for sculptors to be out there in the world, which can be a bad thing, but also there's a humour about the speciality of art.

ID: *So placing objects into spaces to see how they work offers a dialogue for you?*

KW: It's not all the time that something is going to have that extra bit, but if the material fact of a sculpture means it can take its chance, most of the time it's furniture, but if it's a good one, then occasionally it can offer other opportunities for interpretation. So I'm very happy for it to be 99 per cent bicycle rack and on occasion a sculpture that means something to someone. So I'm not at all thinking the meaning I have for it is the meaning that it has to have in some precious way. And once you step back from the studio and into the world, you've got to take your chance with the work; it's wrestling with everybody else's space, it's fighting for space with everything else.

ID: *You mention a previous generation of sculpture. Which generation?*

KW: I'm really fascinated by that body of work by Caro, typified by *Early One Morning* where it's both an explosion into ordinary space and it's a containment of energy internal to itself. For Modern British Sculpture we re-made a bench from Caro's *New Generation* Whitechapel exhibition; it was the moment when notionally the plinth disappeared, but of course there was still a plinth in the room – it was the furniture. There was a big low bench in the space that I wanted to make again because in a way it indicated to me the problem of stepping into ordinary space.

ID: *Which you continue to look at yourself?*

KW: The will towards stepping into the world is something I'm fascinated with in my own work. What is special about studio space? What is it you want from the gallery space, and how do you relate

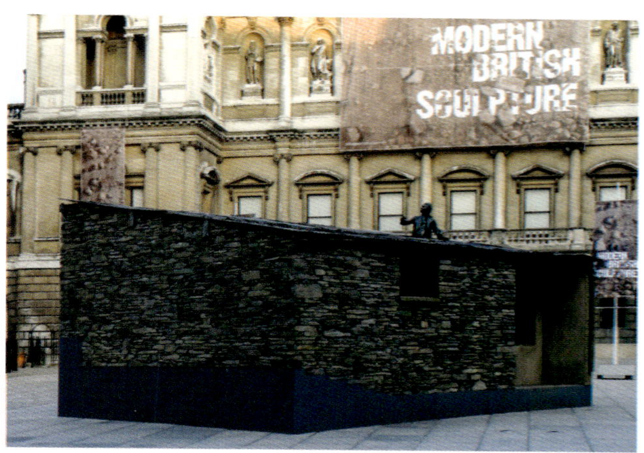

Keith Wilson, *Schwitters' Merz Barn* (2011). Modern British Sculpture, Royal Academy.

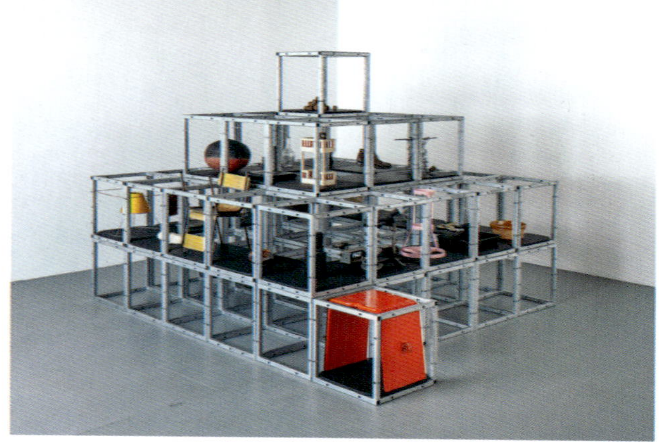

Keith Wilson, *Z is for Ziggurat* (2003). Galvanized steel cubes, painted MDF, found elements, 2 × 3 × 2.5m.

those two to those notional ordinary spaces? What are those different qualities? I love the studio space. I decreasingly love the museum space.

ID: *Have you explored that idea?*

KW: In the Royal Academy show, we placed the Kurt Schwitters' Barn in the courtyard, locked, so in a sense it's the very private nature of the studio space, the inaccessibility of the studio, that is a claim on the subject. So if the Royal Academy is there, notionally to be an institution for artists, we're saying, 'Well, there's another institution for artists, and that's the studio.' And at the moment I am of the opinion that the first thing you should build is the artist's studio, not the museum. So it is a political gesture to say the subject belongs to artists. There is something about making a claim on a subject; otherwise the people at the dinner-party make the claim on the subject. Or the director of the museum makes a claim on the subject, or an art historian makes a claim. While you're alive and able, you have to be punting in as well. That space of the studio is something I really want to put in the middle of the museum – I would really love to open that first. And then, from that, decide what you would need. What does the artist want from the gallery? What does it want from this thing that to me is just an extension

of the studio in public? So beyond making the work and doing the shows, I'm trying to think about these categories of space and what you can do with them.

ID: *And your studio practice?*

KW: I've got a very strange studio. No one really occupies my studio; they never have. I've always joked about how I've always seen myself as a janitor. I go in and I sweep up. There's no real visible sign that I ever do much. I go in, I've got a sofa looking at the canal, I open the doors and if there's food, I'll feed the ducks and I make a coffee and maybe have a chat; then I'll get on the laptop. After all that then I'll go in to have a nosey into the space and I might think, oh yes that's funny, and do one or two bits. But essentially a minimum of work goes on.

My studio is mostly a place where things are given the space to see more or less if they're contenders, and that can sometimes be a long process. There is one piece that has sat there for ten years, and I still have no idea whether it might end up in the skip. Often an exhibition is useful because you can have a skip and a lorry waiting and you make your mind up – success or failure. You know there's no end point for any of this but while you're alive you can still say 'no' and bin it. ∎

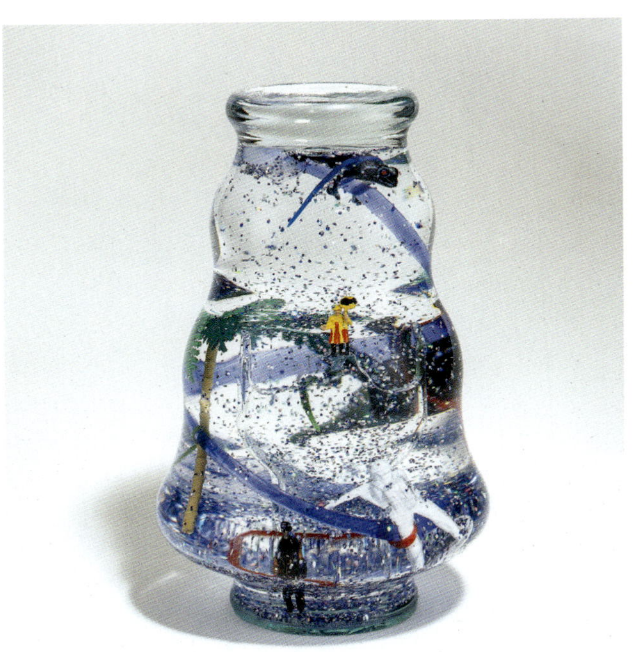

Richard Clegg, *Snow Dooms 1*. Mixed media.

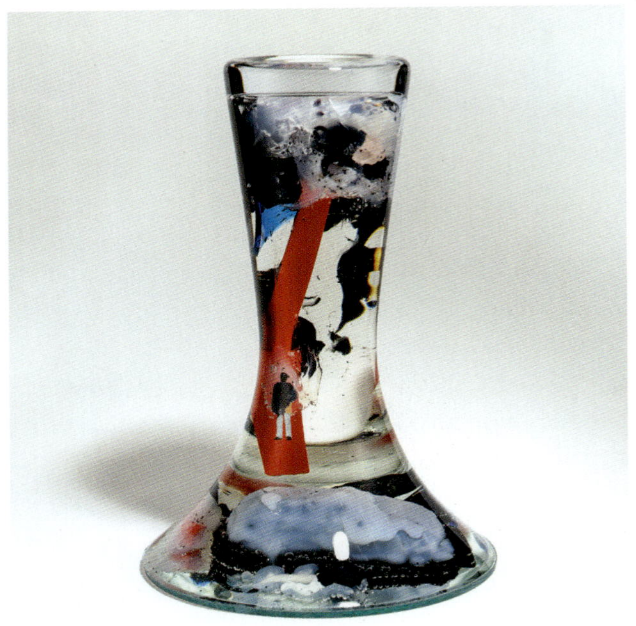

Richard Clegg, *Snow Dooms 2*. Mixed media.

▶ Richard Clegg:
Nature abhors a vacuum

'Mind the gap': the persistent statement greets London Tube travellers at Underground stations. Making the passenger mindful of the cavity, increasing the unease with the void between the train carriage and the platform. It is a mundane, daily reminder of the *horror vacui* – the fear of empty space.

Aristotle first made the statement that 'nature abhors a vacuum'. It was a physical observation that nature would choose at all costs to saturate empty space, that any abyss would be flooded with matter. This was later disproved, but the idiom has endured, of an urge to overcome blankness, that life's imperative is to envelop and fill. In artistic terms, extreme surface treatment (covering all available space with equal detail) has allusions of obsession and mania, a failure to discriminate and discern, of creating an environment of over stimulation, of the eye not being able to rest.

This is a psychological version of space – a repository for neuroses and phobias – and in 2006 Richard Clegg created a series of '*Horror Vacui*'s. Grabbing glassware from TK Maxx, figurines and statuettes from model shops, Clegg constructed inner worlds of spatial angst. Space in this instance isn't empty but full of disturbing scenarios, harbingers involving firemen, doctors and farmyard cattle with globules of lurid silicone casting ominous shadows across the scene.

Titling the series *Snow Dooms*, Clegg built these works in the same way as their anodyne cousin, the snowdome, submerging the scene in water to create an ethereal arena of floating dark matter, refracted and distorted. Influenced by the language of the grotesque and the space of the funfair, the suspension of the elements in water allowed for the construction of implausible relationships.

In an upturned vase, which resembles the profile of a mushroom cloud, a figure points upwards, caught in the maelstrom of swirling particles; above him a hazy construction of violet, green and black hovers

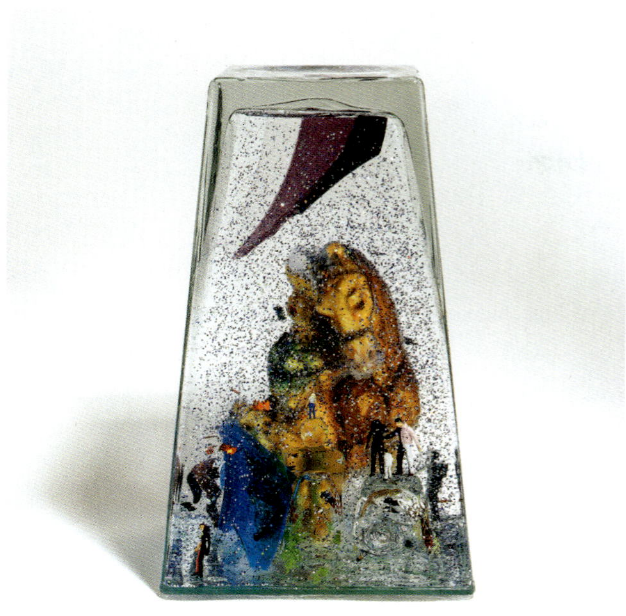

Richard Clegg, *Snow Dooms 3*. Mixed media.

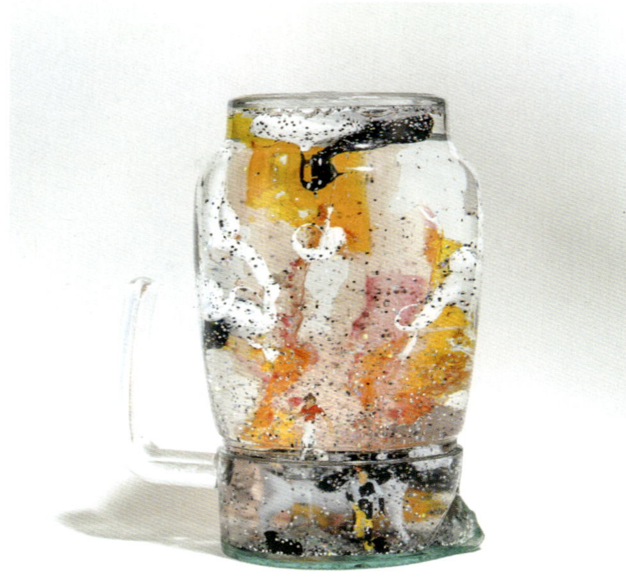

Richard Clegg, *Snow Dooms 4*. Mixed media.

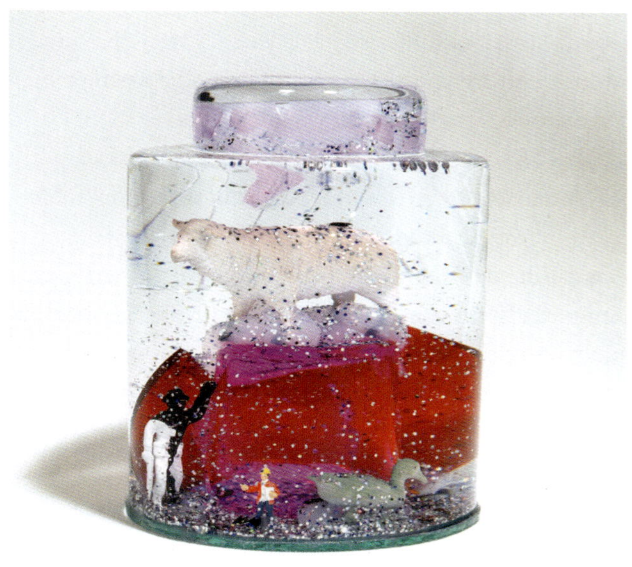

Richard Clegg, *Snow Dooms 5*. Mixed media.

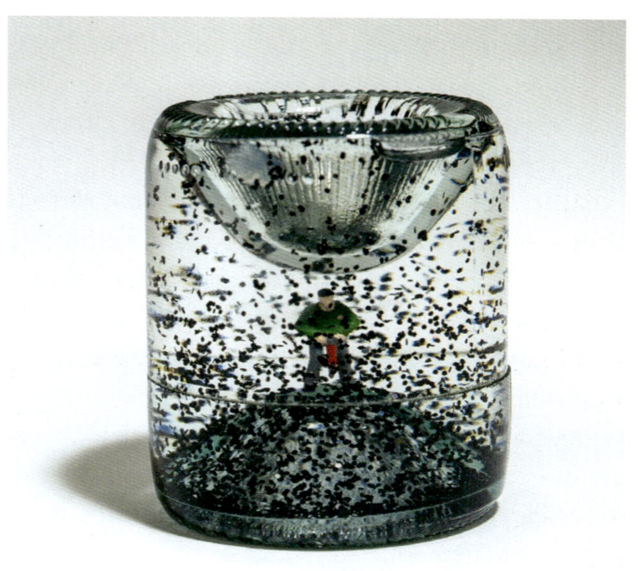

Richard Clegg, *Snow Dooms 6*. Mixed media.

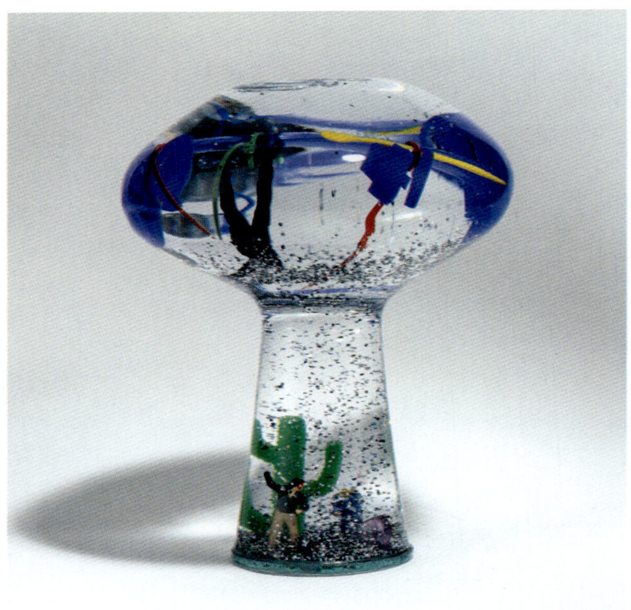

Richard Clegg, *Snow Dooms 7*. Mixed media.

ominously. In another jar a workman with a pneumatic drill stands atop a mound, frozen in a forlorn attempt to escape the condensed space created by the concave arc of the glass hovering above his head.

Clegg worked in series, building within multiple objects simultaneously, sticking objects and articulating an internal space. Saying that he 'quickly forgot about why, the why becoming irrelevant almost immediately', he articulated this imaginative space, considering them as ornaments, as objects of contemplation to view over an extended time. And like the attraction with pleasure beaches, with the tunnel of love, the ghost train, the hall of mirrors, it somehow reveals a disappointment with the world.

The final act is pouring the glycerine-enhanced liquid into them, drowning them, then plugging and sealing the scene. A *horror vacui*. ■

▶ Bold Tendencies

Every summer at the Metropolitan Museum of Art in New York, the roof terrace has prestigious shows of modern masters of sculpture; David Smith, Alexander Calder and Sir Anthony Caro have all featured. It is a stunning way for established work to be shown in the urbane surroundings of midtown Manhattan, the work framed by the iconic backdrop and greenery of Central Park.

Every summer in a multi-storey car park in South London, something unexpected has been occurring. If you follow the path intersected by the multiplex cinema and the railway arches you arrive at a dingy doorway. Stepping through this threshold you begin to climb the dank stairs, sauntering up the internal oil-covered ramps of this archetypal cast-concrete car park, a spiral upwards to the elevated levels. All of a sudden you are confronted by offbeat objects: large-scale experimental sculpture.

This is *Bold Tendencies*: a project that produces an annual outdoor experimental sculpture show of ambitious scale within an inner-city urban environment. The idea of the sculpture park had long emigrated to rural settings for a car-owning public; this was founded by gallery owners Hannah Barry and Sven Mundner, who wanted to facilitate a space for untried propositions.

IAN DAWSON: *How did it all start?*

HANNAH BARRY: I happened to come across this group of artists working out of a large Georgian townhouse. It had ten rooms and in each room there seemed to be something happening, artists making interesting work. So I kept visiting, every weekend from then on, and about six months later, they said they would like to do a show in the house and asked if I could help and that's how it started.

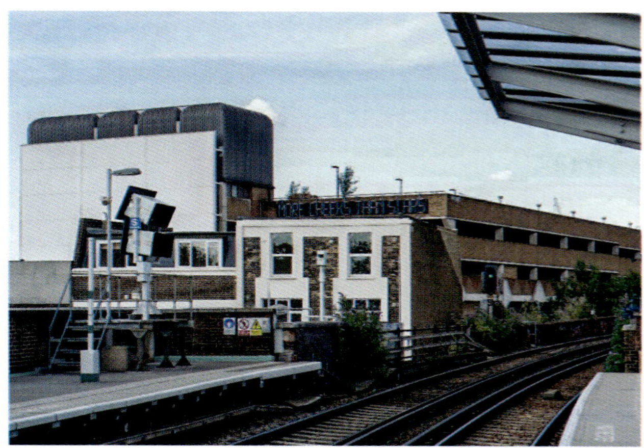

Mircea Cantor, *Bold Tendencies* (2011).

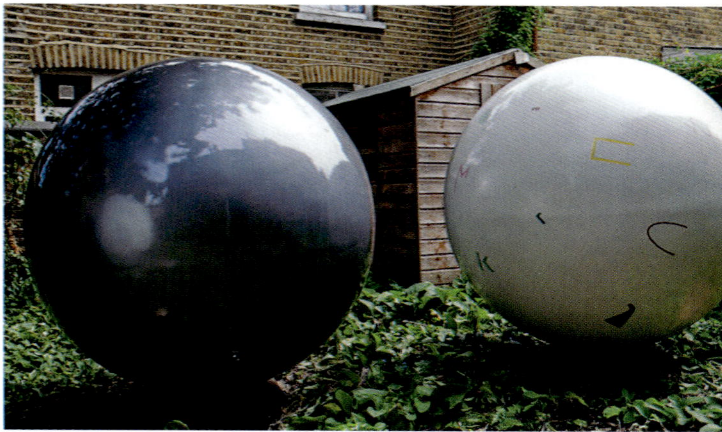

Bobby Dowler, *Lyndhurst Way*.

SVEN MUNDER: It's really important to stress the Hannah Barry Gallery came out of the Lyndhurst Way exhibitions and that it was a necessity as well as an opportunity. The artists needed some support structure and there was something resonating because people were coming to the shows. So there was a dialogue.

ID: *And the first exhibition?*

SM: The first show was called *Ten rooms and a sculpture garden*; the project then grew from one show to become ten different themed exhibitions. They were broad themes: colour and line; the figure; landscape. In one of those shows we wanted to tackle large-scale sculpture, and we called it *Bold Tendencies*.

HB: The Lyndhurst Way exhibitions were about creating a system of opportunity that gave people a set of specific parameters within which they could make progress with their work; that was the point of the structure of the exhibitions programme. That's why they had these very broad titles. And the last one was to do with monumental sculpture; it was something that I felt would be an enormous challenge. If you were to make large-scale sculpture what would you do? There are not many opportunities for people who are experienced, let alone people who aren't versed in making substantial works.

ID: *Where did you stage it?*

SM: We talked to Southwark Council and the first show was at the top of a council office. It was an old Victorian schoolhouse that had a playground on the roof, and the council gave us this space for a one-week exhibition. It has an interesting poetic feel to it, but it obviously was just beginning, and at that point, to be honest, we didn't know very much about the practical aspects of staging outdoor sculpture. But we learnt a lot from it.

HB: The experience of doing the show on the roof without thinking it through too much, the combination of feelings of complete and total freedom because of the proximity to the sky and on the other hand the competition with the vista of the city which is spread out all around you, north, south, east and west – those two things coming together created an amazing catalyst for artists' visions. So the current multi-storey car park is just the grander version of that first rooftop space. The same sky; the same feeling of the city.

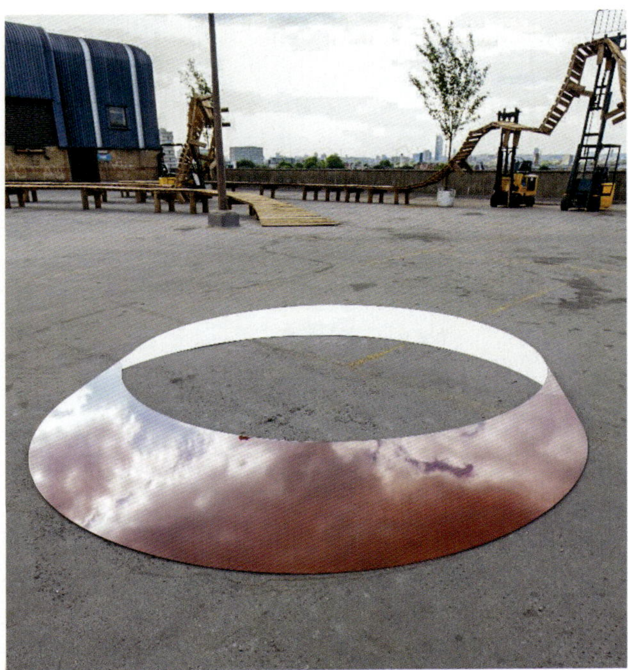

Lilah Fowler and David Brooks, *Bold Tendencies* (2011).

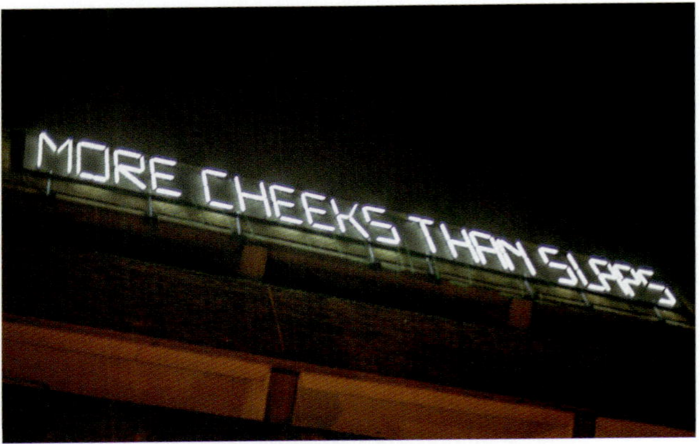

Mircea Cantor, *Bold Tendencies* (2011).

ID: *How did you find the car park?*

SM: We needed better access in order to reach a larger audience, so we then talked to the Council; we were grateful for them lending us the space and asked if there were any other spaces. We looked at quite a few but none were suitable (mostly very exposed and therefore quite difficult to work with). And then the council said they had one last space – we probably wouldn't like it – but it was the multi-storey car park.

ID: *The space that people assume is the least attractive is the most interesting.*

SM: It's such a fantastic place. It's difficult, visually, as an exhibition space because it has very unusual proportions and architectural constraints, but it is the catalyst for making things that usually might have been made in a different way or wouldn't have been made at all.

ID: *And you have a dialogue with the artists?*

SM: We are very keen, whenever we work with an artist's project, that they come and have a site visit. Time and again, we have the proposal and before you know it the artist comes in and completely changes it. This is true for young and established artists. The latest example was Mircea Cantor, who completely changed his work and made something that was quite untypical to date. It is our job to arrange a dialogue between the artist and that space in the right way in order to trigger interesting things. It is an arena for projects that are experimental, that are the best that can be done at that point in time, in that context.

HB: Bettina Pousttchi came up with a number of ideas and then settled on this one, of creating the bollard that identified with the character of the car park yet in their shininess contravened everything about it. They were amusing, they were bent and battered but yet they were very shiny. Pousttchi is an Iranian German artist, who has never really been shown in the UK, but is much celebrated in Europe.

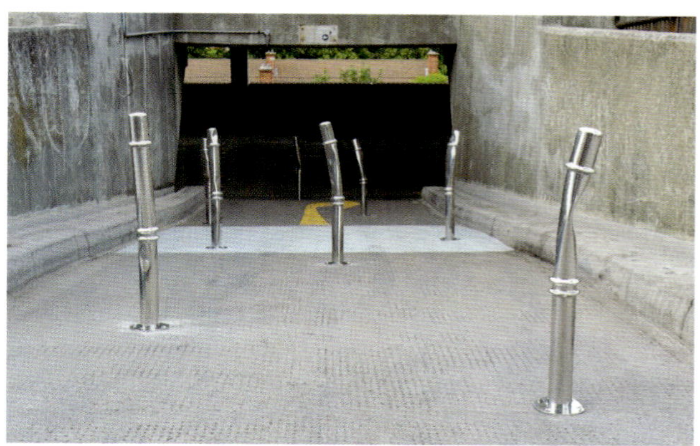

Bettina Pousttchi, *Bold Tendencies* (2011).

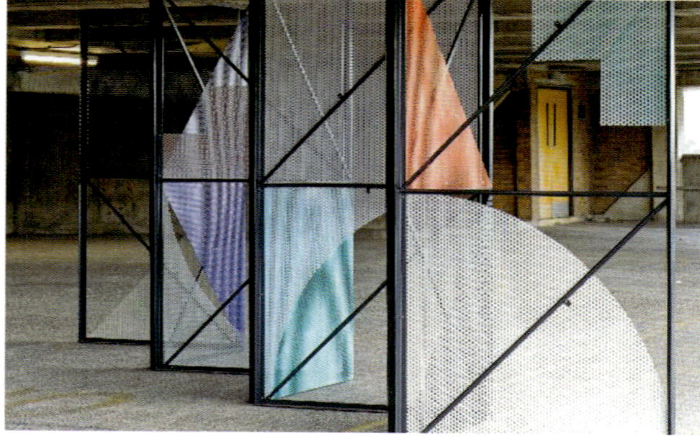

Eva Berendes, *Bold Tendencies* (2011).

ID: *And installation-wise?*

HB: With some works like Eva Berendes' piece it was clear where that was going. It was a piece of architectural folly, with a space in mind; it came made, it just had to be installed.

SM: Then someone like David Brooks had come for a month going up to the top floor every day building his *Boardwalk*, in situ.

ID: *How do you manage the installation?*

SM: We recognize it's important to be open-minded until the last minute, but with some pieces you can't.

HB: There is often a big negotiation with the artist when you do that. I did quite a lot of that this year, but to do with the ins and outs of each particular space itself.

SM: Some pieces you start with because they are immovable, like David Brooks' *Boardwalk*.

HB: And the issue sometimes is that the work is not unmovable but that the artist likes what they are doing, and that is part of the fun of the fair. If you want a great show you have to just keep working on it.

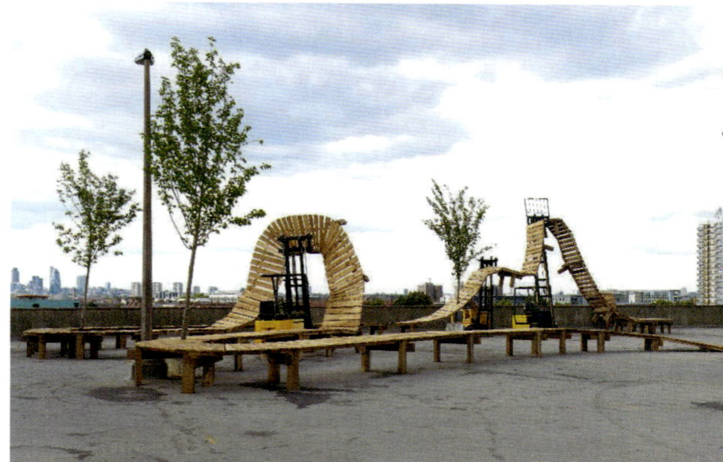

David Brook, *Bold Tendencies* (2011).

ID: *And the spaces have evolved?*

HB: This year we constructed an auditorium on a lower level of the car park, a building made from straw. We initially wanted to have a talks programme, but the talks programme sort of somersaulted into a performing arts programme. We have always done that: with the gallery, our first show was a Bobby Dowler sculpture show where we organized contemporary dance to take place in and amongst the sculptures. We felt it would be illuminating for the audience to have this taking place.

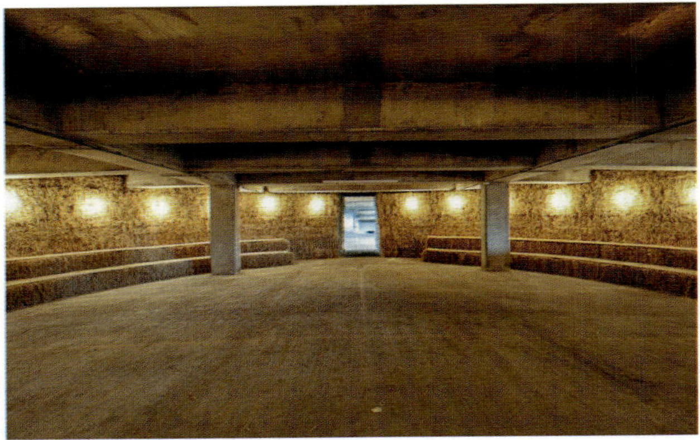

Bold Tendencies auditorium.

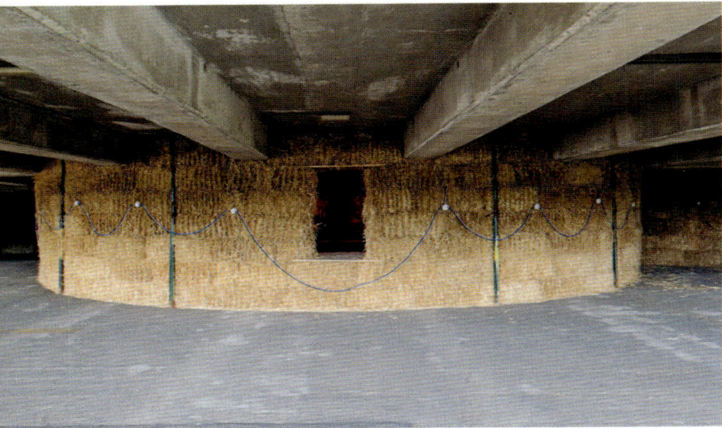

Bold Tendencies auditorium.

ID: *So that is extending the context?*

SM: There is a whole dimension to sculpture that is beyond the physicality of it. There was now room for talks, about car parks, about regeneration; it was connecting all these themes that sculpture was fundamentally connected to anyway, making it visible. It is that richness – there are more layers; there is the sculpture itself, then all these themes that are adjacent, that we are giving a platform to. There may be something in a sculpture or a material meaning and it is beneficial if there is a conversation about it. So that is why we built the auditorium. It takes a lot of effort to get this going but I hope it develops a dialogue between the sculpture and the architecture and an audience.

ID: *You also mentioned performances?*

SM: Igor Stravinsky's *The Rite of Spring* was performed by a hundred young musicians. I was so frightened that the acoustics would be terrible – you know, it's a car park – but it was amazing.

ID: *That continues your proposition of providing opportunity?*

SM: In this case we asked Kate Whitely, a recent Young Musician of the Year, what she wanted to do, and she said she had always wanted to perform *The Rite of Spring*. She took the lead, put the orchestra together, we gave her all the support necessary. It has been the first year of an events programme and something that we are definitely going to develop further.

ID: *And does it go year on year?*

SM: It was a year on year thing, but we have done five years now. We feel we have got a depth of experience, and there is a change in how we are looking at it: we are not just going to the next year – we are looking at the next five years.

ID: *When do you start working on the coming exhibition?*

SM: We begin in the autumn.

HB: It's a big cycle of commitment to get everything done. The logistics are quite intense. So we tend to look at the art now, nine months prior. When you are commissioning new work, it takes a lot of time to get it right.

SM: We are interested in furthering the dialogue of space with art. I don't believe that you can arbitrarily place anything into an alternative space and then make it more attractive. If you don't listen to the art or engage with it, or establish a dialogue with it and if you don't do the same with the space, then you can't synthesize the two, and that's not good, whether that is a perfect white cube or an old warehouse. Sometimes it is easy to place something into an unusual space and benefit from a 'wow' effect, but it also it wears off very quickly. It can work but it is hard work, and the car park has to be continually worked on.

HB: It is interesting what you can do when you have limited resources and just the will to do it. I think it happens quite rarely when something gets made like that. It's a rare experience, with costs.

ID: *What are its costs?*

HB: Its costs are giving up a feeling of safety and stability, and in return you get to work with artists making exciting exhibitions. ■

▶ Fiona Banner

I finally arrive to interview Fiona Banner; she voices her surprise at my interviewing her for a book about sculpture. I am surprised that she was surprised.

ID: *Where do you start?*

FB: I always start with a page, a piece of paper, physically or notionally – I have never purposely set out to make sculpture, and I'm always quite surprised when I do make something that exists in space, something that is discussed as sculpture.

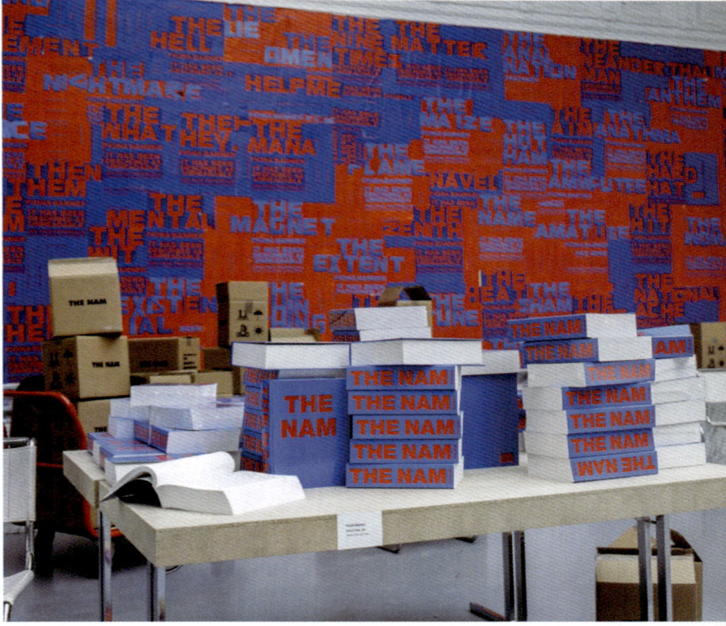

Fiona Banner, *THE NAM* (1997). 1,000-page book, London.

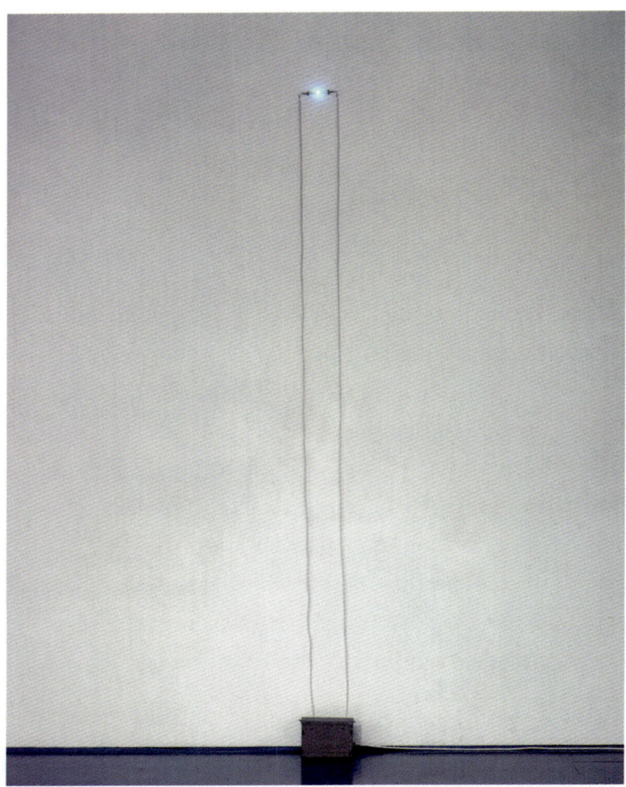

Fiona Banner, *Full Stop* (1997). Neon, wire, transformer, 11 × 1cm.

ID: *And the first time your work became sculptural?*

FB: Probably *THE NAM*, which was technically a book. Though the project was very driven by the content of the book, I also thought of it as an object, something that existed beyond the remit of a book – you couldn't hold it properly, it was a ludicrously oversized paperback that spilt out over your hands and became this object that you grappled with and denied you that fantasy contract that you usually have with a book. So holding it or reading it involved conscious physical engagement. At the time Adrian Searle said, 'Fiona Banner's *THE NAM* is not so much a coffee table book as much as a coffee table', which I liked. It was as much an object as a book, not in an overblown extravagantly bound way; it was a very reduced version of a book, the type set and cover design was utterly generic, to the point where it made it unfamiliar. So perhaps that was the first sculpture.

ID: *The second sculpture?*

FB: That also was related to books and writing. I began thinking about full stops and the difference between a full stop that ends a book and all the others, for instance, the last full stop of *THE NAM*, because it was such a feat to write. I thought, 'Does that have a different weight? Does this mean something different?'

I had also noticed that there were never any neon full stops – small en-dashes but never full stops – so I set about working with a glass blower to make a little hand-blown ball. It's a fragile process: it's very easy to over-blow and pop. So, *NEON FULL STOP*. I liked that it encapsulated a breath – which is in some ways what a full stop is.

ID: *This led to larger ones?*

FB: They were made at a point of crisis where I didn't know what to do. Until that point I had been working with language and words, a substitution for a pictorial language, and that ran out on me – I had a crisis of how to proceed. So I started exploring language *in absentia*, making these very physical sculptures, thinking of them as the opposite of language – massively blown up 3D full stops. They were from different fonts, all very different shapes and sizes: *Slipstream* is this massive great thing that almost looks like a comma, *Helvetica* is almost square – a heavy block, *Avant-Garde* is plinth-like. They are very dumb, they were exploring a dumbness of my own, at the time. It was personal in some senses, about a loss of language. After a while I realized it was quite an articulate way to explore a block or a vacuum… after a while those sculptures started to become a language of their own.

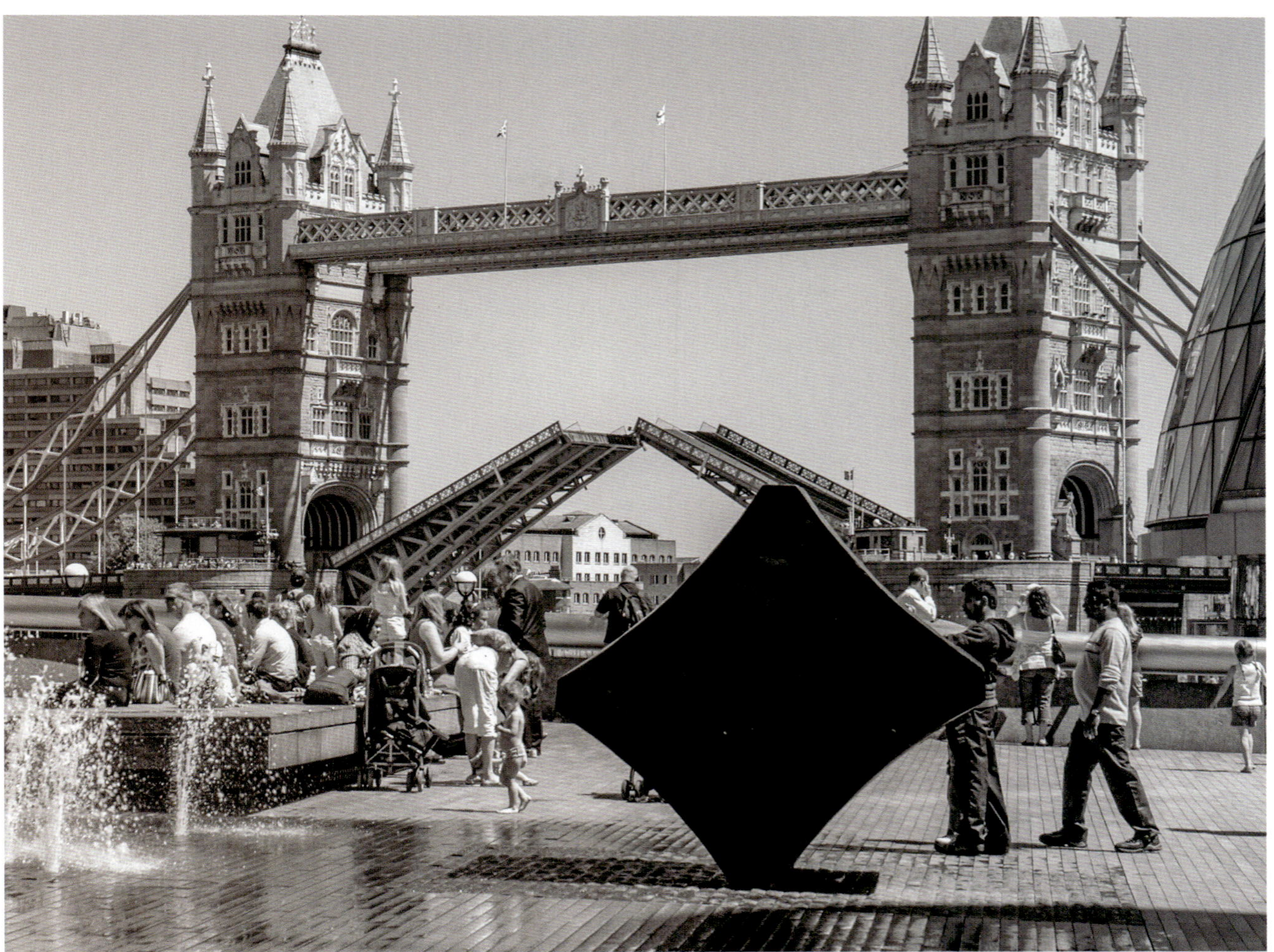

Fiona Banner, *Klang Full Stop* (2003). Bronze, paint,
270 × 270 × 100cm, Installation view, More London.

ID: *A number have been sited around City Hall.*

FB: There are six there, maybe seven, all different. The
one people engage with most, from the font *Klang*, is
like an Art Deco triangle, finely balanced; kids like to
skateboard off it.

ID: *They affect the space?*

FB: As a group they operate literally as punctuation in
space. People negotiate them, people are the characters
in the story, the sculptures the punctuation. As they
are in public spaces, there was a suggestion that they
should be raised, on plinths, but they *are* plinths in and
of themselves; anyhow I wanted the opposite – it was
really important that if they went into a public space
they could be public objects, that they can be urinated
on or graffitied. People do scratch words into them and
I actually find that beautiful.

They somehow create pauses that people negotiate;
tourists have their photos taken, not necessarily
because they are standing by a sculpture but because
they create little landmarks.

ID: *The surface of them is understated yet highly worked.*

FB: I wanted them to be engaging objects. The idea sounds so simple: a full stop, a nothing, a void – but they're pretty tactile, they have a 'made' surface. Even though they are the opposite of narrative – books without any words perhaps – through the surface they contain time and stories in and of themselves.

ID: *You continue to make the full stops?*

FB: I've made them at various stages; at points where I am a bit lost, a sense that there is a pause in studio activity – they are punctuation for me, in that way too, making physical and abstract, difficult space. The act of making them and the time it takes is important; it fulfils a function.

ID: *The piece* Black Bunting, *how would you describe that?*

FB: I've described that in various ways as a big, strung-out painting or an abstract sentence. I saw it as an opposite of bunting: it just creates black space when you look at it, and bunting is defined by its colourfulness, its celebratory nature. I have always felt odd about that piece, and have rarely wanted to show it, though I did recently in America, where it had a different context and connotations. Bunting here is historically nationalistic, celebratory, whereas there it's more typically found in car lots – it's a form of decoration for businesses. So it's about commerce at street level and that was interesting given the current economic situation.

ID: *Where does your unease about this piece stem from?*

FB: I realized what I feel odd about is that it is such an abstract work, that it becomes open to almost any interpretation.

ID: *Where was it first shown?*

FB: It wasn't made for a particular show; it was just something I made for no obvious reason, really. It was first shown in a curated show called *Nothing*, alongside other work dealing with abstract and minimal gestures, then was strung outside the Hayward Gallery.

ID: *How did* Harrier *and* Jaguar *come about?*

FB: Going way back, that work came from drawings (paper again) that I started making when I was seventeen, eighteen. I have a whole bunch of drawings that encompasses every fighter plane in the world. It's an on-going series; I still add drawings. Initially I had just put them in a drawer and then years later came across them, and though it was odd that I'd keep them, and that there were so many – I mean, they weren't particularly good drawings. Anyway I decided to carry on with them. There was an element of anxiety in those drawings because they had come from quite an unconscious place, and they themselves represent the opposite of communication and language: that we are still stuck in this very primitive space, those objects feel very out of date, and it seems extraordinary that we are still vying for power and control through owning these big heavy objects of threat. They are so seductive, but so horrible.

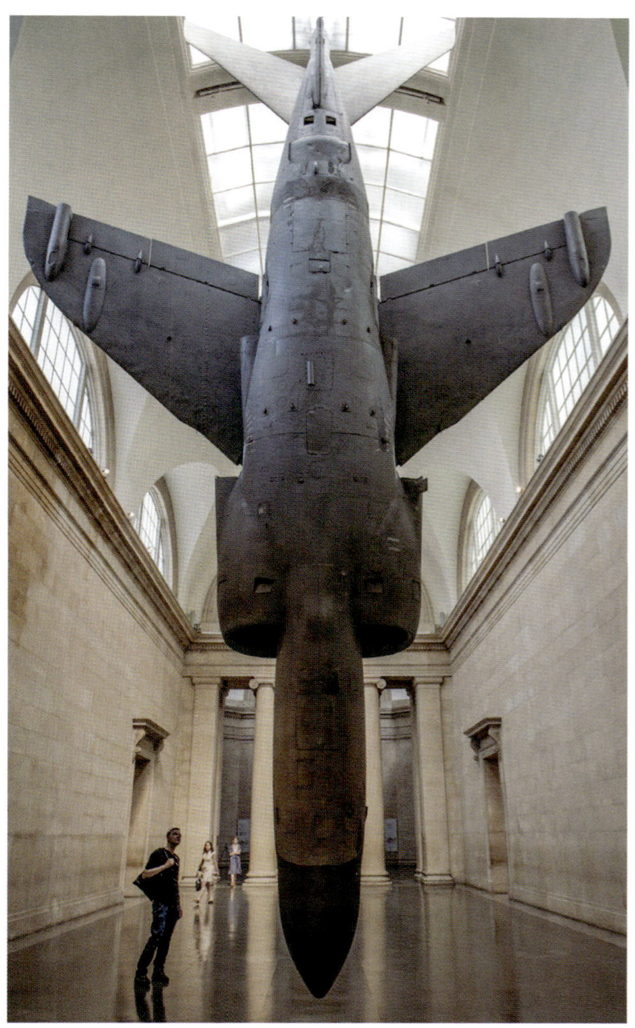

Fiona Banner, *Harrier* (2010). BAe Sea Harrier aircraft, paint, 7.6 × 14.2 × 3.71m.

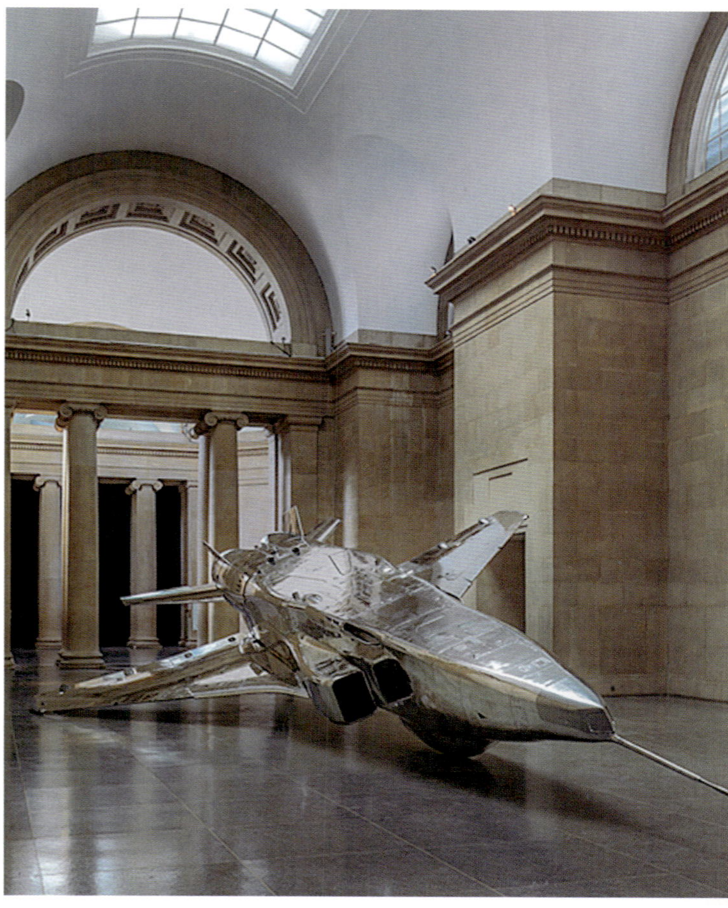

Fiona Banner, *Jaguar* (2010). Polished Sepecat Jaguar aircraft, 8.69 × 4.92 × 16.83m.

ID: *How did you practically manage the installation?*

FB: There was a big discussion about how to get those objects into that space, which was very complex. Especially with the Harrier that fitted the space exactly, both had to be taken to pieces, a complete Airfix job, from an engineering point of view challenging.

ID: *The way they fit the space is extraordinary.*

FB: There is something about the clash between the imperialist architecture and the nature of the objects that worked. But that atrium of Tate Britain, though really big, wasn't built to take really big objects; the building was designed for painting and sculpture of a certain time and a certain scale. They were exactly wrong in that space.

ID: *How did you choose the objects?*

FB: I really wanted planes that were in active service. It was important that they had that currency, the sense that we had all paid for those planes, as taxpayers, that uncomfortable scenario – they belonged to us. I also wanted planes that were quite anthropomorphic. The Harrier, even by its name has a strong link with nature – a predatory bird.

ID: *And the Jaguar?*

FB: Then the Jaguar, which didn't fit vertically, was stripped of its paint and polished; I saw that in the tradition of the nude in some way, the reclining object. In its former life it had been called Buster Gonad in Desert Storm, it had nose art of Buster Gonad with his unfeasibly large testicles on the side of the cockpit. After Desert Storm, and the erasure of the painting the plane kept its name. I really wanted that particular plane but I wasn't 100 per cent sure why. It was really hard to get hold of that particular Jaguar. When it was finally installed on its back in the space in Tate Britain (the first time that I managed to see it from a distance was the night before the opening) I realized then that its two massive, round, back burners on its arse, were the unfeasibly large testicles. That's why it had been called Gonad in the first place – so it confirmed to me that it was a nude reclining as well as being this superfast killer plane.

ID: *It's reassuring that even with such a large project, you have worked with your intuition.*

FB: Making art is all about making decisions. And what's uncomfortable about it is you have to make a lot of decisions without knowing why you are making them. Some things you can articulate and other things you can't or you don't want to. Sometimes it's only at the end that you realize what made you determined to do something.

There's a strange contract there with the unknown – it's always an experiment: you don't know how work is going to operate, even how you're going to react to it, let alone anyone else, and yet it takes a lot of confidence to make something. So there is a contradictory thing there, but that's the magic space. That's the problem with big things: you often need to make everybody else feel secure about the outcome at a point when you aren't. When the stakes are high artists often only deal with the known for that reason, which is why big things often aren't very good.

ID: *What happened to those pieces afterwards?*

FB: There were a lot of discussions about selling the work and who might buy them, and then I realized that was all wrong and that they were public objects. They worked because they were in a public space that was a continuation of the public sphere; because they were such trophy objects, they had this incredible seductive draw, so then the discussion became about what should we do with these objects. They're pretty big, so storage became a concern. In the end I rang everyone concerned and said, 'I've worked it out: ingots – it's the best way of storing metal.' I broke the planes down into small pieces, and I recently went to a smelting factory in Wales and saw them being melted down and poured into ingots, embossed either Harrier or Jaguar. I spent a lot of time researching the life of those two planes; one of them had been particularly active, so it was a relief to kind of erase them.

OPPOSITE PAGE
Fiona Banner, *Slipstream, Full Stop* (2003). Bronze, paint, 149 × 76.1 × 72.5cm, Installation view, More London.

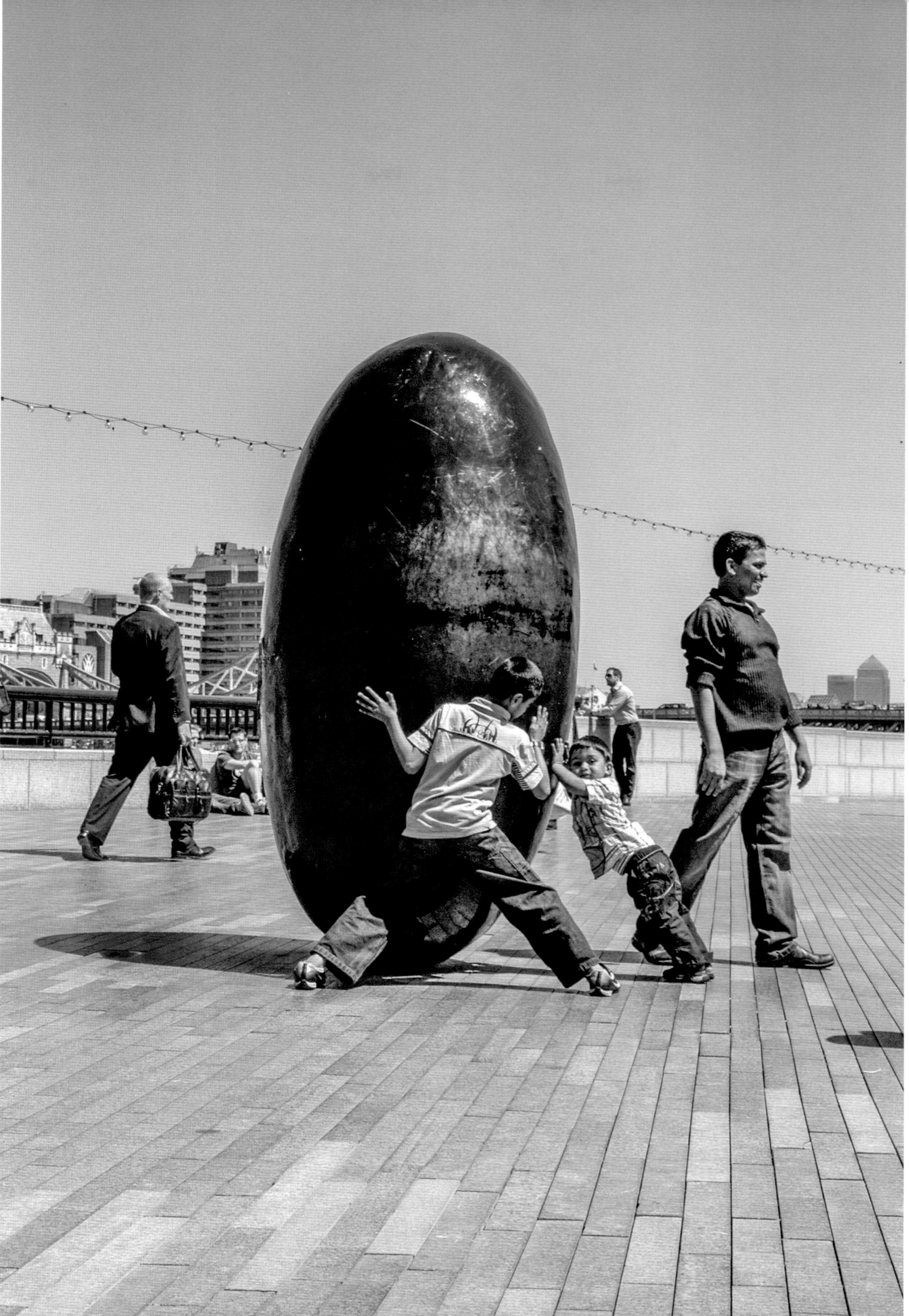

Bibliography

Introduction

Clarke, Geoffrey (1915–), *A Sculptor's Manual* (Studio Vista, 1968)

Craig, Blanche (ed.), *Collage: Assembling Contemporary Art* (Black Dog Publishing, 2008)

Curtis, Penelope, and Wilson, Keith, *Modern British Sculpture* (Royal Academy of Arts, 2011)

Hall, James, *The World as Sculpture* (Chatto & Windus, 1999)

MacGregor, Neil, *A History of the World in 100 Objects* (Penguin Books, 2010)

Smith, Mike, *Making Art Work* (Trolley, 2003)

Material

Ashton, Karen, and Salter Green, Elizabeth, *The Toxic Consumer: How To Reduce Your Exposure To Everyday Toxic Chemicals* (Impact Publishing Ltd., 2007)

Batchelor, David, *Chromophobia* (Reaktion Books, 2000)

Batchelor, David, *Dirty Shiny* (Ikon, 2004)

Batchelor, David, *Unplugged* (Talbot Rice Gallery, 2007)

Burton, Johanna, *Uncertainty of Objects and Ideas: Recent Sculpture* (Smithsonian Institution, 2006)

Humphrey, David, *Blind Handshake: Tilt Trucks and Free Fliers* (Periscope Publishing, 2009)

Meikle, Jeffrey L., *American Plastic: A Cultural History* (Rutgers U.P., 1995)

Newspeak: *British Art Now* (Booth-Clibborn Editions, 2010)

Saatchi Gallery, *Shape of Things to Come: New Sculpture* (Jonathan Cape, 2009)

Smale, Claude, *Creative Plastics Techniques* (Van Nostrand Reinhold Co., 1973)

Process

Arnheim, R., *Entropy and Art* (University Presses of California, Columbia and Princeton, 1998)

Bois, Yve-Alain, *Formless: A User's Guide* (Zone Books, 1997)

Gleick, James, *Chaos: Making a New Science* (Vintage, 1997)

Gleick, James, *The Information: A History, A Theory, A Flood* (Fourth Estate, 2012)

Krauss, Rosalind, *Robert Morris: The Mind* (Guggenheim Museum, 1994)

Morris, Robert, *Continuous Project Altered Daily: The Writings of Robert Morris* (MIT Press, 1993)

Narrative

Bindman, David, *Roubiliac and the Eighteenth Century: Monument Sculpture as Theatre* (Yale U.P., 1995)

Buck, Louisa, *Moving Targets: A User's Guide to British Art Now* (Tate Gallery Publishing, 1997)

Cahun, Claude, *Mise en Scène* (Institute of Contemporary Arts, 1996)

Careri, Giovanni (1958–), *Bernini: Flights of Love, The Art of Devotion* (University of Chicago Press, 1995)

Carey, Frances (ed.), *The Apocalypse and the Shape of Things to Come* (British Museum Press, 1999)

Gelatin et al., *Dionysiac* (Centre Pompidou, 2005)

Gisbourne, Mark, *Cathy De Monchaux Exhibition* (Whitechapel Art Gallery, 1997)

Harland, E.J. and Gillett, J.R. (eds.), *Winchester School of Art Research Anthology* (Winchester Gallery Press, 2009)

Monchaux, Cathy De, *Repleces De La Pulsio* (Fundacion La Caixa de Pensiones, 1996)

Rosenthal, Norman, *Apocalypse: Beauty and Horror in Contemporary Art* (Royal Academy of Arts, 2000)

Woodward, Christopher, *In Ruins* (Chatto & Windus, 2001)

Performance

Ameline, Jean-Paul, et al., *Robert Rauschenberg, Jean Tinguely: Collaborations* (Bielefeld Kerber, 2009)

Brett, Guy, *Force Fields* (South Bank Centre, 2000)

Etzler, John Adolphus, *The Collected Works of John Adolphus Etzler* (Scholars' Facsimilies and Reprints, 1977)

Madrigal, Alexis, *Powering the Dream* (Da Capo Press Inc., 2011)

Sayre, H.M., *Object of Performance* (University of Chicago Press, 1992)

Schimmel, Paul, *Out of Actions: Between Performance and the Object, 1949–1979* (Thames and Hudson, 1998)

Sillars, Laurence (ed.), *Joyous Machines: Michael Landy and Jean Tinguely* (Tate Liverpool, 2009)

Stoll, Steven, *The Great Delusion: A Mad Inventor, Death in the Tropics, and the Utopian Origins of Economic Growth* (Hill & Wang, 2008)

Intervention and Collaboration

Goldberg, Roselee, *Performance: Live Art Since the 60s* (Thames and Hudson, 1998)

Gorschlüter, Peter, et al., *Fifth Floor: Ideas Taking Space* (Liverpool University Press, 2009)

Livingstone, Marco, *Richard Woods* (Lund Humphries, 2006)

Nickas, Bob et al. *Performance Anxiety* (Museum of Contemporary Art, Chicago, 1997)

Smith, Bob and Roberta, *Hearing Voices, Seeing Things. A Serpentine Gallery Project: Seven Artists' Projects Exploring Mental Health* (Serpentine Gallery, 2006)

The Plan

Archer, Michael, *Richard Wilson* (Merrell, 2001)

Hays, Michael K., *Buckminster Fuller: Starting With the Universe* (Yale University Press, 2008)

Iversen, Margaret (ed.), *Chance* (Whitechapel Art Gallery, 2010)

Meller, James, *Buckminster Fuller Reader* (Cape, 1970)

Morrissey, Simon, *Richard Wilson* (Tate Publishing, 2005)

Porritt, Jonathon, *Radical Nature: Art and Architecture for a Changing Planet 1969–2009* (Koenig Books, 2009)

Roussel, Raymond, *How I Wrote Certain of my Books and Other Writings* (Exact Change, 1995)

Tyson, Keith, *Keith Tyson* (Delfina, 1999)

Tyson, Keith, *Geno Pheno* (Pacewildenstein, 2005)

Tyson, Keith, *Keith Tyson: Fractal Dice, September 5 – October 4, 2008* (Pacewildenstein, 2008)

Watts, H. A., *Chance: A Perspective on Dada* (Anne Arbor, 1980)

Formal Concerns

Barker, Ian, *Anthony Caro: Quest For The New Sculpture* (Lund Humphries, 2004)

Burn, Gordon, *Sex & Violence, Death & Silence* (Faber & Faber, 2009)

Early One Morning: Sculpture Now (Whitechapel Art Gallery, 2002)

Fairhurst, Angus, *In-A-Gadda-Da-Vida: Angus Fairhurst, Damien Hirst, Sarah Lucas* (Tate, 2004)

Portelli, Guy, *Modern British Sculpture* (Schiffer Publishing, 2005)

Waldman, Diane, *Anthony Caro* (Phaidon Press, 1982)

Space

Banner, Fiona, *All The World's Fighter Planes* (Vanity, 2004)

Golding, Mel, *Space Explorations* (Space Explorations, 1997)

Graham, Dan, *Rock My Religion: Writings and Art Projects, 1965–1990* (MIT Press, 1993)

Sadler, Simon, *Situationist City* (MIT Press, 1998)

Vidler, Anthony, *Warped Space: Art, Architecture, and Anxiety in Modern Culture* (MIT Press, 2000)

Ville, D.N. *Space Invaders* (James Hockey Gallery, 1998)

Wilson, Keith, *Keith Wilson: Galvanised* (Milton Keynes Gallery, 2005)

Acknowledgements

Thanks

Thanks to all the artists who have been generous with their time and thoughts; I am inspired by their commitment. I am indebted to each of them. Thank you to Clarisse Wisser who has assisted in the collation and ensured that I've managed to finish. Thank you to the continued support of Deborah Curtis and all at The House of Fairy Tales. To Louisa Buck for her support. Thanks to all those who have helped in supplying images and setting up interviews: Clare Gormley, Alexandra Darby, Oliver Hale and Polly Bielecka at Pangolin London, Mary Cork at The Approach, Susanna Beaument, Dale McFarland and Emma Starkings at Frith Street Gallery, Shireen Painter and Nick Dowdeswell at KT Projects, Jackie Honsig-Erlenburg and Pat Cunningham at Barford Sculptures, Tabitha Longton-Lockton at Corvi-Mora, Meri Atkins at Gavin Turk/Livestock Market, Christian Mooney at Richard Woods Studio, Heather Monahan at The Pace Gallery, Guido Poppe and Jerlyn Sarino at Conchology Inc., Marla Ulrich at Kesselkramer. Thanks to Andrew Brook, Christian Carter, Lucy Smallwood and Nick Day, all Winchester School of Art staff who have endured me during the last two years, and to all the sculpture students who continue to make an impact with their energy and enthusiasm.